# The Rebel Yell & the Yankee Hurrah

# The Rebel Yell & the Yankee Hurrah

## The Civil War Journal of a Maine Volunteer

Edited by Ruth L. Silliker
Introduction by Robert M. York

Down East Books
Camden, Maine

Photographs from the Dyer Library, Saco, Maine, and from Mrs. Thelma Haley's private collection used by permission.

All engravings in the text are reproduced from A.H. Guernsey and H.M. Alden, *Harper's Pictorial History of the Civil War* (Fairfax Press), 1866, facsimile edition published by Crown Publishers, New York, 1977.

ISBN 0-89272-186-3
Library of Congress Catalog Card Number 84-51560
Design by Karen Searls
Composition by Roxmont Graphics, Rockport, Maine
Printed by Capital City Press, Inc.

9   8   7   6   5   4   3

Down East Books
Camden, Maine   04843

Dedicated to the librarian and staff
of the Dyer Library, Saco, Maine

## June 9, 1865

*Here we are, some with whole skins, and some not so whole. Others have been left behind. For myself, I can only wonder that there is a bone left in my carcass when I think of the wholesale carnage through which I have passed. My bruises are inward.*

*It is all over now, and I can only regard it as a hideous dream — the smoking ruins, the sodden field, the trailing banner, the slaughtered thousands and wailing families, the roar of cannon, the Rebel yell and Yankee hurrah have all passed away, and we again return to peace.*

# Contents

1    Preface

3    Introduction, by Robert M. York

12    Who Was John Haley?
A Brief Biography

"Haley's Chronicles"

21    Prologue

23    Camp King, Cape Elizabeth *August 6 – 22, 1862*

32    Off to the Land of Dixie *August 23 – October 9, 1862*

40    The Chase Is On *October 10 – December 10, 1862*

55    Fredericksburg *December 1862*

65    The Mud March *Winter of 1863*

77    Chancellorsville *Spring of 1863*

88    March to Gettysburg *June 1 – 30, 1863*

100    Battle of Gettysburg *July 1 – 6, 1863*

109    From Gettysburg to the Wilderness *July 7, 1863 – February 5, 1864*

135    Winter and Spring of 1864 *February 6 – April 30*

141    Battle of the Wilderness *May 1 – 9, 1864*

150    Battle of Po River *May 10 – 11, 1864*

155   Spotsylvania *May 12 – 16, 1864*

159   Battle of Cold Harbor *May 17 – June 9, 1864*

169   The Siege of Petersburg Begins *June 10 – August 6, 1864*

189   Autumn Siege of Petersburg *August 7 – December 31, 1864*

233   Winter of 1865 *January 1 – March 4*

248   The Fall of Petersburg *March 5 – April 9, 1865*

264   Appomattox *April 9th and 10th, 1865*

267   The Long Road Home *April 11 – June 11, 1865*

284   Roster of Company I, 17th Maine Regiment

290   Appendix A: Background on McClellan, Stanton, and Sickles

295   Appendix B: Battles in Which the 17th Maine Regiment Participated

296   Chapter Notes

311   Bibliography

# Preface

I first discovered John Haley's journal in 1981 at the Historical Room of the Dyer Library in Saco, Maine, while researching another Maine personage, Joshua Chamberlain. My first reaction was one of incredulity at the size of the book and the exquisite hand-printed text. I was soon immersed in the story unfolding on the first page and in fantasy I joined young John as he wrestled with his foolish decision to enlist in the army; I suffered his hunger and physical anguish on the mud march and the terror of the Wilderness. Haley's words leapt from the page, as fresh and exciting as though they were written yesterday. As I read further, a note in his handwriting fluttered to the floor: "It is my hope that from these pages some caring generation may find inspiration for direction to undertake the work that they may better understand the cause we served, the cause of the preservation of the Union of States."

I was hooked. John Haley nibbled at my conscience for many months, but the problems of transforming the journal into a book seemed insurmountable. The original work could not be removed from the library (as well it shouldn't), so how was I to edit the 440 thousand-word text for today's reader? The subject continued to plague me; I had to try. The journal should not moulder another one hundred years! Once the decision was made, each piece fell into place as though old John Haley himself leaned over my shoulder directing the project.

I began by struggling through the complete set of tablets wherein Haley recorded his experiences at the time, or within twenty-four hours thereof. To have such a reference source "was richness" itself, (to use a favorite phrase of Haley's) — most books of this nature are written years after the event and are distorted by time. I then turned to the more formal journal, which Haley penned long after the War of the Rebellion. Though I found many passages reflecting political and social background Haley could only have had access to in later years, his finished work remained remarkably faithful to the original notes he had scribbled by the campfire after a battle or a day's hard march through Virginia. The more I read, the more I realized that this was a unique history of the 17th Maine Regiment and the Army of the Potomac.

The Civil War has always fascinated me, and Haley's account brought it shockingly alive in all its horror and heartbreak. But it is much more than a dry history; the author's style and irrepressible wit transform it into delightful reading, a real page-turner. This volume is not, therefore, intended *primarily* as a scholarly reference work.

Regrettably, one of the widespread nineteenth-century social attitudes Haley mirrors is a disdain for the Irish and Negroes. Whether or not he modified his attitude as he grew older is not evident, and his journal treats the subject by expressing the feelings of the soldiers of the time of the war. I have kept these passages in the text and trust that today's reader will understand the context in which the offensive phrases were originally written.

Lengthy as it is, this printed version of "Haley's Chronicles," as he titled it, is only about two-thirds as long as the original. It is not an exact word-for-word transcription, for I have exercised my editorial judgment to make his account more consistently interesting. Haley constantly repeated himself, particularly when it came to complaining about the faults of his officers or criticizing the political views of Secessionists in the South and Copperheads in the North. I have therefore deleted many paragraphs where Haley repeats earlier remarks or where he expounds on some topic to the point of beating it into the ground. Similarly, I have tried to bring consistency to the narrative. Haley tended to mix past and present tenses in the course of transcribing and adding to the original field diaries. I have straightened out these discrepancies where I could. Likewise, I have deleted, or moved to the chapter notes, interesting but lengthy asides that were obviously inserted into the original text long after the fact, my aim always being to emphasize the day-by-day immediacy of a private's life in the field. Spelling and punctuation also have been modernized or corrected. (Haley had a little trouble remembering when *i* comes before *e*, and vice versa.)

Like the author, I found my task of editing the mammoth journal "a strain on [my] fund of patience, but the thought of doing something for posterity has spurred on [my] jaded efforts and kept the interest to the finish." Fundamentally, this is John Haley's personal account in his own words, and no other soldier has ever told his story with more thoroughness and skill. It is as fascinating today as when he wrote it a century ago. I can only hope that John Haley would have been well-pleased with this rendition of his journal, assured that posterity honors the truth as he witnessed it.

My many thanks to the head of Down East Books, Leon Ballou, for recognizing the value of the work; to Steve Podgajny, librarian of the Dyer Library, for his enthusiasm and for gaining permission to work on this project; to my editor, Karin Womer, for her guidance and many hours of labor and caring; and to my husband for his T.L.C. in the long months of arduous toil. Last, but far from least, my thanks go to Dr. Robert York, Maine's official historian, who encouraged me at the inception of this book and who wrote the introduction that follows.

Ruth Silliker

# Introduction

The Civil War is the most popular single subject in American history. More ink has been spilled on it than any topic from the Pilgrim fathers to nuclear war. Historians have analyzed it militarily, politically, economically, socially, constitutionally, diplomatically, and biographically again and again. Thousands of great books have emerged to form a solid core of significant Americana. Carl Sandburg, Douglas S. Freeman, Allen Nevins, Bruce Catton, Frank Owlsley, E. Mertin Coulter, Bell Wiley, Fred Shannon, David Donald, Kenneth Williams, and James G. Randall are but a few of the major historians who have written extensively and brilliantly of the period. They are flanked by a host of others whose books and articles help to round out our knowledge and understanding of the war era.

Although Maine servicemen played an important role in the Civil War, the bibliography of Maine's participation is not large. There are a goodly number of regimental histories (now old) plus John Pullen's incomparable *20th Maine* and *Shower of Stars* (27th Maine), Charles Hamlin's *Maine at Gettysburg*, biographies of Hannibal Hamlin (Lincoln's vice president), generals Oliver Otis Howard and Joshua Chamberlain, and William P. Fessenden (U.S. Senator and Secretary of the Treasury). Also noteworthy are Joshua Chamberlain's *Passing of the Armies* and Sturtevant's *Josiah Volunteered*.

While Maine's Civil War soldiers were writing soldiers — they kept diaries and they wrote frequent and long letters (uncensored) to their loved ones at home — and while many of these have been preserved, very few have ever been published. That is why what Ruth Silliker has accomplished in editing John Haley's very full diary of his three-year enlistment as a member of the 17th regiment — one of Maine's fightingest — is of special importance.

This introduction seeks to provide the background of Maine's participation in the Civil War into which the 17th regiment and Haley will be placed.

Like the rest of the North, Maine was unprepared for war in 1861. Most of the old militia companies had long since been disbanded. Those still functioning were primarily for ceremonial purposes and not ready for combat. When Lincoln called for volunteers after Fort Sumter's capture, there was a hearty response in Maine. Governor Israel Washburn was a strong Unionist and he urged Maine men to step forward, which they did with enthusiasm — so many that recruiting had to be temporarily suspended because no adequate accommodations and materials had been readied to handle them. Of course, in the early days of the war there was a general feeling that the conflict would be short and easy; one big push to Richmond and it would all be over. As the war lengthened and the casualty lists mounted, it became increasingly difficult in Maine as elsewhere to fill the ever-climbing quotas. A draft was instituted to meet the need. Even then, most Maine servicemen were volunteers; there was a stigma attached to the word draftee. There was a financial incentive as well. Those who had to go were anxious to collect as much bounty as possible, and by volunteering in a larger and wealthier community than their own they often fattened their pocketbooks considerably. There was a terrible inequity in this system because the enrollees were credited to the quota or city in which they enrolled rather than to the one in which they resided. This left the smaller towns and rural areas facing a vicious circle of high quotas and diminished numbers of potential soldiers. This situation gave rise to the "Kingfield Riot" of 1863.

Over the course of the war nearly $10 million was paid out in State of Maine and local enlistment bounties. When John Haley signed up in a spurt of group patriotism as a member of the 17th Maine in August 1862, and received $55 from Saco, $45 from the State of Maine, and $25 from the federal government, he felt "very wealthy." In the early part of the war it was possible to avoid service by paying a commutation fee of $300 but this was abandoned after a year. Another way to avoid service was to hire a substitute. This option remained in effect throughout the war and was utilized by Maine men who could afford it. This resulted in many referring to the Civil War as a rich man's war and a poor man's fight.

Maine had its share of skedaddlers, and the extensive Maine woods were a hideaway for those from Maine and elsewhere who wished to avoid service. "Gone to Canada" was the excuse used by some. Maine also had some "copperheads" who counseled against a vigorous presentation of the war. Marcellus Emery, editor of the *Bangor Democrat*, was the most conspicuous spokesman for this point of view. In August 1861 a "respectable" mob of Bangorians destroyed his press. He later resumed publication with a more subdued editorial tone, but throughout the war he remained in opposition and was a principal speaker at peace rallies in eastern Maine in the middle years of the conflict.

Maine did not escape the stigma of desertion. The rate ran above 10 percent for both Union and Confederate forces, and company records for Maine regiments have many notations of desertion — "whereabouts unknown." All in all, however, Maine's record in the Civil War is an honorable, even inspiring, one. Well over seventy thousand men from a total population of just under six hundred thousand answered the call to the colors. Over 10 percent died. The majority of casualties were the result of disease rather than enemy bullets. A large number of Maine regiments served on the periphery of the Confederacy, especially in the Mississippi River area, where they were subject to unaccustomed diseases of the warm climate. Many others succumbed to dysentery, typhoid, pneumonia, and other camp diseases.

The overwhelming majority of Mainers served in the over thirty infantry regiments, while others served in cavalry, artillery, and sharpshooter outfits. Sixty-seven hundred served in the navy or marines. Maine men engaged in every major battle of the eastern theater of war from First Bull Run in 1861 to Appomattox in 1865. Five raw Maine regiments were rushed into action at First Bull Run in July 1861 and, like the rest of Union forces, failed to live up to expectations. Following Bull Run, General George McClellan assumed command of the Army of the Potomac and, by repeated drilling, got a fine army whipped into shape. He took it down the Potomac, expecting to capture Richmond by a flanking movement in the Peninsular Campaign. There were seven Maine regiments with him and all were conspicuously engaged in such actions as Williamsburg, Fair Oaks, and Gaine's Mill, but the campaign failed. The troops were withdrawn and McClellan relieved of the command. A political general, John Pope, succeeded McClellan. He proved unequal to the task, and his memorial became the second battle of Bull Run — a major disaster that left the Federal forces demoralized and in retreat.

Lincoln again turned to McClellan to save the day. Lee's success at Bull Run emboldened him to begin an invasion of Maryland in the hopes of bringing that border state into the Confederacy, or at least providing thousands of new Confederate recruits. The invasion ended at Sharpsburg (Antietam), the bloodiest one-day engagement of the entire war. The 7th and 10th Maine regiments were heavily committed and suffered serious casualties. The noise of the battle (heard 60 miles away) was the first hint of hostilities for the 17th Maine, recently arrived in Washington, D.C., and then garrisoned at Fort Stanton just outside the city. Haley, like many of his fellow enlisted men, hoped to remain there for a long time, but some of the officers were itching for battle and requested a transfer for the regiment. Haley reported that "as far as the men in the ranks are concerned this statement is a gross misrepresentation wholly devoid of foundation. We desire to stay where we are, or in some place equally safe and pleasant."

Antietam blunted Lee's advance and forced his return to Virginia. In that sense it was a Federal victory but in reality it was defeat for both sides. Its most important result was the effect on European leaders. England was on the verge of recognizing the independence of the Confederacy but Antietam caused her to pause, and the danger of foreign interference passed.

Following Antietam, McClellan was again removed from the command. This time he left the army, only to resurface in 1864 as the Democratic opponent to Lincoln in his reelection bid. The new commander, General A.E. Burnside, was guilty of colossal blunders resulting in the terrible defeat at Fredericksburg in mid-December. The 2nd, 4th, 16th, and 17th Maine regiments all fought bravely in this futile assault on entrenched enemy positions. The 16th and 17th were fighting for the first time and did well under withering fire. General Hiram Berry (formerly the colonel of the 4th Maine and currently brigade commander) praised the men of the 17th for their conduct. Although military historians generally place the blame for the debacle at Fredericksburg on Burnside's shoulders, Private Haley thought Burnside an "honest man and a true patriot" who accepted a "command beyond his ability" and who was shafted by his subordinates. Burnside is best remembered for his whiskers; Haley said "no other man we ever saw had such a head." Whiskers do not a general make, though, and Burnside's days as commander were numbered as Lincoln, desperately seeking a winning general, on January 25 turned to General Joseph (Fighting Joe) Hooker as his new leader.

Generally, from freeze-up in late fall to thawing time in the spring, Rebels and Federals alike went into winter quarters — often quite close to each other. Active campaigning usually began around May 1, and 1863 was no exception. After a winter of much cold and snow but plenty of rations (at least as far as the 17th Maine was concerned) the armies were on the move again. This time it was Chancellorsville, another Union disaster. Maine's Oliver Otis Howard, a Bowdoin and West Point graduate who would achieve the highest permanent rank of any Mainer serving in the war, commanded Hooker's right wing in this fight, and he, along with Hooker, is heavily blamed for the

Union failure. In this battle both the 17th Maine and the 5th Maine Battery were badly mauled. Haley's company lost several. Haley himself had a bullet pass through his trousers near the hip and rejoiced that a "miss is as good as a mile." The Confederates lost Stonewall Jackson, Lee's right arm, but the Federals lost Major General Hiram Berry, who according to Haley was "fairly idolized" by his troops. Berry's funeral in his home city of Rockland, Maine, was a solemn event. Vice-president Hannibal Hamlin marched in the procession for his fellow Mainer. The state had lost a good man and the Union a promising general.

His success at Chancellorsville encouraged Lee to undertake a second invasion of the North, which terminated at Gettysburg in early July. Gettysburg became the high-water mark of the Confederacy and a great Union victory. It was also Maine's finest hour of the war. About six thousand Maine men were there as a part of the eighty-five thousand Federal forces opposing over seventy thousand Confederates. Of the resulting twenty-two thousand Union casualties, approximately a thousand were Mainers.

On the first day, which saw more Confederates engaged than Federals, Hall's 2nd Maine Battery and Stevens's 5th Maine Battery were in the thick of the fray and had to abandon their positions on the west side of town as the Federals were pushed back through the town to a defense on Cemetery Ridge. Both batteries lost about a third of their strength. Even more conspicuously involved was the 16th Regiment, which at 4 P.M. was ordered to advance and to hold the position at all cost in order to protect a Union withdrawal that threatened to become a rout. "At all cost" meant 80 percent casualties: 11 killed, 62 wounded, and 159 captured. General Howard was the ranking Federal officer on the field and is generally credited with selecting Cemetery Ridge as the best location for a Union stand. As night fell the Rebels were stretched out along Seminary Ridge while the Union forces were strung out from Culp's Hill along Cemetery Ridge.

On the second day, five Maine regiments were strongly committed. They were the 3rd, 4th, 17th, 19th, and 20th. Gettysburg was a junction of many roads, and the soldiery of both sides was spread out for dozens of miles along roads leading south and west. Many made long forced marches to reach the battlefield and often were rushed into battle without rest or rations. The 3rd and 4th had arrived late in the day of July 1 and became a part of the force Dan Sickles took down Cemetery Ridge to the middle ground between Federals and Confederates. The 3rd was hit by Rebels in the woods at noon and again at 4 o'clock in the Peach Orchard, suffering over 100 casualties. The 4th was stationed at Devil's Den near Little Round Top and in two hours lost over 100 men. (At this time Maine regiments rarely mustered over 350.)

The 17th was many miles away when Gettysburg began. At 2 A.M. on July 2, it began a forced march that brought it to Gettysburg in midafternoon and immediately it was rushed into action. Their corner of hell was the wheat field, where they repelled repeated efforts by the Rebels to dislodge them. With ammunition exhausted, the men of the 17th stood with fixed bayonets, awaiting the final Rebel charge. Only the timely arrival of reinforcements saved this regiment from annihilation. As it was, the 17th lost one-third of its strength. In Company I (Haley's company), two were killed and twenty-two wounded, six of whom died shortly thereafter.

The 19th Maine reached Gettysburg at 1 A.M. on the second but did not see action until 6:30 P.M., when it was committed as part of the Federal force seeking to stabilize the fighting involving Sickles's badly mauled forces. This regiment lost 130 killed and wounded. It was also the only Maine regiment seriously involved on the last day of the battle.

While the 3rd, 4th, 17th, and 19th regiments all gave splendid accounts of themselves, it was the 20th that really achieved immortality on July 2, 1863. Under the brilliant leadership of Colonel Joshua Chamberlain, this regiment, which had marched twenty-five miles on July 1 and was stationed on the Union left on Cemetery Ridge, was ordered at 4 P.M. to occupy and hold Little Round Top on the extreme left of the entire Union line. They beat the Confederates in a footrace to seize this key position and then repelled every Rebel effort to dislodge them. The crowning achievement was a magnificent bayonet charge that utterly confounded their adversaries and resulted in the capture of many prisoners. Chamberlain subsequently was awarded the Congressional Medal of Honor for his valor and action, which literally saved the Union left from being turned by the Rebels. Had the Confederates been successful in capturing Little Round Top, the results of Gettysburg could well have been much different from what history has recorded.

On July 3, having failed to crack either the Union left or right, General Lee, for reasons that still puzzle historians, ordered a frontal assault on the Union center by the flower of Southern manhood under General George Pickett. This futile charge into the heart of Federal strength was both a magnificent and awful moment of the war. The Confederates marching up the hill shoulder-to-shoulder and row upon row presented alluring targets for the Union infantry and artillery, which proceeded to rip huge gaps in the advancing lines. So great was the carnage that the survivors were sent reeling back down the hill in utter defeat. That night Lee began rapidly withdrawing his forces to his beloved Virginia.

Gettysburg concluded as a major Union victory and, coupled with Grant's simultaneous success at Vicksburg, constituted a great Fourth of July present to Abraham Lincoln and the North. Henceforth it was all downhill for the Rebel cause but there were still twenty-one months of warfare and many savage and costly battles before the conclusion at Appomattox in April 1865.

Meantime the 27th Maine, whose enlistment had expired on June 10, had been asked by the administration to overstay its enlistment to help provide a defense for Washington, D.C., in case of a sudden Rebel threat. Of the 865 men in the regiment, only 315 responded affirmatively. The rest went home as scheduled. Fortunately for the ones who stayed, there was no fighting, and on July 17th they too went home. As promised, the Congressional Medal of Honor was awarded to them for their extra service but a snafu resulted in medals being sent to all 865 members of the 27th Maine. At once a cry went up that this cheapened the coveted award. Of course all agreed that the 550 deserved no recognition but the mistake was not fully rectified until 1917, when the award was formally revoked for all. The 315 were allowed to keep theirs as a memento only. This is why the 27th was referred to as the "most decorated" regiment of the Civil War.

It was in this same time frame that the war had been brought home directly to Maine when a Rebel manning a captured fishing vessel sailed boldly into Portland harbor and under the cover of darkness captured the *Caleb Cushing*, a revenue cutter. In the morning, from the Portland Observatory, the cutter was sighted down the bay. A quickly organized rescue party overtook the captured vessel. The Rebels, having discovered that the cutter was unarmed, set it afire and abandoned ship in small boats on the far side. They were all captured but the cutter was a total loss. There was great excitement in Portland for some time thereafter.

Also at this time occurred the Kingfield Riot in northern Franklin County, reflecting dissatisfaction with the operation of the Federal draft. When draft notices could not be delivered in Salem, Freeman, and Kingfield because of local opposition, the governor called out the Lewiston Light Infantry, which was augmented by returned veterans from Augusta, and sent them to the area to enforce the laws. They traveled by train to Farmington, and then it was shank's mare to the front. Instead of being met by sharpshooters hidden behind stone walls and barns, they were met by young girls inviting them to banquet as they approached first New Portland and then Kingfield. After camping overnight at Kingfield and assuring that all draft notices had been delivered, the soldiers marched back to Farmington without incident. To compare this event to riots in New York City and other urban centers is a grave injustice to the rural folk of Franklin County, whose male population had already been bled white.

It should also be noted that the powder mills on the Presumpscot River (Windham and Gorham) were operating full-scale at this time. Over the course of the war they provided the Union with 25 percent of its gunpowder.

Returning to the eastern front, both Rebels and Federals were back in Virginia by late July 1863. Throughout the rest of the year there were many marches, much maneuvering, and minor skirmishes but no major battles. At Rappahannock Station the 6th Maine made a brilliant but costly charge against a heavily defended Confederate position. The 17th spent much time in the Warrenton, Centreville, Fairfax, and Culpepper areas of Virginia without much fighting. In a skirmish at Locust Grove on November 28 the regiment suffered fifty-two casualties. One was Captain Sawyer of Company E and the other was Lieutenant Brown of Company A. Haley commented: "The first-named was a genial, warm-hearted, and impulsive man, liked by all under him. He was deeply lamented. The other was exactly the reverse and was thoroughly detested. Indeed I do believe he was so hated he was shot by some of his own men, for he caused more fellows to be punished than all the other officers in the regiment." Haley, like most ordinary soldiers, was free with his comments about the officers under whom they served. Soon the regiment went into winter quarters and spent a relatively quiet winter.

In the west the 13th and 15th Maine regiments participated in the Texas Expedition (November 1863 through February 1864). In March of 1864 the same regiments along with the 12th, 29th, and 30th participated in a campaign along the Red River.

It was March 1864 when General Grant assumed command in the eastern theater after a very successful career in the west. Lincoln finally had a winning general, though by this time many of the veteran regiments were approaching the end of their enlistments. The new leadership did not prevent the 5th, 6th, 7th and 19th from suffering heavy losses at Spotsylvania in May 1864, however.

Grant's plan of action was to wear down the undermanned and under-supplied Rebels by relentless pressure from the superior Northern manpower and material. For many, this was a slower and more costly process than they cared to contemplate. Haley regarded Grant's overland route to Richmond as a "stupendous blunder," and in early June of 1864 he scorned Grant's generalship, which "consists of launching men against breastworks." Would he still be around to share the ultimate victory? Although the 17th was engaged at Cold Harbor in early June, it was the 8th and 9th Maine regiments that suffered the heaviest losses.

On June 9 Haley confided to his diary that he thoroughly expected to be in Richmond by July 4. On the twelfth they were on the road to Petersburg, which Haley felt should have fallen on the fifteenth. It didn't, and much of the rest of the year was consumed by unsuccessful efforts to capture that city. It was here, on the sixteenth, that Haley and a fellow soldier saw a cannonball coming directly at them. They were rooted to the spot as the ball passed between their heads! It was here also, on the eighteenth, that the 1st Maine Heavy Artillery (a fresh outfit of infantrymen) made a noble but senseless charge against a strongly fortified Rebel position and in the short space of fifteen minutes suffered 115 killed, 489 wounded, and 28 missing out of an attacking force of 950. This was the highest percentage of casualties in so short a period of any Federal regiment.

In this fighting around Petersburg the 1st Maine Cavalry and the 20th, 31st, and 32nd regiments, as well as the 17th, all served with distinction while suffering heavy losses. On the second anniversary of his enlistment (August 6) Haley attributed his survival to "tenacity for life and great endurance" (he later added "short stature"). In late August there was a lull in the fighting, with much fraternizing and trading between the Blue and the Gray; the Rebels had tobacco and the Federals had food, albeit some was of questionable quality. On August 30 Haley traded a piece of flabby salt pork to a Confederate officer who "clutched it as a starving dog would a bone. What could they be feeding on when a commissioned officer deems such stuff edible?"

The fraternization continued despite efforts to prevent it. Haley reported Rebel pickets coming to Yankee "gopher holes" under cover of darkness and cursing the Southern leaders for continuing the war. The Union boys gave them cakes and coffee. Haley said "we are all heartily sick of the slaughter. If left to us privates, we'd make short work of it. Perhaps we can accomplish more by cakes and coffee than by bullets." His diary for the rest of the war makes repeated references to desertion by the starving and almost naked Rebel soldiers.

By mid-September the lull was over and heavy fighting resumed. It was at this time that General Phil Sheridan was rolling up victory after victory in the Shenandoah Valley, and on the twenty-first a 100-gun salute honored Sheridan and his troops. For Haley, fighting was sporadic during the rest of the year and varied from light to heavy. Various duties such as picket, marching and drilling, foraging, tearing up railroads and bridges, building roads, and burning houses occupied the time. On December 25 he wrote, "Merry Christmas has no significance to me."

The drilling was especially distasteful to Haley but it was a pet activity of Brigadier General West (their former colonel). Haley wrote: "If he would have been where we wished him, it would be Fort Kent, Maine, as far away from us as possible." By this time Haley was counting the days until his enlistment was over. On February 18 he noted that he had six months to go. He also noted that Confederate pickets were in full sight but "it had become a policy with us to commit no more murder by shooting a picket down when he is on his post minding his own business." Also, scores of Confederate deserters were coming in daily near the end of February. Haley's outfit saw little action for the rest of the campaign.

On April 3 Petersburg fell, and on the ninth Lee surrendered. The soldiers "shouted, danced, sang, and wept" with joy. The ordeal was finally over. The Union joy soon turned to sorrow with the death of Lincoln. Haley had long been a Lincoln admirer and had voted for his reelection. He reported that a soldier who expressed satisfaction over Lincoln's death was promptly thrown in a frog pond from which he was taken "more dead than alive, coated with green slime and frog spawn." When the dunked soldier complained to the colonel, the officer bellowed, "They served you right, only it's a d—d shame they didn't drown you!"

Maine was conspicuously present at the actual laying down of Confederate arms. Brigadier General Joshua Chamberlain was the Federal officer designated by Grant to lead the Union forces before whom the Confederates surrendered. Colonel Chamberlain had served with distinction in the Wilderness before he received a ghastly wound at Petersburg. Such injuries almost always proved fatal, and fearing the worst, Grant gave Chamberlain a battlefield promotion to Brigadier General. Miraculously, Chamberlain recovered sufficiently to return to duty and served valiantly in the closing weeks of the war. It was a fitting reward that he should be given the honor of accepting the formal surrender, and it was at Appomattox that General Chamberlain, on his own authority, ordered his men to give the marching salute (carry arms) to the brave but vanquished men in gray. This noble gesture from a "magnificent" man (to borrow an adjective from Douglas Freeman, the greatest Southern historian) went far to give a dignity to an otherwise forlorn and woeful moment in Southern history, and it was much appreciated by the men of the South.

In the following days Haley's comrades did considerable marching (probably to keep them busy and to prevent rioting), heard many rumors (some good, some bad), and were subjected to many inspections and parades. On May first they headed for Richmond, which they entered on the sixth. The next day they were on the road to Fredericksburg, reaching that town on the tenth. For days the heat had been almost unbearable. After two more days of marching they went into camp outside Washington, D.C., and began preparations for a grand review before the president and top generals. Haley reports that he didn't participate in the review because he was too short and squat to please the officer who selected the participants!

By June first everything was nearly in readiness for leave-taking, and on the fifth the regiment began its journey on the long road home. After marching into the capital, they followed Pennsylvania Avenue, passed the Capitol, and thence to the Baltimore Railroad station. Following a wearying wait of many hours they were unceremoniously dumped into coal cars for the three-hour ride to Baltimore. After marching across that city they boarded cattle cars.

At Philadelphia they had a "delicious" lunch and then it was on to Amboy and the steamer to New York. From New York a steamer took them to Newport, where they boarded more railroad cars to Boston and finally to Maine. They reached Portland at 6 P.M. and were accorded a tumultuous welcome — truly a royal one. After all festivities had been completed Haley and his fellows were hauled to the old City Hall and "lodged on the bare floor," which was "too filthy for a dog to lie on." Mustering out came on the tenth, and Haley reached home again at 2 A.M. on the eleventh — glad to be alive and gladder to be home.

Ruth Silliker's editing of Haley's mammoth diary is a significant addition to the literature of Maine in the Civil War. It fully portrays the common soldier's view

— a view from the bottom up. Haley speaks freely about food or lack of it, foraging, marching, drilling, picket duty, mud, heat, rain, snow, the waiting and the rumors, the fear of death, the fighting, the stench, the cries of the wounded and dying, the waste, incompetent officers, and other topics best known to the foot soldier. Since the 17th Maine was involved in all of the fighting of the Army of the Potomac from Fredericksburg to Appomattox, this journal is a gold mine of information about the most active twenty-eight months of the war from the point of view of a common soldier.

Robert M. York
Maine State Historian

Flag of the 17th Maine Regiment.

# Who Was John Haley?

Who was John West Haley? His life spanned eighty-one years; he was born March 3, 1840, and died April 7, 1921, of liver and stomach ailments contracted during the war, which had plagued him throughout his life. He was the only son of Nathan G. Haley and Hitty (Mehitable) Barnes Lee. Three girls were also born to the Haleys but all died fairly young.

In his (unpublished) autobiography John writes: "I was born in the little hamlet called Biddeford, on a spot not much more than a stone's throw from Fort Saco, where one of my paternal ancestors, Thomas Haley, Sergeant in the King's Army, was slain by prowling Indians in 1695. The Haleys are among the early settlers hereabouts, and soon became connected by marriage with the First Families of Maine of this locality."

Haley was proud of his lineage, which dated back to 1638 when Samuel Haley settled at Winter Harbor (Biddeford Pool). Another Haley fought with Sir William Pepperrell at Louisburg in 1745, and still another in the Revolutionary War. His grandfather was in the Battle of Lake Erie in the War of 1812 and was captured and confined to Dartmoor Prison. He lived to return home, though he died soon afterward from diseases contracted in prison.

The Nathan Haleys were a hard-working Maine family, and money was far from plentiful. John continues: "I left school before I was through grammar school to earn not only my own living but [to support] some others dependent on me.

"I was employed as alley boy in old number four mill on the York [York Mills, which manufactured fine textiles] at fifty cents per day and counted myself well-to-do. It would at least provide food for us, and I was thankful to be able to corral so much money."

He remained there seven years and finally received the grand sum of seventy-five cents per day. The great Panic of 1857 closed the mill. "For the next nine months there was literally nothing doing in Saco. Potatoes, although cheap, represented a luxury."

He next worked at the Saco Water Power Shop until the Civil War broke out. From his description, his enlistment was more a matter of saving face with his friends than an affair of patriotism:

"In 1861 I concluded I had a duty to perform but hesitated about embarking on this troubled sea. I feared I lacked those qualities which soldiers so much need. And so that year passed and still the matter stood status quo. In the summer the president called for a large number of men, of which 300,000 were for three years and about the same number of nine-months men. A very intimate friend became fired up under this call, also some other friends, five of us in the same class in Sunday School, and we were getting hot under the collar. Our teacher, although one of the best of men, was a bitter opponent of the war and labored hard to knock the war spirit into a cocked hat. So we concluded to enlist but waited still. My friend sounded his parents out and they neither denied nor affirmed. All at once they decided to give their consent if I was going — they never thinking I would — and all the time my going depended on his getting their consent, which I thought they never would give. A high school teacher had just opened a recruiting office, whither my friend sped to enlist August 5, 1862. As soon as morning dawned, he sought my society and informed me of what he had done. While it was brought home to me with an almost paralyzing shock, no grass was allowed to grow under my feet and my name was promptly plastered onto the roll of those who would answer father Abraham's call. This was August 7. And thus the soldier life began for us until death overtook us or the war ended."

Haley served in Company I, 17th Maine Volunteer Regiment from August 7, 1862, the day the regiment was formed, to June 10, 1865, the date it was mustered out. He describes himself as a soldier "below criticism. Poor fighter. Achieved successful mediocrity. Present all the time." It is "present all the time" that emerges as the key to John Haley's character. Suffering from dysentery and liver trouble, he stumbles, falls, is often one of the stragglers on the long marches through Virginia, but he always struggles to get "back on his pins" and catch up with the regiment.

Sick, weary, starving, disgusted with the military, Haley nonetheless was unwavering in his belief in the Union and determined to protect it at all costs. Although he was implacable toward Secessionists, his diary reflects his compassion for the Southern people and his abhorrence of the destruction he saw all around him. His protest against the horrors of war speaks for the soldiers of any century. Page after page, he describes the conflicts he participated in: the Battle of the Wilderness, Po River, High Bridge, Spotsylvania, Sailor's Creek, Cold Harbor, Totopotomoy Creek, Fredericksburg Turnpike, Fredericksburg, Hare House, Boydtown Road, Hatcher's Run, Weldon Railroad Raid, Chancellorsville, siege of Petersburg, Deep Bottom, Gettysburg, Wapping Heights, Locust Grove, Mile Run, Auburn, and Kelly Ford. Few men endured three years of such dreadful combat, yet our mediocre soldier was "present all the time."

June 19, 1865, Haley returned to civilian life and to the shop he had left three years before — the same room, the same boss, the same job. He was too restless to settle back into the old rut, however, and secured a position as a night watchman at the Portland–Saco–Portsmouth Railroad. Here he also worked as clerk and freight agent, then as York County's first telegrapher, but in 1877 the railroad underwent a change of management and he was again out of a job.

Meanwhile he had married Abbie A. Batchelder, and they had two children, Adelaide and George. Having no means of supporting his family after the railroad let him go, he traded his home for a farm named Toad's Island in local parlance. Why such a peculiar name John could never fathom. He wasn't at the Dayton farm long enough to put down roots, for his venture in agriculture ended within a year and he took a position as bookkeeper with the Saco and Biddeford Gas-Light Company. He later spoke proudly of his fourteen years there and his efficient disbursement of funds:

"no less than $40,000 annually, with never a disagreeable word except with one of said customers, the late J.R. Libby."

It was a good position in those days, but this firm also changed hands and John once more was out of work. In 1891 he took a position on the *Times* as its Saco reporter. Although he had written frequently for the local paper, he claims his was an editorial style and "didn't fit in with reportorial work. My employer, a very small female, saw an opportunity to cut off supplies as she had a friend who needed the job. And I was down and out again."

He was next employed by the *Record*, in 1891, to canvass for subscriptions but was "a flat failure, and one month was sufficient." Thus 1891 ended dismally.

When the Dyer Library opened its doors for the first time in 1892 and John was offered the position as librarian, he leapt at the opportunity. He held this position for twenty-eight years. Haley was already recognized as the area historian and was never happier than when in the world of books. He was a voracious reader and devoured everything on Maine history, with a special interest in the Saco Valley, the Indian raids, forts on the Saco River, and the Revolutionary War, leaving his research for today's historian — the Dyer Library's "Haley Collection."

Genealogy was another passion, and his work on this subject is in popular use today. Haley was also an artist of considerable talent, and two of his paintings have recently been discovered at the York Institute of Saco. He was a popular speaker on diverse subjects and also produced a scholarly paper on the history of libraries.

Haley felt strongly that everyone should have the advantage of education, women as well as men. He designated a study room at the Dyer Library for young ladies, a revolutionary concept at the time. Undoubtedly his conviction stemmed from his own deprived youth and the fact that he had a brilliant daughter. Adelaide graduated from prestigious Wellesley College in 1897 and taught in the Boston schools for twenty-five years. Although she was a comely young lady, she never married; Boston teachers were forbidden to do so. Her adoration for her father also might have influenced her. She inherited his passion for research and genealogy and left the Dyer Library a rich legacy of her work.

John Haley had a curious, brilliant mind, and his interests ranged from poetry and philosophy to body-building. In terms of the latter, he was never proud of his short stature and described himself as having an "excess of adipose tissue." He maintained an exercise regime of weight-lifting and long daily walks. His white hair and black frock coat were a familiar sight as he came striding down Main Street. His son, George, was his constant companion and accompanied his father on his long hikes — often to Kennebunkport, a good twenty miles from Saco. Evidently John Haley had overcome his aversion to the forced marches through Virginia, and walking became a way of life and health for him.

He lived in an exciting age of inventions and invested heavily in the American Telegraph-Typewriter Company, doing quite well, it would seem, as he bought a fine house on King Street in Saco and deeded the Haley Field to future generations. His success in the investment world led to a sad chapter toward the end of his life. Others sought his investment advice, and Haley acted as administrator of one friend's estate, advising the widow on the management of her funds. Upon her death in 1917 her son-in-law initiated a lawsuit against Haley, calling him "grossly inefficient" and hinting at worse. The lawsuit was on behalf of the only grandchild, who had been left $500 in the widow's will. Even though bad blood had existed for many years between mother and son-in-law, Haley had repeatedly beseeched the man to petition the widow to make a new will, leaving her property to her grandson. The lad's father brushed off Haley's suggestion; in fact, he rudely resented any discussion of the matter. During the last year of the widow's life she made out two new wills, naming John Haley as recipient of her house and property.

The first knowledge Haley had of the suit came in a letter from the son-in-law's lawyer charging him with gross inefficiency and claiming that he had made poor investments, frittering away the estate except for the house and a few thousand dollars.

Above all else, John Haley valued his reputation and the fact that he was known as a man whose word was as good as his bond. He writes that he picked up his "sword" (pen), and his correspondence from this time is a vitriolic diatribe. His anger knew no bounds, and he referred time and again to his "efficient disbursement of the Gas and Light Company funds." He appealed to, and received, letters attesting to his character, many of them from old commanders such as Hancock and Sickles. The case never went to court because Haley had the house auctioned off, receiving $2,150 (very close to the $2,500 assessed value), which he gave to the grandson. Coming so near the end of a life lived with honor, it was a bitter experience.

A strange coincidence occurred at this time. Haley received a letter from his former commander, General Sickles, begging Haley to rally his old soldiers in his cause; the general was being sued by the state of New York for mismanagement of Park Department funds. What action Haley took is not known — perhaps he was too embroiled in his own troubles — but he had always maintained close contact with brother veterans and was a person sensitive to others' needs.

Like all old soldiers, Haley was proud of the regiment he had served in and was active in formation of the Seventeenth Maine Association. He was involved in the movement to erect a monument at Gettysburg to his old regiment and writes of the emotions that swept over him as he stood on the old battlefield at the dedication ceremonies on October 10, 1888: "We traversed the Wheatfield thoroughly and then went up into the Devil's Den, from there over Round Top and down again to the scene of Pickett's charge. Ah, distinctly, I remember that day when the heavens and the earth trembled, and the fate of the Union hung by a hair. But the thing turned in our favor, and the Rebel tide of invasion was stayed. How quiet now, and yet not more so than it was on that day after the awful, awful carnage men had wrought was over and the sun had set on the Rebel Waterloo."

Another memorial — the Soldier's Monument in Saco — also occupied his attention. The town procrastinated on the project for twenty years. Finally, an anonymous donor came forth and work got under way. Haley insisted that the statue honor soldiers of all wars and that the figure of a woman be included to pay homage to their sacrifice and service at home and on the battlefield. This may seem a contradiction in his character when one reflects upon his remarks in his journal about the wives and sisters who stayed at home while urging their menfolk onto the bloody battlefield, and his comment about his "small female employer" at the *Times*. These were the exceptions, however; he never held the then-popular attitude that women were less intelligent or less valuable than men. He may well have had Annie Etheredge in mind, whom he admired greatly. This courageous and compassionate nurse had endured the carnage of battle as well as any man during the Civil War.

On May 30, 1907, the Saco memorial was dedicated, and Haley delivered an impassioned address on the sanctity of the Union, pointing out that the woman in the sculpture "is here by design." Today, on a manicured plot amidst busy Route One traffic in Saco the Soldier's Monument rests — a woman proudly standing beside a kneeling soldier, one of only two such statues in the country.

Haley, always the writer, used the pen to argue the many causes he held dear. In 1918, the law of 1890 granting pensions to veterans of the Civil War was under fire. His correspondence at this time reflects letters to editors, statesmen, and veterans' associations. He deplored the toll on the American public of $140 million annually and criticized the fact that many received pensions who were undeserving: bounty jumpers, non-service disabled, double-dippers with government salaries, veterans in hospitals and homes for old sailors and soldiers, and those who saw no service at all. Haley received a pension of eight dollars a month for an injury that had led to blindness in one eye, but (he states) many "who have no just claim on the government draw from $12 to $30 and some even more." His correspondence does not imply he feels unjustly treated, only that the American people could no longer support such large expenditures and that the deserving might suffer.

Who was John West Haley? He was an ordinary man who answered his country's call to duty, along with the thousands of other ordinary men. But Haley left an extraordinary gift to posterity: a journal of his day-by-day struggle through the war that tore the Union asunder. Uneducated by today's standards, this man wrote a mammoth journal in a lucid, detailed, often ironic style. His journal is much, much more than a history of the Army of the Potomac. Haley's quick, satirical wit transforms it into a fascinating narrative. The journal published here is one of three Haley hand printed: two recounting his experiences in the war, and the third entitled *Old Battlefields Revisited*.

On August 20, 1919, two years before Haley's death, the *Biddeford Record* hailed his journal as "the most remarkable book in United States." The tremendous undertaking was complete and Haley laid down his pen. He had meticulously hand printed 440,000 words, an estimated 25 million pen marks "without a blot." (The mere act of counting these, let alone producing them with a steel pen, is remarkable.) Most books of this kind are written years after the event and are subject to distortion because of faulty recollection. Although many years intervened between the war and the completion of his journal, Haley was able to report his experiences thoroughly and accurately. During the war he wrote almost every day in a series of notebooks. No matter how weary he was after a hard march through Virginia, he faithfully recorded the details of the day in these field diaries as he sat by the campfire. His journal, organized and eventually penned so long afterward, remains remarkably faithful to his original notes, which are in the Dyer Library archives.

John Haley is especially fascinating as an example of the prejudices fostered by the era in which he lived. He fought for the Northern cause, yet was remarkably intolerant of blacks or Irish immigrants by our twentieth-century standards. Poor soldier though he considered himself, he was willing to lay down his life to insure that future generations would live under one flag unfurled over these United States.

His hope that a "future generation would read this journal and gain an insight into the soldier's life and a true account of the War between the States" is realized in these pages.

For his gift to posterity, we thank him.

The old soldier with his family: John, wife Abbie, daughter Adelaide, and son George (circa 1902).

"We dedicate this monument to all men who participated in wars for the defense of our country. I must pay tribute to the women of this nation, one of whom is represented on this monument. She is here by design. . . through all the war she never faltered in her devotion to the flag. . .at home, in camp, yea, even in the battlefield."—from Haley's address at the 1902 dedication ceremony for Saco's unusual Civil War monument.

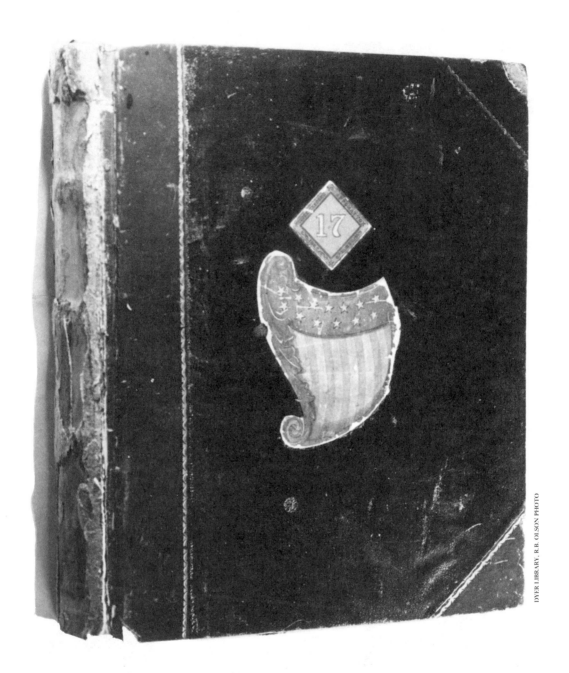

The cover of the original handwritten journal.

# Haley's Chronicles 1862–1865

With Some Observations and Comments
Thereon, Some Wise, Some Otherwise,
but All True

JOHN HALEY
JAN 1863
Co I - 17 ME

# Prologue

Having been an active participant in the late disturbance known as the War of the Rebellion, it has seemed not inappropriate that I should give to those who may come after me, and who may be curious for details upon which history is and will continue to be silent, an account of my experience and observations covering a period of thirty-three months, including all the active operations of the Army of the Potomac from the battle of Fredericksburg down to Lee's surrender at Appomattox Court House.

In giving this account I shall rely principally on my diary for facts. As for opinions, I shall give my own unless I find something more reasonable and conclusive, in which case I shall give credit when I know whom to credit.

In writing on a subject on which there are many witnesses, and where many are so confused by the passage of time that they cannot give a correct account of anything, I expect much adverse criticism. Occasion has not been wanting for me to correct some who would write history and consider themselves well-qualified to do so. One writer affirms that it was "very dark" on the night of May 2nd, 1863, when Stonewall Jackson broke the Union line at Chancellorsville, when in fact it was splendid moonlight, the moon being full and not a cloud in sight. A more lovely night we never saw.

Another writer claimed to have seen General Grant the first time at Mine Run [November 26 – December 2, 1863]. This person must have been blessed with most remarkable eyesight, for Grant was in the West at that time and did not come east till March 1864, when he made his advent in Washington to receive his commission as lieutenant general. And so I might go on and on and show numerous instances of *lapsus memoriae*.

My diary, so far as the facts are concerned, was written at the time the events occurred, or within twenty-four hours of them, while fresh in mind. And as I was an eyewitness of most of these events, I cannot *greatly* err.

At the time of my entry into the service, the war had been in progress about a year and a quarter, and thus far the Rebels had been victorious. The first Bull Run and the Peninsular Campaign had resulted in disaster to our arms. General Pope had also suffered a most inglorious defeat. He had come fresh from recent successes in the West, with a lofty scorn for the Eastern troops. By certain "spread-eagle" devices, and much cheap talk, he hoodwinked the government into the idea that he was the individual who could show Johnny Reb something in the way of fighting that would greatly astonish him. Pope issued an order which was an insult to the entire army, and was a strong reflection on General McClellan.[1]

From the bluster and noise of Pope's advent, let us draw a veil over his subsequent career, which was all the more humiliating. He was a man of dash and patriotism — and some ability — but he accomplished nothing, and the army was again turned over to McClellan, or the "young Napoleon," as some of his admirers chose to call him. As to the propriety of this high-sounding title, I shall leave others to judge who know more about him than I do. Time will, no doubt, set McClellan right when partisan strife has so far subsided as to do justice to *merit* wherever found.

Some called him a traitor, some an incompetent. Hooker called him "a baby," but Meade said, "Without McClellan there could have been no Grant." A middle ground between these views will best serve my purpose.

Soon after McClellan resumed command, he went in pursuit of Lee, who, emboldened by the staggering blow he had given Pope, was now carrying out an idea which had long been doing duty in the cranium of Stonewall Jackson: namely, to invade the North — "Carry the war to Africa."

Lee's army was encountered in Maryland; the battles of South Mountain and Antietam were fought. The Union army was victorious, at least to such an extent that Lee retired across the Potomac. It was a setback to Lee's army, and broke the chain of Rebel successes, and for a time raised the courage and hope of the North.

There is no question as to who won but failed to grasp the fruits of victory. McClellan labored under several disadvantages, one of which was a difference in politics.[2] The prime cause, however, was his elevation to high command so early in the war. Public sentiment was too crude; no man could do himself or the country justice at that time. Too much haste cost us a great many lives and much humiliation. It is by no means certain but that General Scott, even with his weight of years, might have led our armies to victory, but he required time and the army needed a preparation. And when the public heat had subsided enough to allow these two elements to enter into the calculations of our leaders, we began to show the world that not *all* the skill and prowess were on the side of our opponents.

The drowsy lion must have time to collect itself.

# Camp King, Cape Elizabeth

## August 6 – 22, 1862

During the summer of 1862 the North at last removed its gloves and a call was issued for 600,000 troops. It was under this muster that the 17th Maine was raised, and in Company I of that regiment several companions and I signed up. Our enlisting was like many other things in this world; one started and the rest thoughtlessly followed, like sheep over a fence, until six of us had enlisted from one class in Sunday School. Speaking for myself, I had *no* inclination for the business, but once committed in a momentary spasm of enthusiasm to serve under certain circumstances, which I never expected to occur, I found myself face to face with the alternative of going or showing a white liver by backing out. I decided to do as I had agreed and enlisted for "three years, unless sooner discharged." *Shot* or *starved* should have been added to the contract.

Given time for reflection, I had a thousand fears and misgivings. I moved in a dazed sort of way and couldn't believe I had done such a thing. Naturally timid and shrinking, it seemed impossible that I had, even for a moment, thought seriously of going into the service. I consoled myself with the thought that I should, if I lived, have a chance to see some of the country and *might* witness a battle, which I greatly desired, only I wished to be a safe distance from it — a mile at least.

August 6th was the day of enlistment. Ed Eastman was the recruiting officer and William Hobson was captain of the company. Our examination passed off all right. We were accepted and ordered to hold ourselves in readiness to report in Portland whenever they desired our company. And they desired it much sooner than we anticipated — the very next day.

### August 7th.

We were examined again thoroughly, found to be "sound and kind" and were then mustered into the state service by Captain Joe Perry. So another step was taken, and having nothing else to do, we were turned out into the field to run about like a flock of sheep, as long as we didn't run away. I grew homesick for the first time in my life, experiencing a feeling akin to being in solitary confinement. We have not been assigned to any company; we have no quarters as yet; nearly all who are in camp are strangers.

Company I, to which we are to belong, is composed almost entirely of men from York and Cumberland counties, with a few "Oxford bears" sandwiched in. Most of the men are scholars to a greater or lesser degree: sixteen graduates of high schools, nine collegians, two clergymen, and one lawyer. In addition to all this erudition, a decidedly moral tone pervades the company; there are not less than thirty who are really pious, and quite a number whose spasmodic bursts are noticeable because of their violence as well as their obtrusiveness.

It may be inferred, and justly so, that patriotism prompted most of these men to enter the service. As far as my own case is concerned, I lay claim to but very little of what goes by that name. Love of a change, an overwhelming desire to see the country (with certain considerations already named) furnished the key to my conduct.

But here I am, however I came.


The afternoon dragged its slow length along, and the approach of night warned us to seek shelter and something to refresh the inner man. On making mention of our lack of these things, we were referred to Captain Martin of Company B, who was Officer of the Day. We called on this gentleman and were very much impressed with his kindness of manner and entertained the notion that he was the embodiment of all the Christian graces and the very quintessence of suavity and politeness. So impressed were we with his goodness that we felt like canonizing him Saint Martin the Second. His later conduct only goes to show how deceitful a man can be and how he can smile and smile and still be a villain. He proved to be "a wretch so empty that if e'er there be, in Nature found the least vacuity, 'twill be found in him."

But I have anticipated matters. He used us first-rate upon our first meeting, partly because he knew he had been delinquent in providing for us. He ordered his cook to furnish us with as good as the larder afforded. But it afforded mighty little for a set of hungry men. We were soon munching "salt horse" and washing it down with copious draughts of some kind of tea which tasted strongly of turkey stuffing. This we found was sage tea, and a strong dose at that. Bread didn't seem to be on the bill of fare, quite an important oversight of Captain Martin's. What earthly reason there was for giving us sage tea I never discovered. Nevertheless, hungry and thirsty as we were, this *sumptuous* repast went very well.

But no provision had been made for us to sleep, and we again resorted to Captain Martin for aid. He directed us to occupy a Sibley tent, the floor of which was partially concealed by a few wisps of hay.[1] This was to be our bed, which only goes to show what tremendous latitude our language has, when such a misnomer can be perpetrated. Not even a feather for our head to lie on — such luxury was denied us, as the Commissary Department was out of feathers (and everything else, judging from the meagerness of our supplies so far). We concluded that Captain Martin must be a dreadfully facetious cuss if he could call those few wisps of straw a *bed*. But as privates we were not supposed to know anything, so we didn't dispute it. Our officers, by reason of their shoulder straps, are (in their minds, at least) the embodiment of human wisdom. They look down in lofty scorn upon men who are their superiors in everything but rank.

To tumble onto our new bed was our next move. This was a trifle steep for boys who had never slept on anything harder than a straw or husk cot. One blanket was allowed to every two men, which liberal allowance precluded the idea of rolling oneself in its folds to, in some degree, make up for the lack of bedding beneath. Sleep came finally in the "wee small hours," enabling us to forget our hard beds and our lack of hardtack. The next morning dawned on a tired and disgusted set of mortals.

## August 8th – 10th.

The first tap of the drum found us on our pins and ready for anything except a return to our beds. Sleeping on the soft side of a plank is a strong incentive, and we were not long in dressing as we had retired with everything on but our boots. For an hour or more after we turned out there were no exercises of a military character. Breakfast was announced, and we fell in with a cheerful alacrity. It was a slight improvement over supper: salt horse retired in favor of fresh beef, sage tea was displaced by coffee of a good degree of strength. We also had bread, accompanied by a villainous substance masquerading as butter. It proved a sorry apology for the real thing, having the tokens of age and being tall-flavored.

We find everything subject to one condition: we can eat, drink, or wash when we can find the wherewithal to do so. Our first duty each morning is to wash, when water is to be had, then to punish a quantity of soft bread, coffee, and meat. Our second duty is very much like the first, and so is the third. A few men vary the order of exercises, inasmuch as they indulge in only *one* meal, which lasts all day. It is amusing and astonishing to see the amount of grub disposed of in a day. It is also alarming, as we fear it might result in famine later. But idleness is conducive to hunger most assuredly and if they were not gourmandizing, there is no knowing how much worse they might be doing.

We cannot drill as there seems to be no one who knows enough about it to teach us. Several days of this regime have so disgusted and sickened us that we have lost all enthusiasm over the war and desire to depart for home although we have not fired a gun, nor have our officers drawn their "cheese knives" in defense of the Union. By the end of the third day, our military ardor had so abated that a thermometer which stood at fever heat on Wednesday would have been found at or below zero on Saturday with the mercury congealed.

On August 9th those of us from Saco and Biddeford were allowed a short furlough. Most of us had come away so suddenly as to have left our affairs unsettled. As there was a fair chance that many of us would not look upon our native town again, we did what was equivalent to making our last will and testament. Bidding goodbye to friends passed off jolly enough, as no one hinted even at the bare possibility that we should not come back. And *we* didn't propose to throw a pall of gloom over the matter. It might be four years and it might be forever. Who can tell?

## August 11th.

Received the princely sum of $55.00, which the town has voted to give those who enlisted. The men of means showed themselves to be exceedingly liberal. Men must be forthcoming, even if it takes a draft to do it, and it is touching to see the number of persons who are ready, even anxious, to sacrifice their relatives on the altar of their country. This "spontaneous" uprising of the people should teach the South!

Fifty-five dollars is a most generous sum for a man's head. Such high appreciation is almost enough to die for. The state also decided to do the handsome thing and so it came down with the magnificent sum of $45. The general government gave $25 and one month's wages in advance, making about $140 in all. Here is richness, and we consider ourselves very wealthy. I would feel better, though, if we had brought at least as much as the festive negro is worth at auction.

We returned to Camp King, arriving about 9 P.M. Our passes expired at noon but time was a matter of no account; there is no need of our being there anyhow. We were met at the gate by an exceedingly pompous individual in spectacles and a sash, the latter indicating he was Officer of the Day (and the former that he was trying, by artificial means, to appear intelligent). He examined our passes and gave us a look intended to annihilate us, but it failed to have that effect. This caused the spectacles to glare fiercely and the owner of them to vibrate frantically in the most violent exhibition of temper, reminding me of a Chinese official lashing himself into a fury. He looked and acted like a fool, showing his obvious unfitness for command. At first he refused to let us in and made several ridiculous threats. One of our number was foolish enough to remark that this would please us greatly. Thus, our military fledgling decided that the best punishment was to admit us to camp.

One thing was gained by our furlough. We found better accommodations waiting us: straw beds and a blanket for each man. We have also been assigned to our company, which is Company I, under Captain William Hobson, First Lieutenant P.S. Boothby, and Second Lieutenant J.O. Thompson.

These appointments have no reference to the fitness of the candidates. None has any military knowledge to boast of. Captain Hobson was a schoolteacher, Boothby a hotel clerk, and Thompson a Methodist preacher of more assurance than piety, more breadth of beam than learning. Thompson brought with him a crew who seem to regard him with a species of profound awe. If he condescends to notice them, they immediately mount to the third heaven. As for us common trash, we don't expect any notice from him and our expectations are pretty generally met. The men who came with him know their place and understand that the Reverend J.O. Thompson of the remote country village and Lieutenant J.O. Thompson of the U.S. Army are not the same person. He is overbearing and supercilious, and can be patronizing to serve his own interests. Like a little dog who wags his tail in the presence of a big dog with a bone, there is nothing more deferential than Lieutenant Thompson in the presence of his superiors. In consequence, he is not a favorite with the men, most of whom have an unmitigated contempt for airs.

As we are now officered and our noncommissioned officers appointed, we have commenced drilling. The paucity of military knowledge of both officers and privates renders this pretty dull music. One of our sergeants, who claims to be better posted than the average, was corrected so many times by a private that, in sheer desperation, he begged the latter to assist him. This the private refused to do but offered to take over the entire exercise.

### August 16th and 17th.

Were paid the balance of the money promised us to make up the $140. To most of us this seems quite a sum, but it is niggardly compared with other states such as New York, which gives its volunteers as much as $1,500. If only we'd thought of it in time, we could have gone to New York and enlisted there. If one is going to sell his life, he might as well get all he can out of it.

It has been feared that it might be necessary to enforce a draft in order to fill the quota. This has the effect to cause a draft on the pocketbooks of some who fear that a draft might be just inconsiderate enough to gobble them. Hence, their liberality and unconsciousness of the value of money.

The next day our Saco friends came in to visit us and brought some substantial tokens of their regard. While enjoying their company, those who had been especially favored were so overcome with rum as to fall over dead drunk.

## August 18th and 19th.

The 18th was the day of our muster into the United States service for three years. The mustering officer was Major Gardiner, a full-blooded West Pointer who has a crushing hatred for all volunteer troops. How we lived through this day I know not. Somebody surely has formed a conspiracy to see how much the back can carry and not break, how much the flesh can suffer and not die. Several men fainted and fell from the ranks of dress parade but we managed to stand for hours while one company at a time was inspected. We found mustering into the service by a West Pointer a slow, painful performance. Red tape stuck out all over him like porcupine quills. It was with difficulty that he could get near enough to hand us our guns. He stood off and threw them at us. This, we learn, is not intended as a special token of disfavor; it is simply the West Point style.

The inspection continued, every detail undergoing the closest scrutiny. Our West Pointer was determined to find fault with something or somebody. By the time the first three companies were inspected, the rest of the regiment was flat on the ground, except for Jim Jose. He stood as a monument of endurance and folly. If it be not folly to thus punish oneself currying favor with some official snob, then I don't know what constitutes folly.

The ordeal was finally over and only one man was given permission to retire from service, but he has declined. He enlisted to escape domestic tyranny and has no desire to return.

We engage in drilling and otherwise preparing for the business before us. We have company from Saco — wives, mothers, and sisters who come in on some pretense or other almost daily. On Sunday the ladies of Portland made us a dinner of pies, cakes, cold meats, and other luxuries not mentioned in commissary supplies. We have not suffered for anything thus far, due to our Saco friends, but this does not prevent us from appreciating the Portland ladies' attentions. In the afternoon the Reverend Lovering of Park Street Unitarian Church came out and gave us a flowery discourse in which he was pleased to inform us that "all who died in defense of the flag had a sure passport to heaven." This is all very well for talk, but the Reverend evidently doesn't care to try it on. I feel that death is one of those things to which distance lends enchantment, so notwithstanding Mr. Lovering's bland audacities of speech and fine-spun theories, I don't care to cultivate a closer acquaintance with the hollow-eyed monster. It never does furnish much satisfaction to listen to these cowards who talk of pluck but are so destitute of the quality themselves. Why shrink from that which is so desirable as the glory of war? I am just perverse enough to want to share it.

## August 20th.

Drilling and readying for the move we know will come ere many days. Anywhere for a change! We are sick of this inactivity and its concomitant state of mind. It has been rumored that we are going to Annapolis to a military school for three months and are then to be quartered in the forts around Washington. This is a nice prospect and promises immunity from danger and the exposures incident to life in the field. At night we learned we should leave these diggings on the morrow. Our feelings are highly paradoxical: we want to go and we don't want to. Although we dread it, we have a curiosity to know our fate.

There wasn't a great deal of rest for anyone this night. Singing and carousing went on from dewy eve till daylight. About 3 A.M. there was a general turnout, and a most outrageous din and confusion commenced. Our orders are to move at six, and we set ourselves to getting ready. The glare of the burning beds and the gyrations around them, and all the confusion of breaking camp compares favorably with the popular idea of the place of "future uneasiness."

## August 21st.

About 6 o'clock, everything being ready, we entered Portland via Tukey's Bridge. Our speed could only be compared with a steam engine. At one time it seemed we should not live to get out of the state. We marched only a little over a mile, yet were nearly defunct. Some of us young ones bitterly regret we didn't take the advice of our elders to let the war alone. I left a good job, which pays twice as much as this government. We have surrendered comparative ease and comfort to wear out our lives in this drudgery, if we don't get killed first. And now, being fairly in for it, no lament will avail until sickness, wounds, or death give us relief. Before we came to a halt we were ready to aver that there weren't a dozen more breaths in us and that our powers of endurance had been taxed to the utmost. Dust filled our eyes and ears and throats. The sweat ran down our faces, giving them the appearance of animated gridirons. We halted in Commercial Street and then were hustled into railroad cars, packed in like sheep, and the doors locked.

We started out for Boston amid a great hurrahing at a speed of not less than a mile a minute. We flew through Saco so fast that we couldn't recognize friends who had assembled at the depot to see us off, thinking we should stop there a moment. But it was best to go in this way; it prevented many trying scenes.

Our breakneck pace can only be accounted for on the supposition that our officers, some of whom are so mean as to make mutiny a work of grace, are desirous of reaching the scenes of carnage in a hurry. It was about 2 o'clock when we arrived in Boston and, although we had plenty of time, were rushed across the city as though the entire work of saving the nation devolved upon us. A collation had been set for us on the commons, but we didn't have a chance to get even a smell of it. Our transit through the city was too rapid for comfort.

The streets were narrow, and hot almost to suffocation, and thankful were we when we reached a place to stop long enough to get a breath, even a hot one. We halted at the Providence depot in a broiling sun. Several of the men fainted dead away. There was no shade and no water, and when some sought the support of the walls of the building, they were ordered to "Get into line and STAND THERE!"

We stood till patience ceased to be a virtue, then we threw ourselves down wherever we chose, and bade defiance to those who sought to torture us needlessly. We were kept in this position a long time, with a brick wall on one side and a high fence on the other, and not allowed to go for water although suffering the fiercest thirst. If we were prison birds, we should have fared no worse. How strange it seems to us who have enjoyed our freedom so recently to be thus deprived of all privileges. Have we enlisted to secure freedom for others only to give up our own?

As we couldn't go after water, we employed some boys to fetch it at three cents a canteen. A few of the men took this occasion to procure something stronger and more exhilarating than water. Strong spirits thus braced up drooping spirits.

We left Boston about 5 P.M. and made no stops, arriving in Providence just before dark. Only a short halt was made here and then we were off for Stonington. After dark those who had fortified themselves with a canteen of tanglefoot gave the most convincing evidence of its power as a stimulant. Our vivacious comrades proved conclusively that Man can *descend to* the level of the monkey — whether or not *descended from* him — whenever the requisite amount of tanglefoot can be imbibed. They made the night hideous with their howling, ribald songs, and vulgar jokes, swearing frightful oaths and cursing niggers and the administration without stint. Our officers came in for their share of curses — some of them justly. One of our company, especially pugnacious, was spoiling for a fight. He became so boisterous that Captain Hobson took away his bottle and threw it out the window. This so enraged the bellicose Lamberton that he threatened the most blood-curdling things, even to performing a delicate surgical operation on the captain which would release him from further military service, or any other kind of service. A hint from the captain that he would be put in irons had a most salutary effect on Lamberton, and he became as meek as a lamb.

About midnight we arrived at Stonington and were marched onto a steamboat named *Plymouth Rock*, so named, I decided, because of the resemblance of her crew to that piece of rock. Their hearts were stony. The ship's officers were human hogs. They lacked only bristles, which some of my companions averred were concealed about their persons.

The boat was loaded to her carrying capacity when we arrived, but this made no difference. We were crammed and jammed, hustled on board — handled worse than the horses. We were allowed the saloon, the deck, and any other hole we could find.

A few of us couldn't believe such packing of men was conducive to health or comfort and we accordingly made provision to pass the night where the air was less freighted with filthy odors. Some of our men reeked with fumes of rum and tobacco, and a general air of uncleanness that was the natural consequence of our day's exercise. It seemed as if we had done nothing but sweat from the moment we left Camp King. All manner of dirt had a strong affinity for us, and a cabin packed with such material smelled as loud as an old fish house. The spray on deck nearly drenched us, but at least the air didn't cut like old cheese nor cause a fear of congestion of the lungs. Compared with the air inside it was pure comfort.

## August 22nd.

At 4 o'clock we saw signs of approaching dawn, a truly welcome messenger, and found we were approaching the environs of New York. The rest of the sail was delightful and full of interest.

We came alongside the wharf at Jersey City at 7 o'clock and immediately disembarked. On shore we were instantly besieged by a small army of Agents of the Christian Commission who seemed to entertain the reprehensible idea that we were from some remote part of the world where the light of civilization has never dawned, instead of from puritanical New England where Bibles are as plentiful as dogs in an Irish neighborhood. They insisted on giving each of us a Testament although there isn't a man among us who hasn't one already from home. No doubt they judged us by the

New Yorkers who have gone to the front. If they had supplied something for our physical wants, our comfort and gratitude would have been enhanced. We were the subjects of a perceptible "goneness in our innards," having eaten nothing worth mentioning since our last supper in Portland. We accepted the gift out of courtesy and tried to appreciate the motive.

Nothing was furnished us, but some women came around with a villainous compound alleged to be pie. Having in mind the delicious article bearing this appellation in our section, I was simple-minded enough to invest a few of my stamps (postage stamps are in use for change) to the extent of fifty cents, anticipating a feast. My feast was a feast of fancy, soon dispelled by a closer acquaintance with this beastly imitation of pastry. A turkey buzzard could not have eaten one of them without having his gizzard thoroughly demoralized. Unfortunately, I had invested in two pastries and sunk my teeth into one before discovering the disagreeable contents of the so-called pies. Judging from their internal appearance, they were composed of the sweepings of some Irish den, held together by a generous contribution of hair and flavored with grapes. Not being partial to that kind of sauce, I decided to fill up with less pretentious food whose ingredients had less of the charm of mystery.

Soon after this we left Jersey City, and none too soon. Our experience on the boat and with the people ashore made us eager to see the last of the place. It seemed as if everyone we encountered considered it a religious duty to swindle us.

After going a few miles we came to a city over which the railroad ran, and here I deposited my pastries, giving the inhabitants a chance to witness the remarkable celestial phenomenon of a shower of pies. That they were *not* of heavenly origin was attested by the strong flavor of Old Ireland that pervaded them.

As we advanced into New Jersey the scenery became so varied and enchanting that some of us forgot our hunger. Nature and art have here entered into a warm rivalry and implanted a strange beauty. It seemed like a fairyland. About 4 P.M. we received information that Philadelphia was no more than an hour's ride away. Having heard much about the peculiarities of this place, I was curious to see it. We all held a comfortable hope we might find there a morsel of something for the inner man and a chance to reduce the quantity of dirt adhering to us. We were sleepy and tired, dirty and hungry, and as cross as these four ills combined could make us.

We arrived at Burlington, opposite Philadelphia, about 5 P.M. and moved slowly through the town, where we were enthusiastically received, returning the greetings by cheering and waving handkerchiefs. Mine, which was of nice silk and valued as a gift, was promptly snatched by a person on the platform — to my chagrin. Having done duty from the time I left Maine, the handkerchief was not of immaculate purity, but more so than the character of the one who snatched it.

We soon came to a halt, and here General Howard, from our state of Maine, met us and acted as an escort into the city, which we reached by a monstrous ferry boat. Half of the regiment went to a place called the Cooper Shop, and here we found just what was needed. It has been fitted up by private individuals for the accommodation and refreshment of soldiers going to the seat of war. It was perfection itself, and we in our gratitude could but feebly express our feelings.

We were first conducted to a long row of sinks where every man had the chance to wash his face and hands and a clean towel to wipe on. We then had a luncheon fit for a king, consisting of bread and butter, boiled ham, bologna, sausage, cheese, cake, pickles, and coffee. We were directed to eat all we wanted. There was no reason to doubt that there was a plentiful supply, for we could see a room full of bread and another nearly full of boiled hams. Never was a hungrier set of mortals treated to a repast more suited to its needs. When our plates emptied, they were immediately refilled until we could dispose of no more. As I have already elaborately hinted, our appetites were quite sufficient to make an ordinary table look disconsolate, if not utterly discouraged. But here was no cause for solicitude.

It was with many regrets that we turned our backs on the City of Brotherly Love at midnight, when we took cars for Havre de Grace and the long, long road to Dixie.

# Off to the Land of Dixie

## August 23 – October 9, 1862

It commenced to drizzle soon after dark, and by the time we left Philadelphia it was raining hard. The route was thronged with men, women, and boys who were as anxious to see us as though we came from another planet. It wasn't an easy matter getting through the crowd until an increase of the rainfall induced the "better element" to scatter to their homes. The less retiring ones (the "baser" sort, whom many of our men encouraged) persisted in hanging on till we reached the cars, even offering to accompany us to the front. Their invitations were respectfully but firmly declined. There is no doubt many of the men are as base as these lewd women, and they showed it by hugging and kissing them most vehemently. About midnight we started south. As it was dark and I was dozy, I knew nothing of the country we passed through.

### August 23rd.

About 5 o'clock we awoke to find ourselves being run onto another ferry at Havre de Grace to cross the Susquehanna. Solomon was wrong when he said, "There is nothing new under the sun." He never saw a steam engine, or a ferry boat like this one. Had his Royal Nibs lived in these days of steam, his ideas might have undergone a most radical change.

After crossing the river, we waited for the other wing of the regiment to join us. We then moved on to Baltimore, reaching the Monumental City about 11 o'clock. This city is associated in my mind with secession and "plug uglies" and other suggestions of treason and bloodshed.[1]

We marched up the same street where the 6th Massachusetts was assailed and Ladd and Whitney fell, the first victims from the North. And here was one of the most singular coincidences that ever happened, so singular that I can hardly convince myself that it was not design. On the 19th of April, 1775, Massachusetts shed the first blood in the cause of freedom at Lexington. And now in 1861, on the same date, she repeats it, and two of her sons fall dead in Baltimore.

On our way up the street, I noted many marks of bullets on the walls of the brick buildings, but the city was now as quiet — and to all appearances as loyal — as any city of the North. Union flags were flying and ladies waved their handkerchiefs as we passed.

About noon we were marched into the rooms of some kind of a Union organization and had an alleged collation. The building and its appointments, as well as the food provided, were infinitely inferior to what we had had in Philadelphia. This organization would not have been tolerated here a year ago, but things have changed since General Butler taught the city some manners.

Although the Rebels had declared that no troops marching for the subjugation of the South should pass through their city, General Butler quite as firmly said, "They cannot go *under* it, nor *over* it, and they shall not go *round* it!" The batteries of Federal Hill and Fort McHenry added a most persuasive argument to Ben Butler's words so *through* it the troops went.

Union flags now fly as thick as leaves in the fall. Such demonstrations of loyalty cannot be regarded as genuine; under it all there is a deep-seated hatred for everything Yankee. There is not another city more intensely disloyal. As we marched through the streets many women waved handkerchiefs and flags, but my opinion is that it would be more congenial to their taste to be drinking water from a cup made of a Yankee's skull. It is recorded that they wear finger-rings fashioned from Yankee bones and that Yankee shinbones do duty as drumsticks. And these outrages are committed by people who boast of their superiority and affect to despise us as a low-born set whom they cannot tolerate.

We waited at the depot some considerable time and regaled ourselves on melons to our hearts' content. Large watermelons and cantaloupes could be had for six cents apiece, and peaches for a song. It was especially delightful to indulge in these luxuries, which bring high prices up North. One individual was too close-fisted to allow himself to indulge, even at this low price, and contented himself by gnawing the rinds we threw onto a manure heap. I shall withhold his name, as he will doubtless be rich some day and I may need to borrow a little from him.

Having gorged ourselves, we entered the cars again and were soon on the way south, arriving in Washington just as the sun put its last touch of gilding on the dome of the Capitol. It would be pleasant and exciting under different circumstances, everything being new to us, but loaded down like pack mules we can enjoy but little.

We left the cars and passed into a building adjacent to the depot, where a lunch of beef and bread was furnished us. After eating, we lay down in the depot and were soon sleeping. We had not been long asleep when we had orders to fall in and were on the march somewhere. Past the Capitol, out by the Navy Yard, and over the Anacostia, or East Branch of the Potomac, we marched and hauled up on an eminence called Mount Good Hope. Without any attempt at wit, I will say we indulge a good hope of rest for this night at least.

As we have no tents or shelter of any kind, we have only to spread our blankets and tumble into them. The blue arch of heaven is our cover, the stars our candles, as the "gas light of the moon" is not available. Very tired we are, after precious little sleep, and in coming here we have marched at least six miles — or so it seems to us in our dilapidated condition. We are, all of us, so exhausted that we are not capable of judging distance or anything else.

## August 24th.

Sunday morning, and as fine a one as was ever seen. It was thought best to allow us to lie abed as long as we chose, and we chose to lie till 10 o'clock, when the church bells in Washington turned us out. As they struck their confounded din, I was transported in spirit back to New England. I couldn't make it seem like Sunday, nor did it seem as if I were in my own country. War has given everything an unnatural tint.

We lounged around till noon, when orders came to occupy the forts on this side of the city. Company I was assigned to Fort Stanton, a large earthwork mounting sixteen guns: 32-pounders. These, plus hand grenades and muskets, constitute our means defensive and offensive should an invader be foolhardy enough to attack.

Fort Stanton is delightfully situated on a high hill overlooking Washington, with a fine view of the Potomac from Georgetown to Alexandria, including Long Bridge. On the opposite, or Virginia, side of the river, can be seen the Soldiers' Home, Fairfax Court House and Seminary, and "Arlington," late home of General Robert E. Lee and formerly the residence of his father-in-law, G.W.P. Custis, adopted son of Washington. We are surrounded by beautiful groves of chestnut trees, orchards, and grapevines. Were I free and able to reside in such a place, I could ask for little more to make me supremely happy.

It was somewhat sultry inside the fort so we stacked our arms outside. Tents were put up in a little ridge to the rear of the fort and we were lying around in the most careless manner when there was suddenly an alarm that the Rebels were coming. Such a scampering to get under cover I have never seen. Confusion reigned for some moments, and it is certain that some men could not have told their own names, so excited were they. Everybody grabbed for a gun and cared but little whose he got. One of our noncommissioned officers was intensely agitated and had little control over himself. If there had really been any Rebels coming, he would have been about as effective as an old woman of ninety. How we all got into the fort I shall never know. Whether we walked, ran or flew, sailed or blew in is a mystery, but we reached the sally port and found ourselves inside, thankful for a great deliverance.


### August 25th.

We heard no more about Rebels last night, nor did we find traces of any this morning. As we might have suspected, it was a ruse employed to see how we acted in an emergency and to get us into the fort.

Commenced to get acquainted with the terrain. We soon found it is a place abounding with fruit and other luxuries and have an idea we are now settled and provided for. However, this is enemy country and we might expect a visit any time.

In the morning we were told we'd be trained in the use of the big guns as soon as an instructor could be brought over from one of the regular artillery companies on the other side of the city. A Dutchman from Pennsylvania soon put in an appearance and set about the task, but the heat was so intense that he found us indifferent pupils. The heat is just "orfull" and "tremenjous" and threatens to reduce us to the consistency of soap grease. Fort Stanton seems to be the focus of a monster burning glass. Tents offer no resistance and shut out any breeze that might be stirring. Our appetites have dwindled and army rations are a drug on the market. Fortunately it is fruit season, and this we can enjoy. Also, a male Celt comes over from Washington every day with pies, cakes, and milk — in which, no doubt, we are treated to our peck of dirt. We wade in, nonetheless, and swallow our scruples along with these dainties.

### August 26th – October 6th.

Day after day passed by in this monotonous manner. To our practice on the big guns were added lessons on a couple of howitzers and mortars. We have gained a proficiency in handling them, which surprised our Dutch friend, who is better at giving orders than in executing them. After learning the use of the hand grenades, we considered the country perfectly safe, certain that we could hold our own against the combined powers of Europe and the Southern Confederacy.

This arrogance was soon to receive a severe blow. On the 14th of September the Battle of Antietam was fought. We listened all afternoon to the cannonading although Antietam was sixty-three miles away. Rumor had it that we might expect an attack on the forts at any moment. A story flew around that old Stonewall Jackson himself was marching on Washington. We had seen a body of cavalry rush out of the city over the Long Bridge and heard firing in the direction of Falls Church, so we were ready to believe any tale, regardless of its Munchausen flavor.

A few hours later a picket guard was ordered outside the fort. An order for our instant execution could not have caused more despondent looks, blank faces, and ghostly voices. We might as well have spared ourselves the anxiety, as it had no effect on the stony-hearted officers. At last a sufficient number of patriots were found willing to immolate themselves on the altar of their country. And so the detail went out.

The first post was at the sally port and ran thence to the cook house, where there are various corners and angles from which the enemy might pounce on us. The other posts were stationed at points to the rear of the fort on a road running around it. Contrary to all expectations, none of us was gobbled or molested, and when morning dawned we began to be ashamed that we had been the victims of so much uneasiness. After this we had more confidence and didn't give ourselves any concern about the Rebels. Some time later, though, one of our men who was of a very excitable nature imagined that the Philistines were upon him, and fired. We fell in to meet the enemy, but investigation showed only an old cow quietly grazing — utterly unconcerned at her narrow escape from death.

As the weather grew cooler and we became accustomed to the fort, we began to like the place and cherished the hope we might stop here a long time, even as long as our term of service. But this is not to be. Scarcely had we settled down when a few ambitious ones began to pant for glory and devise schemes for its realization. The first step was a representation at headquarters that we — the 17th — are anxious to test the quality of our mettle on the battlefield.

As far as the men in the ranks are concerned, this statement is a gross misrepresentation wholly devoid of foundation. We desire to stay where we are, or in some place equally safe and pleasant. But true or false, the story was believed at headquarters and preparations soon commenced for getting us into the field. Our Major West, who was at the bottom of it all, with high glee began drilling us in field tactics. At this time we were not aware of all this plotting, and when ordered to drill, we continually wondered why. Such movements were of no use in the forts. We soon learned that staying at Fort Stanton formed no part of Major West's plans. He, and a few others who listened to his seductive words, desire promotion, and to secure this are willing to sacrifice lives — and even to *risk* their own.

Promotions at this place must be few, natural causes being all that can be depended on to produce vacancies. Human life is valued at rather a low figure compared with the gratification of their ambition. It is devoutly wished by the men that Major West and his friends might find the glory they pant for — underground.

About the first of October our suspicions crystallized into something definite. It was well understood in the ranks that our stay in Fort Stanton would be very brief, perhaps reckoned even by hours.

A Rhode Island regiment was sent in to relieve us, arriving some days before our departure. A remarkably rich time we had of it, too. We did not agree particularly well; their officers assume too much and put on many airs and frills for men who come from so small a commonwealth, not as large as some of the counties in Maine. Indeed, it is reported that it isn't safe to let a coffee pot boil over on the stove for fear the entire state of Rhode Island will be submerged.

Is it to be wondered then that we were indignant with these fellows and their airs? Also, they had a free and easy way of making appropriations. One of them stole my blanket and left me to get along as best I could. Had it not been for a comrade who had some holes that he called a blanket, and which he placed at my disposal, I must certainly have suffered considerably before another was procured.

We knew that in a few days we should leave these haunts and decided to have a little sport at the expense of the Rhode Islanders. On the last night of our stay we made it warm for them by burning the outbuildings. The rage of their officers was highly amusing to us, it was so impotent. The more we laughed, the more they raved. One of them actually danced about and swore and offered a sum of money for information concerning the perpetrators of this outrage. It didn't work, and we soon retired, leaving them to stew it out while we packed our knapsacks.

It was no small job to cull over our household goods. Much of the accumulation of the last seven weeks must be abandoned, for we are neither pack mules nor camels, although some of the men seem determined to test the question.

## October 7th.

About 7 o'clock we left our snug quarters and waited down at the bridge for the other wing of the regiment. It soon arrived, and we moved over into Washington, went into the Capitol grounds, and stacked arms. Here we were told to await further orders. These were slow in coming, so we passed the time inspecting the incongruous mass of stone called the Capitol.

Our view was somewat circumscribed as Congress is not in session. Consequently, much of the building is not accessible. The rotunda is occupied as a hospital for a portion of those wounded at Antietam. The large insane asylum across the river, many of the private houses in Washington, and tents and houses elsewhere have also been pressed into service as hospitals.

When one considers all these, and the hundreds killed outright, one begins to get an idea of the magnitude and fierceness of this engagement and must concur that General McClellan, who fought against the Confederate's great chieftain Lee, is *not* a "baby," even if Hooker did pronounce him such. Lee was so badly punished that he was glad to sneak off.

The wounded have an opportunity to become art critics, for the walls of the rotunda are covered with paintings (so-called) of scenes in American history, several of them executed by G.W.P. Custis, Mrs. General Lee's father. Having taken a glance at these works of art, we departed not knowing any more about the rest of the building than we did of Windsor Castle or the Tuilleries. We discovered the rest of the building was fastened — as if there was a possibility there'd be anything to steal after Congress had been there.

After dinner some of our men who have formed a select choir sang a few patriotic songs suitable to the occasion and designed to stir up the latent forces of our natures.

Sometime after two o'clock we had orders to get ready to move and we were soon on the road to Long Bridge, but instead came to a halt not far from the Washington Monument. Here we waited again for orders. Just before sunset we crossed the bridge and moved out over the line about a mile, and went into bivouac in a low place in front of a large earthwork. We didn't exactly camp in a frog pond, but the ground is enveloped in a misty shroud that rapidly sent chills up our spinal columns. The fact that we are wet through with sweat doesn't add to our comfort. Such air as this must be burdened with malaria. In fact, I feel full of it and shudder at thought of lying here all night.

In arriving at our bivouac we came through a kind of stockade made of logs sharpened on one end and driven into the ground. It looks as if our generals think they have an army of wild Indians to fight instead of an army of Americans with modern implements and engines of war that could batter that stockade into the smallest kind of kindling wood in fifteen minutes. The Rebel generals will laugh and kick themselves in the ribs if they get near enough to see these tremendous devices for keeping them out of Washington. So much for the wisdom of our West Point engineers, who have more gold braid than common sense.

GENERALS McCLELLAN AND HOOKER. *Harper's Pictorial History of the Civil War.*

### October 8th.
Turned out at 7 o'clock and ordered to move right away. Our grief at leaving this charming place was *not* inconsolable, and a good brisk trot was the best way to take the

chill out of us. A half hour later found us on the road to Falls Church, a small hamlet not more than six miles from Washington. We didn't go quite to it, but turned off in another direction.

On the way out from Washington we passed a large number of dismantled houses, which had been stripped of their boards and everything behind which the enemy might hide. Judging from the size and appearance of these mansions, this must once have been a pleasant locality. Most of the owners are in the Rebel army or in Washington playing the spy. However attractive the neighborhood, we couldn't stop a minute. We marched on and on nearly all the forenoon without a halt.

When a halt was finally called, half the men were flat in the road, or by its side, strewn along for miles. The weather being sultry, and we unused to marching, it is bad enough when we have nothing to lug, but some unfortunates persist in making pack mules of themselves. Those who did keep up were puffing and blowing like porpoises. This racing is enough to exhaust and play out veterans, to say nothing of "green uns" like us.

Many things regarded as necessaries we have now discarded as of more burden than use, leaving them by the roadside rather than leave ourselves there. Men of each company came in with the mounted officials, but it is safe to say that one-half of them didn't arrive till night, and late at that.

Our regiment is assigned to the 3rd Brigade, 1st Division, 3rd Corps. This brigade is commanded by General Berry of Maine, who is at this time sick at home. The division is commanded by General Birney of Pennsylvania, the corps by Major General George Stoneman. Colonel Poe of Michigan is in temporary command of our brigade.

We went into camp near Ball's Crossroads on the spot where a body of Rebels encamped only a short time before — within hearing of the church bells of Washington. We found many tokens of their stay in a pine grove nearby, enough to disprove the theory that they are only half-civilized. They drank whiskey, but aside from this we saw no evidence of their superiority.

When we first made camp, we didn't know how near we were to the city. In fact, we marched not less than eighteen miles to arrive at this place, which on a beeline is only six miles from Washington. This might have been necessary, but I don't believe it. If a rumpus had occurred, we shouldn't have been much better than a flock of sheep. Some of the men didn't get in all this day, and many have gone to the extreme of throwing away much of their stuff that is really indispensable.

The brigade to which we are assigned bears the appellation of the Iron Brigade. But as this designation is laid claim to by no less than three brigades, I shall not use it further lest I confound things. However, it looks good on paper. Its former commander was Phil Kearney, a name synonymous with daredeviltry and recklessness beyond equal. He was absolutely fearless and "longed for the fray." Of Kearney it could be said, "He feared not God, nor regarded the person of men." Profanity was his vital breath; coarseness was his native air. He had wealth, but if he possessed culture nobody ever suspected it. A person who tried to be decent in his presence was almost certain to be overwhelmed by a torrent of billingsgate.[2] He recognized all men as having the right to stand erect, and one must never approach him as a cringing suppliant.

It might be interesting to follow the life of such a character but we cannot for he didn't live long. He was killed at Chantilly while reconnoitering the enemy's picket line. Unknowingly, he had penetrated the enemy line and was ordered to surrender. He replied with a curse, put the spurs to his horse, threw himself forward on the neck of his mount, and galloped off. The Rebel fired and Kearney fell to the ground, dead, remaining in their lines until morning, when he was identified and sent into his own line under a flag of truce. How he came to his end was a mystery, as no blood, bruise, or contusion could be found. The surgeon was about to relinquish the search when he discovered the slightest protuberance just below the ribs. An incision was made and the bullet found. It had entered the body rearward, without so much as breaking the skin, something for which medical history furnishes no parallel.

Kearney was succeeded by General Richardson, who was killed at Antietam, and General Birney raised to the command. If there was a painful lack of dignity in his predecessors, it is fully met in General Birney, for a more dignified individual never mounted a charger. He reminds me of a graven image and could act as a bust for his own tomb, being utterly destitute of color. As for his countenance, it is as expressionless as a Dutch cheese.

When Birney was promoted to command the division, Colonel Berry of the 3rd Maine was made brigade commander, a most excellent choice in both cases. We feel well pleased to be under a general from Maine, thinking it may be to our advantage. If report be true, however, we shall have all the service at the front that the most blood-thirsty officer could desire, even the redoubtable Major West.

## October 9th.

Passed the time drilling, drawing clothing, and otherwise preparing to vacate these parts. Stuart's Rebel cavalry are on a raid up in Maryland and are reported to have surrounded that portion of our army there. It is surmised that he has by this time got so far into Maryland that with a decent alacrity on our part we can capture him. So today we were ordered to go up and "possess the land" and gobble the wily Stuart.

The rest of the 3rd Corps is at Poolesville. Thither we are directed to assemble ourselves and to capture the Rebel chief on the way. But it is generally conceded that there are two parties to any agreement. We have to catch our eel first, before we cook him, and Stuart is a slippery fish.

# The Chase Is On

## October 10 – December 10, 1862

*October 10th.*

It was decided to go in the lightest marching order and to pick out those men who were well and capable. So, during the night of the 10th we were called up and assorted. Those who cannot march far were ordered to the rear. We had an opportunity to test the patriotism of some of the loud-mouthed, bloodthirsty fellows who, when in camp, edified us by telling us what they will do on the battlefield. Almost to a man they now discovered that they were quite too infirm to march. One after another was sent to the rear, proving that their patriotism, like some people's religion, is all in their mouths.

*October 11th.*

Having packed our traps and left them in the barn of Mr. Pyle, hard by, we started on the march with only our blankets, rations, and equipment, in light marching order. We proceeded to the Potomac and crossed at the Chain Bridge, then followed a towpath up into Maryland. We had no rest until noon, when, the generals being hungry, we halted near a farmhouse for them to refresh a little. The smell of meat and vegetables penetrating our olfactory organs was positively aggravating as it was all *we* had of their dinner. We had our revenge by stealing the farmer's apples and making pleasant remarks about our officers that would have affected them about as much as a fly on an oxen's horn if they'd heard.

We made no more halts till eve, when we halted by the roadside in a pine growth, having marched twenty-two miles. Our place of bivouac is near Seneca Mills, if anybody knows where that is. I only know it is in Maryland.

Some of those men who had been so weak that they could hardly wag a tail, or keep anywhere near the column all day, recovered their strength and spirits and went out foraging after the rest of us had lain down to rest. The squalling of hens cleaving the night air announced their arrival at a farmhouse and that "fowl" play was going on.

It is truly astonishing to see the amount of latent energy these feeble men develop when a pig or hen is spotted. Their drooping spirits revive at once and they sit up the rest of the night to cook and cram, making sleep impossible for others. The sizzling of pork and kindred sounds can be heard on every side.

### October 12th.

I made out to get half a night's rest, which was doing tolerably well considering we have no tents and it being quite cool. Back home the mere mention of such a thing as sleeping out in this way would have given me a chill. But here it *must* be done, and I have learned that I can do many things which under other circumstances I should deem quite impossible.

Started out to find where Mr. J.E.B. Stuart is holding service this Sunday. We marched till noon before seeing or hearing anything of that worthy. It was then rumored that he was coming, and with proper vigilance we could bag him as there are only two other insignificant routes by which he could escape. We formed line of battle in three sides of a square — two of infantry, one of artillery — and waited for him. We intended to lie in ambush, the infantry on each side of the road, and the artillery formed across it near the river. By the time he struck the latter and was thrown into confusion, the infantry would close in on him and the game would be ours. With these very pleasant cogitations we laid there concealed in the brush a couple of hours. But, after all this, he had the cool impudence to go off by another route and we lost this opportunity of distinguishing ourselves.

It is said that this daredevil may have actually made a circuit of Stoneman's corps, near Poolesburg, or passed between it and this division, and escaped. It is a wonder the impudent creature didn't undertake to capture one or both of us. After we ascertained that he was gone, we resumed the march and halted for the night near Edward's Ferry.

We had scarcely bivouacked when it began to pour in a most extraordinary manner. It seems to come down in bucketfuls. Unlike Father Noah, we have no Ark, not even a tent or shelter. It has been said that "God tempers the wind to the shorn lamb," but He won't temper the rain to our unprotected heads. Not only does it pelt us on our heads, but it is running down under us in streams. A ditch around us is the remedy for this new difficulty. Precious little sleep will be obtained this night.

### October 13th – 27th.

I don't think the sun was ever a more welcome guest. We soon had a fire going and our blankets and clothes drying, making life a trifle more endurable.

About 9 o'clock we packed up, supposing we were going on the march, but we only moved a mile or so nearer the ferry and went into bivouac on a hill just back of it. During the day our tents went up, and by "borrowing" straw from some stacks near us, we contrived to make ourselves comparatively comfortable.

This is a most desirable place for a camp. The view is extensive, including the Virginia side of the Potomac for miles, nearly to the Bull Run Mountains. The section abounds in beautiful springs, and we have the Potomac and the canal to bathe and wash clothes in. Fruit, milk, pigs, hens, and cattle abound, and we do not allow the animals to wander around camp unprotected. Sometimes appetite gets the better of us and we sally forth and bring them in. The farmers have lodged complaints at headquarters and the provost guard has been set upon our track with orders to arrest all found outside of our lines unaccompanied by a noncommissioned officer. This is a most unsatisfactory state of affairs and causes a heap of dodging around, taking away much of the pleasures of foraging. Profound strategy is resorted to, and by it we keep our *table d'hôte* provided with luxuries. We indulge in fried chicken, pork, and lamb cutlets to our hearts' content.

Colonel Poe, who is in temporary command of the brigade, is very jealous of us and was not slow in giving us the full benefit of his hatred. If rigorous treatment can make our lives bitter, he is determined to administer it. His own regiment pilfers far more than we do, but the guard has a faculty of looking over the Michiganders and letting their optics fall onto us, much further off. We, in consequence, meet with many exciting adventures and enjoy the reputation of being the biggest thieves out.

If Colonel Poe thinks he has gained a victory over us, that only goes to show what delusions the human mind is capable of, for there has been no perceptible diminution of the luxuries aforesaid. A washing excursion to the river or canal gives us the desired opportunity to inspect the crops, some of which — a pig, sheep, or feathered biped — always insist on accompanying us back to camp.

There occurred a little episode recently that opened our eyes to the fact that our Captain Martin is not as saintly as we supposed when we first encountered him in Portland. On the occasion in question he came near depriving Uncle Sam of two men in a jiffy. He was Officer of the Day and, in order to show his brief authority, came prowling around after taps. Hearing some conversation in our tent, he ordered an immediate cessation of it. We at once complied and, hearing him move off (so we thought), commenced again, there being no good reason why we shouldn't talk as much as we chose. The first intimation we had of his presence was a whir-r-r through the air, like a Whitworth shell, a soft voice stealing out on the evening breeze saying "D——n you, see now if you will stop!" Fortunately for us, his number 18 pontoon[1] landed on the tent between our heads, otherwise there would have been an obituary on our untimely demise. We didn't indulge in any further conversation, but came to the conclusion that our amiable friend Martin is a consummate old fraud.


Nothing of any consequence took place until about the 22nd, when we were sent on picket on a strip of land between the Potomac and the Baltimore & Ohio Canal, nearly opposite Ball's Bluff, a place of most unhappy memory so far as we are concerned.[2] We got posted before dark, otherwise it is doubtful if we should have been posted that night. Some of our officers ought to have been posted as cowards, for such they proved to be.

Never were such weird sounds heard at this spot in the blackness of night — moans, groans, growls, and screeches. Perfect blood curdlers! A neighborhood of felines engaged in an Ethiopian concert couldn't have added anything to the racket. Those men who were nervously inclined or superstitious were tremendously agitated. Their imaginations ran riot and they heard very much more than the circumstances warranted. Some of them heard the splashing of oars, and strained their eyes nearly out of their sockets to see who was coming. It was only the Potomac's tiny billows lashing the shore. But there was something weird and ghostly about this place, where so many good men were murdered, that almost stopped our hearts. At no other place have we experienced so much timidity without any real cause. The noises could all be traced to natural phenomena — the sighing of the wind through the trees, the hooting of owls, sounds made by coons and sundry other animals — but all seemed doubly loud and fearful because of the associations of the place.

Some of the men were kept on their posts only with difficulty, and some of the officers were worse than the privates. One in our company, when ordered to go down to the river and see if everything was right, went a few feet in that direction and returned, saying the posts were all deserted. The fact was, he was afraid to go near enough to the front to find the men and instead gave vent to this slander. I saw him dodging from tree to tree in rear of my post, but had no idea what he was about. He was a Methodist preacher, one concerning which it is said, "The righteous are bold as a lion."

In the morning we discovered some of the causes of the sepulchral sounds of the night and concerned ourselves no further with ghosts, ghouls, loons, or Rebels.

Across the canal from us is a large and splendid farm owned by one Snowdon Pleasant, a strong Secesh [Secessionist] sympathizer whose surname is a misnomer, as he is anything but pleasant to us. His apples and pigs *are* very pleasant, however. We had no money to pay for some foraged goods recently and offered him our notes.[3] These he refused to take and entered a complaint at headquarters. Colonel Poe was only too glad to show us some attention. He conceals his hatred under a "keen sense of justice," which he seems to fall back on whenever *we* are the delinquents. Our colonel took sides with the Rebel against us and we were immediately put under guard and not allowed to go out unless accompanied by a noncommissioned officer. No other troops in this division are subjected to this petty persecution. We were held in this surveillance for about a week and put to considerable inconvenience. Some of our officers finally claimed to have procured our release by paying Mr. Pleasant the sum of $300, which they said was to offset a little account we hold against them for eating our rations since we left the State of Maine. The story that they have paid out any such sum is unconvincing. The organ of credulity has not been developed to a very startling degree in this soldier, at least.

The monotony of this picketing excursion is occasionally broken by an encounter with the provost guard. One day there was a suggestion of something more exciting than harassing the guards. There was a lively commotion caused by discovery of a band of Rebels across the Potomac, on or near Leesburg Heights. They were reported to be executing battalion movements. This we regarded as somewhat cheeky, if not a downright menace to us. We communicated the fact to headquarters, who promptly brought his field glass to bear on them and pronounced them Rebels. He said he could see them deploy, close up, and break into column.

We watched them for some time and thought we saw them go through certain evolutions of a military character. So much for imagination, for this indeed was the substance of our Rebels. There were no Confederates across the river, no military evolutions. It was simply a rail fence that had somehow become more conspicuous that day. Imagination, aided by a few doses of commissary red-eye had done the rest. It occurs to me that a man who can see a rail fence cut up such antics as Major West reported must have something to do with *other* glasses than just his field glass. The bottom of a tumbler is an excellent medium through which to take a certain kind of observation.

### October 28th.

Received orders to be "ready to move at a moment's notice." Being still green in this business, we packed up, and although the rain was falling in torrents, we took down our tents and sat around outdoors waiting an order to move. Thus we sat till noon, when we were told there was to be no move that day and that we could go and "make ourselves comfortable." Make ourselves comfortable indeed. The ground where our tents had been was one mass of wet straw and mire; we had shown ourselves idiots, and this ungenerous sarcasm was a fitting climax to our folly. All the time we were out soaking, the rest of the division was in tents, no doubt making merry at our expense. No wonder, for Major West and Adjutant Roberts have seen service in the field and should have known that an order to "be ready to move" doesn't mean to pack up in this way, but a general readiness.

The first step toward making ourselves comfortable was to move to higher ground where the mud was something less than a foot deep. We then put up tents and procured a lot of straw from stacks nearby. So we are out of the mud and, by comparison with our condition in the forenoon, might be said to be comfortable. By these means we will contrive to pass a very decent night.

The prospect of such an early departure from here is a serious disappointment to some of us who have a weakness for the festive pig. For several days we've been watching a gigantic specimen of the female gender, who is giving sustenance to a full dozen juvenile porcines. We had fondly hoped these juveniles would reach a state of maturity to be able to sit at meat with us before orders came to move. But the administration, utterly indifferent to our desires, has chosen this time to order General McClellan to cross the Potomac and find the enemy. Thus a presidential order has, indirectly, given a respite to thirteen pigs. We spared the mother pig for the sake of the children, expecting ultimately to get the whole family; now we shall get neither.

### October 29th.

The order of yesterday was repeated and this time it was "go." We started about 7 o'clock and marched up the river to White's Ford, where we found the rest of the corps, only they had forded the stream, or were doing so, when we reached the river. We were ordered to cross in the same manner, and accordingly made preparation: some stripped entire, some only removed their nether garments, some removed nothing. The sharp, slippery rocks gave the barefooted ones no end of hurts and caused some of them to lose their footing. The current is very strong from recent rains, making the fording difficult and dangerous.

When we reached the Virginia shore, we found that the worst part of this fording business was climbing the bank. Those who had preceded us had dragged so much moisture over the clay that it was slippery as ice. Our ascent was like the old gentleman who "Got up one stair, and tumbled down three." Some did, in fact, fall back and landed in a heap at the bottom of the bank, or at the bottom of the river.

We all finally climbed the bank and, after running a mile or two, came up with the rest of the column, bivouacked some distance farther down the river. Fires were soon built, rails being plentiful, and we settled for the night sometime before dark.

A foraging party went out soon after to see if there is anything eatable in this section. The Rebels have preceded us by a few weeks, but they have been quite sparing of things in Rebeldom, and our party returned well supplied. Those who are too lazy to go after these things themselves can purchase them for a mere trifle: turkey at 25 cents apiece, and other dainties in proportion. The Rebel policy of sparing the people might create a public sentiment favorable to them, but otherwise is barren of good results, as we follow hard behind them. It is *our* notion to "make treason odious," even if we have to eat every turkey, chicken, and pig in Virginia. We don't propose to go hungry when treason stalks abroad in every pasture and farmyard.

### October 30th.

We were detailed to go on picket. Headquarters are at a large brick mansion, which was used by Stonewall Jackson only five weeks ago. There is, perhaps, no design in it, but it seems curious that our generals so carefully keep five weeks between us and this Rebel chieftain.

The owner of this place is Secesh to the core and makes no bones about it. All of which renders his property insecure and his neck liable to a slight extension. His age is somewhat of a protection, being about seventy. But too much chin of his kind has more than once improved the market for rope. Being less radical than some, we let him gabble while we proceeded to gobble such edibles as we had a taste for. An expression of appalling uncertainty crept over his aged countenance as he beheld his stock rapidly diminishing. He looked daggers and penknives at us, but we didn't concern ourselves greatly; turkeys and chickens tasted just as nice no matter how sour he looked.

### October 31st.

We came in from picket and spent the rest of the day cooking the luxuries we captured. Solomon descants upon the choice flavor of stolen meats. I have but little historical data as to Solomon's experience in the meat business, and for myself can only say that I didn't notice any particular richness of flavor.

### November 1st.

Were mustered for two months' pay but didn't see any money. It is just as well, as we have no use for it except to pay the Virginians for what we have taken, a thing not to be considered in respect to our opinion of Secessionists. Nothing special happened after muster, and we laid around on picket as usual until 5 P.M. when we changed camp, moving to Leesburg Heights. In coming here we had a chance to glimpse the wealth of this section known as Loudon Valley. We passed many fine residences and I was much struck with the beauty of the country. One mansion in particular is so elegant that I can only describe it by calling it palatial, more like some ducal palace than the residence of a plain American gentleman. It is owned by ex-mayor Swan of Baltimore (afterward governor of Maryland). Our route lay directly across his grounds, which we entered through a marble gate not less than a half-mile from the house. The grounds are very extensive and embrace a magnificent tract of country.

Mr. Swan's plumage is none too immaculate in respect to the Secession heresy; he departed summarily sometime previous to our arrival, leaving his estate in charge of a lot of niggers, who chattered and grinned like so many monkeys. They were mortally scared, as if they expected to be devoured then and there. But having lunched on chicken and turkey we felt little inclination to sup on crow, so we passed along and didn't molest them or the house.

We halted for the night on the top of the heights. The town of Leesburg is at the foot of these hills.

*November 2nd.*

Sunday, and we have no work or drill. We would have gone out foraging if it weren't Sunday. The country we have just left was teeming with game, but the change here is most notable. It is a most excellent *hunting* ground, in that one can hunt here and find nothing until he dies of starvation. So far as we can see, there is only one old hen, belonging to an impecunious shoemaker. We essayed to lay murderous paws on the bird, but she, being duly impressed with being the sole survivor of her species, went around the house on the wings of the wind and everything else diabolical that could assist her in her flight.

The Rebels have skinned these parts of everything except this venerable bird, who seems to bear a charmed life. We were at last compelled to cry "quits" and let Miss Biddy go free.

I have to record here the most despicable conduct of some dirty fellows who, exasperated by their failure to catch Mistress Biddy, decided to execute a dashing movement on the house. Passing the door, they saw the table set for breakfast. Instead of going in and setting down to eat like gentlemen, they went in, seized the tablecloth, and bore it off dishes and all, to the utter astonishment and grief of the occupants.

This was a nasty, contemptible trick, deserving prompt punishment. But they did not get it, as this family who were robbed are *poor*, and such may be robbed with impunity. The Rebels have already taken all the clothing, carpets, and bedding. I must add, though, that anyone who has seen the destitute condition of the Rebs cannot blame them; they could improve their state by changing clothes with a scarecrow. But with us it is different. We have no such excuse, being well-clothed.

About 1 o'clock had orders to move immediately. We cut across fields in every direction, marched about eight miles, and hauled up near an old brick tavern named Mount Gilead. This tavern looked very homelike and inviting but there was only accommodation for the general and his staff. They took lodgings inside and we were turned into the fields. There was no balm in Gilead, unless we could find it in an old mill nearby.

As we came into the field, each of us took a rail from the fence for firewood. Captain Martin undertook to steal the rail belonging to my chum, who remonstrated with him. Martin threw down the rail, saying with a menacing sneer, "It is all right," whereupon a voice piped up from the rear line, saying, "If it isn't all right, we will make it right in the morning." Shades of Pandemonium, but wasn't old Martin mad when he heard this reply and the fiendish chuckle that followed it! He sought to lay hands on the "impudent upstart" who had the audacity to sass the great Martin. (The adjective *great* I use in reference solely to the captain's size 18 feet, which a few days past came so near to depriving my chum and me of what little brains we have. It is a wonder to us that the general does not utilize Martin's shoes instead of hauling around a pontoon train. Martin would not be pleased to know that the chap who claimed the rail and the one whose remark so irritated him are the same whose heads he threatened on that occasion at Edward's Ferry.)

As soon as we had stacked arms and unslung our trappings, we started out to view the fields. In the old mill we found some flour, and it was soon doing duty as something resembling griddle cakes. We disposed of them all and would have licked the platter if there had been one on which we could have executed this ill-mannered trick. A dirty, smoke- and grease-begrimed tin plate and tin dipper have to serve as our entire culinary department. We boil potatoes, fry pork, and make coffee — all in our dippers. Army life in the field is an excellent school for teaching how little our actual needs are, especially in the matter of dishes. We see at once what the poet meant when he said, "Man wants but little here below," and in the army we can verify the other line of that stanza: "Nor wants that little long."

### November 3rd.

Marched nearly all day and camped for the night near Goose Creek, not far from Upperville, outside yet another old mill. More fritters for supper. Here also was a cornfield of ample dimensions, and we took in a "right smart lot of it," as the Virginians say. A couple of cows across the way were speedily added to our bill of fare. Supplies are mighty uncertain around here. Feast one day and fast the next.

### November 4th.

Went on picket on Goose Creek, a sluggish stream emptying into the Potomac just below Edward's Ferry. All was quiet until night, when we heard a deal of rustling in the bushes. We couldn't tell whether it was Rebels, hogs, or snakes making this everlasting rustle, rustle, as if the woods were full of some disturbing element. It was just far enough off to make it imprudent for us to leave our posts to investigate.

We bore this state of affairs until daylight, when we sent out a detail to find the cause. Instead of Rebels, they found a drove of lean hogs who fled at our approach, all but one old masculine who was the only one having any claim to fatness. (The others were so lean as to require a blanket to make a shadow.) The old fat one commenced to show fight. Sergeant Richard's bayonet pinned him to the ground. When dressed, he made pork enough to last us as long as we live, but after the pig was put into the spider he continued to puff and froth. It reduced our gustatory pleasure in pork to the minimum and we had no stomach for it after all.

We remained on picket all day. Heard a brisk firing over among the hills, near Ashby's Gap. We could see the smoke and hear the rattle of the smaller guns when the wind was favorable. This was our first hostile meeting and excited us not a little. We later learned that it was caused by the appearance of a few Yankee cavalrymen in the same place where some Confeds were camping. An altercation over the proprietorship of the land ensued, and the Rebels found it expedient to depart southward via Upperville.

The execution of this movement was about as sudden as its conception. They passed through the town in the most undignified haste in a cloud of dust, now and then a pair of heels cleaving the air. The ladies of Upperville had a feast prepared for the defenders of their charms after the invaders had been driven out, but so sudden was the flight of their shining knights that there was no time for such collations. In this latter I can sympathize, having had a similar experience when we were hustled through Boston. Our cavalry pursued the Confeds as far as the Gap and then returned. It seems as if the Rebs might have seen enough of us today to cure them of their absurd notions that they can do such astonishing things.

### November 5th.

I was on picket till noon, when we were ordered to join our command immediately. Having done so and drawn rations, we started right off on the march in a southerly direction.

The first town we came to was Middleburg, a place of considerable importance for this section. It contains two or more churches, some nice houses and stores. The churches have been converted into Union hospitals for wounded from the battle of Antietam and from the late fight [first battle of the Wilderness]. Many private dwellings are in use for the same purpose. Several houses have Union flags flying, this being policy. Some ladies even came out smiling, waving their handkerchiefs at us, though Satan never hated holy water more than they do us. Still, we flatter ourselves that they cannot be wholly indifferent to our sleek and comparatively tidy appearance compared with the scarecrow condition of their own men. We smiled on them very graciously, molested no one, but marched quietly through as though it were some Northern town.

We turned down a street to the right and were soon out of Middleburg and on our way to the mountains, which seem to loom right in front. Rebels, or some portion of our army, had been just ahead of us, for there were campfires all along the road and the mountains were enveloped in smoke.

We marched all afternoon and hauled up for a few minutes at White Plains, a station on the Manassas Gap Railroad. While we paused there, an engine came down the road and it seemed so like an old friend that we gave a cheer. A demonstration of this kind may seem childish, but I am not chary of my dignity and confess to a weakness for anything reviving memories of home. "Home, sacred name, at thy endearing sound / What forms of ravished pleasure hover round."

It is now quite plain that we are not very far behind the Johnnies. We don't appear to be pressing them very much and soon hauled up for the night near Salem. As it was dark and we were very tired, we laid down without making any preparation for rain, which was imminent, and which came down in good shape about midnight. Piling out in the darkness and rain and mud in strange country isn't a bit amusing. We dug a ditch, and by the time we lay down again, the rain had ceased. We learned a lesson that should prove worthwhile in our future careers as soldiers: dig a ditch around the tent when it looks like rain at night.

## November 6th.

Got up early and were ordered to move at 7 o'clock. That hour found us on the road, moving for the Bull Run Mountains. We don't know what McClellan is about, but his movement looks like maneuver. He menaced Lee at the gaps of the Blue Ridge and then struck out as though he proposes to cut Lee's communications. Lee, not knowing which of these movements is real, or which is the feint, has divided the army in the valley to meet either, and thus opened the way for McClellan to whip them in detail.

We soon came to Thoroughfare Gap, a narrow and rugged defile in the mountains where the Rebels could have bothered us immensely if they had only been there. It was mighty slow work, halt and close up all afternoon, till it seemed we had scarce life enough to put one foot ahead of the other. By the time the rear of the column passed through the gap, the van of it was way off across the valley toward Bull Run, and we thought we never should live to get closed up. But we did, and came into camp about 7 o'clock, having experienced the hardest march we've been subjected to thus far. We went into camp a few miles north of Warrenton and about the same from Waterloo. Never was the ruddy glow of oak and chestnut rails more welcome, or our dish of strong coffee more exhilarating. The sky was threatening as we retired, and we anticipated rain before morning. Instead of rain, we have snow. Glad we are, too, for we have seen all the mud we want for several weeks at least.

## November 7th.

No marching orders today, and as the Dutchman said, "We don't vas sorry." A few of our men went to spy out the land and found something well worth seeing. It is a large plantation owned, or occupied, by a Confederate "widow" named Lee, whose husband is in the Rebel army (not in heaven as she purports). It is a curious fact that there are many Virginians who have died but whom we believe increase the Rebel army in corresponding ratio.

Mrs. Lee has been left in a comfortable condition by her liege. She has a splendid plantation on which are five hundred hives of honey and other eatables. Here is an opportunity we might not have again. When Mrs. Lee discovered what an affinity we have for honey and other good things, she made the astonishing and appalling revelation that she is a relative of General Robert E. Lee by marriage.

Finding that this didn't have the desired effect on us, she all at once recollected that she was of French extraction and would call on her government to protect her. This didn't interrupt our work in the least, as we care no more for France than we do for the King of Dahomey. She informed us, in terms no wise complimentary, that no tears would be shed at our absence, no matter how short our stay. So, we prepared to take French leave, and take some honey along too. The cold weather is especially favorable, as it makes the bees stupid.

Each two men bore back to camp a hive of honey, and as we advertised Mrs. Lee's pretty thoroughly, her sales were just immense; not less than three hundred hives came in. Others invested in pigs and sheep, large numbers of which were running around loose. We didn't feel enough interest in their genealogy to ask whether their pigships' names were Lee or Fitzhugh. The claim of being descended from French or German families is a dodge by some Rebel sympathizers to save their property, and might work with some who are more anxious to conciliate those powers than we are. We care no more for foreign powers than we do for the man in the moon.

The provost guard were sent out to protect Mrs. Lee, but their services were too late. Our camp could be said to "flow with honey," if not milk. We could not eat it all and disposed of it in diverse ways. To the members of our own regiment we gave it; to the others we sold it. This caused much comment. We have just malice enough in our composition to enjoy it, for had not these same fellows enjoyed it when we were in durance vile under Colonel Poe's chastening rod at Edward's Ferry?

## November 8th – 15th

While here we had another example of that devilish disposition which activates some people. An old colored woman was washing out some small articles in a nice china bowl. One of the men came along and snatched the bowl from her. She remonstrated with him, but all to no purpose; he moved away a few steps and dashed it on a rock. He ought to have paid a fine equal to ten such bowls and been put on extra duty long enough to take some of the kink out of him and teach him a little decency.

On the morning of the 8th we captured a squad of of Confeds, and of all the forsaken-looking creatures we ever saw, they capped the climax. They wore every color and texture: bed quilts, carpets, anything to keep out the cold and cover their nakedness. Their hats were quite indescribable. They didn't appear particularly down-hearted at being captured.

We stayed here until 5 o'clock, then started out for Waterloo, on the upper Rappahannock, and passed through the town. If I have ever experienced solitude, it was here. Dilapidation was visible on every hand; even the bridge over the river threatened to dump us into the water as we marched across.

Next day a feint was attempted on the enemy, whose rear guard made a stand — a little artillery duel that resulted in the discomfiture of the Rebels. In a day or so we moved back into a piece of woods, thinking we would camp there awhile. A sutler from another regiment came to supply our wants, but his supplies were meagre, and our pocketbooks ditto or worse, so we derived but little benefit.

We cannot find so much as a feather in this section. The only eatables, outside of army rations, are a few nubbins of corn and some cabbage stumps that taste exceedingly good. We rummage the woods for nuts, acorns, and persimmons. The latter are a powerful astringent and aid materially in checking a too rapid digestion of the little food we have. This alternate fasting and feasting isn't especially agreeable.

It was during these days that the public demanded the removal of the Blue Ridge or of a certain beloved general. After a long and stormy session of the Cabinet, it was decided to be easier and more economical to remove the general. As the Blue Ridge has no aspirations for the presidency, the Cabinet has decided to allow them to continue, thus the official axe has fallen on "little Mac's" neck.[4]

There are those who insist that it is from incompetence that he has been removed. But the soldiers, who are not so steeped in prejudice that they can see nothing but party, claim he has submitted to one reduction after another of his forces until he has a smaller army than Lee although we are the attacking party. The soldiers believe he has accomplished nothing short of a miracle in saving his army.

Burnside, commander of the 9th Corps, succeeds McClellan.

### November 16th.

This afternoon we moved east again and camped just outside the village of Warrenton in the Piedmont section. General Berry joined us here and took command of the brigade, Colonel Poe returning to his own regiment, for which we are devoutly thankful. Old Poe has treated us so badly we have no fear of anything worse.

There is a great current of dissatisfaction in this army caused by McClellan's removal. His old men feel he has suffered a great injustice and have nothing complimentary to say about the administration. General Humphreys went so far as to remark that he "wished the Confederates would get into Washington and drive the whole d——d abolition posse into the Potomac." This came very near to being flat blasphemy and he was made to feel the consequences of his remark. It is quite plain that until this feeling is allayed, no commander will be likely to succeed with this army. It is the theme at all times and all places, growled out at the mess table, around the campfires, and on picket. We think "little Mac" the smartest and the most ill-used person on earth and are convinced that nothing can crush the Rebellion unless he is in command. No stone is left unturned to keep alive this feeling of distrust among the privates and lower-grade officers. Burnside has to contend with all this festering and fomenting.[5]

AMBROSE E. BURNSIDE. *Harper's Pictorial History of the Civil War.*

### November 17th.

It is rainy and cold but we were ordered to set out as soon as we drew rations. The pork was so mean that we consigned it to the flames, and most heartily wished we could have served the ones who furnished it the same. (I was idiotic enough to think that an "unclean" thing could be clean so I toted along about ten pounds of it, planning on a great feast. This piece of folly brought its own punishment, for no amount of boiling or frying had the slightest effect in rendering it eatable.)

About 7:30 we started for Richmond, mud nearly ankle deep. We didn't stop till night, when we hauled up at Fayetteville. There was nothing visible which we could possibly torture into even a suggestion of a town.

A jolly row took place, which went a good way toward showing how hard it would be to stop this army if it ever did become mutinous. We were turned into a field and, as it had rained hard all day, the ground was anything but dusty. Water stood in sheets all over the field where we were to lie down for the night. We'd had a hard day's march over the worst kind of roads and were played out. To lie in wet blankets at this time of year is too suggestive of chills and fever to suit us. We spied a dwelling not too far off, flanked by numerous hay or straw stacks, which seemed to exactly meet our needs. The house was guarded by a provost guard, and an officer of the guard was inside stuffing himself and making eyes at the woman. The sentinel ordered all who approached the straw to "go away and let that straw alone!" Everybody obeyed the order except a very sick man from the 37th New York. He wouldn't drop his armful of straw, so the officer ordered the guard to shoot. The man fell, seriously but not fatally wounded, and managed to crawl back to his regiment. Then there was the devil to pay. His comrades rushed out to avenge the insult. For a brief period pandemonium reigned.

The entire division was ordered under arms, for no one could guess how this might end. When the officer who had ordered the shooting passed the victim's regiment, he was violently set upon and cudgelled over the head and ears. It seemed as if he *must* be killed. The mob took rails from the fire and smashed him over the head, thus literally "heaping coals of fire upon his head." Now that officer knows the effects of a shillelagh wielded by a wild Irishman. It is nothing short of a miracle that he didn't immediately require the services of an undertaker.

He deserves all he got. Although I am not in favor of mob law, still there are cases where justice can be accomplished no other way. A private might complain till doomsday and it would be only so much the worse for the private, as the officer always escapes punishment and subjects the private to the most vigorous persecution. If that creature had been killed on the spot, perhaps the managers would begin to understand that human life is worth more than Rebel straw stacks.

By midnight the house of Mr. Rebel was consigned to the flames, which was hardly a fair proceeding, as he didn't do the shooting, nor order it done.

### November 18th – 20th.

We marched nearly all day on the 18th. Progress very slow. Road phenomenally bad and growing worse. Nothing of importance occurred. We passed through Morrisville, which thriving municipality consisted of one house on fire and fast disappearing. We bivouacked near Bealeton Station on the Orange & Alexandria Railroad. Rained all night, and by morning the roads were impassable for mules and horses. As we cannot go without them, we have laid here for another two days.

As there is one house in sight and another down the road, this must be a "-ville" or a "-ton" or a "-burg," but we can find nothing of the sort on any map. In the matter of mud, our camp is as bad as the road, while overhead it would make a good smokehouse. In the midst of all these evils, we have found some comfort in a garden nearby, even a lot of cabbage stumps — a luxury suited to our station and means.

## November 21st.

It neither rained nor shined, but made strong threats to do both. We started off in a southerly direction, and about noon had the immense satisfaction of seeing the sun. We halted for dinner and awaited orders.

We tarried here, the junction of the Fredericksburg and Stafford Court House roads, about two hours and then resumed our march. About dark, we came to a halt not far from Falmouth, hauled up in front of a large old house ("Boscobel") overlooking a wide stretch of land extending beyond Fredericksburg. As soon as we had unslung knapsacks and stacked arms, we were in pursuit of wood and water and anything to contribute to our comfort.

As far as we can see, this section of the country looks as if a grasshopper would have to handle himself pretty lively to find enough grass to survive. No vegetation, only some monster trees in front of the house and a brush fence. As the fence was the only thing that promised to burn, the place was denuded of fences.

We lie down expecting to go over the Rappahannock the next morning and possess the city and the heights in the rear of it.

## November 22nd and 23rd.

We thought we would surely cross the river on the 22nd but soon learned we are waiting for pontoons, which were promised to be here. This is an upsetting state of affairs when we reflect on how much depends on our getting over there before the Rebels concentrate their forces and make it impregnable. As a move is out of the question, we decided to gather sticks and try to build fires, for it is cold and snow has fallen.

We find it no light task to get a fire or keep one, all we could get for free being green pine. We built stockades of the heavy wood and cooked coffee by burning the green boughs.

Our shelters are exceedingly rude specimens of architecture. The New Yorkers built up by digging down: they dug a hole and put their shelter over it. *We* dug a place, built a stockade of the earth and pine logs, and put out shelters on top of *that*. The advantage to our plan is obvious. In rainy weather the dug-outs will be nearly submerged, while we will be high and dry. This being our first attempt at this kind of work, it must not be inferred ours are perfect to the architecture or appointments, but we consider ourselves quite clever. One very desirable addition is a chimney to carry off the smoke instead of drawing it down into our house. It was claimed by some that our chimneys are all wrong side up. To our dismay, we soon learned that they were right. Our houses soon filled with smoke and our eyes almost washed out of our heads. We shed enough tears to pickle all the beef we draw in two days. Our sufferings were most excruciating, and we came to a unanimous conclusion that either the fire must go or we must.

And here I will explain my remark as to our pickling beef. We have only drawn it once and the quantity was *very* small. This we smoked over the green pine and swallowed without seasoning or salt. If one can conjure up a more unpalatable mess, I desire to know its name.

Our stock of bread was soon very low, and for two days we have had nothing but coffee, which we have been saving in the hopes that when we reach Richmond we can trade it for something to eat. We know that coffee is a luxury throughout the South, bringing fabulous prices. In consideration of all the ills we endure here, we have named the place "Camp Starvation."

### Thanksgiving.

While our friends at home suffer through roast turkey, mince pie, and plum pudding, we cram ourselves on air pudding. At night we drew some fresh beef, which we put through the smoking process and devoured. This didn't satisfy our appetites and only set them clamoring for more. The more ravenous ones went out to where the butchering was done and stripped the fat from the entrails. One fellow with more cupidity than conscience cornered the market in lights [lungs], which he sold for ten cents the half pound. Those who indulged in this luxury derived very little satisfaction; chewing lights is very much like chewing froth.

### November 25th.

Although so hungry that we couldn't think of anything else and so weak that we could hardly stand without swaying, we had a review. General Hooker desired to see how Kearney's old division looks after the campaign that has just closed. This has been a year of awful fighting, beginning with the movements in front of Richmond and ending with Antietam. Hooker found us looking mighty cross, but this was our first review as a regiment and we put our best foot forward. Consequently, we made a most creditable appearance and won the commendation of our commander, General Berry.

### November 26th – December 10th.

We continue to suffer and starve on, enduring cold, hunger, homesickness, and other illnesses. Plenty of smoke and but little fire. Wood and water scarce, rations scarcer. All this time we awaited the pontoons that had been promised as soon as we arrived. They came on the 9th of December, eighteen days after us, long enough for Lee to concentrate his entire army and fortify the heights behind Fredericksburg.

# Fredericksburg

## December 1862

*December 11th.*
While it was yet dark we were suddenly startled by the boom of a cannon, quickly followed by another. These were the prelude to an ever-memorable battle.

Instinct told us what was coming. The shudder that passed over our frames as we answered to the roll call on this chill December morning was not altogether the result of the weather. We knew it was the "cannon's opening roar," and the long expected and dreaded day had come at last. The ball had opened and we should soon be dancing. By the time it was fairly light, we had orders to move immediately. By 7 o'clock the cannonade had become a roar, and the city was enveloped in a cloud of smoke and mist.

Our guns on Stafford Heights opened on the doomed city, and there was an almost continuous line of fire from Mrs. Scott's Hill on the right to Pollock Mill on the left. We soon started, and had an idea that we were to advance over the river at once so we began to brace ourselves for the shock. Mingled fear and curiosity filled our bosoms as we moved along. Curiosity to see a battle and to know how we should act in our first fight. Lurking under it all, the fear that we should fall in the fray. I am sure that some of us actually wished ourselves at home.

We didn't cross the river immediately but turned off to the left and marched down the river to a place called the Brooks Farm. Here we hauled up, listening to the terrible roar of nearly two-hundred guns belching fire and destruction on the city. Burnside was carrying out his threat to lay Fredericksburg in ashes if the Confederate forces didn't evacuate it within forty-eight hours of his ultimatum.[1]

The shelling of the city was not for the purpose of destroying property, but to dislodge the Rebels occupying the houses and stone walls near the river, thus preventing our troops from laying pontoons. But the shelling didn't dislodge them, and so no progress was made in crossing. Finally a crew crossed over in pontoons and eliminated the sharpshooters, and the troops were soon driving the Rebels through the streets and lanes of Fredericksburg toward the heights in rear of town. A running fire was kept up through the forenoon. At the same time, shelling was maintained and a large portion of the city was rendered useless. One third of it lay in ashes. The firing was kept up all day at intervals, and after dark the sky was lit by the glare of shells.

We passed the day on the Brooks Farm, and for us it was a day of terrible suspense. Nothing could be seen because of the mist and smoke enveloping the city, but we could hear the firing and cheering as one regiment or brigade after another crossed the river and entered into the fray — the deadly fray. And when I use this phrase it is not idle chatter. There is a meaning to it which the soldier comprehends.

THE BRIDGE AT FREDERICKSBURG. *Harper's Pictorial History of the Civil War.*

It means all that is implied in the fearful and determined struggle of two immense armies, doing all that military skill and ingenuity can do to secure success. Terrible in earnest and prepared with all the accouterments of modern war were these combatants. And this says nothing of the great advantage of position held by the Confederates.

As we laid there hour after hour hearing all this, our imaginations ran riot and we expected every moment to be ordered in. It was not an easy matter to keep our men within hailing distance, so eager were they to catch a glimpse of what was going on. Up to noon there had been no battle, only the fighting in the streets. After sunset we moved down into a piece of pine woods and bivouacked for the night. We had no news of what our army had accomplished and were in a state of appalling uncertainty.

It may be supposed that Lee did all he could to prevent our army from crossing, but this is a mistake. He wanted us to cross, expecting to destroy us or drive us into the river. The Confederate generals know they have an almost impregnable position and an attack by our army on the front means nothing short of destruction.

While we waited, a little transaction occurred that gave us another exhibition of Irish enthusiasm.[2] The celtic heart can surely fire up in the shortest time imaginable. General Thomas F. Meagher of the Irish Brigade rode along in front of the line, and his appearance was the signal for an outburst that was almost deafening. But for the cannonading, it must have been audible over in Fredericksburg.

Howard's division holds the city this night, camping in the streets not far from the river. No reports except that an infant was killed in its cradle by the explosion of a shell in the house. (It is said that the child was left behind when its parents cleared out — a queer kind of parents, if the story is true. But most likely this story was circulated for a purpose — and we know *that* purpose.)

General Burnside gave the city ample notice of his intentions. It is probable that if the inhabitants of the city had requested the Rebel army to vacate, it would have done so. Instead, the inhabitants of Fredericksburg chose to be very patriotic. Result: ruin!

In the rear of the city is a line of heights running from a point just above Falmouth to Hamilton's Crossing, about two miles below the city where the Fredericksburg and Richmond Railroad crosses the old stage road to Richmond. At this point the ridge descends to the lowlands of the Massaponak Creek. Marye's Heights, in the rear of the city, are said to be well-fortified. These hills are laid out in natural terraces and well-adapted to defensive operations.

It is on these hills that the Rebel Army is drawn up to give battle. We have General Meigs to thank for the elaborate Rebel preparations. Lee's army is commanded by Longstreet, Stonewall Jackson, and A.P. Hill. On these cognomens the Rebel wit has made quite a pun. It runs thus: "Before they can get in here, they must go over a *stonewall* and up *longstreet* and climb two *hills*." The worst part of all is that it is true; we must do these very things to succeed.

Our command is Hooker, Sumner, and Franklin, a trio of veterans no less celebrated that the bumptious individuals who command the other side. General Franklin is considered an especially able officer, and Hooker a very dashing one. Sumner is the soul of patriotism and not given to jealousies and growling as some others we know. As for Franklin, he is very envious of Burnside and exceedingly angry over McClellan's removal. Burnside might, with reason, suspect Franklin of treachery. Instead, he has entrusted Franklin with a highly important part of his plan (if he *has* a plan), and put him in command of nearly one-half of our army.

## December 12th.

Didn't move for the day. Kept out of sight of the Rebels until after dark, when we moved down into a grove of oaks not far from the river. This movement was owing to our division (Birney's) having been borrowed by Franklin as a reserve, ostensibly, but actually to further his designs against Hooker. Franklin thus weakened Hooker. He also intended to throw this little force over the river instead of his own larger one.

We were allowed to build only the very smallest fires and to make no noise. We didn't know just how near we were to the enemy, this being a new section of country to us, and it was dark and overcast so we couldn't tell anything as to our whereabouts. I made coffee and then retired with dismal forebodings. What is before us? Possibly this might be my last night on earth. Even worse, ere the setting of another sun I might be mangled and bleeding. Such thoughts crowd in upon me and prevent me from sleeping.

## December 13th.

A memorable day for some of us. We were out betimes and soon had the coffee kettle simmering and the pork sizzling. We had our grub, and then laid around awaiting orders.

A portion of Franklin's corps was engaged with the enemy over the river, and we were ordered across to support them, not knowing whether the entire Grand Division was there or not. Great was our surprise, as we emerged from the woods and came in sight of the river, to see no less than four lines of troops lying on the ground while a comparatively small force engaged the enemy.

We pushed over the river and moved up the old stage road to Richmond and came to a front near a fine residence, the Barnard House. On the side of the road, next the house and in lieu of a fence, were an embankment and a ditch. We couldn't take advantage of them then, although under severe fire, for we had something else to do. The small force sent over earlier by General Franklin had accomplished prodigies of valor and had pierced Lee's lines. At that moment, had it been supported by another division, there is no doubt a lodgement could have been effected. But they looked in vain for support and were compelled to fall back.

As they neared our group at the old stage, or river, road, the Rebels in hot pursuit, we came to a front and fixed bayonets. As soon as the Pennsylvania Bucktails, who were in front of us, cleared out, we charged on the advancing Southrons, giving them a volley as we moved. Shot and shell fire flew in all directions, reminding us of what an old nigger once said under similar circumstances: "See dar, Hell has laid an egg."

We were soon the recipients of as many of these favors, or "eggs," as we could attend to, and they kept us ducking and dodging in a lively and bewildering manner. The first in our company to receive an injury was Sergeant John Libby. A fragment of shell smashed his hip. He took it coolly and patiently, although judging from the nature of the wound, it must have been very painful. He smiled and tried to appear unconcerned, but it was a ghastly effort. He was carried to a brick house in rear of us used as a hospital.

We were in the immediate presence of death. One in our company, when a shell burst near the head of our regiment, supposing it was a Union shell fallen short, exclaimed, "I should think they could get a better aim than that!" Another, who saw the gun on the Rebel side that fired it, replied, "You devilish fool! I should think it was good enough." At the same time, he bowed very low to escape pieces flying around our heads. No harm was done beyond a slight breaking of the ranks.

Our regiment formed in the road to dispute the further progress of Johnny Reb. The first volley from our guns compensated somewhat for the havoc the Rebels had made in the ranks of the Bucktails, who were now thoroughly demoralized. They were out of ammunition and forced to fall back and save themselves, if possible. There was no order in the manner of their coming off. Each was taking his own time and motion. Some, with broken legs, were carried on the shoulders of others who had been hit in the head or otherwise disabled. But for such timely assistance from their comrades, many must have been left on the field to the mercy of an exultant foe.

Our arrival was opportune and quickly showed Mr. Johnny that in the matter of charging, two could play the game. Our regiment is larger than many old brigades in both armies, and when we blazed away, we made a hole visible a long way off, as in the case of the Georgia regiment. The dozen or so left must have wondered what struck them — earthquake, tornado, or lightning.

Our regimental loss was twenty, Company I lost one. We were now ordered to lie down, but not willingly, as we had more curiosity than fear and wanted to see what was going on. General Berry paced back and forth in the rear of us, an old slouched hat pulled over his eyes. He ordered us to keep down, out of sight and out of range: "Boys, don't expose yourselves any more than you can help. You'll have a chance to see all you want to. The State of Maine is looking at you and expects every man to do his duty today."

This little speech stirred us wonderfully, way down to the bottom of our boots, making us wish we were back at home. Some of us still stood up and tried to peer into the Rebel lines, whereupon General Berry ordered, "Lay down, men! Lay down! I am here to take care of you, and I'll do it if you will let me and will obey my orders."

After things settled and there was no immediate prospect of an attack, we took a position in rear of the embankment by the side of the road. This was a judicious move as it gave us protection and, at the same time, a good range. The Rebs spotted us and commenced a lively cannonade, which hastened our move.

Strangely, not a man in our company was hit in passing through this storm of shot and shell, but there were some hairbreadth escapes not soon forgotten. We laid here till about 4 P.M., when there were indications of Rebel movement. We moved to the front and formed ahead of a battery somewhat to the left of our first position. This was a rifled battery, and it sent its missiles with horrible force. If the Rebels had known what was there, they'd have looked before they leapt.

We hadn't long to wait, as the Rebels commenced to cannonade our lines about half past four, preparatory to a charge. Our battery replied, and shells went whizzing over us so near that we hugged old Mother Earth most affectionately.

There was a single gun nearly opposite belonging to Stuart's horse artillery and under command of Major John Pelham. This conceited party must have thought he could silence our battery. His was a large gun and threw a much heavier missile. Our gunners ceased firing for a minute, and never was sixty seconds better employed. They sighted and fired. That shell created a profound sensation in Rebel circles. It burst exactly under Mr. Pelham's gun and not only dismantled the same, but mixed things up dreadfully. Two men and a boy were killed by that one shell. It wasn't necessary to duplicate the dose. The indefatigable Pelham — the incomparable Pelham — and the rest of his crew made great haste to depart. No more cannonading that day, nor did the Rebels make the contemplated charge in which they had, no doubt, expected to capture our forces or drive us into the Rappahannock.

This was one instance of Stonewall Jackson's timidity. It is said he "stood with his watch in his hand, counting the minutes till the sun went down" and then put it up and relinquished his design. A curious ending for so promising a movement. The Rebels probably cannot understand it. I do. That cannonading probably reminded him of the costly and fruitless charge his command made at Malvern Hill last June, when they were mowed down by the hundreds.[3]

Night soon settled over the scene of carnage, and after getting something to eat we laid on the ground, but not to sleep. Our ears are continually saluted with the cries of the wounded left on the field to the mercy of weather and Rebels, their sufferings heightened by cold and thirst. Who can depict such horrors? These wretched men lay crying, groaning, and begging for water and help in the most agonizing manner, and we unable to rescue them. The rustle of a leaf or the crackling of a twig might send a shower of Rebel bullets into our ranks. We had an illustration of this soon after settling down. Something caused the pickets to commence firing, and it increased to such an extent that it was feared a general engagement might be the result. We got up and packed our things and put our knapsacks up in front of our heads as a breastwork, much like the ostrich hiding its head and leaving the rest of its carcass exposed. (We learned better the longer we stayed in the show.) I was mortally scared and could not imagine what I should do on picket on such a night. It is a dreadful night even for old and tried soldiers.

A reconnoitering party passed along our front about the time the row was ending. Although close to our line, and with the pickets in front, one of this group displayed the most ridiculous fright. He dodged and ducked in a most comical manner. Each time, this affected the others. The officer in command of the squad drew his revolver and threatened to transfer its contents to the fellow's head. This proved to be a good remedy for the soldier's nerves.

After this I tried to rest, but no sleep could be obtained, listening to the wounded and unable to help. Their fate, or a worse one, might be mine before another sunset.

How fortunate for the peace of mind of the women of our land that they do not know all these things. In giving their sons and brothers to such a cause how little they know what they are doing. The peculiar feature of war is that each expects *someone else* to fall. The horrors are not mitigated by the Rebels, who, it is said, stripped our dead and wounded and left them to suffer. It is hard to credit this, for I believe the Rebels *are* human, but such acts are diabolical. One cannot blame them — to bury a good suit of Union clothes when they are nearly naked in winter would seem foolish. The system of African slavery that has prevailed here so long has, no doubt, destroyed much of the finer sensibilities of the Southern people, even of the better class. But that institution is fast approaching its end.

This day has been a most exciting and eventful one. It was our regiment's first experience under fire, and a whole lifetime has been crowded into it. It was expected that we should show the white feather. This formed no part of our plan; still, no man can tell as he sits in the chimney corner whether he is a brave man or a coward. In accordance with this belief, a couple of New York regiments were placed in rear of us to keep us in line. But, horrible to relate, our gallant support soon struck out and left us to do as we chose. All efforts of their officers were utterly unavailing, and they fled from the presence of the enemy. On the contrary, our regiment behaved so well it merited the encomiums of General Berry.

## December 14th.

It being Sunday, we made no demonstrations, and the enemy, also of a devotional turn, made no disturbance until afternoon. As we are suspicious that they might attempt to get a hold on our flank, it was deemed necessary to throw back our left so that our flank rests on the Rappahannock. After this a flag of truce was sent to protect our men who went out to bury the dead and bring in the wounded. The Rebels thronged the works opposite and gave us an idea of the number of our opponents. Most of them are clad in blue, so it is a plain case that our dead have been contributing largely to the Rebel wardrobe. The truce was limited by the Rebels to two hours, consequently we didn't even get all the wounded, and the defunct ones were left unburied.

Officers, Union and Rebel, found time to meet on the picket line and wet their whistles, then separated. As our stretcher-bearers were bringing in a wounded man, a Reb picket discharged his piece and one of our men was minus a toe. Perhaps this was accidental, but we chose to regard it as an exhibition of treachery. After the truce ended, the pickets resumed firing incessantly till darkness put an end to it.

I have almost forgotten to describe an occurrence during the truce. A.P. Hill, one of the ablest Confederate generals, sent his compliments to General Berry and begged to say, "I have never seen a brigade so skillfully handled on a battlefield." This was not an unmerited compliment, only it wasn't General Berry's brigade that he had handled so well, it was simply the 17th Maine. The way we had double-quicked down the old Richmond turnpike under fire, come to a front and delivered a volley, and then charged, is not easily surpassed.

After dark we drew rations of corn or rye (in a liquid state), though we would have much preferred it in palatable pork. There are times when whiskey is needed, this being one of them, for it is damp and cold. We have been worked hard and are nearly used up. We have also come to the conclusion that we should be relieved. We have been over here forty-eight hours and are well aware that there is nearly a whole grand division lying on the northern bank of the Rappahannock, which has not participated in the fight at all.[4]

## December 15th and 16th.

We were routed out before daylight and marched off the field. A feeling of relief came over us, thinking we were going to the rear for rest and refreshment. But to our almost infinite astonishment and disgust, we were marched onto the field after daylight as fresh troops. This piece of unmitigated rascality no doubt passed for profound strategy with those who ordered it. The idiot who concocted it should be riddled with as many bullets as there were lives sacrificed. This was one more case of wholesale slaughter, of which there have been several. Two days and nights on the battlefield without rest when thousands of fresh troops lay close at hand doing nothing is a bit steep. I don't believe there is any precedent for it in this army, unless it was Fitz-John Porter, last summer, when he caused Pope's defeat.[5]

Nothing of unusual interest going on during the morning of the 15th till about 10 A.M., when the Rebels kicked up an awful smoke and smother. We had no idea what could be going on unless they were destroying things preparatory to evacuating this section. If all the camp equipage of the Rebel army had been piled up in a heap and burned, it wouldn't have made any more of a smother. It was surmised that an attack was to be made under cover of the smoke, but we waited in vain. After a while, one of our batteries decided to give them an eye-opener and in response received convincing evidence that, whatever else might be the cause of the smoke, the Rebels had not yet evacuated. They responded by throwing old gun barrels, railroad iron, and anything handy. One of our men declared that they threw over a whole blacksmith shop, anvil and all — a kind of anvil chorus with cannon accompaniment. Whatever it was, it made an awful whirring and whizzing. A gun barrel struck at the right of our regiment, sounding like a rickety whirlwind, and buried half its length in the ground. General Burnside sent word to them that he would retaliate with chain shot. This had the effect to bring them down to such missiles as are authorized by the laws of "civilized warfare" (if this last phrase is not a most ridiculous paradox).

Firing soon ceased and was not resumed this day. Something quite unexpected turned up about 9 in the evening. Just as we had concluded that we were going to pass the winter over there, we received orders to pack and to make no noise, not even a whisper. While we were wondering what manner of movement this indicated, an order came to march. It hadn't dawned on us that we were whipped, as we knew that only a very small part of General Franklin's command had participated — or even crossed the river. So we inferred that we were moving to some other portion of the field to be in readiness for the conflict on the morrow.

We hadn't long to wonder, for we soon discovered we were in rear of the Barnard house and steering straight for the Rappahannock. The truth flashed upon us that we were on the retreat with none to relieve us. The pontoons were muffled so that our tramping wasn't heard. Otherwise, we might have had more help than was compatible for a safe crossing.

We were soon on the northern bank of the river and, under the circumstances, not sorry to be there. It isn't often that men are subjected to such treatment on their introduction to war. The Rebels (barring the 49th Georgia) have had it all their own way.

By 3 o'clock we were all across except for a Zouave band,[6] which laid down to sleep and didn't get roused when we moved off. The bridges were all up by daylight. After going about a mile from the river, we were permitted to lie down for the little time left before daylight, but not to sleep. Hardly had our weary bodies struck the ground when a storm of wind and rain struck us. We had been guilty of a consummate folly in lying down without putting up our tents. By the time we had them up, it cleared off, and we didn't need shelter. Virginia storms come and go without much ceremony, and the sun came out bright and cheering soon after dawn. The Rebels, discovering our absence, hastened to pay us their respects, but their firing was entirely at random and no one was hurt.

We then marched farther away from the river. After several hours of marching and counter-marching, finally hauled up on the side of a hill not far from the festive locality we call Camp Starvation. No campground could possibly be found that is more conducive to death and destruction. The air is just laden with miasma, and the ground reeks with poison and chills.

## December 17th – 22nd.

With this promising future we went into camp and commenced to put up shanties by driving down some stakes and then weaving brush between them. We have exhausted all the wood, and as for water, it is hardly in sufficient quantity even for drinking purposes. A rich vein of typhoid was soon struck and in a few days was in full blast. We have encamped where swamp water is taken into the system in doses anything but homeopathic, and miasma taken in with every breath. The drainage of the mule stables on surrounding hills and the fumes from dead mules are active agents in decimating our ranks.

For several days nothing of any consequence has occurred, excepting deaths. In fact, these didn't seem to be of much consequence only as they raise the oft-repeated query: "Who next?"

This place, Camp Pitcher, was named in honor of the major of the 3rd Maine who fell at the Battle of Fredericksburg. This officer was held in high esteem in his regiment but he derives no honor from having his name associated with a hole like this. Short rations, bog water to drink, malaria inhaled with every breath, homesickness, and, added to all this, an incompetent surgeon. Is it any wonder that we are being swept off at the rate of two per day? The muffled drum and death march are more regular than our rations. Most of us have lost our courage and expectation of reaching home, or even dying on the battlefield — a fate less cruel than dying here by inches.

A New York trooper whose regiment was up on one of the hills informed a visitor inquiring for the 17th Maine that "most of it is up under the big pine yonder" (our burying ground) "and the rest are down in the frog pond."

General Stoneman, our corps commander, rode through camp one day and remarked that he "wouldn't keep a dog in such a hole," but he gave no order for a change. So we stay and die off like sheep while all around us are hills and elevations dry and healthy, with plenty of wood and a hope of clean water. We are on the shortest rations, the roads being in horrible condition and the Aquia Creek Railroad not in running order yet. The mules are hard put to haul an empty wagon, let alone a loaded one.

Some of the men (following the example of their superiors) got tipsy recently and became quarrelsome. They were made to go into the water up to their knees and stand for two hours, or as long as an officer saw fit. Another punishment for a refractory private was to put a barrel over him on which was painted in large letters "Rum Did It." The punishment was mortifying, not deadly, and I only complain that it was not administered to all alike. William Shakespeare said, "What in the captain is but a choleric word, in the private is flat blasphemy." Not much has changed since old William's day. Perhaps it should be added here that teams that are detailed to carry whiskey are sorely needed to carry bread, but our only redress is to grumble.

## December 23rd.

An order was read on dress parade from General Birney complimenting us on our conduct in the late fight and admitting us to the order of The Red Patch, an organization including all the regiments in Kearney's old division. We didn't know we'd done anything especially meritorious, only tried to do our duty as we understand it. But if this is cause for special commendation, we accept it.

Each man in this order is expected to wear in a conspicuous place on his cap a bright red patch, diamond shape. Kearney's division flag was of this color, and when Jeff Davis's minions saw it on the field, it gave notice that the "one-armed devil," as they called Kearney, was coming. As for Kearney, it seemed there was something not of this earth in the spirit that spurred him in action. He coquetted with death and dallied with danger. His division lost none of its prestige under such leaders as "fierce Birney and Berry." Kearney was a wild Irishman from New Jersey, and a goodly portion of the division are the same. Then there are three Maine regiments, the 3rd and 4th, and now the 17th. Our troops from Maine prove themselves as good as the best, and that is the record they have received from all who have commanded them.

## December 24th.

Today occurred the first death in Company I from sickness since we entered this infernal show. Dan Hill of Biddeford concluded he had seen enough and "handed in his resignation." For some reason, our company has until now been exempt from the destroyer.

It is rumored that there are sundry boxes and mysterious parcels over at Stoneman's Station directed to us. We retire to sleep with feelings akin to those of children expecting Santa Claus. We have become very childish in some matters — grub being one of them.

### December 25th.

Went on a detail making corduroy roads. It was a dismal day but rendered quite endurable by the anticipation of what was in store in our boxes. On returning to camp, I was informed by my tentmate that there was no parcel at the station bearing my name. My mental thermometer not only plummeted to below zero, it got right down off the nail and lay down on the floor. Seeing this, my tentmate made haste to dive under the bed and produce the box, which he had brought from the station during my absence, and in but a few minutes we were busy discussing the merits of its contents. Most of the men have been remembered, and any that have not received something from home are allowed to share with their more fortunate neighbors.

### December 26 – 28th.

Nothing but the usual routine of camp duties: guard, picket, police, an occasional inspection, washing, cooking, and cutting wood for ourselves and officers. We had a feast too in these three days, and gorged ourselves well.

### December 29th.

A division drill by General Birney on the Brooks Farm. We were out two hours, and for those who like this kind of thing, it went well. On this occasion we had with us old "Dutch Mary," a female whose adipose tissue is quite remarkable, as is her agility. She is the "frau" of a Zouave, who persists in eating her sauerkraut *mit hans* and in drinking her schnapps. She cooks and washes for the officers, thereby earning an honest penny.

When a battle rages, she is on hand to minister to the needs of the wounded. When in camp, she sometimes drills with the men, as today, and she can go through it as well as any. The way her legs fly when executing a wheeling operation reminds me of some swift-moving insect. Some writer has remarked that the two most awkward things in Nature are a woman or an elephant trying to run. I agree with his estimate of the latter, but he is a bold slanderer when he classes women with that most awkward of animals, especially a woman as nimble as Dutch Mary. With her tight Zouave suit on, she looks like a man. One private, thinking to have a little sport at her expense, once came up behind her as she was washing some clothes at the brook, and kissed her. She seized a wet shirt and belabored him right and left, pursuing him out of camp, to the great amusement of his comrades and chagrin of himself. When next he felt in a jocose frame of mind, no doubt he didn't take Dutch Mary as the object of his mirth.

### December 30th and 31st.

All quiet on the Rappahannock. This day closes the record of 1862. We have been in service five months and are quite familiar now with military matters. Having had a taste of most everything in this business, we have decided that, on the whole, it is not to our liking. We have experienced marching, picketing, fighting, and exposure to all sorts of weather. We started out with 1040 men and officers; at this time, we haven't much more than half the force we had in the beginning. A very few have been killed in action, some have died of wounds, more from sickness, and others have been discharged for various aches and pains. Others are back in some hospital having a soft time. Apparently we are doomed to stay right in this old swamp till we are dying or dead. I shall abandon all idea of living any longer than spring "if we don't get shet of dis yer misery" before long.

# The Mud March

## Winter of 1863

### January 1st, 1863.

The first day of the new year has been spent clearing up and readying for a review announced for the next day. Such reviews generally indicate forward movements in the near future. General Burnside, smarting under a severe castigation and the criticism of his enemies, naturally has a strong desire to retrieve his late disaster. So, such a forward movement might occur at any moment.

### January 2nd.

A division review was held by General Birney on the Brooks place. The Rebels have the advantage in this respect as most of our movements are in plain view while they are hidden in the woods. Our only means of ascertaining what they are doing is by means of a balloon, kept up a great part of each day, that holds telegraphic communications with headquarters. This method of communications the Rebels cannot interrupt.

### January 3rd and 4th.

There has been nothing of any importance except getting ready for another review on the 5th. It is to be a grand review — a kind of swell affair — and we retire with great expectations. Although Burnside has been in command since November 7th, we haven't seen him yet.

### January 5th.

Grand review of General Hooker's grand division by General Burnside. This is one-third of the Army of the Potomac, a larger body than we have hitherto seen.

General Burnside appears to be a very modest, unassuming man. His modesty could be profitably imitated by some of his inferiors, for while he came onto the field destitute of all the pomp and pageantry of war, some of the brigadiers actually seemed to bend under the weight of gilt buttons, yellow sashes, and other paraphernalia. Particularly noticeable in this respect was General Carr, who seemed determined that no one should overlook the fact of his being a general. When he came clattering down the line we at first took him for General Burnside, his whiskers being of the same cut. Carr was a fine specimen of conceited flatulency, and when General B. did put in an appearance we very soon saw the difference.

No other man I've ever seen has such a head as Burnside. I had seen a picture of him and knew him when he approached. The bands played "Hail to the Chief," and although he may not be considered a great commander, it wasn't inappropriate. He possesses certain moral qualities that cause men to respect him and consider him a great and good man. That he was not successful in the late battle wasn't entirely his fault. If his subordinates had done their duty instead of plotting against him, the results would have been otherwise.

After we passed in review, we returned to camp. On the way we passed General Berry's headquarters, and he came out to greet us. He has just had a fever and lost all of his hair, giving him a venerable appearance. It was startling to us, as we saw him only a few weeks before with his black hair and whiskers.

Berry has been promoted to command of the 2nd Division of this corps. (The 3rd Division is commanded by General Amiel Whipple, of New Hampshire, the nastiest man I ever saw in uniform. This isn't a very flattering remark to make of a general but candor compels me to state that he looks worse than a Rebel. There is no outward sign of rank.)

### January 6th.

The division was paraded to witness the reward meted out to privates whose "precarious pegs" have too good an opinion of them to stand by and see their body abused. When an officer's legs are thus shaky, they are frequently braced by promotion, and if this doesn't work he is allowed to resign under some specious plea such as ill health or pressing claims.

Francis Hermon of the 1st New York was the individual suspected of desertion. He was marched round three sides of a square of soldiers to impress on them the enormity of his crime. His head was shaved and he was escorted out of camp to the tune of the "Rogue's March." "He deserted his comrades in the face of the enemy," says the record. This youth belonged to that regiment placed in rear of us to keep us from running. He wasn't the only guilty one, but they couldn't drum out the entire regiment.

The Maine troops thus far have had no love for that particular tune and its accompanying exercises: shaved heads, branded hips, and a procession with bayonets at their heels. The New Yorkers have different tastes, and the "Rogue's March" is sweeter music to them than the whistle of bullets or the screaming of shells. Perhaps we shall have the same feelings when we have been in the show as long and have endured as much as they.

### January 7th – 18th.

Nothing worthy of note except that two more of our men decided to go into "eternal bivouac" under the big tree on the hill: William Powers on the 11th and Jerry Smith on the 17th.

### January 19th.

Paraded again to witness another highly elevating exhibition. A man from the 37th New York had his head shaved and a *C*, for coward, branded on his hip. Branding a human being like a pork barrel is a relic of barbarism. Before the curtain rose on this scene, an order was promulgated saying we "must not express any approbation or disapprobation at anything we might witness today." Several disregarded this injunction and expressed their disgust at these proceedings and their contempt for the executors. Any commander who thinks we would honor such a display is ignorant of the American character! We haven't lost quite all our sense of decency, nor our courage to rebuke such uncivilized spectacles.

### January 20th.

We learned the key to yesterday's performance. We were routed out at daylight and ordered to move at 7. We moved at 9, and if good judgment had been used, shouldn't have been moved at all. After getting into line, we were read an order from General Burnside: "Recent successes in North Carolina and other parts of the Confederacy have so weakened and divided the enemy that the commanding general deems this an auspicious time to strike a blow for the Union." After this we marched upriver to Bank's Ford and went into camp, intending to cross at daylight, divide the enemy's forces, and whip them by detail and smash them generally.

Although every precaution has been taken to keep our move a secret, the enemy knows of it and we found them all ready. Long before daylight they had sent up signals informing the line where the attack was to be made. This didn't make any difference, as the weather alone was sufficient to insure failure. About midnight a most violent rain and wind set in, and by daylight the roads were in horrible condition, impassable for anything but men. Pontoons, teams, artillery, and ambulances were mired. All our ammunition had to be brought from the wagons by details of men walking through mud up to their knees. Burnside must have seen what was evident to us, that the situation was hopeless.

After it was agreed that no present advance was practical, another fellow and myself, being equally curious to see how things stand in Rebeldom, decided to reconnoiter the enemy's position. Accordingly, we sallied forth to get a squint at the people across the raging Rappahannock. We wallowed and waded and floundered for the space of forty minutes and then found ourselves near the banks of the river, which were not far from perpendicular. How it is proposed to get our artillery down over them is more than we could fathom. Rebels were concealed in the woods mostly; here and there one could be seen straggling round over the fields, lugging wood or searching for water and forage. In fact, we saw nothing that would indicate the presence of anything more than a strong picket line. Here and there clouds of smoke rose over the trees, warning us that in fact the woods are full of them and that any attempt to cross over would be followed by a second Ball's Bluff of colossal proportions.

Some waggish Rebels have painted on an old barn door this insulting inquiry: "Burnside's stuck in the mud. Why don't you come over?" We didn't come over, but wallowed back to camp.

At night a generous dose of stimulant was served out all round and matters assumed a very lively hue. Some of the New Yorkers air their eloquence at our expense, spoiling for a fight as the Irish always are when they have had an "odd sup." As their chance of getting at the Rebels is as small as their desire to do so, they exercised their pugnacity on each other. Judging from the howling, I'd say a good number of them have been converted into sausage meat. Noise is an Irishman's special prerogative.

Our regiment, being a bounty regiment,[1] came in for a goodly share of the New York slang, which is very rich and very expressive. One thing that seems to

THE CAMPAIGN IN THE MUD. *Harper's Pictorial History of the Civil War.*

afford them immense disgust is the thought that the State of Maine should "pay $200 for a hundred-pound man." Their ire was inexpressible when they were informed that Maine has in fact paid as high as $400 for that amount of avoirdupois. Some of our boys returned this torrent of billingsgate in kind; however, the incident passed with nothing more serious than a war of words.

### January 22nd.

Found us enjoying neither rain nor shine, but a threat to do both. While it was yet dark, two of our men were seized with a thirsty fit and went off in pursuit of the aqueous fluid and failed to put in an appearance that day or night. It is conjectured that they knew of some spring in Her Majesty's dominions.

We remained here all day, laying corduroy roads to get the artillery and teams over. At night we built rousing fires and tried to dry ourselves. We passed a quiet night as the boisterous ones of the previous evening have settled down to a cooler condition.

### January 23rd.

Turned out early and supposed we were to move quickly, but 11 o'clock found us still there. A little later we got started, turned our faces to the foe, and moved on to a camp we left a few days before. It was a weary way, the mud ankle deep, and progress slow, but most of us reached camp by sunset.

Our feet are well encased in the soil of Virginia despite the most frantic efforts to shake it off. The quantity of soil that has changed places in the last twenty-four hours would furnish a subject for geological speculation, and I flatter myself that these wise ones might scratch their craniums over it in undisguised perplexity.

### January 24th.

An event of unusual interest occurred today. The paymaster arrived and disbursed some old green rags with Chase's photographs on them. By a singular coincidence the sutler came up the same time. Neither of these characters amounts to much without the other.

This was our first pay since leaving Portland. In consequence we felt very rich. This delusion was quickly dispelled after one visit to the sutler's. When one has to pay the price of a cow for a pound of butter or the price of a barrel of flour for a dozen cookies, even the income of a Rothschild or Belmont couldn't long stand the pressure. What we should regard as hardly fit for soap grease at home is sold for *butter* at 60 cents per pound. Cheese is a trifle less expensive, being only 50 cents. If we received what the government allows for rations — or even the half of it — we would not submit to this extortion. Instead we are stinted and pinched in every way. We seek relief where we can find it, and money has become of no account compared with the overwhelming desire for something to eat. "Hang the expense!" is our motto; "Hang the quartermaster!" our most fervent ejaculation.

It is asserted that it is impossible to get rations over the roads. This is true sometimes, but the muddy condition of the roads is not chronic. When they *are* passable, even a minimum of good judgment should suggest the propriety of hauling up a lot. We are convinced that we are the victims of systematic robbery.

### January 26th – February 19th.

About this time, soon after the so-called Mud March, General Burnside, at his own earnest request, was relieved of command of the Army of the Republic. He had made a similar request after the battle of Fredericksburg and been denied. But now there was so much distrust on all sides that the administration yielded to his petition.

And now it is "Fighting Joe" Hooker who is called upon to show his skill. With his habitual modesty, he has remarked that with a certain force he could "drive the Rebels to Hell or anywhere else." The administration's plan doesn't involve so extensive a campaign, only that we go as far as Richmond. General Hooker is at last in the position he has so long coveted (according to report).

Within a week a change was perceptible in our cuisine. Our larders began to fill and we had no occasion to patronize the sutlers, who no doubt wish Joe Hooker in the sultry locality to which he threatens to drive the Rebels.

Not only has the quantity increased, but the quality has improved and we enjoy all the variety afforded by government, of which we have previously been defrauded. Now we have more than we could possibly eat — no thanks to sutlers or commissaries. General Hooker had immense bakeries built, and in a few days we were enjoying delicious hot loaves of bread, the mere sight of which is better than a pound of the measly, wormy hardtack we had been served so long. Besides this, there are beef (fresh and salt), pork, beans, peas, rice, and potatoes, as well as other vegetables, pickles, candles, coffee, sugar, and condiments of all sorts, with the exception of Worcestershire sauce. Our diet is generous and our spirits rise high in consequence. We no longer desire death, nor suffer a weakness that makes the slightest labor a burden. General Hooker once remarked that "men who are fed well will fight well." This is excellent logic, and we like the first part of it immensely. Hooker's popularity shows how closely the stomach and emotions are allied.

### February 20th.

Up to the 20th of February nothing occurred but the common routine of camp life. The weather is unusually severe and we have been treated to many a snowfall. We are stationed up the river not far from Bank's Ford, a dismal and forbidding place.

My first post on this day wasn't far from the river, which at this point is exceedingly turbulent. On the opposite bank I espied a huge Confederate sitting grim and composed. I approached him for a chat, if our voices could be audible above the rushing Rappahannock, but a nearer view revealed that my Confederate was only a large grey boulder, so my social intentions came to nought.

The night was phenomenally dark and cloudy. The post to which I was next assigned was on the side of a hill in the heart of a dense pine thicket. In getting there we fell into ditches and gullies, over stumps and rocks, and were whacked around in great shape. Finally reaching the post in a bruised condition, we found it favorable for sleeping, for no Rebel or anything else could possibly approach us without arousing us. We didn't think any enemy were near us, but still had an uneasy feeling, knowing we are in a section where it is an act of great merit to kill a Yankee.

A little incident happened at the riverside this afternoon. As our Officer of the Day came down from camp to inspect the posts, the Rebel vedette opposite sang out, "Officer of the Day. Turn out the guard!" The Rebels promptly turned out and presented arms. I presume this was a Confederate joke, and not a bad one either.

### February 21st and 22nd.

Morning ushered in a gloomy, overcast day. A storm was brewing but held off until late in the day. At last it came down and I have never seen its counterpart in Virginia. In fact, New England might strain herself considerably and not produce anything so fierce.

Went on post at a house nearby at night but didn't get *into* the house. Instead, we waded outside in eight or ten inches of snow for two hours, then laid down in a brush house, or shelter, and shivered out the remainder of the night. The fires all died down, leaving us in a semi-congealed condition. We passed the night without slumber and when we threw off our blankets in the morning and looked about us, found we were in "a bed and shroud of the beautiful snow." Not so beautiful as poetic license would have us believe. We were nearly frozen, and as soon as daylight appeared we crawled out of our shelter. And it was lucky we did, for but a few minutes later the whole thing, not less than thirty feet long and with an immense body of snow on it came down with a crash. If we had been under it we certainly would have been crushed to death.

No relief was sent, and we were allowed to go down and occupy the negro huts connected with this plantation while our officers stayed in the main house.

The man of the house (a somewhat prominent character — a judge, I think) is suspected of being too communicative with the enemy. It was from this house that the signal went up informing the Rebels where we intended to cross the river during the late Burnside fiasco. The judge was subsequently invited by our government to make an indefinite stay in Washington. His family has been left alone, and are in no mood to entertain Yankees. They were especially horrified when asked to furnish us something to eat. The old lady declared (with trembling voice indicating weakness from lack of food) that they had nothing, positively nothing, in the house to eat. Her rugged appearance, and that of others in the household, belied this. A hint that we might search the premises refreshed her memory and she remembered having some ham and eggs.

"Starving" on ham and eggs! Here's richness. It was a good way to die, and we were glad to run the risk of dying under such conditions. We were as self-sacrificing as the old rat who hid himself to starve in an enormous Cheshire cheese. In a short time a goodly quantity of ham and eggs was stowed away under our vests, much to the disgust of a bevy of female Rebels.

An immense pile of rails was near the house. Seeing no other fuel, we carried them to our shanties to insure no repetition of last night's experience. We shortly had them crackling on the hearth, dispensing warmth and light. We are having a right jolly time tonight — no guard duty, no picketing, in fact no restraint of any kind. There is plenty of hard bread, pork, and coffee, and we lack but one thing for comparative comfort. There is no place to sleep except the bare floor. This is so disgustingly filthy as to make our flesh creep. However, it is much better than staying out in the snow and wind.

This being the date when George Washington was added to the census of old Virginia, a salute was fired in camp — on the Union side. Not having the historical item in mind, we mistook it for a row with the Johnnies and breathed more freely when the truth dawned on us. If the venerable Washington were here, he'd have seen a lot of scared Yankees, one of whom continually expressed the opinion, whenever a gun was fired and he could cease his teeth from chattering, that "Stuart's cavalry must be making a rage!" At night this private was further agitated by hearing the colonel's horse kick against the side of the barn, mistaking it for cannonading. He groaned, "O my God, what a life a soldier's life is!" We encourage his misery all we can, and no doubt he will pass a most wretched night.

### February 23rd.

Returned to camp this morning. On the way in we encountered the 19th Maine in rear of Falmouth. They were lugging the snow from their company streets in hard-bread boxes. What foolishness will come next? There's no telling, for the officers, having but little to occupy their minds, hatch up a great many foolish things.

Reached camp about 3 P.M. and immediately drew a ration of whiskey. General Hooker is a firm believer in spirits of this kind and, if rumor is true, he and his staff devote a great deal of time to "inspecting quarts."

### February 24 – 28th.

We enjoyed a season of comparative rest and quiet; we built miles of corduroy roads and have improved the "Old Dominion" to the extent our needs demand.

### Month of March.

Went on picket about three miles from camp on the road to Bealeton Station the first day; out three days and had a good easy time. It was much pleasanter than in camp, with plenty of wood and much purer water. (When I came in I found some tokens of remembrance from home. I was not suffering for food but these were welcome for a change of diet.) This place in line we occupied for the remainder of the month and went on picket two or three times.

The number of deaths has decreased as we become acclimated, and we were getting settled when there began to be rumors of a move.

### April 1st.

We were victimized and made the subject of a *sell*. Before daylight we were ordered to get ready to move immediately and we turned out in a grand rush. After waiting awhile, we recollected the date — April 1st.

The enemy *had* crossed the Rappahannock — seventeen cavalrymen who came to spy out the land — but our men had chased them back over the river. One thing is certain, if they have the slightest idea of how destructive of life this section is, they would let us rot here. It has proved more fatal to our regiment than several Fredericksburgs.

### April 2nd.

No excitement today. We were ordered to decorate our company streets with pine and other evergreens. We worked like beavers, and our camp presented a gala appearance with festoons and arches and all manner of cunning work. There have been rumors of a move, but today entirely reassured us. We have no doubt that our generals intend to remain here till the Spring campaign opens after the roads settle.

## April 3rd.

To our surprise and disgust we had orders to change camp. It isn't changing camp that disgusted us, but the thought of how much labor we wasted decorating our camp yesterday when it must have been known that a move was contemplated. Camp was broken about nine o'clock and we marched down the river three miles to a place called Belle Plain. We went into camp in a range of hills on a neck of land between two rivers, a most delightful site. Had we moved here immediately after Fredericksburg, there is no doubt that several of our comrades would still be with us, eating their regular allowance of "peas on a trencher."

## April 4th – 7th.

Two hills were selected for this camp; the officers have their tents on one, and we put ours on the side of the other, with a deep gully between. There is an abundance of building material and fuel, and plenty of pure water. In less than a week we have built a camp that General Sickles, our corps commander now, pronounced the best in the Army of the Potomac. However this may be, we do have some fine specimens of architecture, considering that our tools consist of axes and knives. The rest of our brigade are posted in rear of us on adjacent hills, and the entire division is close by. Here we can eat, drink, and be merry, and keep clean. We even have an excellent drill ground, which, since we must be drilled constantly, is not a matter of indifference to us. Our camp is quite a curiosity and has been visited by the following generals: Sickles, Berry, Birney, Mott, Whipple, Carr, and others. We named it Camp Sickles, in honor of our corps commander, a braver or better looking officer it has not been our pleasure to look upon. He is a gamey looking bird.

DANIEL E. SICKLES. *Harper's Pictorial History of the Civil War.*

## April 8th.

An unusual event occurred: a review by no less a personage than the president, who was accompanied by Mrs. Lincoln, their youngest boy, Tad, and a host of Washington officials. The army, numbering 90,000, was all in sight at one time, and a fine sight it was. Two corps, the 11th and 12th, were at Stafford Court House. These were in addition to the above-named and were not in the review.

Mr. Lincoln is one of the plainest of men, while his wife is quite the reverse. He has a kindly expression that made us forget his plainness. Mr. Lincoln on horseback is not a model of beauty such as an artist would select. A more awkward specimen of humanity I can not well imagine. It shows him off at a horrible disadvantage. There was a fearful disproportion between the length of his legs and the height of the horse. It seemed as if nothing short of tying a knot in them would prevent them from dragging on the ground. Add to this his round shoulders and a hat stuck on the back of his head, and one can visualize how he looked.

## April 9th.

Mr. Lincoln and suite reviewed the 11th and 12th corps at the Stafford Court House. Our brigade was detailed to do escort duty to His Excellency. We went down the road a mile or so, formed in two lines facing each other, and our distinguished guests passed between.

As Mr. Lincoln rode by, I noticed that he was weeping. Why he wept I know not — whether he was thinking how many had fallen, or how many will soon fall. It might be neither. But this I do know: under that homely exterior is as tender a heart as ever throbbed, one that is easily moved toward the side of the poor and downtrodden. He is probably aware that a battle cannot long be deferred.

I can guess as much as this. A review of this entire army means something of more important character than just to please the president. And so, as I wended my way to camp, a feeling of uneasiness and horrible uncertainty possessed me.

## April 10th – 27th.

A few days later we were reviewed by Lord Lyons, British minister to Washington. Still later by Governor Curtin of Pennsylvania, generals Hooker, Sickles, Birney, Berry, Whipple, and Graham. Somebody seemed to want to be gazing at us all the time. Several other governors of northern states visited, and each one of them had to see how we looked in line. And thus the days passed till April 27th, when General Berry, having received an additional star on his shoulder, thought we would like to see his new adornment and came over to our camp to pass a portion of the day.

We were glad to see him and note this evidence of his increasing popularity. An after-dinner speech was next in order, and he didn't spare his praise of this regiment. He spoke in high terms of our neat camp, our appearance on review, our conduct in the late battle of Fredericksburg, and wound up by calling for "three cheers for Joe Hooker and the next fight." These we gave, then gave "three for General Berry," "three for the Union," and "three for everybody," at General Berry's suggestion.

After this display of vocalism, we returned to camp to speculate as to when and where the next fight might be. That it will be soon, no one can doubt. And that it will not be far away is equally plain. All orders confirm the first of these statements. The extra luggage has been sent to the rear, and also the sick and those unable to go far.

### April 28th.

Governor Coburn of our state put in an appearance, accompanied by a member of Congress named Rice and the Honorable Sam Holden of Portland, all of whom had the conventional dose of "taffy" to give us. Governor Coburn is, without exception, the most wretched speechmaker that ever burnished the cushion of the governor's chair. What sin have we committed that we should be so punished, and on the eve of battle, too? He acted more like a great, blubbering school boy than like the Governor of Maine. The sum total of his remarks was the sum of all flattery, piled on so thick it fell off in great chunks. He informed us (confidentially) that "the 17th has the best record of any regiment from the state." If this wasn't the seventeenth time he said this to as many different regiments, it was only because he hasn't seen that number from our state; some of our regiments are much farther south than the old fellow dares to risk his carcass. His flattery was not as exhilarating as he expected. We have heard similar language before and know we have to pay for it. Blood will be the price.

In the afternoon we were suddenly aroused by the blast of a bugle blowing "pack up." This gave us a chill, and before we recovered our equilibrium, an order was received to march at two o'clock. But we didn't go till four. We moved down to the Rappahannock, very near where we crossed at the battle of Fredericksburg, and bivouacked for the night. We have a notion that we might be going to try the heights again.

# Chancellorsville

## Spring of 1863

*April 29th.*

Rose early, and it was supposed that a crossing would be made right away. Colonel Merrill called on the chaplain to offer a prayer. This performance didn't aid us a mite; it only unfitted us, if anything, for it reminded us of the danger of being wiped out before night. But we were agreeably disappointed this time, for we only moved down into a hollow out of sight of Mr. Johnny Reb and stayed there the rest of the day watching two monster balloons circling overhead, taking observations in Rebeldom. One of them was named *George Washington*, and by a singular coincidence hovered almost directly over the spot where Washington's father died. The Rebels, some of whom are very superstitious, might have thought it was Washington's spirit come to rebuke them. It suggested to my mind a new method of warfare by carrying shells and dropping them where they would have the most effect. But of course it was much easier to *plan* than to *execute*.

At night we were mustered for two month's pay, which we feel sure some of us will never live to draw. A battle is imminent and well we know that any attempt to reach Richmond via Fredericksburg must be attended by a fearful loss of life and limb.

*April 30th.*

There was an absence of any immediate battle and we were moved to a piece of woods where an order was read from General Hooker congratulating us on our past achievements and saying, "The enemy is now in a position where he must come out and fight us on our own ground or ingloriously fly."

No doubt General Hooker intends and expects to do all he advertises — and he advertises extensively. But there are but few plans that provide for all contingencies; something is left out of the calculation, and a general must have the fertility of resources to think and act quickly outside the usual routine of military commonplaces. There are many things the rebels insist on doing, to our disgust, that frequently upset our calculations and plans.

After the reading of General Hooker's grandiose order, we started on the march and night found us about fifteen miles up the river, not far from Bank's Ford. It was so cold that our blankets froze to the ground. Being very tired, we nonetheless soon fell asleep and dreamed of home.

### May 1st.

Turned out stiff and sore and feeling very little like marching. As soon as coffee was disposed of, we set out. The 1st Corps (General Reynolds's) had crossed the river early at U.S. Ford, and we were ordered to follow at once. We did so and halted near an old Rebel camp until about 2 P.M., when we moved nearer the front and went into a piece of woods. Here we passed the rest of the afternoon, momentarily expecting orders to the front. We could hear firing and see hundreds of wounded going to the rear — a great demoralizer.

Just before sunset we were ordered to the front and soon found ourselves in Chancellorsville, an old country tavern on the Orange Plank Road. There is a junction of roads here. The Plank and Turnpike roads unite and continue thus a couple of miles, then diverge again. The road from Ely's Ford, also the U.S. Ford road and the "river road" from Bank's Ford form a junction, making it a place of considerable importance. We found troops of the 2nd, 5th, and 12th corps engaged there, but it was about dark and the strife soon ended for the day. We bivouacked by the side of the road and nothing disturbed us but a miserable bird who persisted in singing "Whip I Will" — an evil omen, the old troops say. I take no stock in this superstitious nonsense. The singing of a bird can affect the result only so far as men might give credit to the story. If men believe that they are whipped, of course their first object and aim is to prove it.

Chancellorsville is not, as its name might imply, a village but a country tavern kept by a widow of that name. We met her and another female clad in deepest mourning making their way toward Fredericksburg, where Lee's army is, a portion of it no farther off than Tabernacle Church. I suspect that one, at least, was no woman, but an infernal spy who had assumed that disguise.

On the afternoon of the 30th, while coming up the road from Falmouth, we met a decrepit old man and woman going to the rear. If I had been in command, there'd have been an overhauling of the apparel of the female portion of the pair to see if it hid contraband. Females or no females, they should have been detained until the battle was over. There is no doubt that the Confederates obtain much valuable information in this way. Deference to the sex prevents our officers from doing anything that might be construed as rudeness.

Not far from Chancellorsville is the house of Melzi Chancellor, or Dowdall's Tavern. Where any American ever found such a cognomen is a wonder. It is neither scripture nor Dutch. It is almost as bad as Polish names, to pronounce which one has to sneeze three times and add a "-ski" at the end. General Hooker has displayed a reckless disregard of the consequences to the jaws of his staff by selecting this as his headquarters.

### May 2nd.

Commenced to rise about daylight, and the first thing that greeted our optics was a female rising up from the ground. It was none other than that heroine of the war, Annie Etheredge, and a braver soul cannot be found. She is always on hand and ready to bear the same privations as the men. When danger threatens, she never cringes. At the battle of Fredericksburg she was binding the wounds of a man when a shell exploded nearby, tearing him terribly, and removing a large portion of the skirt of her dress. This morning she was surrounded by soldiers on every side, laying outside with no covering but her blanket, but such lodgings must have been selected voluntarily, for there isn't a man at any of the headquarters who wouldn't gladly surrender his bed and tent to her. She cooks for General Sickles on the march, and about an hour later we saw her coming to the front with coffee and food for him.

Almost perfect quiet prevailed for hours in the forenoon. The enemy made no demonstrations, nor did we. It was apparent that General Hooker was on the defensive. Sometime about noon General Sickles discovered a Rebel wagon train moving across his front toward Gordonsville. Word was sent to General Hooker, who prounounced it a retreat. In the meantime, pending Hooker's orders, General Sickles ordered Birney's division to advance and assault this column and develop the enemy's intentions. A battery also opened on the Rebels and drove them off the road. We advanced as ordered, and soon came up to the rear guard, which we drove into an unfinished railroad cut and captured an entire regiment, the 23rd Georgia.

Undoubtedly, we would have captured more and delayed the Rebel column further had we not suffered a vexatious delay at the very outset. A supporting battery moved just in time to cut our regiment in two. Major West rushed at them with drawn sword and fiery imprecations, threatening to brain the drivers if they impeded our progress any further. The battery officers were not disposed to test his sincerity. We were soon closed up and moving to the front. The battery galloped on behind and gave the rebels a good shelling while we moved forward into some scrub oak and stirred up their skirmishers in front. Randolph's battery came up and took position on our right on a road, either the Plank Road or one leading into it. The firing of this battery evoked no reply, in a measure confirming our suspicions that the Rebel column was on the fly. We hastened to rush after them.

Just in front of us was a railroad cut. A regiment from Georgia had taken refuge there, and we came along and gobbled them. It proved to be Jackson's rear guard, and if by giving up a regiment he could capture a division, and such a one as Birney's, he would have done a good day's work. But he had still larger game in view. However, we knew not his design and we pursued our way, hoping to capture the train, which proved to be only an ambulance train instead of wagons. The train, and those on the other side of it, moved right along undeterred by us. Our force was too insignificant to cope with Jackson's command but, like the fly on the ox's horn, we thought we were burdening them. So we worked along slowly and appeared to be making headway. We were simply fooling with fire.

Toward night we were halted and ordered to back down the road a short distance, supposing we were to bivouac there for the night. Only a short time passed before we were ordered to fall in and make no noise. Another order followed quickly: "Fix bayonets!" We stacked arms and rested for a time.

And now let us glance at the situation and discover, if we can, why we were in such a fix, for this it proved to be.[1]

Stonewall Jackson's force, whom we had dallied with all afternoon, had moved around in front of the 11th Corps (Howard's) and rushed them suddenly, routing them completely. The Rebels were, in consequence, to our rear, and we were cut off from the rest of the army. When old Stonewall got through with the 11th Corps, we knew we'd receive his attention unless some way could be devised to check him, enabling us to reach our main army again.

About 11 o'clock the colonel sent for the line officers. Something desperate was in the wind. The officers gathered in little groups and, after conversing a few minutes, separated, shook hands and expressed the hope they "would come out alive." Such affectionate demonstrations are not customary, certainly this indicated something more than stacking arms. No portion of the Manual of Arms includes an exhibition of such tender solicitude.

It was a lovely evening. The moon was full, not a cloud in sight. Every object was as distinct as if it were day, except in the shadows of the forest. As we moved out into the road, our bayonets glistened in the moonlight like the rising and falling of waves. It was a magnificent sight, not to be soon forgotten. About midnight, the hour at which "graveyards yawn," we were ordered forward "Into the jaws of Death, into the mouth of Hell." The enemy was much nearer than we realized, for no sooner had we entered the road than we were greeted with a deafening crash of musketry. It came near to being a fatal volley but the Rebel shots went over our heads instead of through them. This I cannot account for except that the Rebels were so excited they failed to note the lay of the land, which was much higher than the road. We know they were awfully scared, for they had just come out of a bad scrape and were all cut up. An attack from this quarter was entirely unlooked for and came upon them before they had fairly got their breath.

The most remarkable circumstance was that not a man was killed, or hit even. But we were mortally scared. The 40th New York preceded us and were as fortunate as we in the matter of loss. The scare wasn't confined to the privates; officers dodged hither and thither, some of them so frightened that they couldn't have told their names. Everyone was in an uproar, scurrying for cover before another volley. Marching in as we did, "in company by company," we took it for granted that the enemy was much farther off and that we should wheel into line of battle and attack, or receive an attack in order, but here we were receiving a fire in the flank, fearing we'd be cut to pieces before we could put ourselves on the defensive. One of our men turned end over end and finished up this remarkable gymnastic performance by divesting himself of every sign of military toggery except his clothes. Such a panic ensued as I cannot describe — officers begging, threatening, and swearing, but all to no purpose. Discipline was a dead letter. Men were as sheep huddled together, each intent on saving his own precious head.

General Ward, who had charge of the movement, was in such haste to reach the rear that he ran over two men, one of whom died a few days later. But for the timely arrival of General Berry, we might all have been run down, shot, or captured. A few orders from him settled the business and we quickly formed again, ready to charge down the Plank Road. At the same time a battery came up and soon the shells were screaming and bursting over the Rebel lines. We had been making the most dreadful havoc in their ranks the first of the evening, but of this we were unaware. Also, we did not know that at that very moment the great General Jackson was hovering between life and death, quite undecided which to favor. He had received three terrible wounds from which the blood poured with great force.

This knowledge took the fight out of the Rebel army and, undoubtedly, was the reason they did not attack more fiercely. We fell back out of the road and laid down in the edge of the woods to pass the rest of the night. Sometime after this the Rebels, under Stuart, crawled toward our lines and bivouacked almost under our very noses, a most impudent proceeding. As we didn't suspect their presence, we laid down feeling quite safe. Perhaps our proximity was unknown to them, or on the other hand, they might have been congratulating themselves on our easy capture in the morning.

Old Stonewall has done an exceedingly good day's work for the Confederacy and lifted a great burden from General Lee's shoulders.[2]

## *May 3rd.*

Our pickets were called in between three and four o'clock, and we prepared to move back to a new line at daylight. Just as we started, a yell greeted our ears and the Rebels swarmed from the woods at the very spot where we had slept. They waltzed out as gaily and confidently as though we were their legitimate property. As we had been marching off in line of battle, we had only to turn about and face them. This chilled their enthusiasm somewhat and gave us time to reform our lines on top of a slight elevation.

Three or four of our men dropped behind the elevation to escape the enemy fire, and as we moved off by the right flank toward Chancellorsville, the Rebels moved in and scooped them in. These three worthies will thus have the pleasure of traveling to Richmond, arriving there in sore distress, and of being insulted by a lot of old crones who will no doubt call them "Yankee scabs" and other pet names.

The rest of us continued until we arrived at a clearing west of the Chancellor House and then came to a front and prepared to receive the enemy. It was but a few moments before they came on, howling and dancing like devils or redskins. Their manner of advance was such that neither artillery nor musketry fire seemed to have the slightest effect in checking them. They didn't come in a dense line as we did, but strung out in a skirmish line. West Point tactics were ignored and they adopted Indian fashion. Our men were falling fast, and our artillery horses faster still. The poor, dumb animals lay on the ground mutilated and suffering, seeming to appeal for relief.

The Rebs, seeing the batteries thus disabled, rushed for those in front of the Chancellor House, intent on capturing them. But at that moment Hayman's brigade executed a charge and the Irish Brigade dragged the guns off. With the exception of one caisson — exploded — we lost no artillery. Two men from Company I were killed and several wounded in this charge. The dead were J.H. Goodrich and John G. Libby, both good fellows. The last words of Goodrich were, "God save me!"; those of Libby, "Let me lay down and die."

After the withdrawal of the battery, the Johnnies crowded us so that another change was soon necessary. It is astonishing how these creatures will fight. Nothing seemed to check them, and we kept falling back, but contesting every step. When we reached the clearing a few rods west of the house we made another stand, and the battery we had saved was soon working as pertly as ever. In moving one of the heavy siege guns, it became mired. General Hooker dismounted, put his shoulder to the wheel (literally), and helped push it out. The effect was electric, and plenty of hands rushed to extricate it.

The battle didn't rage much longer. About 10 o'clock Chancellorsville was in the Rebels' possession and we held only the roads leading to the fords of the Rappahannock, from which the enemy attempted to cut us off. When Sickles notified Hooker of this situation, Hooker ordered Slocum of the 12th Corps to dislodge them with a charge. This charge prevented the Rebs from gaining the desired end, but we could not hold the ground, and it was abandoned, as were our dead and wounded.

Exploding shells soon set the woods on fire, and many a poor fellow was offered up as a sacrifice. Generals Sickles, Whipple, Birney, and others exposed themselves recklessly, trying to restrain the further progress of the enemy.

General Hooker was everywhere, in the thickest of the fray, a conspicuous mark for sharpshooters, of course, because he was mounted. A few moments after freeing the siege gun he galloped down to the house now being used as headquarters and while there met with an accident that deprived us of a commander for some time. He was leaning his head against a post of the piazza when a shell whizzed through the house and struck the opposite end. The heavy concussion knocked General Hooker senseless.

It has been asserted that Hooker was unconscious from a too generous patronage of the canteen. He doubtless is a close observer of canteens, as are most of the other generals, but no one could have been so soon overpowered by drink who only a few minutes before had shown such agility on the field. A man accustomed to his potations is not so easily overthrown.

A few minutes before the accident, we had heard General Sickles say to him, "They're whipping us badly."

Hooker replied, "Well, Dan, the boot will be on the other foot directly."

Whatever his plans, they were now locked in his own bosom, and they remained so just long enough to upset our apple cart.

Hooker was carried to a tent and laid for some time in a stupor. He was aroused by nausea and got up to vomit. He had just left his bed when a shell came right down through the center of it.

This was certainly a hairbreadth escape for General Hooker. Such escapes are very common, and some people even counterfeit them. One of these latter cases came to my attention today. General Ward took a pickaxe and, after making an incision in a tree above his head, called General Sickles's attention to it, saying, "See how near the d——d Rebel came to hitting me." No doubt he has had narrower escapes this day, as has General Sickles, who is said to have remarked as his aides kept falling around him, "I guess they mean *me*, Birney."

This morning our army suffered an almost irreparable loss in the death of General H.G. Berry, our first brigade commander. When I say that General Berry was loved by this brigade, I use no idle phrase. He was shot by a sharpshooter, who must have been up in a tree, while rallying troops to fill a breach in our lines. The bullet passed down through his shoulder and heart, killing him almost instantly. He was carried off the field on his horse, supported by two of his aides, a sad sight to us who fairly idolized him. He was our general, from our own state, and we were justly proud. When his body was set down in front of Hooker's headquarters, he wept for a dear friend, exclaiming, "O my God, Berry, why wasn't I taken and you left?" He kissed his dead friend over and over again, and seemed utterly overwhelmed and broken.

General Hooker felt very keenly the unfavorable turn the battle had taken and was heard to exclaim in the anguish of his spirit, "I wish to God someone would put a bullet through my head." This was after his own injury received at the Chancellor House.

It is regrettable that General Sickles cannot be the senior in command now, for he has a perfectly clear head and is, so far as danger is concerned, a fine specimen of majestic indifference.

General A.W. Whipple of our 2nd Division was the next to fall after Berry. He was also shot in the heart and carried from the field mortally wounded. How any bullet ever pierced General Whipple's armor of dirt is a mystery of mysteries. I considered him perfectly safe from any missile weighing less than a ton, having a casing of dirt of unknown thickness supposed to be invulnerable.

About this time, half of our regiment became detached and wandered down to the river, not discovering their mistake until stopped by the provost guard. (The fighting was over before this occurred.) They must have got lost again on their way back, as they didn't arrive until about 4 P.M.

The right of the regiment was ordered to the rear of the breastworks. In going there we passed the field hospital, where the surgeons were cutting and slashing human flesh right and left. They had a pile of arms and legs there nearly as large as a Virginia strawstack. After taking position, we were constantly subjected to shelling and danger of death by falling limbs.

FIELD HOSPITAL. *Harper's Pictorial History of the Civil War.*

Toward sunset an impression prevailed that the Rebs were about to do something desperate, and we prepared to give them a reception. Our "heaviest regiment" was ordered to the front. This order emphatically pointed to the 17th of Maine. A battery was sent out in front and we went ahead of them. If the Rebels charged, the battery was to give them grape and cannister; if that didn't settle the business, we were to give them a volley and charge them. As they didn't come, this little program went by default. Our disappointment was not unmixed with gladness, as an encounter of this kind must cause some destruction to our side. We remained out all night and were not molested save by the lonesome whippoorwill.

If it is a fact that misery likes company, then those who have parted with their limbs today may derive some comfort in the thought that an equal number on the other side are thus bereft. It would be much more like patriotism to contemplate the sacrifice as one made for *principle*, and though the Rebels are, in our judgment, wrong, still some of them must be conscientious.

Our company lost no men except the ones taken prisoner early in the morning: George Whitten, Lewis G. Whitney, Cy Buker and William Perry. In addition were those who fell in the charge about 9 A.M.: J. Goodrich, J.G. Libby, John Kendrick, and E.W. Tibbetts. At the same time this writer was wounded in the pants near the hip. This was rather a close call, but a miss is as good as a mile. Had the miss been any less, someone else would have to chronicle these events.

### May 4th.

We were called in from our advanced position and stationed in rear of the works. One of the New Jersey regiments was sent out on picket still farther in advance. They moved across an open field in splendid style until they came to some woods. Here a Rebel volley met them and they about-faced and came back across the field in a decidedly short time. (Such conduct, and that of the 11th Corps, makes one cease wondering at defeat.) The Rebels followed them in and a lot were gobbled. General Griffin's brigade captured seven stands of colors and 2000 Rebel prisoners. General Lee showed his disapproval of this by giving a vigorous shelling. Later it was understood that all this charging and shelling was a blind to attract our attention while the larger portion of Lee's command turned back to Fredericksburg to attack Sedgwick, who had crossed the river in obedience to General Hooker's orders and had carried the Heights. Thus situated, Sedgwick could fall on the Rebel rear whenever the auspicious moment arrived. But not content with the measure he had attained, Sedgwick pushed onto the Rebel rear. Old Early returned and laid on Sedgwick's rear, thus Sedgwick fell into the very trap Hooker had planned for Lee.[3]

Hooker could have saved Sedgwick if he had known of his predicament in time. But the deed was done and Sedgwick was now in for it. He could only do two things: surrender or (perhaps) hold his ground until night, then sneak out and cross the river at Bank's Ford. Sedgwick was enveloped on three sides and it was doubtful that he could get out. The Rebels closed in on him and tried hard to crush him. They didn't accomplish this, and after dark he recrossed the river.

All this time Hooker was doing absolutely *nothing*, and here is a great mystery. Lee held Hooker all day with a skirmish line while he paid his respects to Sedgwick. Thus our left wing is crippled, as our right was on the second of May. Carelessness on the right, disobedience on the left, inaction in the center. The condition of things must now be eminently satisfactory to Lee, who just a short time ago was in a most embarrassing position.

Night found our own regiment just where we had laid all day. We lost no men, nor did we fire a gun.

### May 5th.

We had an idea that something exciting might be done today, but waited for hours without receiving any orders except to strengthen the works. So, we began to think that nothing of an aggressive nature is to be done. Hooker is probably waiting for the enemy to come out and fight him on his own ground, or ingloriously fly. But they don't seem disposed to do either although General Hooker's plans and orders anticipate one, if not both, of these things as dead sure. Occasionally a picket shot was exchanged, otherwise quiet prevailed. The Rebels annoyed our men much by firing on them as they crossed a field when they went on picket. Our men are unable to return fire as the enemy is concealed in the woods and exchange *their* pickets under cover.

Night found us still here and not particularly satisfied with our position. We expected better things.

### May 6th.

We awoke this morning to find a first-class Virginia rainstorm in full blast, and ourselves as wet and wretched as it could make us. The Rappahannock rose nine feet in as many hours, endangering our communications to such an extent that we had to take up one pontoon bridge and add it to the other two so as to cover the distance from shore to shore. Even then, it was feared that they might be swept away by the turbulent flood.

General Hooker immediately called a council of his corps commanders to discuss whether to remain and fight, or to return while it was possible to do so. It was decided almost unanimously to retire. Nothing could be gained by staying, while much might be lost. The activity of the foe indicated that a movement of some kind was on foot. General Hooker gave the order to retire. The position was too perilous — an exultant foe in front and an angry river behind were too much for his stomach.

After dark we commenced to recross the fatal Rappahannock. It was very dark and the rain incessant, hence our progress was exceedingly slow. The roads were indescribable. We would make a few rods, then halt and stand still and shiver. This continued all through the night until our patience was utterly exhausted, and our bodies too.

### May 7th.

The dawn found us on the south side of the stream and in momentary expectation that Lee would discover our absence and pursue, in which case we should remain on that side of the river until exchanged from Richmond.[4] Still, we longed for morning, for darkness aggravates all ills.

While poking along as fast as my "precarious pegs" would carry me — wet, worn, and weary — an aide of General Sickles came along and urged me, with others, to make all haste to reach the river. Having a vaulting ambition to do that very thing, we picked up our pace and soon were floundering in a pool of liquid mud.

After daylight we moved along with less delay and about 8 o'clock landed on the northern bank of the Rappahannock, thankful to have escaped from another disastrous attempt to go to Richmond via Fredericksburg. This was the second abortive movement of this kind. It cost us many lives and limbs, much treasure, and nearly destroyed the morale of our army. Soon after crossing the river, we passed the 11th Corps, with whom we exchanged greetings of a highly uncomplimentary nature. Yet, it is not the men who are to blame, for no man could stand such an attack as this had been. General Howard should have been fully prepared, but he wasn't; hence these jeers.

We halted not long after for breakfast of soft salt pork, wet hardtack, and coffee strongly tinctured with the Virginia mud, for the water was very thick. Some of us had an extra ingredient in the shape of homeopathic pills.[5] Having broken a few bottles in my knapsack and thinking them mostly sugar, I didn't bother to pick them out of the coffee. I learned later that that was a dangerous and stupid thing, and unless something of an opposite nature wasn't administered shortly, others would draw my rations. I would have no need of them.

As soon as we had eaten we moved on. It continued to rain and the mud was simply appalling, but being in a hurry to reach camp, or Washington, or somewhere, we allowed no trifles to stand in our way. In some places where streams crossed the road, they became streams of liquid mud so stiff they couldn't run downhill. Many of our men fell by the wayside, utterly played out. When night arrived they were miles to the rear. Not a particularly cheery prospect when one is out of rations, wet, chafed, weary, with no fire or means of making one. Tired almost to death, and not caring much whether we lived or died, it is little wonder our spirits were below zero.

These are some of the beauties of war, and I am quite sure that the war would be of very short duration if the political leaders on both sides could have a taste of conditions in the field. They would cry out for a truce on any terms. (Not so with the men in the ranks, for with few exceptions they ask for no terms that do not have as a preliminary the surrender of the Rebels.) When I speak of leaders I mean that class of men who, far removed from scenes of danger, can afford to be very stiff in the back. In contrast, our officers, except field officers, have to endure as much as we do.

I moseyed along in the most agonizing manner, my heels galled to the bone, my boots full of mud, grinding into the flesh at every step until it seemed that nothing more could be endured. But I reached camp at last and laid down, nearer dead than alive. Some men who were quite able to walk had been hauled in the ambulances. One such passenger threw a stack of guns down on his head and posed as a wounded man, turning up at the division hospital with his head bandaged. His cheek was boundless. With this exception, our men behaved splendidly and did honor to the old Kearney Division.[6]

### May 8th.

Had an order this morning from division headquarters to send 200 men on picket. It wasn't easy to find that number for we all have a strong inclination to stay put, having already seen all the exercise of this kind we want for one week. We had no rations, many were nearly barefoot, and all were sore and stiff. But military orders are not to be set aside, and the detail was soon formed.

One, however, positively refused to budge a hair and insisted on being his own judge as to his ability to go out. As a rule I don't believe in insubordination, but there are times when one is driven to it in self-defense. This was one of those cases. I didn't go on picket this morning, nor did I ask any surgeon to excuse me from duty, thereby incurring the displeasure of a certain noncommissioned officer who insisted that one or the other must be done. The surgeons, whittlers of human flesh and sawers of bones, are often moved more by their individual likes and dislikes than any medical knowledge. Some surgeons are no more fit for their position than a cow is for teaching the languages. Hence, my reason for declining to appear before one. In my condition, which was one of excruciating torture, the thought of going on picket was tantamount to committing suicide.

After about two hours of fooling around, the detail was completed, save *one*. If anybody had been looking in the right direction, they'd have seen this writer making his way over the hill in a very feeble manner and seating himself on a stump to witness the imposing pageant of the detail leaving camp. The detail went as far as corps headquarters and were then sent back. On their return, we all drew rations, rested, and filled up.

## May 9th.

The detail was again called for and this time it went with a much better grace. All but a few who had the usual complaints. A chronic grumbler is worse than chronic diarrhea, which is at least a private trouble. The army is a most excellent place for the grumber to develop his talent. One would have be to an improvement over old Job himself not to complain when called upon to march ten miles or more when his heels are already galled to the bone.

## May 10th – 31st.

A couple of days more and the pickets returned, the stragglers came in, and matters had settled down into their old ways. Within a week, only those thoroughly acquainted would have suspected that we have been out of camp at all.

Nothing of any consequence was done for several days. There was simply the usual routine of camp life and the presentation of "Kearney medals" to those whose conduct was especially meritorious in the late fight. This was a most foolish and unjust performance. Had the thing been reversed and the medals, two to a company, been given to those who had been notoriously cowardly, it would have been just right. Wearing a badge for cowardice would be a novel way of punishing offenders. We returned to camp, confident that the country is now safe for some days.

Twice now we have been led as sheep to the slaughter. Twice have our plans miserably miscarried without proper cause, and somebody is to blame. Human life ought to be worth more than old bones. General Hooker is not wholly to blame; Howard is deserving of the strongest censure for allowing Jackson to flank our right; Sedgwick, although brave, capable, and patriotic, disobeyed orders and got himself into a trap, nearly losing all his command. However, after he was so cut off, if General Hooker had moved promptly from Chancellorsville, Lee's army would have been held in a vise. If Sedgwick had held the city and Hooker had held onto the position gained on May 1st, Lee would have been in a still more precarious condition and the movement by Jackson would never have been made.

Again, on Sunday, General Hooker allowed the 3rd Corps to stand the brunt of battle and be mutilated when he had 37,000 troops on the flank of Jackson's column who never fired a gun. This will no easy matter to explain, except we consider the injury Hooker sustained at the Chancellor House. It is fair to infer, however, that General Hooker had communicated to *some* of his subordinates his intention to bring up this column to the attack. But neither Couch, who was next in command, nor Meade assumed the responsibility, and the movement was never made.

And thus ends my account of the Battle of Chancellorsville, an engagement which was bloody, fierce, mysterious, and most barren of good results to us.

# March to Gettysburg

## June 1–30, 1863

*June 1st – 3rd.*

Had a holiday on the 1st in which we made merry and did about as we pleased, even to getting tipsy on stimulants going by the colorful names of old budge, tanglefoot, red-eye, or bug juice.

The New Yorkers had a great day of it, playing hurdle races, catching greased pigs, and shinning greased poles. But the chief diversion was seeing how much old rye they could put themselves outside of. Some of McClellan's admirers loudly lauded that individual, drawing invidious comparisions between him and the present commander, General Hooker. They demanded three cheers for "Little Mac," and when one of Hooker's staff demanded three for Hooker, the 37th New York showed him they had a greater faculty for fisting than cheering. He was pummeled almost into jelly and nearly torn from his horse. It was feared he would be killed, but he finally cleared himself and galloped off. Thus closed the day, and I had no regrets, for it had been productive of little good.

A day or two after, an event occurred that generated considerable activity in our camps and promised an early interruption of the quiet now prevailing. The army of General Lee has for some time been preparing to move somewhere but in what direction is unknown to our commander. Whether it is to be an advance or a retreat, no one knows. It seems improbable that they are in any condition to take the offensive so soon after the late fight; nor can any satisfactory reason be given why they should retreat.

It is claimed that the Confederates are encouraged by the general condition of affairs, but I don't see it in this light. True, they have won a victory in the last two engagements, but our army is again buoyant and ready to be led to new fields of conquest — or defeat.

*June 4th.*

A division of Union cavalry, under Kilpatrick, crossed the Rappahannock and surprised the Rebel cavalry at Brandy Station, capturing their headquarters tent and gaining possession of a copy of Lee's plan of invasion. This was the rear of Lee's army. The van has started north. Our spies must have been napping. All we can do is put ourselves in motion, and General Hooker has decided to do just this as soon as his army can be made ready. It is not a light matter for an army of 80,000 men, lying in camp quietly, to be put in motion without preparation. A portion of the Confederate force is reported already up in the Shenandoah Valley and menacing Washington.

### June 7th – 10th.

Went on picket on the Warrenton Road. At this time of year picketing is a pleasant pastime. We were out three days, and it was fair all the time. Rumors from camp followed us and every fresh arrival brought news. Everybody *knew* just where we were going.

At the end of three days we returned to camp and found the rumors have crystallized into positive orders. The sick and the sutlers have all gone, and we have orders to move the next day. This is definite enough, but where are we headed?

### June 11th.

As soon as we had eaten our frugal breakfast, we found ourselves ready and awaiting the final order to go. It was not until about 2 o'clock that the bugles blew the "general" (or pack-up), and by 4 P.M. we were on the road, travelling north. Supposing Lee to be still occupying the line of the Rappahannock or Rapidan, we assume we are en route to Washington or the upper fords of the Rappahannock for the purpose of turning Lee's flank. The column marched about fifteen miles on the Warrenton Road and halted for the night.

Myself and another, who were not equal to this amount of exertion, decided to take shelter at Hartwood church, a small brick structure. On entering, we were struck with the number of texts and embellishments executed in charcoal on the walls. The seats have been torn out, the windows and doors smashed, and the walls covered with obscene characters and writings. A body of Union cavalry did this dastardly desecration of the house of worship — a sufficient commentary on the characters of these dirty caricatures of patriots. No matter if it *is* a Rebel house of worship; its character should be a protection against vandalism. Such treatment of churches is a disgrace to the much-boasted civilization of the nineteenth century.

### June 12th.

Those of us who camped here rose at the first sign of dawn and went in search of the column. There was no difficulty finding them for the road was lined with sleeping stragglers. The main column was about a mile from the church where we halted. They would have been on the march before we reached them if they hadn't waited for the 6th Corps to execute two deserters. This is supposed to terrify any who might entertain similar ideas.

We marched about twenty miles and camped for the night not far from Bealeton. Those of us who fell out yesterday did the same today but with one difference: today we had a pass from the captain and Dr. Hersom. We cannot run with the horses in the condition we are in, and the heat is fearful. Three of us bivouacked under a large tree in rear of some teams. We passed a comfortable night and woke up wonderfully refreshed, for the nights in Virginia are deliciously cool even in hot weather.

### June 13th.

Turned out at daylight and moved down to the corps, which we found in a nice grove near Bealeton Station. We laid here all day as a continual stream of troops passed by in the direction of Manassas. No cars passed on the railroad, and we have seen no other signs of life in the neighborhood. I have no idea why a station was established in such a place, nor why any human being settled here.

### June 14th.

Still at Bealeton and the army still filing past. It must cover a good number of miles. Spent another night here as the army kept coming, hour after hour. We would be much pleased to move out as quickly as possible for there is no water in the vicinity except one spring a mile away. Scarcely anything grows in the arid soil. It is difficult to get sufficient water for drinking, and as for ablutions, a mud puddle would be deemed an inestimable treasure. There seems to be a prospect of rain, and we hope it will rain sufficiently to lay the dust, which in this region is phenomenally abundant.

About midnight we were turned out to draw rations. The unseasonable hour was not explained but presumably it is because tomorrow is Sunday. It would be a wicked sin to desecrate the day by drawing rations. Such piety in these quartermasters is truly affecting and in glaring contrast to our impiety, for we see no sin in drawing rations whenever circumstances require or permit it. To hold inspections and dress parades is sanctioned, but to feed us hungry mortals is a deadly sin!

### June 15th.

Nothing of any consequence until 5 P.M., when we received the long-expected order to "Dust out of this!" We marched to Kettle Run, halting for the night between that and Warrenton Junction. This place was considered of much importance during the early part of the war. The buildings are now charred ruins, and the tall chimneys stand out in the moonlight like ghostly fingers pointing skyward. One can easily imagine the spirits of the departed generations flitting around the ruins and sighing at the folly of their successors.

As I gazed on these ruins of what were once (so far as I know) happy homes and cheerful firesides, I could do no less than pity the Virginians and wish they had been guided by reason rather than swayed by passion. All this to carry out a false idea of independence. What had they ever been if not independent? And where is their boasted freedom now? There was never anything so near akin to despotism in this country as is now being enacted in the so-called Southern Confederacy.

A few hot-headed demagogues have dragged the State of Virginia almost into beggary and turned their once beautiful country into a desert. Virginia, the garden of this union, is now overrun with weeds. "Poor old simple Virginia," exclaimed Governor Pickens of South Carolina when he learned that it had passed the ordinance of secession. He was shrewd enough to see that the border states must bear the brunt of the fighting.

The Virginians doubtless thought a bold front and one or two victories for the Confederates would so demoralize us that the war would soon end. But they reckoned ill. All pride and courage are not monopolized by the Rebels.

To encourage the Rebel heart, improve the Rebel commissariat, and secure the recognition of England, a movement north is now in progress. The Confederates are elated at the ease with which they have twice disposed of our army within six months. They now plan to draw our army away from Richmond and gain a breathing spell. They also hope to replenish their wardrobe from the abundance of the North.[1]

*June 15th.*

The march began about 7 A.M. The air was almost suffocating, and as we advanced and our canteens became empty, matters assumed a serious turn. The dust in the road was scalding and, as one person remarked, "was thirty feet deep." The soil of Virginia was sucked into our throats, sniffed into our nostrils, and flew into our eyes and ears until our most intimate friends would not have recognized us.

On no other march have we suffered so with thirst and heat. It was but a short time after the water gave out that the effects of the march and heat began to be apparent. Men fell by the roadside to die from sunstroke, but notwithstanding the fact that more than a hundred had fallen out and others were on the verge of it, no halt was made until 10 o'clock, and then we hauled up in an open space where not so much as a mullein stalk was visible. The only suggestion of water might be at a couple of houses a mile off. My tongue was now an "unruly member" and "vaunted itself and was puffed up." It required more room than I had for it. Consequently, I lolled and could only perform respiration through my nose.

Water must be had. We made a wild scramble for the house and found a well, but there was such a rush that the bucket collapsed and smashed into pieces far below our reach. Just at this moment the bugle blew and we could tarry no longer. Our hearts sank at the sound. As we were about to start from the house, I spied an old barrel at one corner of it. The barrel was about one-third full of something resembling ale in color and protected by a scum an inch deep. Into this my dipper was plunged and twice emptied without stopping to taste or smell. This horrible substitute for water was much like the turtle soup of the Scotchman, "It would 'na stay doon." I was soon relieved of the mess, but not before my internal department was fearfully demoralized.

It was but a short time before it was evident that more of us must succumb to the dreadful heat and thirst. Desiring to keep up if possible, I strained every nerve, hoping that the leader of the column would come to his senses and haul up. Any such hope was doomed, and I soon grew sick at the stomach and lost my eyesight. Two comrades, Stacy and Bradbury, enabled me to reach a spring by the roadside, where prompt measures restored me sufficiently to move on in a couple of hours and join the column, which had finally halted soon after I dropped out. Had I fallen alone and been left in the sun, a few minutes more would have placed me beyond recovery.

General Birney now seemed to conclude that such "scratching gravel" could be endured no longer, and we resumed our march with a deliberation of movement quite as marked as was our former haste. There were frequent halts for rest until we reached Manassas about sunset.

Various rumors flew about as to the cause of the fearful rushing of the forenoon, most of them too foolish to repeat. The probable reason was a fear that the Rebels would get possession of some point in the neighborhood of Manassas essential to us, thus menacing our rear and Washington. But once we had passed a certain point there was no danger, so we were not hurried after noon.

We were soon in camp and thankful for the chance to sleep. As we could get no water and were unable to make coffee, we soon had our blankets on the ground and tumbled into them. We were just chucking ourselves under the ribs at the thought of a good night's rest when a sound greeted our ears that nearly congealed the blood in our veins. It was the bugle at brigade headquarters blowing "Pack up." In a few minutes we were in line ready to depart for regions unknown. Supposing that a new danger menaced the line, perhaps the Rebel army snapping at our heels, we marched several miles and at last hauled up at a ford on Bull Run.

Fear of a Rebel surprise was the cause of our being sent here. General Heintzleman, who commanded the defenses of Washington, had the same notion and he, too, sent out a force to picket Bull Run — but on the other side of the stream. Not knowing anything of this, when we spied them pacing back and forth, we supposed them to be Rebels. If Heintzleman's troops had shown the slightest "advance" on our position, they would have been promptly met by fire from us.

Things must be slightly mixed when Union soldiers picket both sides of the stream and both expect the enemy from the other side. There are other bulls than Bull Run around here! No thanks to the authors of this one that we didn't shed fratricidal blood. We watched them closely all night and, no doubt, they did the same. They allowed us to approach and get the water we stood so sorely in need of. And so ended a day of great suffering from heat, thirst, and dust.

## June 16th.

As soon as daylight put in an appearance we discovered that the party across the stream wore blue. The surprise was mutual. As there was no occasion for this double picket force, we withdrew and took position near a line of old works thrown up during the previous battle at Bull Run.

We laid here all day near the Run, refreshing our weary carcasses. From the high bluff we can see a goodly portion of the Bull Run battlefield, the Bull Run Mountains, and Thoroughfare Gap. This section of country is quite in contrast with the part we have just passed through. This is too lovely a landscape to be desecrated by war, but hundreds of our countrymen have fallen here, and at least one peaceful citizen — the widow Henry — was shot as she lay in bed sick. Virginia is a beautiful country, and it is no wonder that its inhabitants are proud of their state. I could live here forever and ask for nothing better, only exemption from disease and death.

## June 17th.

Laid still till noon, when we received orders to move. Marched to Centreville, only three miles distant. The heat is truly infernal, and only the shortness of the march saved many of us from sunstroke. On the way we passed over the locale of the famous battle, or charge, of the Black Horse Cavalry, which body of Southrons came very near total annihilation by a regiment of Yankee "mudsills" from Michigan. This Rebel cavalry was composed of sons of very wealthy Virginians and claimed to be of noble blood. Well they might have been, but a bullet had the same affinity for one of them that it had for the lowest mudsill in our army or clay-eater in theirs, and the cream of Virginia troops had their saddles emptied by the common herd from Michigan.

This Black Horse cavalry was so colorful it bears time for description. They were mounted on the best blooded steeds that could be found and they were gaily caparisoned. The men wore black-velvet clothes with broad-rimmed hats surmounted by large black plumes and other tinsel by which they aped "ye knights of old." They were excellent riders and could do many daring deeds. But all this counted for naught when a volley of Yankee bullets ploughed through their ranks. Many tokens of their stay lay about, and for relic hunters this is a charming spot, but having all I care to lug, I won't add any relics to my collection.

We reached Centreville about sunset and bivouacked for the night just outside the town. Most of the Army of the Potomac is nearby, as are some nine-months men who belong to the outer defense of Washington.[2]

## June 18th.

Laid here all day, resting and roasting. It was intensely hot and if we didn't suffocate, it wasn't because the conditions were unfavorable.

Centreville, of which we have heard so much, is a miserable little village of no importance except its strategic situation. It is considered the key to the defenses of Washington. During the day some of our nine-months men from Maine came over to visit. They look very nice, as if they are just out of the bureau drawer and intend to return there immediately. We are lousy and filthy and, curious to say, not ashamed of either condition. They are tokens of service rendered, which these fellows can lay no claim to. Some expressed contempt for our condition. Had these knights of the bandbox been through what we have the past six days, perhaps their white collars and gloves and gold braid would be at a great discount. We had no regrets when these "parlor soldiers" left. Although dirty and covered with vermin, we made no apologies to these fellows.

Just after sunset we started out on a march with no idea where we might be going except that it was in a northerly direction. It commenced to rain in fine old Virginia style, and in less than an hour the road was a mass of liquid mud up to, even over, our ankles in many places. This is partly due to the peculiarity of the soil, which is like brick dust.

It was so dark that one couldn't see his hand before him, or as one wag remarked, "So dark that bats ran into each other." Occasionally we passed a farmhouse with a light burning — a sign of life that gave us comfort. About 9 o'clock we saw a glimmer in the sky, which indicated the close proximity of somebody in bivouac. We soon hauled up for the night in an open field with not a sign of wood.

## June 19th.

Referring to my map, I find we are near Gum Spring. Soon after rising we went on picket and were posted in a field near some farm houses in the rear of the division. The inmates of said homes were soon made acquainted with us and, for a trifling consideration, seemed pleased to furnish us with all the luxuries of the season. Our visits became so frequent and protracted that our officers resorted to several stratagems to deter us. Among other things, they reported guerrillas in the vicinity, and that several of our men have been found murdered. Although these yarns were received with a grain of salt, they had the desired effect on many, though some daredevils continue to come and go as they please. They fear nothing so much as an empty stomach.

This afternoon a body of Rebel cavalry encountered some of our fellows at Aldie. The long and short of it was that Mr. Reb left that section quite hastily and the Yankees pursued him as far as the mountains. The 1st Maine Cavalry under Colonel Duffie won a great name in this engagement. We were anxious listeners to the firing, expecting to be sent up to assist at any moment, but the 1st Maine Cavalry had the affair well in hand.

After dark we were treated to a scare that came near to breaking our lines all up. The residents hereabouts have driven their cattle into the woods to keep them out of our way. After dark the cattle came piling in, and the clatter of their hooves as they leaped a rail fence nearby startled us extremely. Despite our agitation we fixed bayonets and prepared to receive cavalry. One of the men from Company I discharged his gun and ran away from his post, leaving us in suspense as to where he was or what was the occasion for firing. We searched far and near for his remains but could find nothing so we supposed he had been shot and dragged out. Our speculations were entirely out of place, for he was, in fact, making excellent time in the direction of the reserve, where he poured into the ears of the commanding officer a marvelous yarn of great Rebel flank movements.

The Rebel flanking party turned out to be some small cedars scattered around the field. When the facts in the case were ascertained our fleet-footed picket would have been court-martialed but for the intercession of Captain Hobson, who said he is a good soldier. The man is not actually a *coward* but he is sadly deficient in judgment and knowledge, having no more sense of propriety than a three-year-old. (I assume he did as well as he could, for he doesn't even know how many weeks there are in a month. Captain Hobson at one time threatened to put him on extra duty for six weeks if he disobeyed an order again. He retorted by saying, "I don't care if you put me on for a month!" This caused an audible smile all around.)

### June 20th.

Returned from picket and found the division has moved up to a point much nearer town, as dingy a place as I ever saw except Waterloo, Virginia. The only building in town that is not absolutely shabby is a little church, just built. Wendal Phillips once remarked that the church is the milestone that shows how far public morals have advanced, but in this case the score or more of dilapidated buildings in the town speak quite as eloquently of the decadence of morals and pride. Gum Spring derives its name from a mineral spring in its midst, the water of which possesses rare medicinal qualities. Nothing could be clearer or look more inviting than this spring, but the taste is hardly equal to the looks.

We were not long in "doing" the town and discovering what might be of interest therein. We then meandered into the nearby countryside and found a stream large enough to wash in, whereupon we started for camp with murderous thoughts intent, determined on a war of elimination against dirt and lice, both of which we have had in the most lavish abundance ever since leaving Camp Sickles. The dirt we washed out of our clothes made quite a tract of new land — and it must have been exceedingly fertile.

### June 21st.

Nothing stirring to mar the serenity induced by the state of the weather except a brigade drill by General de Trobriand. During the drill there was a slight passage of arms between the general and Colonel Tommy Eagan, a broth of a lad of Celtic origin commanding the 40th New York.

Tommy has never forgotten the insult to his nationality caused by de Trobriand's elevation to the command of the brigade and has signalized his displeasure in sundry small capers more fitting a small boy than an officer. On this occasion he actually attempted to take the reins into his own hands. The general soon made it very clear who was commander of the brigade, including the vociferous Tommy. We had a two-hour drill and returned to camp.

Blacksmiths Department, Head-Quarters.

Stables and Negro Servants' Tent.

General Hooker's Tent.

**HEADQUARTERS.** *Harper's Pictorial History of the Civil War.*

The broad and level fields stretching in every direction offer a chance for drill our officers cannot resist, so we have enough of it here. After drill we wage war with the lice attacking us. Nothing short of boiling our clothes will rid us of them.

### June 22nd.

A goodly portion of this day was spent in frantic efforts to reduce our stock of lice. We were never in such a fix before, and I hope we may be spared from any more of such severe experience. No move today so far as we know. We are covering so much territory at present that we know but little of the other corps.

### June 23rd.

Much excitement in our regiment this morning. Captain Hobson had taken under his protection a nice home-cured ham, from which he was anticipating much enjoyment, but some person or persons unknown appropriated the same to his own use last night. The resulting remarks from Captain Hobson were exceedingly voluminous as well as rugged, and he expressed a burning desire to crush the villain to indescribable atoms. Camp was searched but nothing discovered that could throw any light on the abduction of this precious bit of pig. It is unfortunate for the captain that he has such a small tent; there wasn't room inside for both his feet and the ham. (Lieutenant Thompson, who is also blessed with particularly large extremities, has taken the precaution of building an ell onto *his* tent for the special protection of his feet.) If the captain had only left his feet out of doors instead of the ham, he would have saved both, for no one would have undertaken the task of carrying off the former.

Although we laid here all day, no other episode occurred to attract my attention.

### June 24th.

Had orders to move, and 7 o'clock found us in line. We marched in a northeasterly direction and soon came to Rockwell, a lively town of one stone building, either a schoolhouse or a church, or both. There is no apparent need for either, for there wasn't a sign of humanity except for one man who told us the name of the place.

About 11 o'clock we halted opposite Edward's Ferry. Thinking we had marched far enough to rest and get some dinner, we built fires and set our coffee on. No sooner had we done this than we were ordered to move on, with a promise of rest and coffee the other side of the Potomac. After crossing, we heard nothing more of dinner or halting. The afternoon wore on, followed by darkness, and still no halt. Ye gods! I began to think I could stand no more of this. A drizzle had set in about noon so the towpath was very slippery and marching exceedingly tiresome, for we slipped back as fast as we could proceed.

We didn't halt until we reached the viaduct over the Monococy, a distance of thirty-five miles from our camp of last night. A few of us, thinking no halt was intended, fell out before reaching Monococy, taking for lodging a ditch by the side of the towpath, our shelter a rubber blanket over some rails. This proves to be the best room in the house, as those who crossed the viaduct have to lay down in mud while *our* bed is wet grass. We are so completely played out that we don't notice our poor accommodations as much as we would ordinarily.

The viaduct is an excellent specimen of engineering skill, doubtless one of the finest in this country. While a portion of our division was crossing, an old pack mule decided to show his peculiarities. He planted himself squarely in the path and resisted all entreaties to move on. He seemed to have several relays of legs and was right handy with them. As he couldn't be taken to the rear and access was not to be had from the front, a flank movement was executed and he went splashing into the canal, the pack on his back dragging him to a watery grave. There he was left with his four heels standing above water — a solemn warning to evil-doers. As the Virginians say, a mule is real "peart" with his heels.

### June 25th.

It was with many sighs and grunts of relief that we beheld the dawn of day, though it was still raining. We were terribly cramped and chilled and were very glad to get up. We soon crossed over to the rest of the division and found them wallowing in mud up to their ankles. About 8 o'clock we started for Point of Rocks and arrived about noon, bivouacking alongside the Baltimore and Ohio Railroad after marching six miles.

We found a store not far away and hoped to get something there to tickle our palates but, to our great disgust, the entire stock in trade of this apology for a grocery store were a few salt fish and a couple of hams that looked a thousand years older than Adam.

### June 26th.

It was a lovely day, the sky teeming with light, the ethereal blue unsullied by a single cloud. We expected to start early but it was about noon before we did. General Hooker passed along at 11 o'clock and we soon followed, halting at Jeffersonville long enough to eat the regulation peas on a trencher (salt pork and hardtack). We then marched through the town with colors flying and our band playing the national airs.

The young ladies of the town, dressed in holiday attire, responded with smiles and the waving of handkerchiefs and small flags. There was every appearance of gladness but it might be only affectation after all. They are either intensely loyal or devilishly deceitful. We marched only a few miles beyond the town, though far enough that the men won't go back to bask in the sunlight of the smiling females. We halted for the night quite early.

In these days we are making short marches, moving slowly, for General Hooker must be sure that Washington is covered, and he must move slowly in order to prevent Lee from dashing back in his rear.

### June 27th.

Marched from Jeffersonville to Middletown and camped near the town in an immense wheatfield. These wheat and cornfields are enough to ravish the heart of a New Englander, who is accustomed to seeing them only in the smallest lots.

Some young ladies came out of a house as we passed, and sang "The Red, White, and Blue" and "The Star Spangled Banner," and other songs calculated to fan the fires of patriotism. They were dressed all in white, carrying little flags, and appeared intensely loyal to the North. Everything here has the air of solid comfort, peace, and plenty. Harper's Ferry can be seen in the dim distance. Through the gap the misty outline of other mountains melts into the horizon, making a picture of indescribable loveliness, a paradise on earth.

### June 28th.

Marched into Middletown and then took a northerly direction, which brought us about noon to Frederick City.[3] As we entered the environs of the city, the Negroes came out in troops, treating us to cherries and grapes and other luxuries of the season. There was no mistaking the spontaneity of these demonstrations. There was no end to their smiles. It seemed as if they couldn't do enough for "Massa Linkum's" men.

We made as much show as possible in getting through the town. There was no end of bunting and the most elaborate floral decorations. The people turned out with so much enthusiasm that one would have thought they'd never seen a soldier before. We were told that Bradley Johnson, one of their own citizens, had marched a Confederate brigade through the city only a few days before but no demonstrations of any consequence had been made then.

Some of our generals were covered with wreaths and flowers. Especially noticeable in this respect was General Pierce, our brigade commander, who is said to be the handsomest general in this army. General Sickles came up and joined his corps. (He has been away sick.) Also, General Hooker has been relieved, at his own request, and General G. Meade appointed to the vacancy.[4]

After dinner, and the return of a celebrated spy who had been into the Rebel lines, we marched all afternoon, camping for the night near Walkerville on the Baltimore and Ohio Railroad. During the evening our camp was enlivened by the presence of many ladies and gentlemen who promenaded until midnight. This was a delightful change from the usual; we are generally shunned as though we are an epidemic.

One individual living about a mile from our grove cooked up a lot of eatables and furnished them to all who saw fit to call on him. I couldn't get up steam enough to go so far from camp, but many did avail themselves of the opportunity to get a good square meal. The donor of this lunch could be no mean spirit, for some of our men expressed themselves as "satisfied," which I would not have thought within the range of possibility. To bail out the Atlantic Ocean with a pint dipper is about as feasible.

### June 29th.

Left the vicinity of Walkerville and marched to Taneytown, passing through a dingy little village named Woodboro. We halted a few minutes in the shady street. We were outrageously hungry and were also irritated by the conduct of certain females who lived here. A couple of us approached a house from which issued the savory odor of gingerbread. Having a quantity of the prevailing currency, we sought to purchase some. The vigorous old female who appeared to be the manager informed us that there was nothing in the house to eat. This assertion conflicted with certain observed facts, namely the odor of gingerbread and the sight of a shoulder-strapped individual already in the house munching pie. We indicated our supreme contempt and disgust for him and his pie while he replied with a series of the broadest and most unmitigated grins as he frantically continued his effort to get outside of a whole pie. Finally, at another house, I secured one slice of bread, for which I paid twenty-five cents.

Our next halting place was Taneytown, where we were mustered for two months' pay, which we didn't get then. We also drew shoes and other things. A large mail shipment awaited us, the first we have received since leaving Camp Sickles, with an average of six letters apiece.

There are reports about the Rebels of a startling nature. They are at York and threatening Harrisburg. They have demanded $100,000 of York or the town will be reduced to ashes. The same demand was made on Chambersburg and the place was fired, with hundreds rendered homeless. These towns are only a few miles away. We are lessening the distance rapidly and will mete out punishment for this Rebel insolence.

Wrote home today: "We expect a great fight soon, if the Rebels are in Pennsylvania as reported." We reckon they will soon enjoy a rest from the work of pillage and wanton destruction for a kind not quite so agreeable.

## June 30th.

We moved to Emmettsburg and hauled up about a half-mile out of town, only two miles from the Pennsylvania line. It is a small town in population, but about as large as South Carolina in Secessionist sentiment. I have seen nothing like it, not even in the heart of Virginia. It has never fallen to my lot to see such a malignant set of countenances.

Before the war it must have been a place of considerable business, but fully one half is now in ruins and the business section lies in ashes. There are two colleges nearby and, before the fire, there had been foundries and shops. Most of the people are Catholics — a large church of this denomination is in use to shelter the homeless.

We passed the remainder of the day near a farmhouse where we procured some bread and ham. It was intensely hot but a shower made it a bit more endurable.

# Battle of Gettysburg

## July 1 – 6, 1863

### July 1st.

We made no move until noon, when we bivouacked nearer the college grounds. Close by is a gap in the mountains where it was feared the Rebel cavalry might make a dash and get in the rear of our army. We could guard this gap with a small force, so two brigades of Birney's division were left here and the rest of the corps moved on to Gettysburg. The 1st Corps (Reynolds's) and the 11th Corps (Howard's) met the enemy there quite early in the morning and, with Buford's cavalry, kept them at bay. Reynolds was killed in the early part of the day and the command devolved on Howard until the arrival of Hancock about 4 P.M. (There seems to be a disposition on the part of some to overlook the fact that General Howard is entitled to a portion of the credit for securing the position of defense on Cemetery Hill and for holding it several hours.[1])

The brigades of de Trobriand and Ward passed the night here. We threw out pickets and then laid us down to dream and to dread the morrow. Now that we have encountered Lee's army, we expect a battle no less spirited than that of Antietam.

### July 2nd.

We were turned out about 3 o'clock and ordered to get breakfast though we hadn't a solitary thing to lay our jaws to except coffee. Some hadn't even this. The first order was followed by another to move immediately, so we started and marched until we hauled up for coffee. Before the water was even warm, an aide came from General Birney telling us to move right on. No delay must be allowed as we were in danger of being cut off from the rest of the army.

Lee's army was extending to the left and wheeling around so as to envelop our left and cover the road we were then on. We moved with all diligence and marched four or five miles, halting again, by General de Trobriand's order, to make coffee. The same result as before: another imperative order to move right away. Not a moment too soon was this order obeyed; less than fifteen minutes after we passed, the Rebels swung around across the Emmettsburg Road in rear of our column. It is a wonder that we were not treated to a demoralizing flank fire. Nothing but ignorance of our presence explains this lack of attention on the part of the Confederates. As we came up the Emmettsburg Road, we had an army on each side of us. There was considerable firing going on, with the bullets whistling over our heads, and we seemed to be in considerable danger.

We met a large number of citizens coming from Gettysburg and going toward the Rebels. They were loaded down with bedding and clothing, probably all that some of them saved from their burning houses. About two miles from the town, we turned off to the right into the fields and moved to the rear some distance. We came to a lane and turned to the right near to what was called the Peach Orchard and also near the house of one Rose. It was about 10 A.M. when we arrived and commenced maneuvering, but we didn't settle into position until 3 P.M., when we finally got into line in rear of a strip of woods not far from the Emmettsburg Road, slightly to the right of Sherfy's Peach Orchard.

Our line had been formed less than an hour when the picket firing, until now quite slack, became exceedingly lively and gave evidence of something of a more serious character. We double-quicked down to the left, across a wheat field, and came to a front in rear of a stone wall. The right of the regiment was protected only by a rail fence bordering a piece of woods through which the Rebels were rapidly advancing. Aided by the stone wall, we opposed ourselves to their further progress and, for a time, were quite successful. The Confederate advance was very impetuous, and our skirmish line, although exceptionally heavy, was brushed away as chaff before a wind. This was due to no fault on the part of the skirmishers, but to the size and momentum of the attacking column, which comprised nearly *one-half* of Lee's army — the flower of it at that. By the time our line was formed, the Rebel column had arrived at the opposite edge of the woods, and although we opened a brisk fire on them from behind the wall, it didn't seem to check them much. As they drew nearer, our fire began to tell on their ranks, which were more dense than usual. We peppered them well with musketry while Randolph's battery, which was on a gentle rise in rear of us, served a dose of grape and cannister every few seconds.

There was a dreadful buzzing of bullets and other missiles, highly suggestive of an obituary notice for a goodly number of Johnny Rebs, and we could see them tumbling around right lively. A great number of our own men were sharing the same fate. I'm confident that we could have held a reasonable force at bay, but they were strongly reinforced. Our ammunition now began to run low and the troops on our right, being flanked, gave way, exposing us to a heavy flank fire. The troops who gave way had only a rail fence in front of them, while we had a stone wall, which sheltered us well until our flank was uncovered. Even then we didn't hurry about leaving. The batteries in our rear still continued to pour destruction into the Rebel ranks, and it seemed nothing short of annihilation would stop them.

At this point, while shot, shell, spherical case, and cannister filled the air, General de Trobriand, our brigade commander, rode down into the wheat field and inquired, "What troops are those holding the stone wall so stubbornly?" On learning it was the 17th Maine, one of his regiments, he ordered us to "Fall back, right away!" But we didn't *hear* the order. It isn't often that an order to fall back in a battlefield is disregarded. The old fellow didn't quite comprehend this state of ours. We had good reason for our action. This stone wall was a great protection and the Rebels were straining every nerve to get possession of it for the same purpose. So, we held it till our ammunition was exhausted and we had used all we could find on the dead and wounded. If we could hold on until reinforcements or a supply of ammunition came, all would be well. Otherwise, no one could tell what direful woes might befall us. We knew the fate of the army hung on the result.

General Birney, our division commander, next came down and ordered us away from the wall, saying we were in grave danger of capture. We knew that the moment we abandoned our position the Rebels would seize it. But we couldn't hold it without amunition, and as the troops on our right gave way, we saw it was now time for us to go. We fell back a short distance, and as we ceased firing the Rebs advanced to the wall. Some of them climbed over it and began to press us so hard that General de Trobriand ordered us to make a stand. We told him we were destitute of ammunition.

"Then you must hold them with the bayonet," said he.

We halted and formed under his direction. This checked them momentarily, but only a moment, for they saw our condition and knew they had the field unless someone came to our aid. One other thing gave them great confidence: They had been told that the Army of the Potomac had not yet arrived and that they were facing only raw troops.

At this time a portion of the 5th Corps was thrown in to reinforce or relieve us. No sooner did they encounter the enemy than they broke, and the first thing we knew they were running past us to the rear and leaving us to the Rebels closing in on three sides. The battery on the knoll poured the grape and cannister into their ranks but some of them came up to the guns and were literally blown from their muzzles. Blood poured out like water. Both sides understood the value of this position: If the enemy could take it, they would have the key to our line and would be between us and Washington. Nothing seemed to stop them, and it was a foregone conclusion that the game was nearly up. Some of our men cried as they beheld the victorious Rebels advancing and no resistance being offered.

We had hoped for victory. Had we been properly supported and supplied, it is morally certain that things would not have gone this way. Now it looked decidedly black, but in the midst of our gloom and despondency, a gleam of hope and light darted across our line of vision. A cheer rent the air and was heard above the din of battle and the Rebel yell. The 6th Corps, or a portion of it, had just arrived from Westminster, thirty-six miles away, in time to swing into line and give the exultant Rebels a volley in the face and eyes, which staggered them. It was our turn to show the Johnnies that they had met something more than the "raw militia of Pennsylvania," and they fell back to the region of the wheat field. We bivouacked near the Taneytown Road for the night. How any of us escaped is a mystery that eternity alone can unravel.

Soon after the arrival of the 6th Corps, General Sickles lost his leg and was carried off the field in an ambulance. He was smoking, as coolly as if nothing had happened. General Birney assumed immediate command of the corps, which, with the 2nd, was under command of General Hancock.

Sickles is a great favorite with this corps. The men fairly worship him. He is every inch a soldier and looks like a game cock. No one questions his bravery or patriotism. Before the war he killed a man who had seduced his wife.[2] A person who has the nerve to do that might be expected to show good qualities as a general where daredeviltry is a factor.

But I must continue my account of the deeds of this day and the effects thereof. The 6th Corps relieved us about 6 o'clock. An injured companion and myself were very nearly surrounded by the Rebs when, at this point, we encountered the division of the 6th Corps coming into line. They checked the advancing foe and saved the day. The last wave of Rebel aggression was stayed and began to recede from the ridge in rear of the wheat field. We fell back near the Baltimore Pike and bivouacked, tired and hungry, for no rations had yet appeared.

Company I suffered as little as any in the battle: We lost two noncommissioned officers, corporals Mitchell and Robertson, mortally wounded. Privates Stacy, Jordan, Kimball, Roberts, and Brand were treated to Rebel mementoes in various parts of their anatomies. Lieutenant Adams had his finger torn off, and Tasker's gun had a Rebel bullet welded into it.

Other companies suffered greater losses. Those on the right, in rear of the rail fence, had it much worse. On our left, at the Devil's Den and near Round Top, there were some hand-to-hand encounters, sticks and stones doing valiant service. The 20th Maine saved Round Top, while the 3d, 4th, 16th, and 17th did their share in the day's work. Our gain was slight, but we have prevented Lee's forces from carrying out their design. Lee threw in half of his army, so a repulse was more than we had any reason even to hope for. Thus, we feel much cause for congratulating ourselves.[3]

## July 3rd.

We turned out early. Hunger had such a grip on us that it dragged us forth. Most had not eaten in thirty-six hours and felt we could devour a horse or a mule, provided it hadn't been too long defunct. The teams with rations didn't arrive until 9 o'clock. After filling up, we had orders to take position in rear of the 6th Corps, somewhat to the right of where we were engaged yesterday. During the forenoon there was nothing but an occasional crack of the pickets' rifles, and we rested on our arms.

Shortly after noon there were signs of activity in the Confederate lines. Artillery was being massed on Seminary Ridge and the same was true of infantry, although the woods concealed them. About 1 o'clock the Rebel cannon opened on us, and ours were soon replying. For two hours there was probably the greatest artillery duel ever fought on this planet. The air seethed with old iron. Death and destruction were everywhere. Men and horses mangled and bleeding; trees, rocks, and fences ripped and torn. Shells, solid shot, and spherical case shot screamed, hissed, and rattled in every direction. Men hugged the ground and sought safety behind hillocks, boulders, ledges, stone walls, bags of grain — anything that could give or suggest shelter from this storm of death.

We hardly knew what it meant, but some of our generals did, and preparations were made accordingly. General Hunt, chief of artillery, ordered our gunners to cease firing in order to cool the guns. No sooner was this done than the Rebels, supposing they had silenced us, began to come out of the woods and form in line of battle.

As soon as all was ready, the column commenced the march. Our guns opened on them with solid shot and shells as soon as they were within range. This had no effect except to huddle them closer. As they drew nearer, our guns increased the havoc in their ranks. Solid shot and shell, then grape, cannister, and spherical case ploughed through their lines and rattled in their midst, sweeping them by the hundreds from the field. But on they pressed, bravely and firmly, closing up on the colors as gap after gap opened in their ranks.

A 32-pounder on Round Top fired down the line obliquely and took out as many as twenty files. Even this didn't arrest their progress. Just before the charge,

GETTYSBURG. *Harper's Pictorial History of the Civil War.*

while the air was reeking with death, General Hancock, whose front Longstreet was covering, rode slowly from right to left of his line and encouraged his men to hold.[4]

At this time the Confederates had reached the Emmettsburg road and, having two fences to climb, all suggestion of alignment was lost. They were now little other than a mob, but they came on and on. They were determined to come in spite of grape, cannister, and bullets. Our division and many others hastened to the scene to take part in the closing act of this drama.

On they pushed, delivering a withering fire. But our fire was equally destructive, and they soon presented a bloody and desperate appearance. No troops could resist the awful attack to which they were exposed. It was a sheet of fire, backed by a wall of steel. They couldn't reach the wall and *live*.

The Confederates were now treated to a heavy flank fire, and this seemed to take all the gimp out of them. Many fled in confusion to the rear, pursued by the troops of Hay's division. Hundreds, aye thousands, threw down their arms and came in as prisoners where they had vainly sought to come as victors. Most of those on the left of the Rebel column remained — dead, wounded, or prisoner. The Union troops, by a simultaneous attack, now closed in on them, capturing all who did not seek safety in flight. Many threw themselves on the ground to escape the merciless storm of missiles hurled at them; others held up their hands in token of surrender. "He that outlives this day, and comes safe home,/ Will stand a tiptoe when this day is named."

By 4 o'clock the repulse was complete, the victory won. Thousands who two hours before were in the flush of manhood now lay dead, dying, or prisoners. The Confederates staked all and lost.

No one can describe the scenes of this day. We who were participants were in such a maddening whirl that we can give but little that is intelligible. Babel was perfect order compared to the confusion of these two hours of bloody encounter. Then all was still, the carnival of death was done, and we took a breathing spell.

At the close of the charge General Hancock fell, severely wounded. He sent word to General Meade of the repulse and advised an immediate pursuit, but nothing was done.

This was Lee's third attempt to pierce our lines. July 1st on our right, July 2nd on our left, and today our center. On each of these days success seemed to perch on the Rebel banners at first, but was wrested from them. It is certain that General Lee regards this action as a crisis in the affairs of the Confederacy. He would never have made this charge, putting his best troops into the venture, had he not felt certain of success. His feelings as he saw his troops mowed down must have been quite indescribable.

His admirers claim that Lee is very humane. This may be so, but he witnessed the slaughter of his men from the cupola of the seminary and, from the very first, it must have been plain to him that if any of his men reached the Union line, they could never hold it for an instant. Lee's troops learned the folly of attempting to charge across over a mile of open country against an army quite as large as their own, more or less protected by embankments, stone walls, and boulders, and with a superabundance of artillery.

As soon as this charge ended, silence settled over the scene. A painful silence, broken only by the sigh or groan of some poor mangled victim. Where but a few moments before the smoke of battle, the cannon's roar, the rattle of musketry, the groan, the cheer, the prayer, the curse had filled the air, there was now profound stillness as though the very elements were appalled and stood mute. A fitting climax to this dreadful struggle, the details of which are indeed sickening. "O stay not to recount the tale./ 'Twas bloody, and 'tis past./ The fairest cheek might well grow pale,/ To hear it to the last." How many firesides in the North and South are plunged today into deepest sorrow? Just a few short hours, and thousands are torn and mangled, better dead than living.

I imagine from my own feelings that every one of these cherished the hope that *he* would come out all right, or at least alive, and prayed that this might be the last struggle. It *was* the last for many of them.

About dark our division was sent out on picket in the field in front. It has never been my lot to see and experience such things as on this occasion. The dead lay everywhere, and although not a half day has passed since they died, the stench is so great that we can neither eat, drink, nor sleep. Decomposition commences as soon as life is extinct. As we cannot sleep, we pass the time bringing in the wounded and caring for them. The dead are frightfully smashed, which is not to be wondered at when we consider how they crowded up onto our guns, a mass of humanity, only to be hurled back an undistinguishable pile of mutilated flesh, rolling and writhing in death.

No tongue can depict the carnage, and I cannot make it seem real: men's heads blown off or split open; horrible gashes cut; some split from the top of the head to the extremities, as butchers split beef. Some of the Rebels are very bitter toward us although we do all in our power to alleviate their sufferings, even exposing ourselves to danger to do so. One of our officers crawled on his hands and knees to give a wounded Rebel a drink, and came near paying for it with his life when another Rebel, near the wounded man, fired at him.

It pains me to state that some of our own men taunt these wounded with their lack of success and engage in political arguments, apparently forgetting how incongruous that business is. This custom is by no means monopolized on our side. It is to be deprecated, however, as it in no wise softens the asperities of war and helps keep alive sectional hate. The men who indulge in this kind of lingo soon learn that the characters and sentiments of their opponents haven't changed with their condition, and though the Rebels acknowledge our kindness in caring for them, they still claim that they are *right* in their attempt to destroy this government.

Among the wounded is a little, flaxen-haired boy from North Carolina who is only fourteen years old, giving credence to the report that the Confeds rob the cradle and the grave. To keep the ranks full, they take old men beyond the military age and young ones who haven't reached it, and hustle them to the front.

### *July 4th.*

Morning found us still busy bringing in the dying and dead. Soon after daylight we advanced our pickets and found that the enemy had departed. Finding the Rebel works vacated, we fell back to a hill where the air wasn't so thick from the smoke of battle. We had scarce taken off our knapsacks when it rained like a sieve. We should have been prepared, for we know that all heavy cannonading is followed by violent rain. Many of our wounded, whom we had placed on the banks of a stream because water was handy, came near being drowned.

## July 5th.

We laid here all day, watching to insure that the enemy didn't make a backward spring. Knowing his desperate condition, we suspect that Lee might turn on us and, by a flank movement, secure this much-coveted situation. The 6th Corps started off on their flank to intercept the flying enemy, if indeed he is flying. We should be quite pleased to know for certain, as we have some fears. It seems incredible that we have whipped them. It hasn't been customary to let this army whip anything. The last three days have been a trifle more to our taste than the Peninsula, Fredericksburg, or Chancellorsville. This new experience for Lee's army must be demoralizing, and a vigorous push at this moment might result in their destruction or capture.

The general belief among our army is that one day of honest endeavor could wipe out Lee's army and practically end the Rebellion. It was a foregone conclusion that success here for Lee would have meant the downfall of the Union; his defeat means a Rebel collapse.

At night we received news of the fall of Vicksburg. This sent a thrill down our spines and helped raise our spirits, for we have suffered such an appalling loss of generals in this encounter that we feel quite blue. Generals Reynolds, Hancock, Sickles, Webb, Weed, Vincent, Hazlett, and Graham, besides many lesser officers, have been killed, wounded, or taken prisoner.

But the fall of Vicksburg and the defeat of Lee here at Gettysburg must make the Confederacy tremble to its foundation.

## July 6th.

We moved back into a pine grove on the hill and laid there all day. My impression concerning this section is by no means flattering to the inhabitants. A Rebel victory would have left these people at the mercy of Jeff Davis's minions and it would have been eminently just and right.

After all we have sacrificed for them, the women have the contemptible meanness to charge us two dollars for a loaf of bread that could be bought for seventy-five cents in Rebel Maryland. Even the proverbially mean New England Yankee would blush to ask twenty-five cents for it. One old female sauerkraut had the sublime and crowning cheek to cut a loaf into twelve slices and ask twenty-five cents a slice. If it be asked why we allow ourselves to be so swindled, the querist must put himself in our place and he will very soon understand that there are circumstances where *money* does not occupy the first place in one's affections.

The town isn't entirely destitute of patriotism, for here dwelt old John Burns, who, when battle was imminent, put on his "store clothes," picked up his old musket, and sought the post of danger. He is over seventy-six years of age and quite infirm, but contrived to knock several Confederates off their pins. He was wounded twice and run over by both armies, but contrived to reach home at night. In contrast to his patriotism is one of the wealthy citizens, who harnessed his span of horses and rode out to meet General Lee as he approached the town. He invited the general to his home when he (Lee) should occupy the place. General Lee gave him a look of ineffable disgust, delivered a lecture on patriotism, and wound up by ordering one of his aides to confiscate the horses. General Lee is a traitor to the government that educated him and to which he once promised allegiance, but he cannot tolerate a recreant to one's state, claiming that allegiance to the state is first.

# From Gettysburg to the Wilderness

## July 7, 1863 – February 5, 1864

### July 7th.

It continued to rain but we had orders to march, and we marched. The roads were in an abominable condition, mud over our ankles, about the consistency of lard. To use a female expression, it was "perfectly horrid." But it's an ill wind that blows no good, for it was the wind which overturned a cart of potatoes, three of which fell into my hands. Several weary miles were beguiled by anticipation of the treat in store when a sufficient halt would be made to cook them. No halt was made until Mechanicstown, where it was decided to pass the night.

Like so many towns we have passed through, this one seems to have attained its growth a century ago and relapsed into genteel decay. The only suggestion of business is a broken-down harness maker. The inhabitants were not overjoyed to see us, but we had the satisfaction of knowing that the feeling was mutual. We were more concerned about how and where we would pass the night.

Fifteen miles of such marching is enough to tire an iron horse. We had just settled down when a brigade guard was called to look after the horses. Being one of the victims, I hustled into my harness — with heavy eyes, heavier feet and heart. As we were near total exhaustion, we didn't put up shelter, and a few hours later it rained torrents.

"The wise man seeth the rain coming and hideth himself under a tent. The fool sleepeth out of doors and is punished." My punishment didn't end with the drenching; I had to try to sleep under the same blanket with J——k H——n. To bivouac with this person is to bivouac with a swine of the genus *Homo*. Grunting and groaning, turning and twisting, snoring and gurgling in his throat, and stoppages in his nose — all indicated the difficulties under which he labored. Even a man who can sleep in a sawmill would be fixed by such a racket. Not a solitary wink did I get, while he slept like a person with a clear conscience and good digestion. It seemed as if nothing short of the last trumpet could wake him, and it would have to be no ordinary blast, either.

### July 8th.

We all rose sick, tired, played out, and crosser than a dozen she-bears. I'd guarantee that we could have turned water to vinegar just by looking at it. Our clothes and blankets were wet and heavy and we had no chance to dry them. Such depression swept over me that I suffered a collapse of nearly all my powers so that it was almost impossible to proceed when the column was set in motion at six o'clock.

While at Frederick we saw a man dangling by the neck from a tree. He had been caught acting the spy, and a search of his boots revealed plans of all our fortifications, the number of troops in this army, and much other information of value to the Rebel government. This particular batch of information never reached Richmond, as he was at once hoisted into the air and his body left there as a warning. It is singular that men will run the risks of the spy when they know the consequences of this course if caught. If any men can be said to take their lives in their hands, these men do.

We marched through Frederick, Middleton, and Keedysville, and halted for the night on a part of the battlefield of South Mountain. Scarcely had we composed ourselves for sleep than we were routed out by a series of demoniac yells that curdled the blood in our veins. We scrambled for our shoes and equipment and the pickets fled their posts in dismay. The cause of all this hubbub was a bunch of drovers with cattle, making all the hideous noises they could invent. As soon as we ascertained that it wasn't the whole Rebel army, we retired for the night and this time we slept.

### July 9th.

On the march again about 7 A.M. and marched all day in the vicinity of South Mountain. Made no halt worthy of the name until mid-afternoon, when we made a short stop on part of the battlefield of Antietam. We had barely got our knapsacks off when the order came to resume the march. We crossed innumerable wheat and corn fields, also Antietam Creek, and passed the Dunker Church, where the contest had raged so fiercely that the woods nearby were thoroughly riddled. Such desperate fighting has had but few parallels in this war.

We had a mail today, and when I opened a letter from home I discovered that some infernal thief has robbed me of a five-dollar bill — money that can ill be spared by those who sent it or by the rightful recipient, for I am by this time penniless.

### July 10th – 15th.

About 3 A.M. on the 10th we turned out and moved about a mile, then formed in line of battle in the woods. We had marched fifteen miles altogether, it was said, and overtaken Lee's army. It began to look as though we were going to crowd him just the least mite.

We laid there till 3 P.M., neither side doing anything of an aggressive nature, then moved to the right, out into open country and nearer the front, to a place called Fairview. And we do get a fair view of the Rebel works, which are immediately to our front. We supposed we were to charge them at once. Vice President Hamlin passed the day with us, no doubt also expecting a jolly row. The only protection Lee's army had was a stone wall, which our artillery could reduce to a shapeless mass in no time.

But it wasn't permitted. Perhaps Meade didn't want to disclose the fact that Lee's army was at that very moment trying to get across the Potomac and was farther from us than *we* had any idea of. We laid there, and no attempt was made to arrest them all the time they were working like beavers to get away from us.

The river was swollen so by the late rains in this mountainous region that the Rebel pontoon bridges were inadequate, and they had to cut up their harnesses to make straps with which to lengthen their bridges. A portion of the Rebel army went over at Falling Water, the rest at Williamsport.

It is quite impossible to guess, even, how many men Lee had here. (We didn't see any in the works.) It certainly is a curious feature that two such armies should come so near together and not have a clash of arms, unless by design.

On the 11th we were up betimes, expecting to see a trial of strength and skill between the two armies. The Union army is flushed with victory for the first time since I joined it; the Rebel army is the stag at bay, and might be supposed to be in a reasonable degree of desperation. I do not misrepresent the feelings of the army when I say that we were bitterly disappointed that Lee's army was not destroyed before crossing the river, or driven into it as the Rebels drove our forces at Ball's Bluff. We were eager for the fray and firmly believed that one good, earnest day's work here would break the backbone of the rebellion. (We were anxious to do it and have done with this carnival of bloodshed and other evils of war, but this would bring the end of the war far too soon to suit the devilish leeches who coin dollars out of human misery and blood.)

Nothing was done except that General Meade called a council of his corps commanders to see if it would be advisable to attack. Incredible as it may appear, a majority of them decided it was *not* advisable. This is about what we should expect of General Meade. There must have been a time in these past few days when half of Lee's army was on the other side of the Potomac and half on the nothern side and at our mercy. *That* was the time to strike a blow and whip the entire army, demoralized as it must be.

But they have escaped. As the matter stands now, I strongly suspect that *we*, and not the Rebels, are whipped. Thus depart from our grasp all the fruits of a great victory.

## July 16th.

Laid in this place nearly all day. About night, when it was certain that the entire Rebel army has put the Potomac between us and them, we moved out and captured the stone wall and rifle pits.

We camped for the night in the wheat field of an old Secesh farmer. His friends the Rebs took all his livestock, and now we, his enemies, took possession of his wheat. What we didn't tread down we cut up to make beds of. The ground being very wet, we must do this or lie in the mud. Mr. Secesh cannot derive much pleasure from the fact that whatever inconvenience or loss he is now subjected to is wholly due to the secession scheme he helped encourage.

At this place we got some insight into the Rebel cuisine when we found a pig trough that has also done duty as a mixing trough. How extremely meager must be the provision for these troops when their supplies are of such a primitive nature. It is related that one time when Lee's army was exceptionally reduced on rations he saw a private eating persimmons. Lee asked the private if he didn't know that such highly astringent fruit were not fit for food. The private replied, "I'm not eating them for food but to draw my stomach up to fit my rations."

## July 17th.

We marched about three miles and came to a gap in the mountains where we encountered a body of troops under General French, who has come down from Harper's Ferry with orders to join the 3rd Corps and assume command, by reason of seniority. When the Confederates captured Harper's Ferry, they would have done us a great service if they had toted French off!

He is so repulsive in appearance as to invite nausea at the sight of his bloated and discolored visage. He looks a perfect old soaker, a devotee of lust and appetite. One eye has a habit of blinking, which makes it seem drunker than the rest of him. He is the meanest looking general I have ever seen and yet he did excellent service at Fredericksburg.

We waited now for his men to pass to the head of the column and fell in behind, marching till past noon, when we halted at Pleasant Valley — aptly named, for a lovelier spot I never saw.

## July 18th – 19th.
Several days were spent here at the foot of Maryland Heights enjoying much-needed rest.

General French, desiring to give tone to his own troops — whom we call "French's pets" — demanded that we admit them to the Order of the Red Patch, an honor only allowed to Kearney's division. He took great offense at the exclusion and issued a manifesto threatening "to raise the shroud of the chivalrous Kearney" and invoke his displeasure on our conduct. (If Kearney's shroud could have been raised so that he could get his feet in contact with the rear of French's pets, he would have made it very lively for some of them, as cowards were his special abomination.) Some of French's troops are *not* cowards but his actions make them appear so. If danger menaces in front, they are pushed to the rear; if in rear, they are marched to the front. General French's order we regard as a mere literary curiosity that provides mirth from all who hear of it. He was, no doubt, drunk when he issued it.

## July 20th.
Our interlude at Pleasant Valley came to a sudden termination with an order at 4 P.M. to move immediately. We were soon on the road to Harper's Ferry, reaching it about sunset. We wasted no time in passing over the Potomac, through the town, and over the Shenandoah River. Moving around the base of Loudon Heights, we marched a short distance and bivouacked for the night.

Previous to retiring I must indulge in a trifle of "gush" over the natural beauty of this place. It is a small village situated at the confluence of the Potomac and Shenandoah rivers, which have cut a passage through the mountain range. Here Nature has made a kind of Gibralter. Maryland, Loudon, and Bolivar heights rise up like three giant sentinels holding guard over the town. They tower up hundreds, perhaps thousands, of feet perpendicularly and appear like vast fortresses.

It seems as if an army once lodged there could *never* be dislodged except by starving it out, but it has, in fact, been reduced two or three times by the Confederates.

It is possibly the most picturesque spot in the United States. They are not the highest or grandest mountains, but the situation is spectacular. Three states converge, two rivers unite, and three tall mountains rear their bold, rocky fronts, with the town nestled at their feet.

As we passed through the town, we noticed the engine house where John Brown made his fight and had his skull nearly clove in twain by the sword of Colonel, now General, Robert E. Lee.

There are those who consider John Brown a martyr. If he was such, it was to his own fanaticism. Slavery is wrong, but his method of getting rid of it certainly wasn't right. No doubt his action did precipitate the conflict now raging and thus aimed a blow at American slavery. Brown paid the penalty of his folly with his life. He was a misguided old man whose motives might be right but whose judgment was decidedly weak. No man can allow his mind to run in one groove all the time without becoming more or less insane on that subject. Fanaticism is the sure outgrowth of a nature like his.

### July 21st.

Nothing of a stirring nature going on, and we only traversed six miles into old Virginia. Near some gap in the mountains we bivouacked for the night, and a strong picket was thrown out, for we don't wish to be surprised.

### July 22nd.

All quiet on the Potomac. Not even the squeal of a hen or the cackle of a pig was heard. We passed the day in much-needed rest.

Wrote home this afternoon. As there was a conspicuous paucity of writing fluid in my inkstand, I used blackberry juice and found it did excellent service.

### July 23rd.

Marched about eight miles down the Loudon Valley and halted for the night near Snicker's Gap. We anticipate a visit from Rebels trying to get through one of the many gaps in the mountains as a short cut to Richmond. If they reach the upper Rappahannock or Rapidan, they can strike their line of defense. We make but little effort to restrain them as long as they journey toward Richmond and don't menace us or Washington. Much of our enthusiasm over Gettysburg has petered out and we have settled back into our old-time indifference (or, more properly, our dread of fighting). On the other hand, the Rebs are still smarting and not anxious to renew combat. They move down one side of the mountain range, we travel on the other.

We laid here this day and night, and also the next.

### July 25th.

Marched a few miles and camped between Ashby's Gap and Upperville. Our situation is lovely and it seems too bad to desecrate it by war. So many homes destroyed and farms laid waste. War blights everything but the fat contractor, who, like the undertaker, thrives on that which brings sorrow to others.

At this locality we see a large number of horses' bones bleaching in the sun, the result of a cavalry engagement on November 4th, 1862. The Rebels made a stand here, and here some of them will stay until Gabriel's horn shall call them up or until the elements absorb them, which is by far the most reasonable solution.

### July 26th.

Started from Ashby's Gap about 2 P.M. and marched a few miles up the valley. It was a hard, sultry trip, taxing even the strongest of us. Not being one of those, I took it quite leisurely, having a standing order from Captain Hobson to fall out when the sun is too hot or the march too severe. We passed through Upperville and Piedmont, and as the mountain shadows lengthened came into Manassas Gap and turned into a field on the right.

From the odor of bruised vegetation under our feet, we judged this to be a potato patch and thought of the feast in store for us when we could dig and roast them. We actually contemplated the feat of converting our stomachs into human potato pens. The darkness prevented us from seeing anything except with the eye of faith, and with this we saw sweet fields arrayed with living green potato tops. However, after the most vigorous clawing we failed to find what we so much desired and came to the conclusion that what we had mistaken for a wealth of potato tops was only a patch of villainous ragweed. From such a pitch of expectation the fall was quite severe. The bottom dropped from our stomachs, and we retired for the night to prevent them from getting any lower.

### July 27th.

After a swallow of coffee in lieu of breakfast, we moved up into the gap still farther. It now looked as if the monotony was at last to be broken. A battery was soon in position and the 17th Maine ordered to support it. We advanced some distance to the front and formed in line of battle. Company I was detailed as an escort to General Birney's staff, who were ordered up into the mountain as an observation post.

The Rebels were about five miles away down in the valley and not likely to interfere. We observed next that there are oceans of blackberries on the mountain. Our comrades, so far as we could see, were diligently engaged in making blackberry jam. While we packed the berries into us, we watched the Confederates, who were crossing the Shenandoah River in three columns, one each of infantry, artillery, and cavalry. They looked like so many long, gray serpents, winding along through the wheat fields far below. After crossing the river, they massed their forces in some woods at the base of the mountain, as deliberate in their movements as though we were a thousand miles away or as though they thought McClellan was in command.

The Rebel object was not to fight, but to escape; ours seemed to be the same. They simply wanted to detain us here at this gap while their main force pushed on through Chester Gap, a shorter route to Richmond than through the valley. They made an appearance of massing, but in reality only a small force was formed.

And what were our generals doing? They were napping, simply napping. Company I was on the heights, filling up with blackberries, and taking in the soul-enchanting view. We could see clear across Virginia, eighteen miles in one direction and fifteen in another.

This elevated position we held till 1 o'clock, when orders came to descend and join the regiment. This meant to prepare for the sterner phases of war. Soon after we joined the division, it moved up farther into the gap and, inadvertently I think, stirred up the Rebels, or their skirmish line, which was really all there was. We soon had them into a gentle cow trot over hills and fields until they reached a place where they had two small brass pieces on a hill.

Now, instead of moving right on and dislodging them, our line halted on a ridge opposite the Rebel position, in a very exposed condition, no artillery within two miles and most of our generals farther away than that. The Confederates quickly assessed their advantage and opened on us with their artillery. We were lying on the side of a hill, heels up, heads down, our dark clothes showing distinctly against a background of faded grass. Thus we were left to artillery and sharpshooters without the least likelihood that they would err on the side of mercy.

The shells from the two brass pieces opened several gaps in our ranks and came much nearer than we deemed safe for our corporeal substances. Much too near for the comfort of our sergeant major, whose heels couldn't be found soon after one of the shells made a call in his vicinity. This caused Mr. Bosworth to execute a series of tactics not laid down in any system of tactics with which I am acquainted. It became at once apparent that this battery must move, or *we* must, unless we were to be slaughtered as coolly as so many pigs.

Word was sent to General French explaining our position. That inebriated person was enjoying the seclusion of a house about three miles from the action, in the company of old General Ward and a jug of whiskey. Old Blinkey could not be made to understand our predicament.

There seemed to be an excellent prospect that we would stay right there and be peppered as long as our Rebel friends' ammunition held out. At this critical stage, a certain private rose up and declared that he didn't intend to be killed or maimed and called on us to follow him over the hill. The effect of this invitation was startling; about fifty sprang to their feet and started to follow him. This caused our officer, who had hidden his precious carcass behind a bush, to yell, "Lie down!" He promised to go and see that we were moved to a safer place. I was glad to have him leave. Aside from any question of personal benefit, I should have grieved sincerely had anything happened to him, for he has a large heart and sympathetic nature. Hence, I respect him and would have gone as far for him as for any officer I could name.

General French and General Ward were both in a highly exhilarated condition by this time. The 3rd Corps was virtually without a commander this day, and so there was no action on our part until near sunset, when General Spinoza, a brigade commander, made a sortie on the Rebels. The fierceness of his attack surprised them not a little. He pierced the enemy line and showed its frailty. When the fact that we had been detained by so small a force flashed into our minds, it was too late; the main part of the Reb army was now on its way toward the upper Rappahannock. Had we pressed them as we ought, we could have struck Lee in the flank.

General Spinoza's command had crawled up a ravine and, when directly between us and the Rebs, bounded over the hill like deer and startled the Johnnies with but trifling loss of time or men. The General's order was right to the point, "Give them hell under the coat tail!" The order wasn't particularly military in style, but it was understood and acted upon. As a result, several Rebs laid themselves down for a long rest, never to rise in this world unless some friendly hand should raise them up to give them burial.

(It is not in good taste to joke in so serious a matter, but there is a ludicrous side to these matters which the soldier discerns more quickly than does the person who sees death only often enough to shock him. We are so much in its presence that although we fear and dread it, we yet are not impressed with it as those who see it but rarely.)

When we learned what fools the Rebs had made of us, we were so mad our teeth hung out. While we fooled around, they made track for Richmond with all speed, gaining a day's march. It is the second time this month Lee has evaded us.

Night soon settled over the scene, and we bivouacked on the ground where we fought.

*July 28th.*

Went out early in the morning to see if the Johnnies had gone. (Well, *we* knew they had, but Old Blinkey couldn't get it through that wooden head of his.) We moved to the vicinity of Front Royal and found a mere handful of soldiers guarding the remnant of a wagon train. Their determination to fight came to a sudden halt with the appearance of our cavalry on their flank. The Rebs fled, making far better time than we ever could, not being encumbered with the clothing and impedimenta common with us. They have next to nothing: an old quilt or piece of carpet for uniforms, no tents, blankets, or food. *How* they live will always be a mystery to me.

If we of the North were called upon to endure *one half* as much as the Southern people and soldiers do, we would abandon the cause and let the Southern Confederacy be established. We pronounce their cause *unholy*, but they consider it sacred enough to suffer and die for. Our forefathers in the Revolutionary struggle could not have endured more than these Rebels. A resident of Maryland who lost two sons — one in the Union, the other in the Confederate army — is said to have remarked as he stood over their graves, "God knows which is right." We are apt to always deem our own cause as right, clinging tenaciously to our reasoning although we might be grossly in error.

A nation preserved with *liberty* trampled underfoot is much worse than a nation in fragments but with the spirit of liberty still alive. The Southerners persistently claim that their rebellion is for the purpose of preserving this form of government. We claim the same thing, the difference being, mainly, that the South maintains that the Constitution sanctions the monstrous absurdity of a man owning his brother man in a "free" country. As slavery pays in a pecuniary sense, it is quite easy for the Southron to believe it is justified by Divine authority. On the other hand, we of the North *couldn't* make it pay, so we are convinced that it is "the sum of all villainy." Our plan is more profitable; we take care of no children or sick people, except as paupers, while the owners of slaves have to provide for them from birth till death. So, how we view the issue depends on what kind of *glasses* we use.


As there was nothing further to do, we countermarched and arrived at Piedmont. After we went into bivouac, a portion of the division was made to stand in line for two hours, in marching order, for yelling "Hard Tack!" at General Ward as he rode past. Although many haven't eaten for a day or two, and are nearly insane from hunger, they should realize such behavior will not help. General Ward was formerly a prize fighter and, no doubt, much brutalized. He regards human life much as an angler does the worm he uses for bait.

Present rations are about enough to keep a chicken in fair order. If only I had kept an account of the rations drawn since I entered the show, it would furnish some very interesting statistics for people who advocate the minimum of food. We are victims of systematic robbery by the quartermasters, and knowing that our good Uncle Sam *pays* for a generous diet although we have it not makes us doubly exasperated. To use a most inelegant expression, we could eat a corpse and chase the mourners. At night we draw a half ration of bread, a whole ration of beef and coffee and sugar, which is immediately devoured but with mighty little satisfaction. A trip to the sutlers is then in order, in which we are sure to be fleeced.

NEGRO QUARTERS *Harper's Pictorial History of the Civil War.*

### *July 29th.*

Started early and marched to Salem, a dilapidated town, dingy and old. Much as we usually enjoy going through villages, we were glad to get out of this one, for the ruling passion of the place was filth. Everything that slavery has touched seems to be filthy. We came to another town further along, vastly different, named Warrenton. It reminded me more of a New England town than any place I have seen for a long time.

Just before reaching Salem we stopped to eat. The woman at whose house we were on guard had planted a little patch of ground but the 2nd Corps skinned it completely the previous night. Twelve hours later, we were enacting the dreary and senseless farce of guarding *nothing*. Her entire dependence has been swept away as clean as an army of locusts could have swept away a wheat crop. One of our number, being possessed of a five-dollar bill from the Bank of Virginia, was able to offer her some pecuniary aid. Others of us also purchased some biscuits of her at a somewhat tall margin of profit, contributing not less than forty Confederate dollars.

Although it is Sunday, the people of Salem seem to have forgotten the character of the day, for they were ready to trade with us for any coffee or salt we could spare. They offered a very generous allowance of bread and cake for these articles but we had none to spare, so we couldn't pander to their tastes or to our greed. At Warrenton we found matters more in keeping with the day. The people had evidently been to church and were now sitting in the most comfortable manner on piazzas and under trees, giving me a strong remembrance of home.

We got through the town at last, and night found us camping in a beautiful spot about three miles out. There was a nice house in the grove, which the owner abandoned at our approach. Not being the ghouls so often pictured, we left it alone. It is no wonder the natives distrust all soldiers, for this section has been overrun no less than five times, first by one side, then by the other.

### July 30th.

As no orders were received to move, we put up shelters and drew rations. Wood is scarce and water insufficient to keep a chicken supplied. It is an aristocratic section of country, so our generals forbade depredation of any kind. None of the aristocrats objects to our putting up shelters, so we did, and serenely lay down for the night.

### July 31st.

We drew clothing, which is an immense relief to many of us. Some had only one leg to the pants, and some possessed a most heterogenous collection of rags in all stages of dilapidation. We were just at the point where a shirt collar and boots were considered "full dress." Our scanty wardrobe does very well while we are away in the woods of Virginia but can hardly be considered sufficient when marching through cities and towns, as we have been doing of late.

In the afternoon several of our commissioned and noncommissioned officers were sent home to recruit in Maine for us. Our ranks are so depleted that guard, fatigue, and picket duty come all too frequently, so we look forward to any accessions to our ranks to lighten these duties.

At night our teams returned from Warrenton with supplies, which came by rail direct from Washington via the Orange and Alexandria Railroad. In addition to army supplies, some of us had from home boxes of cakes, pies, and et cetera. Unfortunately, some were on the road too long to be edible but those who have abundance in good condition share with those who have none. Most of my comrades are in no way niggardly about sharing good things.

After dinner we were ordered to "dust out of this," and we moved down the road about four miles and went into camp a quarter of a mile from the Rappahannock River at what was once a famous southern watering place named Warrenton Sulphur Springs.

### August 1st – September 13th.

If our last camp was beautiful, this one is superb. In antebellum times it was to the South what Saratoga Springs is to the North. The secession flame was well fanned here and much villainy concocted, but the chickens are coming home to roost, as the deplorable condition of the place attests. It boasted a hotel, parks, and mineral springs of rare excellence before Pope's and Sigel's columns devastated it last year. The peaceful Rappahannock flows within ten rods of the hotel. The spring is in the center of spacious grounds, enclosed in a marble basin, covered with an octagonal building and shaded by grand old elms. The hotel itself has a grand portico three stories in height, and on each side is a two-story wing extending back and enclosing the grounds. In addition, across the street, are a machine shop, a billiard hall, and a "Rowdy Hall," a place where the young bloods of the South could develop the science of rowdyism without disturbing the elder bloods in their machinations against the Union.

Rowdy Hall is the only part of the property left in a presentable state. We converted it into a division hospital, while General Birney and his staff encamped on the hotel grounds. The coffee-coolers took up abode in the wings of the building.

Most every evening Birney's staff organizes a theatrical show of some kind and we have much fun and entertainment out of it. It is marred only by the thought that this excellent campground must soon be abandoned. We have abundant rations, plenty of good water, the river to bathe and wash clothes in, and a mineral spring, which has no superior as a sanitary agent. The spring water is a most inveterate foe to malaria. Its taste bears great resemblance to the rinsings of our gun barrels or to an egg whose virgin freshness is a thing of the past, but we all take our regular allowance daily. Our picket line is not an eighth of a mile from camp. Soft bread is furnished daily, and with the help of the sutler we live high. Blackberries are plenty. Having enough to eat and little to do, we enjoy ourselves. We put up poles and covered them with brush, shading our company streets in a fine manner.

Some of our men swam across the Rappahannock a little farther downstream and stole some sheep. This was a most glaring sin, as it has been prohibited, and the only way of atonement was to make a "heave offering" of a good quarter of it in the direction of the commanding officer's tent. In such cases, he usually finds some extenuating circumstances or fine technicalities by which justice can be satisfied by a simple reprimand.

Not long after this a little affair occurred which caused quite a breeze in camp. A drunken aide from General French came to camp and insisted on "inspecting feet." Such an order ought not to surprise us; General French is about as prolific in eccentricities as Stonewall Jackson, only not in the same direction.

### September 14th.

We whiled away five weeks at Warrenton Springs in this pleasant manner but on this day we were ordered out on the Warrenton Road to have a division drill. We had just barely formed in line when an order was received from General French to return to camp and get ready to move immediately. It was now 5 o'clock and we we knew we would probably make a night march. This was a damper on us, for we were hoping to stay here many days yet, if not all winter. But "Go!" was the word, and go it was. We were ready in about half an hour to go where fate or General French might decree.

The order to move is utterly unexpected and different from the usual in that we had no warning. All we know is that the Rebels have driven in our pickets and there is the possibility of a row. We marched down the Rappahannock about five miles and camped for the night near Lawton's Ford, not far above Rappahannock Station.

### September 15th.

Crossed the river at the above-named ford and marched all the forenoon, fording the Hazel River also. These streams being only waist deep, no pontoons were laid. Fording the stream wasn't too bad, but when old French sat on his horse and insisted on our "keeping our files dressed" while we forded a stream whose bed was covered with large, slippery rocks, we thought we had reached the lowest point of absurdity.

I have sometimes inquired of myself why we are punished with old French and can only come to the conclusion it must be for the same reason old Grand Ma'am Halleck was appointed General in Chief at Washington, viz, "For the sins of the people." This must be one of the things that an old lady once spoke of as "the ways of an unscrupulous Providence."

We did get over the river and worked along slowly through the day and about midnight came to a halt in a big cornfield, which is said to be only a short distance from Culpepper Court House. We made a supper of roast corn and retired for the night.

### September 16th – 19th.

Turned out when it suited us the next morning and breakfasted principally on corn. Afterward we had a mock battle in which corn figured as ammunition. It was a spirited engagement. About ten o'clock we moved a short distance and went into camp. We proceeded at once to make ourselves comfortable and for the past week have been engaged in fortifying ourselves for the inclement season we might pass here.

The sutler came up, bringing with him plenty of whiskey and ale, and until his stock was gone there was a carnival of drunkenness among the shoulder straps. From the field officers down to the lowest noncommissioned man, they have been as drunk as owls.

### September 20th.

Went on picket in rear of our camp. Nothing appeared or troubled us although we ventured out in various directions in search of something edible. All was as quiet as we could desire, and we enjoyed a freedom from restraint not possible in camp. This picketing was real fun and we hated to go in.

### September 21st.

Morning dawned and found us much refreshed by the vigorous air of this time of year. I was sent on picket near the house of an aged Baptist divine named Reed. Having a curiosity to know somewhat of his composition theologically and politically, I called on him and found an old fellow of at least three score and ten. He came nearest to being a Union man of anyone I have seen dwelling south of "Mason and Dixon's line." He claimed to have opposed secession long after that tidal wave swept old Virginia out of the Union. It was a useless, hopeless task to try to stem the current, positively dangerous to his person and family. Parson Reed is disgusted with the war in general and Jeff Davis in particiular, but he hugged the popular delusion that the war has depleted the North alarmingly, that business is stagnant and grass grows in the streets of New York. I flashed a ray of light into his mental darkness and astonished him considerably by informing him that if he should visit the North he wouldn't know that anybody was gone, and business was never so good. I left the old man with a good-sized flea in his ear, but before leaving I exercised the Yankee prerogative of swapping jack-knives with his grandson.

### September 22nd and 23rd.

Went out on picket in the same locale, and when we returned to camp the second night, we found a bunch of recruits had arrived and made themselves very familiar with our tents and rations. They eyed us keenly, spoiling for a fight. When we found out the extent of their depredations, we were more than willing to oblige. A more precious set of villains I never saw, reckless bounty-jumpers and cutthroats scoured up between New York and the British Provinces. Doubtless they have enlisted several times and jumped a bounty on each occasion. They have found the right regiment if they wanted trouble! However, there was no help for it, and we must make the best of a bad matter.

*September 24th – October 5th.*

A few days passed drilling and preparing for active service. At the same time we got ready for cold weather, thinking we might pass the winter here.

About the first of October the 6th Corps, which had been out on the Sperryville Pike, was sent to Mitchell's Station, farther to the front and near the Rapidan. The 3rd Corps was ordered to fill in the resulting gap. This movement occupied our time until the fifth, when we pulled up stakes and went into camp in a beautiful chestnut grove on the Sperryville Turnpike.

*October 6th.*

Most of us put up tents with a goodly number of boards in them, the former occupants of this locality having left a lot of them on the ground, a plain indication that some people hereabouts have suffered at their hands.

Being in a somewhat broken-down condition, some of us contemplated a furlough, but on a more mature deliberation it was deemed inadvisable, and we abandoned the idea and decided to "stand in our lot and place" as long as possible and fall by the wayside when we can do no better. It has been a task to keep up with the army since that dreadful, almost fatal march across the plains of Manassas last June, when hundreds fell and others rose only as wrecks of humanity.

*October 7th.*

Were paraded near camp to see a man drummed out for refusing to do duty when he claimed to be sick. The surgeon, insisting that it was only feigned, would not excuse him. I have no opinion in this particular case (or indeed any other), not knowing the man or the surgeon, but I can assert most positively that many men *have been* excused from duty who were far more able to do duty than were others whom the doctors refused to excuse.

The scheduled event didn't occur. *Why* I don't know, but it is possible that when the time came the man was too feeble to undergo the ordeal, if indeed he was alive. We returned to camp at sunset.

*October 8th.*

Nothing of any importance in a military sense happened, but we drew clothes for the winter. In the afternoon a reconnoitering party was sent out toward Sperryville. Enough was seen to satisfy General Meade that a Confederate force is hovering on our right flank. Another party, sent out from our regiment under Captain Sawyer, returned about midnight and reported no enemy in view.

But the enemy is not far off and our line of retreat is menaced. The danger is imminent and there is need of prompt action. General Lee is a desperate man and must feel all too strongly the grip we have on him. His region of supplies has been narrowed immensely and the section he occupies is destitute of water and wood. This little strip we occupy is rich in the things he needs for the subsistence of his army. In order for Lee to force us back, he has menaced our right by throwing a force across the river in the direction of Warrenton.

## October 9th.

Having recently drawn a full set of winter clothing, it occurred to us that the next best thing would be to wash up our dirty linen and have things in order. Some of us had just plunged our clothes in the brook and were beginning our laundry work when the bugle at division headquarters blew "Pack up!" The blast was echoed at brigade and regimental headquarters. The sound froze our blood, for such a sudden movement indicated something quite out of the ordinary.

We fell in as quickly as possible and were soon in line of battle facing Sperryville and on the right of the Pike. This line was maintained only a short time until another was formed in rear of it and we started, we supposed, for the Rappahannock. We hadn't gone far before we were again brought to a halt and faced about while the engineers destroyed the bridges in our rear and felled trees to obstruct the roads. This took all night. (While we were thus delaying and trying to prevent Lee from following in our wake, he was marching *around* our flank and crossing above us, thus gaining a day's march.) In the afternoon Colonel West joined us and, if any disturbance is to be made, we are glad to see him. Otherwise, we much prefer his absence. He is a kind of necessary evil.

## October 10th.

About 7 o'clock we started for the rear and had gone but a short distance when we were halted for the 2nd Corps to pass, this being their day to lead the column. "Blinkey's pets" were accorded the same privilege, but not for the same reason; he wanted them in the safest position possible.

It was noon before the other troops had passed. We started off immediately, but had not gone more than the length of the regiment when a woman ran out of a nearby house and informed us that a body of Rebel cavalry was lurking in the woods. No doubt these wily Confederates intended to sweep down in the rear and gobble the sick and stragglers. A halt was made and a line of battle formed while the 40th New York was deployed as a skirmish line and the 17th Maine moved across the field on their left to support them. The Rebels were in a piece of woods directly in front of us. As we neared the woods, we were greeted with a yell and at the same time a body of Rebs moved off at a brisk trot toward Culpepper. Scarce a shot was exchanged, and soon we were en route for the Hazel River. This little diversion was done to hold us while Lee's forces crossed the river above us. We were not molested again till near night, when another attack was made on the rear of our column. The Zouaves gave them a volley or two and they fled precipitately.

We halted shortly after on the low lands of the Hazel River while the pontoons were being laid. This took about two hours. While we lay here on this low ground, a cold mist settled over us, penetrating every fiber of our beings, and chilling the life nearly out of us. If we were ever thankful to move, it was at this time. We crossed over and soon came to the North Fork of the Rappahannock. No pontoons were laid here, although the water was much deeper than in the small stream we had just crossed and we were in a far worse condition. It was midnight when we crossed and, having waded waist deep, we were exceedingly chilled, our spirits as drooping as our clothes. But wet as we were, our position was such we dare not build fires, and so we laid down to sleep, if possible, and to dry ourselves under our blankets.

Most of the officers were toted over the river on the shoulders of a fellow called the "Moose Hunter." He charged them twenty-five cents apiece for the service, and in a few minutes his finances swelled to five dollars. I'd much enjoy seeing our officers share with us in some of the "good" things of life. Surely a cold bath at midnight would be just as good for them as for us.

We crawled into our blankets and tried to warm ourselves, but it was like lying on an iceberg with another one for a cover. There was no remedy except to get up and run around, and this we were too tired to do. We shook enough that night for a juvenile earthquake, and they must have felt it even over in Maryland.

## October 11th.

The column started, but I didn't, and as the army couldn't move without me they soon countermarched and came back to the river. They had orders to "observe the ford," so I didn't have to observe it alone. And the shaking I was doing wasn't because I was scared. I was trying to get warm, but this was impossible as a full-blooded chill was in operation. So, it was shake, shake, shake all day. At one time I had five blankets over me, and as many overcoats, but like Harry Gill, my teeth "chattered, chattered, chattered still," and my stomach and liver felt as if they were being squashed.

Dr. Hersom's attentions and those of my tentmates were unremitting, and the proper remedies brought relief in the course of the day. The enemy moved across to the northern bank of the river, and had we displayed the proper amount of skill, our corps would have crossed to the south side and interposed between them and their capital. This would have checkmated them in this little enterprise. We are here to stop the enemy from crossing the river, but the Rappahannock has many fords, and if the Rebels desire to cross, it is no easy matter to prevent it.

## October 12th.

Started in earnest this morning and made a march of about twenty-four miles, not an uninterrupted one. At Auburn the Rebels placed themselves in our rear and showed hostile intentions, bringing us to bay. The first intimation of this was a bullet through the hat of General French. Had it gone through his heart or head, it would not have grieved us. We formed immediately in line of battle and prepared for an attack. The Rebels, no doubt thinking we were going to attack them, retired precipitately. We soon resumed the march, but the writer was compelled to fall out and take more leisure in coming to camp.

To fall out was not a pleasant prospect. Sick, in a strange section of country, with enemies on every hand, and liable to capture any minute, I became depressed. My spirits sank even further as night descended with the column long since out of sight. Here and there, a fellow straggler indicated the line of march. I traveled a short distance with a member of my company. We sustained a severe shock and concluded we were surely gobbled when we heard a great rustling of leaves, which we thought was at least cavalry bearing down on us. Just as we were about to give up, a drove of hogs burst out of the woods. My traveling companion soon after fell behind me and was left to come up when he could. I arrived at bivouac about 10 o'clock, two hours behind the rest of the regiment. I marched from about 7 A.M. to 10 P.M. with only the interruption at Auburn. We have camped for the night near the beautiful village of Greenwich.

### October 13th.

The column was early on the march and, being more indisposed than yesterday, I was stowed away in an ambulance by Dr. Hersom. I rode all day, and such a ride! I could not have endured it a single hour but for an utter inability to proceed any other way. We are on the race with the Johnnies, who are trying to capture our wagon train. The roads are in such a condition that we were bumped and thumped all over the lot. Our teamsters were nearly dead with fright, and half of them were out of the road into the ditch. Of all the cowards in the world, commend me to the army teamsters!

Several daring attempts to capture the train were made by the Rebels. It is a prize well worth their while as there are 5000 wagons and hundreds of ambulances. They didn't succeed, nor did they bring on any action until after sunset at Bristoe Station, a splendid situation for a fight. The Johnnies were foolish enough to attack us behind the railroad embankment. As a penalty for their folly they left 700 men and seven cannon behind. Our loss was trifling. Their attempt was not so much in the nature of an attack as to occupy a position already occupied by the 2nd Corps, and it isn't the custom of this corps to allow the enemy to occupy the same breastworks with them. They gave the Rebels a reception befitting their rank (and they are quite *rank*, too), mowing them down in rows.

From the heights of Centreville, whither the ambulances had pushed and parked, we watched the fight till after eight o'clock. It was a fine pyrotechnical display. The flashing guns, the fiery trail of shells as they shot through the air, made an exhibit of fireworks equal to any Fourth of July on record. General Warren was the Union commander, General A.P. Hill the Confederate, although Lee is in the immediate neighborhood with his entire army. The Rebels fought with a desperation defying explanation on any other ground than that they are fearfully hungry and want to capture the train's supplies.

We had hoped that Lee would attack us behind the works at Centreville, but he probably remembered Gettysburg. Although well satisfied with the results at Bristoe, we could have dealt the Rebs a more disastrous blow if they had attacked us there.

Centreville is more strongly fortified than Washington. It is really the outside line of defenses of that city, with line upon line of defenses, here a fort, there a fort. Near Centreville is "Chantilly," the home of the Rebel's General Stuart. It would be just like that wily general to visit his old homestead and carry off the guard! It was near here that Kearney's rashness culminated in his death at the hands of a Rebel picket, an irreparable loss to the Union. It is sure that if Kearney were living, he might be in command of this army and Lee would not be chasing us back to Washington without us offering battle.

### October 14th.

Marched from Centreville to Fairfax Station, about fourteen miles from Washington and not far from Mt. Vernon. It is intimated that we will pass the winter here, and a requisition has been made for camp kettles and other necessities. Some body of troops must have been having a soft time here when the news of Lee's approach startled them; they had stockaded tents with *stoves* in them. A little later in the season we would doubtless have found lounges, rocking chairs, and feather beds.

## October 15th.

Still stopping at the same hotel, and we truly have no objections to putting in the chilly season here. Went on picket on a road leading to Mt. Vernon and came in at nightfall. It was my intention, when I first discovered our proximity to the resting place of George Washington's distinguished remains, to drop a little pathetic brine over them. Being quite feeble today, though, I had to forego that pleasure. Perhaps it is just as well, as I have not the conventional amount of veneration for that cold, austere figure.

## October 16th.

The only excitement today was an execution for desertion. A fellow from this division (Birney's) deserted about a year ago and has been playing the guerrilla since. Emboldened by his success, he became careless and was captured. I did not attend the affair, being in one of my spells of trying to shake the ground. I underwent a process of disintegration all the afternoon. While lying here, I heard the band play the "Dead March in Saul," and when the fatal volley was fired, I nearly jumped out of this world. My shakes ended at night and I felt like a new man in the morning.

## October 17th.

Today was memorable because we received General Sickles at night. As he passed along our lines, he was greeted with such rounds of applause as to convince any man of his unbounded popularity. The best of it was that it was genuine, for if ever a general was idolized, it is Sickles.

## October 18th.

Our hero of Gettysburg was today made the recipient of a present from the men of his corps — a carriage and span of horses costing $2000. This present wasn't made because General Sickles is poor (he has ample means). This sum has been contributed voluntarily, each man deeming it a pleasure to do so. General Sickles lost his leg at Gettysburg, and this gift is a token of our regard. This corps is proud that we were once commanded by a *man*, although now under the imbecile French, who doesn't command the confidence or respect of a man under him.

## October 19th – November 2nd.

We stayed here two days and then struck out for Manassas Junction. We halted long enough for dinner and then moved on to Bristoe Station, where the enemy had been encountered on the thirteenth. Here the ground was well-littered by the debris of battle: dead horses and men, besides accoutrements and arms, showing that Johnny Reb must have suffered considerably at our hands. It is certain that he lost *ten* to our *one*.

We stayed here a few days until hearing a rumor to the effect that Lee was working around on our left flank, toward Brentville. Accordingly, our lines were changed to conform with the new order of things. The corps moved to Brentville and changed front almost to rear. This was Saturday, and we remained till Saturday night. Most of us had retired when the cry to "pack up!" was heard. This is the most disagreeable of all sounds, especially at night, and the more so now that the doctor has pronounced my ailment to be congestion of the liver. Any sudden start is sure to produce very disagreeable sensations in the vicinity of that organ. We packed up and moved about two miles, bivouacked, and sent out pickets.

Next morning we had orders to go into winter quarters, and preparations were made to cut down the forest. By nightfall several houses were in various stages of completion. Here this farce ended, and when at 5 A.M. we were routed out and ordered to move at 7, I was glad I had not been able to procure the axe long enough to do much towards the building of *my* house. We moved at 9 and traversed the same road as we did coming back here. Soon after starting, Old Blinkey French got lost. In our seemingly aimless wanderings we forded a stream, then after going a couple of miles, found we must go back and ford it again, having gone no less than six miles out of our way. We reached Greenwich before night, but we ought to have been there by noon.

The next day we moved to the vicinity of Warrenton Junction, which is as far as the railroad has been relaid. Large details of men were at work on it, but progress is slow, the more so as we move farther away from Washington. As fast as the rails are laid, some portion of the army advances to protect it. General Meade being a very cautious bird, everything has to be just so methodical. Our advance is thus quite slow. Meade's design seems to be to avoid a collision with the enemy and to get as far as possible from Washington to winter and, perhaps, to menace the Rebels.

## November 3rd – 6th.

A detail of three men from each company was sent to Gainesville to guard a train going there for supplies. We found the place to be the smallest, dirtiest, and blackest spot imaginable. It consists of not over five buildings, innocent of paint or other embellishment. The Manassas Gap Railroad runs throuth the town, but I can't imagine how either party derives any benefit from the union. We waited here an hour or so, then returned to camp via Greenwich, where we stopped to take tea at a Mrs. Jordan's.

Greenwich is just the reverse to Gainesville in that it is neat and shady and has an air of comfort about it. Mrs. Jordan may — or may not — have been glad to receive us, but we were more than happy to see her table and to observe that she was a much better cook than we have heretofore encountered in our wanderings over old Virginia. It was a great treat to sit up to a table and "eat tea," as a Frenchman once said. This was a pleasure I had not enjoyed since getting into this show.

Her table was well supplied, but we privates didn't get the first cut. Of course the shoulder straps got all the dainty morsels, so our happiness was considerably marred. Those at the first table had roasted fowl and its concommitants, and they derived an immense amount of gustatory enjoyment therefrom. Those of us who dined last didn't get any nearer to the roast than the gravy. (This was a fowl wrong.)

Had our lack of grub been due to anything but their excessive gluttony, and if they had been charged extra, we should not have thought so much of it. We found Mrs. Jordan's biscuits very nice with the turkey gravy, though — so infinitely better than hardtack that under its influence our feelings were somewhat mollified. We didn't eat more than a dozen biscuits apiece, and only refrained from making a hearty meal because Mrs. Jordan, or the flour, gave out. Some of our men were so empty when they began that it was said those who sat near them could hear each mouthful as it fell on the chair.

Mrs. Jordan charged us for both bread and meat, although it was mighty little meat *we* saw — not enough to keep a healthy mosquito in order. We paid her 50 cents apiece and departed, arriving in camp about sunset, glad to get through a tiresome, troublesome journey.

We occupied this camp till the railroad was completed to Bealeton, when we moved in that direction. We were glad to be shed of the place, which was worse even than Bealton for scarcity of wood and water. By going a mile or so one might obtain enough water to make coffee and wash for the day. This area is part of the Plains of Manassas, destitute of anything but sand and stunted oak and pine. Being green, the wood refused to burn. We were not sorry to learn on the evening of November 6th that the railroad was completed to the Rappahannock and we would leave this infernal region in the morning.

## November 7th.

We were up till midnight the night before, drawing rations, and we hardly appreciated being called to turn out at 4 A.M. But that was the hour we put our shoes on, having orders to march at 7. For once, be it said to the credit of General French, he was ready to start at the time planned. We made a forced march of 18 miles, and about noon halted at Mount Holly Church, a small brick edifice near the banks of the Rappahannock. Across the river was Kellyville. While we made a hasty meal of bread and pork, pontoons were pushed over the hill, preceded by a skirmish line. The Rebs mistook the latter for a picket line until it was too late and our troops opened on them. We couldn't wait now for the pontoons. Part of the division crossed upstream at a dam, and coming down the line, scooped the Rebs one way while we took them in front.

We took about 300 prisoners, mostly North Carolinians of the kind which Virginians call "the triflinest set" because they say "we 'uns" and "you 'uns" and other like phrases, which are no more "triflin' " than some of the Virginian provincialisms. The Virginians dusted off and left these "triflinist" fellows to bear the brunt of the action. The main body of the Rebels fell back into some woods a mile or so from the river while we laid down on the ground and awaited further developments, which wouldn't begin until the right wing of the army advanced as far to the front as we were. General Sedgwick, with three corps, was fighting at Rappahannock Station, six miles upstream. Once a crossing had been forced, he was to connect with our right. He had a difficult task, as the Confederates have some very formidable works there. His forces made a direct assault and captured the works, but at a tremendous sacrifice on both sides. A goodly number of prisoners and quantity of arms fell into Sedgwick's hands.

No move was made by us that night. After dark, pickets were thrown out and we built huge fires to dry ourselves.

## November 8th.

Sunday, and we expected a row but were happily disappointed as the enemy moved off in the night. We decided to investigate and so proceeded until we connected with Sedwick's wing, which we found marching along the Orange and Alexandria Railroad. We "jined drives" before reaching Brandy Station. Each corps massed in solid column, making a magnificent sight as they moved over the hills. At this time we could hear cannonading at the front. It was Kilpatrick and Custer, driving the Rebel rear guard through Culpepper.

We only got as far as Brandy Station and went into bivouac near Fleetwood, in a swamp. It has always been a mystery why swamps are so often selected for us to bivouac in when there are miles and miles of high and dry ground all around us. Fortunately, on this occasion our regiment didn't end up in the lowest part of this spot.

### November 9th – 24th.

We moved up on a high piece of ground on the right of the railroad, Carr's division taking our place in line. Our new position gave us command of the railroad for several miles and a good view of the surrounding country. But we found no wood to speak of, nor timber to construct houses. So again we took up our beds and walked down into a pine growth a half a mile nearer Culpepper. Here timber is plentiful, and we commenced immediately to build a camp — until an order was promulgated to suspend building operations for ten days. This intimation of a move dampened our spirits but we didn't stop work altogether — made ourselves partially comfortable.

Some of our lady-killing gentry made herculean efforts, while here, to capture the affections of a Miss Botts, daughter of John Minor Botts, M.C. from this district, whose house is contiguous to our camp. The citadel of her affections surrendered at last to a sergeant in a Massachusetts regiment.

At the end of ten days the work of construction resumed, and by night two companies had their houses up. We have the material cut for ours but we think we discern the incipient stages of a move, so we suspended action. This is very wearing to our patience, but there is no remedy.

### November 25th.

Had five days' rations piled onto us and received orders to move at 5 o'clock next morning. This seems to indicate something more than rumors. I don't generally like suspense, but prefer it to sudden starts, for since my unfortunate illness last June, these things utterly unnerve me. This is true of three out of every five of us who have bowel or liver troubles.

### November 26th.

The weather being a little open, the move is postponed until tomorrow, thus giving me another opportunity to rattle my skull cavity trying to think what is up. As I am not in confidential possession of General Meade's intentions, I have no clue or handle by which a solution can be reached.

### November 27th.

All things being now ready, we pushed out on our expedition about 7 o'clock and marched all day, crossing the Rapidan at Jacobs Mills and halting for the night not far beyond. We met no resistance at our crossing, but some who crossed above or below us were stubbornly opposed. We all got over before night, but it is deemed prudent to advance no farther into enemy country as it is nearly all woods.

### November 28th.

Were ordered to move promptly at six. Although it was barely daylight, old Blinkey was "fuller'n a goat." He didn't comply with orders in respect to time, and soon proved as far out of the way in respect to the route. It is not uncommon for this general to be muddled any hour of the day, but it would have been better for us if he had surrendered the command this day to the canteen.

Our column was put in motion at 8 o'clock, two hours behind orders. All went well until we came to a fork in the road. We should have taken the left; we took the right and followed it until three or four o'clock, when we encountered Johnson's division of Ewell's corps and were soon into a brush with them. We should have been at Robertson's Tavern, instead we were on the Turnpike in the Wilderness. The direction we took led into the road on which the Rebel column was marching to Mine Run, where Lee has strong lines of entrenchment.

The Union forces have orders not to attack or bring on an attack until each corps is in its place. French delayed the entire army over half a day by his blunder, giving the Rebels time to strengthen their works, which are well-nigh impregnable.

The Rebel column kept us at bay till late in the afternoon, when they attacked us with great spirit. General French's pets, who had been at the head of the column, became nervous, so much so he couldn't trust them to "precede him to glory." So he ordered our division (Birney's) to relieve them. It was marvelous to see the way they put danger behind them, and any who were slow in their movements received added impetus from an army shoe, vigorously applied — a long-desired opportunity for gratifying our personal spite.

They were not the only white-livered individuals this day. Certain of our own officials made themselves conspicuous at the front by their absence. One tried to induce a fellow to vacate a position behind a stump, but the soldier put his fingers to his nose and made a motion of contempt.

We moved to the front, and so did the Rebels. The Battle raged for the next hour. Neither side seemed to gain any ground, or lose anything but *men*. The Rebs got on the right flank of our regiment and nearly cut off one company. Our officers urged us to increased exertion; they threatened, remonstrated, and did everything except go to the front themselves. One in particular displayed an unaccountable vehemence, and the result was that we held our own until dark, when the Confederates withdrew, leaving us the victors. We moved still farther to the front and to the left, bivouacking on the farm of Widow Morris.

We had fifty-two killed, wounded, or missing. Among the first were Captain Sawyer of Company E and Lieutenant Brown of Company A. The first-named was a genial, warm-hearted, and impulsive man, liked by all under him. He died deeply lamented. The other was exactly the reverse and was thoroughly detested. Indeed, I do believe he was so hated that he was shot by some of his own men, for he caused more fellows to be punished than all the other officers in the regiment. His whole aim seemed to be to catch the men in some trifling violation of orders and then have them punished out of all reason. At the Resurrection morning he will probably be found crawling out of some other person's grave whither he had been to see whether the rightful occupant hadn't done something punishable.

This battle at Locust Grove was fought on the Union side by one division of the 3rd Corps (Birney's), French's pets doing only the running. There should have been no fight here — we never should have been on this road. However, in view of the demise of Lieutenant Brown, I fully absolve General French for the blunder. Whoever sped the bullet did this regiment an inestimable service.

Doubtless some hold similar views concerning this writer. I encountered a leaden missile in this battle, and but for a slight deviation from the course it was pursuing it would have entered my diaphragm, with fatal results.

## November 29th.

Last night, I was on picket with Jose, Kilham, Holmes, and Lambert. It was an uncommon cold night for Virginia, but we found enough to keep us warm. We had found a rare thing: a farmhouse full of eatables. More, we thought, than the necessities of the inmates required. Intending to be neighborly, we proceeded to lay out such things as we had need of — and we had need of everything. Most of the night was spent in bringing in poultry, mutton, pigs, fruit, and flour. So intent were we in securing these trophies that morning dawned before we tasted a mouthful. Having then something else to do, we had to put as much as we could in our haversacks, leaving the rest for whosoever saw fit to care for it.

After daylight we visited the premises again to see if there was anything else to take care of. A few defunct Rebs were outdoors, and a few who were *not* so defunct. The wounded ones we turned over to the owner of the house with an injunction to care for their wants. After attending to matters in the house, we headed for the barn without any suspicion of Rebels hiding there. We had with us a fellow who always saw a rat under every bag of meal, however, and the moment he entered the hayloft, he acted accordingly. He fixed a bayonet and thrust it into the hay, from which direful sounds issued. A half dozen Johnnies were soon set on their pins and sent to headquarters. Two others allowed that they wouldn't stay with us, but an urgent invitation from Jim Jose, and his persuasive rifle, changed their minds. Although Jim was the sole proprietor of these two subjects, Captain Green captured the honor. He is senior captain, now that Sawyer has been killed, and desires this little incident to advance him toward his commission as major.

About 6 o'clock this morning we came in to where we passed the night. The Rebels could be heard chopping in front, but this had been going on all night. We stayed here about an hour, eating and stowing away grub, not having seen such bounty since we crossed the Potomac at Leesburg a year ago. In fact, we had to leave behind a good quantity of it, which was probably rescued by the ones we took it from.

About 9 o'clock Old Blinkey was sober enough to start, and we took the road we should have followed yesterday. After marching awhile, we struck the Gordon-ville Turnpike near Robertson's Tavern, followed this for about four miles, and found ourselves in front of Mine Run, where the Rebels have some of the most formidable works we ever saw. They are approached in front over low, marshy ground through which flows the sluggish stream called Mine Run. The Rebels have dammed it, and it now overflows for our special benefit. There was plenty of *damning* on our side of the fence as well. We spent the rest of the day fooling around and didn't get settled into line until night, an intensely cold and bitter one. The moon is full and all our movements clearly discernible to the enemy, even without fires. Our brigade laid up in a pine growth out of sight.

## November 30th.

When we awoke, we were pretty thoroughly chilled. We turned out and ate something, then changed front and held a line directly opposite the one we held last night. No other move was made, and everything was quiet until noon, when Colonel West called the officers together to discuss the nature of a move to be executed at 2 P.M. He informed them that a charge was to be made the whole length of the line and, as it was to be a desperate one, the officers must lead. The nature of the ground to be traversed, to say nothing of the strong entrenchments to be encountered, spread consternation in the ranks. It was necessary that the officers should set an example to insure even the mildest hope of success.

So far as my knowledge goes, no man expected to come out alive. Most of them marked their names on slips of paper and pinned them to their blouses, should anyone survive to deliver the messages to their families. The word *fail* was not to be considered, nor any other that would discourage any man. It seemed we were about to throw ourselves away, for there is a fatality attached to this part of Virginia. The two roads on which we now are run directly to the battlefields of Chancellorsville and Fredericksburg.

General Warren was to charge the enemy's right (our left) and his guns signal us to assault in the center and secure fame or death. Death! That word seems far more terrible here than at home, where one might die of disease, surrounded by one's friends. We waited two hours for the signal but it didn't come, and at the end of that time we learned that General Warren declared that the move would be productive of nothing but slaughter to his men. General French adopted the same view, and I cheerfully place this to his credit as a partial offset to his many blunders and shortcomings.

Night finds us in the same place we were this morning. We have drawn half rations and try to fancy ourselves comfortable, if this is possible under such hostile circumstances.

BUILDING WORKS. *Harper's Pictorial History of the Civil War.*

### December 1st.

Were permitted to enjoy a morning nap until daylight. After a miserable apology for a breakfast, we were ordered out to support the 4th Maine battery. At 8 o'clock an artillery fusillade opened along the entire line. This elicited about as much notice from the Rebs as would peas from a pop gun. They threw only one shell, which struck the ground on the right of our regiment and bounced over several men, striking them on their backs without injury, then passing along the right of the line slowly. One of the men, thinking he could stop it, put out his foot and when the shell struck, it broke his leg short off. This was a most curious incident and perhaps wouldn't happen again in ten thousand battles.

Our firing was of short duration as there is no fun in quarreling alone. We then proceeded to build some works for protection and laid behind them the rest of the day and night. It is the coldest night we have ever known in Virginia, the ground frozen solid as a rock. Although we keep rousing fires going, it is all we can do to keep from congealing. Our only remedy is to sit near *over* the fire as we can. If we lay our heads to the fire, our pedal extremities suffer, and if our feet are warm, our heads lodge a complaint for ill treatment. These are some of the pleasant feet-ures of army life on a winter campaign in Virginia. (This execrable pun only goes to show that my mental facilities have suffered somewhat from this exposure.)

### December 2nd.

Moved back into the woods, but did not gain much comfort by the move. A large number of cattle were butchered and distributed, but the measure of our needs is so great that it was another case of dividing the five loaves and two fishes among the multitude. Our bellies were far from satisfied and we gnawed bones like dogs, stripped fat from the entrails with as good a relish as ever an Eskimo ate a candle or chewed a piece of blubber. This greediness is partially the result of the extraordinary cold, and partly due to the fact that our rations have dwindled to next to nothing.

Our division was held in this position all day to keep up a front while the rest of the army meandered home to camp. Somewhere about 9 o'clock we started in the same direction, but not before firing some buildings close by. We moved across lots till we came to the Orange Plank Road, then the Brock Road, which led us to the Germanna Plank Road. This we followed till morning, finally arriving at the Rapidan.

At the very outset of this march the writer became, in a measure, incapacitated. A fellow who preceded me in crossing a frozen stream held onto a frozen stick, which he let go in time to catch me in the left eye, injuring that member so much that I feared the sight was destroyed. On this occasion I had a little set-to with Captain Moore, who, not being aware of the mishap, was disposed to hurry me along. Having the axe on one shoulder and the gun on the other, one eye closed and the other in a very moist condition, I was in no mood for any interference from any source. I hinted that I would drop the axe on the head of any who might be this meddlesome. The captain threatened to make this the subject of a complaint for insubordination.

Some of my comrades soon after relieved me of the axe, and I contrived to keep up wth a portion of the column, arriving at Germanna about 6 P.M.. The road was strewn with stragglers. Many others, who didn't straggle, slept in the ranks while marching. This has been a short campaign, but a very severe one.

It was a splendid evening, the moon full, the sky clear, and the air cold and bracing. Fires were built all along the road to direct the column and bewilder the Johnnies. If there hadn't been guides stationed at the crossings, we should have been as bewildered as the enmy.

### December 3rd and 4th.

As we recrossed the Rapidan, thankful to be alive, I noted an immense hole in the side of its northern bank, which I mistook for a cave but which I learned was Culpepper Mine, from whence this ford derives its name. As soon as we were over, a band near the end of the bridge piped up, "O Ain't We Glad We're Out of the Wilderness." We rather thought we were, and a hearty "Amen!" rose from every throat.

After disposing of a dipper of coffee, we started again in the direction of camp and marched a half mile or so, then halted until afternoon. We then marched six miles or more and halted till midnight, then resumed our march and reached our old camp about 7 A.M. on December 4th, ready to drop from exhaustion. On our arrival, a detail for picket was called immediately and those remaining in camp were held in readiness to move at a moment's notice. Some wag put a notice on a tree, saying, "The great moral show advertised by Lee and Meade has been indefinitely postponed." It is not certain that Lee has postponed his part, but no hostile demonstrations occurred during the day.

At midnight there was a cry, "The Rebels are coming!" It proved to be only a big scare, and we were permitted to lie down again and sleep.

### December 5th – February 5th.

For several days, when not occupied worrying about the Rebs, we were in a jolly muss with some New Yorkers who had the sublime impudence to claim the timber *we* had cut for our camp before starting on this movement. There were words and blows, but no serious injuries. Our stay was short; a change in line made it necessary to move about a mile, separating the 17th from the New Yorkers.

Building a camp in a place like this involves much hard labor. After cutting the material, we had to carry it on our shoulders over a mile. We had just completed the work when, to our disgust, we were told to vacate. This was the result of a disagreement between the government agent and the Honorable John Minor Botts, who owns most of the land in this county, as to the price for the wood and timber destroyed. Botts claims to be a Union man, but he wanted his price, disregarding the protection we have given him from the Rebels. This is the same Botts who is father of the girl whose devotion to a Union soldier is somewhat pathetic. Old John finally gave the paternal blessing to the young couple, but he didn't relent on his decision about us.

We moved next onto a tract of land owned by the County of Culpepper. Although it was a Sunday, we commenced building another camp as there was about a foot of snow on the ground — we considered this as good an argument for working on Sunday as if an ox or ass had fallen into a ditch. There was a prospect of more snow and it was imperative that we get shelters up.

It didn't snow right away, and in a few days we had a good camp. We named it Camp Bullock, after a Philadelphia gentleman who has given Birney's division 7000 pairs of mittens.

It seems that we might winter here, and we very much desire to because wood and water are abundant and we are contiguous to a railroad so we can expect a reliable supply of rations. All in all, we are situated as well as could be expected in an enemy's country.

Nothing of importance has occurred for some time except the execution of a private from the 4th Maine "for cowardice in the presence of the enemy." Doubtless there are cases of *desertion* so glaringly aggravating that they should be dealt with summarily, but no man should be shot like a dog for *cowardice*, this not being a matter within the control of the individual. Some will, I'm sure, urge that a coward of this type shouldn't enlist. This would be good logic if it could be shown that all men know themselves. But they do not. Men are moved by great popular currents, and enthusiasm of this kind is often mistaken for courage. We cannot judge men by the mere fact of enlistment. They are honest and patriotic and no doubt meant to do all they enlisted to do, but it is one thing to *talk* about "staring Death out of countenance," and quite another to *do* it. Alas for human calculations, they so often miscarry.

While at Camp Bullock, we have had a quiet, easy time. We have had a far worse scare from smallpox than from the Rebs but prompt measures prevented it from spreading.

During a portion of the time at this camp, Colonel West, of our regiment, has been in command of the brigade. Contrary to expectations, under him we have greater freedom from arduous labors and more liberty than ever before. Several complaints have been lodged against us at his headquarters but were dismissed and the petitioners given prompt permission to withdraw.

One particular case is fresh in my memory. Several of Company I were on guard at the commissaries. Unbeknownst to us, the commissary sergeant had devised a wily scheme and we guilelessly fell right into his trap. We helped ourselves to certain articles of food such as sugar, beans, sauerkraut, and bread, all of which we needed. Major West dismissed the complainant at once with the uncanny remark that "The men have taken only what *belonged* to them." Not knowing of his decision during the day, we sat on something worse than nettles for some time, thinking that if we were brought before a hostile court we would be severely dealt with. But the day finally wore away and we received no punishment other than our own mental lashings.

Most of our time passes very pleasantly, and we suffer less from hunger and exposure than in any camp thus far. In the immediate vicinity is a country seat where we now and then secure a dainty morsel. The occupant of the house, a Mr. Bennett, has used us very well indeed. He professes to be occupying the house for its owner — one Yancey, supposedly in England — but he displays too much zeal for a hireling. The brigade officers use his best room as headquarters. On one occasion I rendered him a slight service, and he invited me in to breakfast. Thinking this invitation simply a courteous condescension to one he must regard as immeasurably his inferior, I declined the invitation. This house is situated on the Culpepper Road, and all its surroundings and belongings bespeak elegance before the war.

This is a good section of country around Culpepper, and to spend a summer here would be no catastrophe.

# Winter and Spring of 1864

## February 6 – April 30

*February 6th.*

The month of January passed without incident, but this morning a sudden call came at five o'clock with orders to move at seven. This was not much to our liking for we'd had a notion that we were to stay at Camp Bullock for the winter.

We were very prompt and moved at 4 P.M., only nine hours behind time. We waited on the Culpepper Road till five P.M., when the corps was ordered forward to the Rapidan via Culpepper Court House. Short as the distance was that we marched, the writer and another (Augustus F. Bradbury) were so exhausted that we were sent to the hospital at the Barbour Mansion, a large, three-story brick building. It commenced to rain soon after we left the regiment and the mud grew soft and slushy. Darkness set in and, although I was tolerably familiar with the ground by daylight, it was now impossible to find anything, and I became so weak I fell down three times before at last reaching the hospital sometime before midnight. Arriving there, I was directed to a nigger hovel — a more disgustingly filthy hole I have never entered. But this was no time to question the facilities. I must go in or sleep in the fields, and my condition precluded that idea. At least it was shelter. All feelings of repugnance were drowned in the desire to lie down and rest.

I had been ordered to leave the contents of my haversack in the kitchen but by a slight lapse of memory I hadn't complied, a special intervention of Providence. Having taken a lunch, I was soon asleep.

*February 7th and 8th.*

My experiences and observations while at the Barbour House were not favorable to the management. Although declared by the doctors as unfit for field service, I didn't choose to stay there for more than two days. If it were two weeks, my accounts would close for good on the twentieth of February. The condition of those who have been there any length of time is abominable. Men suffering from chronic diarrhea need something more nourishing than dish water soup or chicken juice to recuperate and fit them for the front.

As far as I could see, the corps of unfeeling nurses and attendants have an excessively good time at the Hotel Barbour. They are domiciled in a large brick mansion occupied by a family of female Rebels. Here all live luxuriously on the supplies the Sanitary Commission sends from the North for soldiers in the hospital. Said soldiers sleep outside in tents. (This is unavoidable on account of their numbers.) I have heard much about the treatment our men receive in Rebel prisons but it can not be much worse than this so-called hospital.

I informed one of the stewards that I was opposed to staying any longer and departed at sunset, glad to get away from the place.

WINTER QUARTERS — ON PICKET. *Harper's Pictorial History of the Civil War.*

### *February 8th – 26th.*

I was exceedingly happy to rejoin our division. Things have been quiet for the space of three weeks. We encamped between the Rappahannock and Rapidan rivers, along the Orange and Alexandria Railroad, and passed our time in the usual routine of camp exercises, drill, guard duty, and picketing. There is always wood to cut, clothes to wash and mend, equipment to clean, and cooking to do.

It may be inferred that we don't have much idle time. The officers have parties, and a theater was soon built of logs and covered with a canvas borrowed from the Christian Commission without their knowledge of its intended purpose. Plenty of actors were found among the staff officers and their "wives," who are passing the winter in camp. We have raised a band and furnished instruments for them at a cost of $400. There are also gymnastic poles, footballs, and other means of killing time, which otherwise would hang heavily on our hands.

Our picket line extends from the Hazel River to the Sperryville Turnpike on the left, center being at the Culpepper County poor farm, which hotel the writer once visited while on picket near there. It is a substantial affair of stone, one story in height and covering three sides of a square. There lived here an old Negress, 104 years of age, truly a venerable person. (She died soon after my visit, no doubt the result of a too free use of tobacco, for she was an inveterate smoker.) How many interesting events in the world's history transpired in her lifetime. Since her birth, this nation has grown from a few feeble colonies to one of the great sovereign powers of the world. She lived during three wars and saw the onset of this one, so important to her race. Few people are privileged to live through such changes. This is a digression, but I think it appropriate to pay a passing tribute to this aged African. If she had been a white person, she would have been feted in grand old Virginia style.

### February 27th.

We were somewhat disturbed this morning to see a portion of the 6th Corps going in the direction of the Rapidan. As we have not been informed that a move is contemplated, we know such a move is irregular. Supposing it to be only a raid, we don't expect to go but have been kept in a state of feverish suspense nonetheless.

### February 28th.

The agony of expectation was broken before daylight, when we were turned out and ordered to move at 6 o'clock. We were not only in line on time, but moving, serpentlike, toward the antiquated town of Culpepper. We reached it about nine and passed through. This was the writer's first visit to the war-worn old town and, while I was not in raptures with it, yet it had an air of comfort, the more so as a storm was brewing and any kind of shelter looked enticing.

Soon after leaving the town, we turned off toward Cedar Mountain and shortly came to James City. This busy metropolis consists of the following valuable real estate: two dwellings, one with barn attached, one old carpenter shop, and an old mill — all expecting to tumble to pieces soon. Why such a pigmy hamlet should be called a city is a mystery. The main avenue is a lane terminating in a pasture into which we marched. Another lane intersects this one and passes over a hillock dignified by the high-sounding title of Thoroughfare Mountain.

We halted in the shadow of this hill and formed in line of battle to support the 6th Corps, which has advanced to Madison Court House and Charlottesville. They crossed the Ravenna River near one of these places and surprised a Rebel outpost of cavalry and artillery, capturing several pieces of the latter and over 100 horses. When the Rebel cavalry woke up, the Yankees had fled.

We who were left here passed the day "seeing the town," getting acquainted with the names of the streets and public buildings. At night a storm of sleet and rain set in, but we are provided for such an emergency and have tents up, well stockaded with boards from James City.

### February 29th.

Rain and snow fell alternately according to the caprices of Dame Nature. Our ears were saluted with the sound of artillery firing in the direction of Madison Court House. We didn't know to whom we were indebted for this racket, but were aware that the 6th Corps was inspecting that section. Later, we learned the nature of the difficulty. The Confederates were posted on the Rapidan and Ravenna rivers — both of which streams in our New England would be called *brooks* or *runs*.

The Johnnies were considerably surprised to have us appear in February, and I confess we are inclined to agree, for we thought that the Burnside Mud March and Meade's Mine Run fiasco had shown our command the folly of attempting a move at this time of year. This is our third attack since we went into winter quarters in November. It has been a season of unrest to us and the Confederates, but what has demoralized us has elated them to a corresponding degree. Their army is sure that God is on their side. This idea is especially prevalent in Stonewall Jackson's old command, for they are just as superstitious as when old Jack was alive, and their leaders take excellent care to foster the belief, for it spurs men on to fight like demons.

During the afternoon Major West returned from furlough, remarking as he rode into our midst, "You can't go into a fight without me!" This statement has an element of truth in it, for we do like having him around when there is trouble. We feel he has the ability to get us safely out of a bad spot, for he has few, if any, superiors as a tactician and would, in this respect, make an excellent commander. If a battle is imminent, we are glad he is here; otherwise we much prefer his room to his company. The amount of space occupied by his carcass would suit us much better empty, for he is downright fussy, and the title "fuss and feathers" would sit as gracefully on his shoulders as on General Scott's.

Our Major West is a brave man when it comes to offering *our own* services. This happened at Chancellorsville, and Mr. West was the victim of a good-sized snub for his officiousness. He was emphatically informed that when his regiment was wanted, it would receive orders through the proper channels. This cooled his zeal somewhat and made him less forward in volunteering his services. He isn't commander of the regiment, and we shouldn't have taken orders from him if he *had* received the permission he asked.

He is just dying for a chance to jump over Lieutenant Colonel Merrill, who has been in command since Colonel Roberts resigned previous to Gettysburg. Colonel Merrill doesn't coquette with death nor dally with danger. He believes there is danger enough when men do what they are *ordered* to do, without offering to assume the share belonging to others. He isn't ambitious enough for promotion to risk his own or other lives unnecessarily.

West is all courage and dash, but with no feeling. He only regards men as a means to accomplish an end, that end the "West end." He is intensely selfish and will use anybody as a stepping stone to gratify his ambition. He is imperious and overbearing. Colonel Merrill is the exact opposite, sometimes too much so for the good of the regiment. He often allows men to address him more familiarly than they would a corporal in the regular army. This is laxness of discipline which, in some cases, can only be detrimental to himself and others whose notions might be formed by observing this. Colonel Merrill is too tender-hearted for a warrior, but he perhaps has more of *true courage*, for it requires a heap of moral courage to admit a deficiency of physical courage in a place like this. A lack of moral courage, by contrast, has held many a man on a battlefield. This observation is based on my experience of nearly a year and a half of fighting.

We laid in this place all day, and for lack of anything else to do the men indulged in the most childish actions, hardly behaving like veterans of several battles. The first thing they did was to mutilate an old mill whose wheel refused to turn. They set fire to the old thing, and when it failed to burn, they cut the posts nearly off and with a slight pressure sent it crashing into the gully below. Then they took all the pulleys, carried them to the top of a hill, and rolled them down. A couple of wagon wheels and a log were improvised into a cannon and sham fights carried on. Thus the day passed with these and diverse other ways of killing time.

Being so far from camp, we were grateful when the storm ceased at sunset. Fair weather might bring a battle on the morrow, but it is desirable nonetheless. Most of us have managed very fair quarters in spite of the place. Walt Rounds, Frank Sweetser, and the writer put in this night together.

### March 1st.

Expected to move toward the enemy but were mistaken. We soon learned that the 6th Corps was on its way back, and the forward movement was abandoned. We passed the day here waiting for orders.

### March 2nd.

We commenced a crablike advance, returning by way of Culpepper Court House. We arrived in camp about 1 P.M., and each company took its former place and settled down to the old routine.

### March 3rd — April 30th.

[As he rewrote his journal, Haley did a considerable amount of editing on his diary entries for the early spring of 1864. The revised text that follows thus includes a considerable amount of after-the-fact explanation of the politics, personalities, and strategies of that time. —Ed.]

The latter part of this month General U.S. Grant (who had won some successes in the West) was appointed commander of all the Union forces, with the title of Lieutenant General — Revived. He soon commenced a reorganization of the Army of the Potomac. The first thing was a vigorous weeding out of some of the general officers. The corps were consolidated so that the number of corps commanders was reduced one-half. Generals Sykes, Newton, and French were invited to step down and out. They were considered in some way unfit for high command.

The corps commanders are now as follows: General W.S. Hancock, Commanding 2nd Corps, consolidated with a portion of the 3rd; General John Sedgwick, commanding 6th Corps, consolidated with a portion of the 3rd Corps; General G.K. Warren, commanding the 5th Corps consolidated with a portion of the 1st Corps, and General Burnside in command of his old 9th Corps. General Meade is in command of the whole, and General A.A. Humphreys is Chief of Staff.

It was a heavy blow to veterans of the old 3rd Corps to sink their identity in another body, but they made a gain in one or two respects. Under General French, the corps had a more than even chance of losing whatever reputation it has, while under Hancock there isn't any such contingency. And while the 2nd Corps might absorb most of the future honors, nobody would confound the doings of Birney's division with any but the old 3rd Corps. We have our generals and our distinctive corps badges. One other thing: there are no troops in the Army of the Potomac who wouldn't feel proud to fight under Hancock, Warren, or Sedgwick.

For a short time we didn't exactly know where or to what we belonged. A feeling of homesickness pervaded camp. It was a dull and dreary time of year, and we had an unsettled feeling. All in all, though, we were well pleased at the turn of events, for we had felt for months that a discordant element in this army was preventing a union of purpose, without which no success could perch on its banners. This war must cease to be a machine for the manufacture of political capital.

Presumably acting on some strong hints as to who the jealous and sore-headed ones were, Grant picked out the worst offenders. Fitz-John Porter was cashiered and Franklin sent away under a cloud. Now French, Sykes, and Newton went too, forced to retire to the bosom of their families. I cared not where they went so long as they could do no further harm to this army.

It was openly hinted that all the trouble was in Washington, fostered by Edwin M. Stanton, Secretary of War, and his coterie.[1] The people, through their leaders Horace Greeley, Henry Ward Beecher, and others, demanded that Stanton and Halleck cease their interference. So, when General Grant made it a condition of his acceptance that there should be no meddling in his conduct of the war, he sustained the wishes of an outraged country.

In accordance with the changes noted, our division moved over the railroad in the direction of Stevenburg, highly elated with the orders. The situation was vastly superior to our last. It was originally a Rebel camp, and they had much better shelters than ours, as this camp was composed of houses rather than the crude huts we built. These were built of logs covered with split shingles — houses such as the poor whites of the South live in. Each house accommodated eight men. There were real floors and greased white paper windows, which although not transparent, admitted light. It was a pleasing novelty to live in a house large enough that we didn't have to go outdoors whenever we turned around. We had been so cramped that we scarce had room to have our shoes in our huts with us after removing them.

Such an excess of happiness was too good to last. And it didn't last long, for after two weeks we were moved to a place farther to the front, where we built a rough camp of the old sort.

Soon after coming here our peace of mind was rudely disturbed by the antics of one Dan Butterfield. This person was Chief of Staff to somebody, and invented the most diabolical scheme for robbing the pickets of whatever degree of comfort they might have enjoyed hitherto. If there could have been a fine of one cent for every oath uttered on his behalf, some of the men would have sworn away their entire month's wages in a single night. Our regiment was on picket only once during this time, but contrived to make way with some powerful English. At the end of three days we returned from picket safe and sound (no thanks to D. Butterfield).

From this affair, which occurred in April, we have done no more picketing and but little drilling, but are continually harassed by reports of a move. Surely it must come soon. The mud is drying rapidly, and the approaching warm weather furnishes sufficient guarantee that the rumors will soon crystallize into fact. The sick and sutlers have been sent to the rear, also the extra clothing and women, and everything indicates an early move.[2]

# Battle of the Wilderness

## May 1 – 9, 1864

*May 1st.*

This day found us busy preparing to move forward. Rations and ammunition were served out and various other things were done indicative of an early departure. We would be depressed but for the hope that this campaign will positively be our last and also that it will be decided in our favor. And so, although dreading it for its uncertainty as to whose life will be spared or whose sacrificed, we are sure it will be brief and, correspondingly, with a small loss of life.

*May 2nd.*

Another day like yesterday, and the suspense so great that it would have been a relief to go. By no means unconscious of the importance of the work to be done, we have no doubt that Grant will give them as hot a fight as they have ever engaged in. We are ready and willing to enter into an earnest contest to bring about results at once good for the country in general and ourselves in particular.

What is wanted is men who regard the disruption of the Union as a great calamity and its preservation as infinitely more important than any set of men or any party.

*May 3rd.*

The Anniversary of Chancellorsville. Everything packed but the tents. We remained thus all day to confuse the Rebels, who could see everything from their lookout across the Rapidan. At sunset our tents were all standing as though nothing was to occur, but later confusion and hubbub reigned where a couple of hours before it was as quiet as a Quaker meeting. After everything was ready, we laid down to await further orders and, if possible, catch a little nap. About 9 o'clock came the long-expected summons.

At 10 o'clock we marched out under the somber starlit sky. It was a solemn procession that wound its slow length along toward the various fords of the Rapidan, on the opposite side of which Lee's forces waited for our movement to develop. Physically, some of us were in a wretched condition. For myself, I can say that this all-night march was more dreaded than battle.

We moved on through the interminable forest and endless night. The winds tossed the leafless branches of the trees, seeming to moan and shudder. There was none of the usual hilarity and enthusiasm that attend the breaking of camp. This army has so often been led forward only to be driven back, torn and bleeding, that it has almost lost hope. Though Lee's ranks are decimated and our own have been largely augmented, and we hope for a short and decisive campaign, yet none have the courage to prophesy anything but defeat.[1]

The design is to get in between Lee's army and Richmond. This would flank him out of his entrenchment on the Rapidan and compel him to fight at an immense disadvantage. All of this high planning involves the absurd proposition that Lee will be found napping. But they reckon ill who underestimate Lee; he is said to sleep with one eye open.

## May 4th.

We marched all night with no halts, not even for coffee. About 10 A.M. we crossed the Rapidan at Ely's Ford, continuing until 2 P.M., when we halted for dinner. After resting awhile, we pushed on, and long before sunset reached the breastworks occupied by the 11th Corps when they were driven off by Jackson one year ago day before yesterday. The scene and date were anything but inspiring. True, there might be nothing ominous in such coincidences, but they do have their effect on morale. Hooker has been strongly censured for allowing himself to be shut up here in the Wilderness. Is Grant to repeat this stupendous piece of folly? It looked very much like it as we drew up in front of Chancellorsville.

We found its ruins looking just as we had left them a year ago, and concluded that we would stop here for the night. After forming in line near the Plank Road, we were about to prepare for rest when an order came for the 17th to go on picket. (This was, to *one* at least, a most unwelcome order, for I was in a very weak condition due to the forced march of the night, followed by the heat of the day.) We went on picket and were posted on a road, which I think is the same one Jackson marched over after he started for our right flank.

It would be a trifle singular if, surrounded as we are by soul-harrowing memories, we were not apprehensive. We comfort ourselves with the rumor that Lee has only about one-third of our force.

It is said that this region known as the Wilderness is infested with poisonous serpents whose bite is fatal to man or beast. I have not heard of any deaths from this cause, but if the dreaded Moccasin does dwell here, we have an enemy more to be dreaded than the Rebels. Man is not in love with death even in its most seductive form, but to die from snakebite must be one of the most repulsive.

Near our post is an old well, the water of which has a most horrible flavor. I desired no second taste. I later heard, but do not credit the report, that after last year's battle a lot of defunct Rebels were piled into that well. If such was the case, several of us have just been treated to a dose of the extract of treason. Well, we cannot change it now. I, for one, hadn't strength enough to throw it up, horribly suggestive as it was.

Were I at home and feeling as I do, I would be in bed, but here I am, sitting up without rest for 48 hours. Some don't mind it. They are like the festive mule and their powers are practically unlimited. But I don't belong to that species. Deprived of sleep one night, my system is in a state of collapse. I may be pardoned for introducing this much of personal matter; we are of little importance in detail, but each of us helps make up the grand aggregate.

## May 5th.

About daylight we were called in from picket and found our division ready to move. We drew a ration of beef, but barely had time to warm it before the column was in motion. We passed out through the Cedars and by the Furnaces, places made historical by our experiences of last May, and then moved slowly in a southwestern direction. Our orders were to head for Shady Grove Church on the Catharpin Road, six miles south of Parker's store on the Orange Plank Road, where another corps was directed.

From the orders given this morning, it is evident that Grant and Meade thought Lee would hustle himself off to Richmond. When, at an early hour, the heads of columns moving westward on the Plank and Turnpike roads encountered a force of Rebels moving to take the Union forces in flank, Meade thought it only a small force making demonstrations, so he hoped to prevent them from getting back to their entrenchments at Mine Run. However, this formed no part of their plan, as was soon apparent from the furious way they pitched into Warren and Sedgwick. They meant business. Lee must be near with his entire force. It would be incredible to presume he would pitch into an army of this size with anything less, even if he entertained only the hope of checking our advance so he could withdraw his forces under cover of darkness.

The 2nd Corps, under Hancock, might naturally expect to sustain the first shock of battle. Soon after starting we had thrown out flankers, and we expected to hear the crack of musketry at any moment. We had gone as far as Todd's Tavern when we became aware of trouble. Aides were hastening hither and thither, and we proceeded to move not in the forward position, but back along over the same route we had just come.

The Rebels were making desperate efforts to seize the Brock Road. If they succeeded, they would cut Grant's army in two. So, we were rushing to connect before Lee should break through, or drive our forces opposed to him at the junction of the Brock and Plank roads. This was a desperate predicament to be in, for the Brock Road is the very one Jackson moved on last year when he made his flank movements. Lee was very aware of its importance and now strained every nerve to possess it.

When we reached the junction of the roads, we saw the most awful confusion reigning. Numerical superiority was seen here at its worst. There were more troops than could be utilized, almost a huddle. The roads were narrow and the woods and underbrush very dense. It was a dreadfully mixed-up mess. The enemy was rapidly pushing in this direction and, if they gained the junction, we didn't know what our Ulysses would do.

When we reached the place of action, it was difficult to tell who was who. The brigade commander was tearing and swearing. His English was exceedingly vigorous and confusingly copious. In marching and countermarching, our division and the 2nd became sandwiched in a most remarkable manner. General Hayes, who always has a select litany of imprecations to dispense, was cursing one and damning the other.

"Get out of the way, you d——d white patches," he exclaimed with vehemence to the 2nd Division. And to a cavalryman who happened to hit him in the leg as he passed, he yelled, "G——d d——m your old heels!"

It seemed doubtful that we could get into line soon enough to save this locality, for the troops on our right were hotly engaged. Berdan's sharpshooters were out as skirmishers in our front, and they kept the enemy at bay, so that we soon had a line formed. We advanced at once and very soon became involved.

SKIRMISHING IN THE WOODS. *Harper's Pictorial History of the Civil War.*

Nothing could be seen except trees and brush. All we could see of the enemy was the flash of their guns. This was guide enough, and we blazed away at them. We soon had them started, or they fell back by design to draw us from the road. I don't know which; I only know they did fall back and we followed until darkness closed in on this region of the "shadow of death." From 4 o'clock on we were into it all along the line, hot and heavy, teeth and nails, nip and tuck. It was a continuous roar of musketry, rising and swelling like the sound of surf pounding on the shore. Neither side could use artillery, with the exception of one section on the Plank Road.

About dark the roar died away and we began to look around. We have gained a little ground, but lost heavily in men. There is every reason to believe that the Confederates have suffered as greatly. The last thing they attempted, without success, was to wedge themselves in between our right and the troops of the 5th and 6th corps.

Matters are exceedingly confused, and some of our men sleep in the Rebel lines, but not as prisoners. Major Mattox, of our regiment, who was temporarily in command of the sharpshooters, was taken prisoner. I can't think of any officer I'd sooner part with, for he was very pompous and had yards and yards of superfluous red tape about him.

Our own company loss in this engagement was one killed (Daniel Brown), two mortally wounded, and seven wounded to a lesser degree. Shortly before leaving camp it was remarked to Daniel Brown that he would not get out of fighting in this regiment as he had done in two others. His reply was, "If I go into any fight, I hope to Jesus Christ that I shall be shot before five minutes." This malediction on his own head came upon him with painful fidelity, and he fell before he had fired twice. Such speeches are better left unsaid. Those who heard him make it recalled it when they saw him fall and witnessed his agony. His yells could be heard distinctly above the din of battle.

Frank Sweetser and Fred Loring were the two men mortally wounded. The former was shot in the lower abdomen; the latter had his hip crushed. I must bear testimony to the patience and heroic spirit displayed by these two young men. Frank was a warm personal friend, and my feelings may be imagined when I saw him writhe in pain. Never was there a young man of sweeter disposition, generous and warm-hearted. I couldn't have thought more of him had he been my own brother. Fred was my tentmate and a fine fellow. He didn't possess Frank's generous and cheerful nature, but he was much esteemed by me.

Four of us made stretchers of blankets and poles and carried them to the Brock Road, where the field hospital was. It was not less than a mile from our line of battle, and yet it seemed like ten as we struggled through the tangled underbrush of the Wilderness. Sweetser begged constantly for water, which he threw up as soon as it was down. Fred's patient and uncomplaining manner, in spite of what must have been the most excruciating pain, was astonishing, for he was only a lad in his teens. His conduct was the more conspicuous in contrast to the other wounded men all around us who were groaning, praying, begging, cursing, and yelling with pain and rage. He made not a sound save now and then a sigh or low-spoken request. Sweetser died soon after midnight when they were taking him and Fred off in an ambulance to Fredericksburg, where every house is a hospital.

At this field hospital, where hundreds of men lay wounded with no one to tend them, I passed most of the night. Not far from the boys whom I was caring for was a wounded Irishman who kept up a perfect fusillade of yells and groans to attract attention. At frequent intervals he would raise himself on his elbows screaming, "Murther! Murther! MURTHER!"

The events and fatigues of the last three days have so unstrung my nervous system that a blow from a twig would, I believe, prove fatal. During the engagement in the Wilderness this afternoon I became so weak that I could not stand up, and I bled at the nose like a stuck pig. How I ever did my share of lugging Loring and Sweetser to the rear is something I cannot explain. It was nothing short of superhuman exertion.

### May 6th.

I awoke to find the troops had gone forward in obedience to an order from Grant to attack all along the line at daylight. Jack Brine and I began to search for our division. We moved out to the front, but they were gone. They had the Rebels on the run and kept pushing them for two miles. We found no traces of them for a long time but finally ran afoul of a fellow who said our division had moved in a left oblique direction across the Plank Road. We followed for a couple of hours, then gave it up and decided to do no more running until we found out something more definite.

Our troops had moved with wonderful celerity and had turned the Rebs right out of their blankets, pursuing them for two miles. No one knows where our division would have driven them if Hancock hadn't felt it imperative to halt and make some kind of an alignment. His left used the Brock Road as a pivotal point, while his right swung around toward and across the Plank Road, so that his corps was nearly parallel with the Plank Road. When Hancock halted, it gave Lee the opportunity to form his line, and as soon as the fresh troops had arrived, the two Rebel divisions advanced simultaneously on Hancock and commenced pushing him back. So impetuously was the assault made that the Union troops melted before it and soon came rolling back to the Brock Road, followed by the exultant Confederates.

Here we joined them. It was just as well we hadn't made any further efforts to find them, as they hadn't been anywhere near where we had supposed them to be. At first our side had it all our way, but when the Rebels turned, it was the Union troops that suffered. Company I lost twenty men. When it reached Brock Road, only seven could be found, and one of these had had a mighty close call — a bullet cut a furrow over his head from front to back, as clean as ever a razor shaved hair. There was no organization, no alignment, or much of anything but a mob.

Other companies suffered as much, or worse. Major West, our regimental commander, was wounded in the thigh and sent to the rear. Other officers were put off their pins. General Alexander Hayes, our brigade commander, was instantly killed while leading his troops. He was really a brave old fellow, or perhaps reckless might be a better term. He once commanded a division but in the recent reorganization he was reduced to a brigade command, where it is said no brains are needed.

We were not under Hayes long enough to know him well. He was continually soaked or steeped in whiskey, and it was to this article that he was indebted for his death. There is no saying that he might not have been killed anyway, but I *can* say that that particular bullet would not have killed him except that the strap on his canteen became entangled, and as he tried to adjust his mouth to the mouth of the canteen, the bullet went through his head.

Our Major West is the greatest loss, for we are desperately short of regimental commanders. For a leader at such a time a clear head is needed, and most of the officers are besotted with whiskey.

Our line is now the Brock Road, and this must be held at all hazards. Otherwise, we have no exit from the Wilderness except to go back to Chancellorsville, perhaps Fredericksburg. If that happens, Lee will be between us and Richmond.

Before we formed in line, the Rebels were onto us in a furious charge. Lee had massed all his available forces in one supreme effort to overwhelm Hancock and get possession of the junction of the Plank and Brock roads. It was a desperate encounter. Longstreet's command was on us, yelling like devils. Our breastworks were set on fire. We fell back a few rods, but seeing the Johnnies pour over the works, we retook them instantly.

In this affair, General Longstreet was severely wounded in the neck and carried from the field, and all further attack was abandoned. Panic and confusion reigned and came near resulting in a rout of the Union forces. This was partly due to an excitable aide of General Birney's who ordered some troops to swing around and face the enemy. Instead, his order brought them back-to. The mistake was discovered in time to avoid disaster and deliver a volley in the faces of the enemy, no thanks to that excitable aide, who didn't know his right hand from his left.

The Rebels soon started in the direction of Orange Court House. Their demoralization may be imagined when it is known that a lieutenant in our regiment captured eighteen of them with only his revolver, while they still were all armed.

Soon after, the excitement died away and we were ordered to the rear. We started toward Chancellorsville, but had not proceeded far when we were ordered to return to the front. We about-faced and came back to nearly our original position.

This is the second night in the Wilderness. We laid down for the night near where the last fighting was.

## May 7th.

This morning the command of the regiment devolved on the redoubtable Captain John Perry, of Company D — a very earnest man, and as ignorant as he is earnest. His lack of knowledge is apparently bottomless. He has a quaint way of mixing rustic remarks with his military, which isn't sanctioned by any book of tactics. For example, when one of his company failed to "Dress Up!" he threatened to "keep him shelling pig corn for a week." Another highly sensible and lucid remark (or rather threat) of his was, "I'll have you court martialed. I'll have you shot. I'll have you tied up to a tree!" Why a man should be terrified by a threat to tie him up to a tree after he had been shot is not clear.

This particular morning John dragged us into and through all the mire he could find within a radius of a mile, and at last posted us in rear of the 14th Brooklyn Zouaves in a swamp of black mud and ooze. At noon we were ordered to stir up the Rebels. We made a movement up the Plank Road, trying to discover the whereabouts of the enemy and to ascertain if he was engaged, and whether a visit from us would be regarded as an intrusion.

General Birney and staff moved up the road while the infantry marched along each side in the woods. This affair came very near costing the general his life. He and his staff had proceeded but a few rods when a bundle of rags by the roadside (which they had supposed was a dead Rebel) suddenly raised itself, took aim at General Birney, and fired. That Rebel *was* defunct shortly after, riddled by our bullets.

We moved but a short distance and came in sight of some blankets put up as if for protection from the infernal heat of the sun. On coming nearer, we saw them suddenly pushed aside to disclose a Rebel battery, which sent a storm of cannister whistling about our ears, killing and wounding quite a few and sending the survivors flying in the opposite direction. Such agility as we displayed hunting for the rear has few parallels in this war.

Captain John Perry was first and foremost in finding his way to the rear. He kept yelling, "Halt!" but failed to set an example, except in the way of speed. We could hear the voice of our gallant officer, but nothing was visible but two coat-tails and loose heels enveloped in a cloud of dust.

Our line never wavered in its flight to the rear until it reached the works at the Brock Road. The Rebels followed, and we expected they would attack, but instead they withdrew after giving us a sample of their peculiar vocalism.

Night found us again at the junction of these two roads, which have to be held until we get out of this terrible Wilderness. After dark General Grant and staff rode down to the left of our line. Not more than five minutes elapsed before we heard a report that they had captured Grant. This yarn was probably circulated to take their minds off their empty haversacks, for "Lee's Misérables" fare pretty badly, and all sorts of means are resorted to to keep up their flagging spirits.

We now laid down in rear of the second line of works until about 11 o'clock, when we were routed out and moved a few rods. We then fell down again to sleep. I had reached an advanced state of somnolency when a tremendous clattering of horses' hooves aroused me and I sprang upright, supposing it to be a Rebel cavalry attack. The suddenness of the start gave me such a shock that it nearly turned me inside out. When I came to, my knapsack had disappeared. I searched for an hour and a half, but gave it up, concluding that some infernal thief grabbed it. And now my wardrobe is exceedingly limited, though I soon found a shirt and a pair of socks. There is one comfort in not having many clothes — I now have less to lug.

The cause of the disturbance was never established. A log was my pillow the rest of the night, but I slept well and didn't stir until morning.

## May 8th.

Turned out at daylight and expected to move immediately, but didn't start till near noon, when we commenced by the left flank. We know we haven't whipped Lee, nor has he succeeded in dividing our army in the center. Lee still has the advantage inasmuch as his army could be concentrated and a blow struck on some weak or exposed part of our line. Our great disadvantage is that we don't have a general who dares take the risk of attacking Lee in full force.[2]

We moved to Todd's Tavern, and fortunate it was for us that the distance was short, as it was intensely sultry and we had to fall out often. Our suffering from heat and thirst cannot be described on paper. About 2 o'clock we moved down into a line of works on the Gordonsville turnpike. Our pickets in front kept up a continual fire, and we expected an attack from the Rebels at any moment.

The 5th Corps advanced out on the road, but found the Rebs too strongly entrenched for them to make an attack. It may appear strange that with a force nearly three times as large as Lee's we are so often compelled to fall back. We certainly are superior in numbers, but he is superior in quality, the reason being that his forces have unlimited confidence in their commander while we have little or none in ours. We can see that whatever success attends Grant must be by sheer brute force. No strategy, just hammer, hammer, hammer, until the enemy is flattened.

The 5th Corps fell back before dark, and the Rebels, seeing them draw rations, became so wild they rushed in on them, driving them just far enough so that the rations were left between the two lines. The Johnnies exerted themselves heroically to get hold of these rations, for they are mighty hard up. After dark the 5th Corps moved out again, being reinforced, and recovered the bread. That the Rebs stand sore in need of rations I know firsthand, for I had the pleasure of investigating one of their haversacks today. The only food it contained was dry meal — no coffee, meat, salt, or sugar.

Our loss today was only one. Lieutenant Judkins, of the brigade staff, had his head shot off while carrying an order. Judkins was a great favorite, and if I had been consulted, I could have named several other persons I'd rather part with.

By midnight our lines had been so strengthened that we should have been quite pleased to have the Johnnies come on. Lee hasn't obtained a positive victory, but the results are still disappointing to Grant, who came to the command of the Army of the Potomac with the declared opinion that it has never fought its successes out. He expected, at one blow, with his immensely superior numbers and without the aid of strategy, to clear the road to Richmond. Perhaps, disillusioned by the experience of the past few days, he now will be willing to essay a new route and to attempt a strategic operation.

We passed the night here. All firing stopped at dark.

## May 9th.

Changed place slightly this morning, moving just across the Gordonsville Pike, which runs at right angles with our line. We waited till noon but nothing happened, and there being unmistakable signs that the enemy was concentrating on our left, we moved in that direction. We marched till night without seeing anything of the Rebs. Just before dark our advance came in contact with them and gave them a parting salute as they went over the Po River. They had no resistance worthy of the name.

We halted in the neighborhood of an old church, and a part of each company was sent out on picket. Our last sight of the Rebs tonight was of them taking observations from the corner of a barn. We made a gesture to them with a shell or two, and as they disappeared in the woods, they sent a shell whizzing over us. We didn't pursue them any farther. This country is thickly wooded, giving them almost unlimited opportunities to harass us. Not being acquainted with this section, while Lee and his generals are entirely at home, we are placed at a great disadvantage. All through the forests are innumerable lanes, cowpaths, and roads, and every dweller hereabouts is more than willing to *lead* Lee's men and to *mislead* ours. What else but defeat can we expect from such conditions?

After we went into bivouac, the 17th was sent on picket, the first time we have been called upon as a regiment since leaving camp. Fifty men, under Captain Richards, were posted on the banks of the Ta, the rest of the regiment held in reserve at the intersection of two roads and close to an old church. One of these roads leads to Spotsylvania, the other to Gordonsville. The night is perfectly quiet, not a sound along the entire line.

# Battle of
# Po River

## May 10 – 11, 1864

*May 10th.*

"The orb of day had hardly struck a match" when we were ordered out and put in a condition to procure an appetite. Although rarely without an appetite for breakfast, I often find myself without any breakfast for my appetite, thus I sometimes make the mistake of confounding matters, as some people mistake potatoes for principle and dyspepsia for deep religious feeling.

The 4th Maine, under Colonel Walker, and the 17th Maine, under Major Briscoe of General Birney's staff, moved out on the Gordonsville Pike to ascertain the position of the Confederate forces in the vicinity of Glady Run, a tributary of the Po River. Having crossed this stream on the ruins of the bridge, the 4th Maine pushed on in the road, while the 17th moved to the left and forward in line of battle. The wisdom of such a movement as this was not apparent to us, for the moment we began to separate, our flanks were in the air. The farther we advanced, the wider grew the gap, our lines being at right angles to each other. If this arrangement was in accordance with Briscoe's original intentions, he is a stupid, drunken cuss, for he was dividing his forces in the presence of the enemy and making a breach between them, which in case of attack invited disasters irreparable.

Of the actual position of Lee's force we had no knowledge. It might be a long way off or it might be close by. Soon after deploying we passed down into a hollow. This was Glady Run, and on the high ground of the other side we saw something that we mistook for Rebel skirmishers. We thought them uncommon civil to allow us to approach so near without making some kind of show of hostility. When we all had crossed the stream, we prepared to charge, but a nearer view showed them to be nothing but stumps, which by some singular circumstance were situated equal distances apart on the end of the hill and all of a line.

This bugbear now disposed of, we moved on and reached a point perhaps a mile and a half from the Po. A clearing showed another run, and we were just starting up an eminence in the woods when suddenly the familiar *Whish! Whish!* and *Zip! Zip!* informed us we had at last stirred up our nest of hornets. We immediately put ourselves in position to engage them. It didn't take long for us to find out that we were working at a decided disadvantage, both as to position and numbers.

They were well-supported and had entrenchments, while we were out on open ground and far in advance of any of our army, our right flank in the air and our left the Devil knew where. Briscoe now urged us on, but we refused to move another step in that direction. He grew livid with rage and swore several shocking oaths in quick succession, but this didn't move us a hair. The bullets became more and more plentiful as we stood behind the trees, trying to make up our minds what to do. To go farther was to invite annihilation of our entire force. To advance was folly; to retreat promised death or wounds at best. Briscoe swore, threatened, entreated. It was no go. He then tried to bully us by drawing his sword and threatening to "cut our d——d heads off," but we didn't budge. We firmly refused to sign our death warrants or be driven or bullied any further by him or any other drunken pimp. Just at this moment, as he was trying to get us to advance again, a bullet struck his horse, nearly unseating him. He kept to the road all this time and would have been brought down but for the fact that the enemy could hear him giving orders to us to go forward, and no doubt they thought we should soon all be their game. Seeing now that they were not likely to accomplish this purpose, they turned on him and peppered his poor old nag. Briscoe wheeled about and put the spurs to what was left of the animal. With surprising agility and brilliancy of execution he made tracks for the rear, yelling as he departed, "You must all now look out for yourselves and, if anyone gets out, he might have a chance to make coffee."

What an incentive to action — the privilege of making coffee. Major Briscoe is one of the last whom I would have thought capable of such a cowardly and unfeeling act. Had I not been an eyewitness and participant, it would be incredible. No thanks to him that we were not shot or gobbled and sent to Richmond to enjoy a spell at Libby Prison or Belle Island.

Thought of the terrors of these dens proved sufficiently stimulating to make us attempt an escape and to succeed. We moved over the ground in a manner calculated to astonish our Southern friends. The Rebs pursued us with all the speed attainable, but we, having so much more at stake, almost *flew*. Also, we had the promise of Briscoe's coffee to spur us on. And we did outrun Johnny Reb and did come first to the river. A goodly portion of our flight was through a section of underbrush so dense a rabbit couldn't have skinnied through without leaving behind most of his hair. By dint of a great deal of puffing, sweating, and blowing we worked out of the thicket.

The Rebs in the meantime had projected themselves through the gap between us and the 4th Maine and seized the road and the crossing. Seeing this, we made no attempt to reach the crossing, but jumped into the stream and made our way across. It may be said that all this scrabble caused us to indulge in sundry unscriptural remarks concerning the Rebels in general and Briscoe in particular. We jumped into the Ta with a strong suspicion that we should sink to rise no more, the water being of that peculiar color that prevents one from seeing the bottom. If we could swim with our duds on, it was well; otherwise we would drown.

The shots of the Rebels grew nearer and nearer and we couldn't stop to deliberate. So in we went, but instead of disappearing beneath the river, we found ourselves standing on the bottom with water only up to our waists. Such a sudden halt was too much; it nearly upset my equilibrium. (I was affected very much like the cow who was struck by a locomotive and thrown into a field nearby. She wasn't hurt, but she was much surprised.) I had on long-legged boots, which soon filled with water. I had to stop and turn it out, thereby exposing my corporeal substance to considerable risk. But no catastrophe came to pass and I was soon out of the way.

We floundered out on the other side, and when Johnny Reb saw we had eluded him, he grew red in the face and commenced to pepper us, even firing at a lot of our wounded who were being brought across. This chivalrous conduct on the part of our Southern "gentlemen" is unbelievable. They call us "vulgar Yankees," yet I never knew a Yankee so vulgar as to fire on wounded men who were being carried from the field.

Captain Richards and the fifty men posted at the bridge fell back and joined us after doing their best to hold the crossing till we could get over. After catching our breath, we moved up and bivouacked in the same place as last night. Barlow's division were the only troops in sight and we were ordered to conform to their movements. Barlow was acting as a decoy to draw the Rebs out so our men could pay them back for our little excursion. We stayed with Barlow's division until it crossed the Po, then decided to find our own and do our fighting with them.

The Rebels were allowed to approach so near us on the other side of the river that we could hear the orders of their officers. As we came over the Po we received a murderous discharge of cannister and spherical case, which rattled over and around us like pebbles in a bladder, tearing the clothes of some and the bodies of others. A fellow in front of me had the flesh torn from his back — as one would strip a salt fish — but he moved right on, apparently unconscious of his hurt.

The enemy seemed to entertain the conceit that they were coming right over the Po as they had the Ta, but they found themselves confronted by a wall of bristling steel and a volley of musketry. They made the most determined efforts to get over, and our men were equally determined that they wouldn't. The fight soon became exceedingly hot and extended down the line. There was a continual roar, like the voice of many waters: the crash of artillery, the yells and cheers of the combatants, the groans and cries of the wounded, and the general confusion of charging and counter-charging. This continued throughout the day. I regard this as one of the hardest days of fighting this army has ever seen. There was no cessation from the time action commenced till darkness mercifully closed this day of slaughter.

It seems as if all Rebeldom concentrated here with the sole purpose of crushing us. How could General Lee, with the meager forces said to be under him, have held and punished an army three times his size? Where was Grant? Where was Meade? Have they no strategy, no plans? If the enemy's loss was as severe as ours, they must be nearly annihilated.

Preparations were made to fall back to Fredericksburg. The road was widened, and other things done to meet an emergency. A number left in the ambulances, which traveled hour after hour, all through the night, in a continual string. Those of us who had been engaged in the affair of the morning became separated from the rest of the division, and the surgeon ordered us to the hospital in the rear, saying, "You boys have done enough for one day." But we desired to find our regiment and didn't want any part of a hospital as long as we could avoid it; the sights and sounds there were too much for any except the strongest nerves. We were finally compelled to give up the search and take a rest. I, for one, hadn't life enough left in me for any further exertion, and I sank down to pass the rest of the day in a little strip of timber close by the Fredericksburg Pike.

The great, dark woods are filled with dead and wounded from both sides. Blue and Gray sink side-by-side in its gloomy thickets and slimy pools. Neither side appears to have gained much from this struggle in the Wilderness[1].

A very sad affair occurred today. The 6th Corps was heavily engaged and met with a great loss in the person of its much respected commander, Major General John Sedgwick, or "Uncle John," as the boys called him.

He was trying to infuse some of his courage into the men of one of his batteries. It was an important position, but sharpshooters had killed nearly all of its gunners. The few remaining knew it was only a question of moments until they would all be down. General Sedgwick stepped up to the gun, remarking, "See, there is no danger here." The words scarce left his mouth when a bullet struck him under the eye and he fell into the arms of a soldier standing nearby. Thus fell one of the best of generals and truest of patriots.

Darkness ended the fighting for this day. Our army didn't fall back as we had feared, but kept its front intact on the Po River. Myself and some others from Company I held our own in the woods and refused to be dislodged. We passed the night here.

## May 11th.

Another day of carnage infernal. Started out this morning to find our command, a portion of which gathered during the night not far from our place of bivouac. A nucleus formed, around which we soon gathered quite a respectable body. Soon after joining them, the division was ordered to move to the front and relieve troops who had been holding some works under a galling fire front and flank. The position could not be abandoned without putting our right in jeopardy, and it must be held until another line could be established.

Our advance was attended with extraordinary danger. The Rebel sharpshooters were posted on the other side of the river in such a manner as to cover our approach no matter *how* we came. An enfilading fire caused any of the troops in the line who had the temerity to raise their heads to sink quickly to the ground. We didn't advance in line of battle, but moved down into a ravine and threw forward one company at a time, double-quick and at trail arms. In this manner the entire line advanced with but small loss. Cy Wardwell, who also went by the alias "Pink Eyes" (bestowed on him by Major West), was shot in the hip. A person with a greater claim to pure and unmitigated cussedness than this same Pink Eyes I have never had the pleasure of meeting.[2]

After getting into these works we found it conducive to longevity to spread ourselves on the ground as thin as the butter on a slice of boarding-house bread. We passed two hours in this "condenser" and then, another line having been formed, General Hooker ordered us out by the left. It was expected that we should lose heavily in doing so, but our loss was quite insignificant, though Lieutenant Richards was severely, perhaps mortally, wounded in the throat. Owing to the lay of the land, we were saved from annihilation. To one not familiar with war, it seems like a Munchausen yarn to say that in the midst of all this death only one man was hit in our company.

A singular incident occurred while we were lying in these works. The writer found a Bible on the ground and was importuned to read something to comfort the men, who felt there was but a step 'twixt them and eternity. I decided to read whatever passage the book should first open to. Singularly enough, it was the most appropriate that could be found even if I'd searched the entire Bible. It ran as follows:

Give ear unto my prayer and hide not thyself from my supplications. Attend unto me, and hear. I mourn in my complaint and make a noise. Because of the voice of the enemy, because of the oppression of the wicked, they cast iniquity upon me, and in wrath they hate me. My heart is sore pained within me, and the terrors of death are fallen upon me. Fearfulness and trembling are come over me, and horror hath overwhelmed me. And I said, O, that I had wings like a dove, for then I would fly away and be at rest. Lo, then would I wander away into the Wilderness. I would hasten my escape from the windy storm and tempest.

This and other selections seemed to comfort some of the men amazingly.

After getting into the new line of works, we passed a most wretched day. It rained and drizzled until mud was the prevailing power, and when darkness set in, it was *black*. We had orders to move about 10 o'clock, but in what direction we could not tell.

Soon after we started, a shell rushed through the air over our heads and with a horrid whirring sound went crashing into the woods in our rear. This was probably a signal for the guidance of the column. We marched for several hours in what appeared to be a southerly direction, and then stumbled into a camp of slumberers. The first indication we had of their presence was a terrific string of impious oaths. We moved right on without pause.

Soon we arrived at another camp and, as they had no fires or sentries posted, we marched over them as well, knocking down stacks of guns and treading on heads and other portions of human anatomy. The air was sulphurous with their responses, but we were in no position to make apologies or arguments, and pushed right on, leaving them to sleep.

About 2 o'clock we struck General Augur's camp and found them all astir. Concluding that they had just come in, we were pleased to consider this an augury that we should have a chance to rest. O vain delusion! They were just breaking camp to follow us.

Hancock marched round to the point where Grant indicated we might make a breach in Lee's lines, near Spotsylvania Court House. The wind sobbed drearily over the meadows and through the trees, rain fell steadily, and the night was so dark men had to almost feel their way.

# Spotsylvania

## May 12 – 16, 1864

*May 12th.*

Hour after hour passed, and daylight began to dawn just as we came to a halt in a low, foggy place, so chilly that our teeth chattered and our frames shook like leaves. The mists of morning were very heavy and settled over us like a pall. About 4 A.M. we formed in line of battle, but no foe was visible. The cold, clammy truth dawned on us that we were not far from the enemy and we would soon lessen the distance.[1]

There we stood in the drizzle, all orders given in whispers, and although we knew we faced a dreadful battle, we were not sorry to hear the voice of Chanticleer, announcing the dawn of a new day. There was something terribly weird in this massing of troops at this time of day, in the hooting of owls as the dark figures of men moved through the pines, in the sobbing of the wind through the wet trees. The order to move to the attack wasn't half so disagreeable as one might think.

In a moment the whole force of men, not less than 20,000, sprang forward and a grand charge began. We have stormed no such formidable entrenchments ever before. The loss of life on our side would have been truly sickening but for the fact that we caught them napping.

The Rebel pickets didn't stop to dispute our passage, but rushed pell mell over the works. We gave them an "all wool" yell and tore after them. It is said that this yell awakens men two miles away. Granting that noise is sometimes quite effective, there are times when silence is better, and this was a case of the latter. We would have lessened our danger if we had abstained from yelling.

It was seemingly but a moment before the first line was in our possession. The Rebels were now awake and had several lines and crosslines of works. Could we hold what we had? For a time it seemed as if only a negative answer could be given. "Here for ten minutes war never saw more terrible fighting," says one eyewitness.

We had gained a foothold, and if not dislodged, we would soon be on Lee's flank. Every Confederate realized the desperate situation and every Union soldier knew what was involved. For a time, every soldier was a *fiend*. The attack was fierce — the resistance fanatical. We captured one of their strongest entrenchments, but it was done in a tempest of iron and lead, in a rain of fire.

We sought shelter from the storm behind stumps and trees, anything that offered a suggestion of safety. Many of those most in advance crouched on this side of the Confederate works, and when joined by others, moved over and made a feeble attempt to carry a second line. It was useless. The force of the blow was spent, so far as Hancock's troops were concerned. If we held our own, we should do well, and we were soon tested in this regard, as Lee concentrated his forces with a view to hurling all he could spare against this spot to recapture it.

We took 3,000 prisoners, forty pieces of artillery, and two generals — Stewart and Johnson. Two privates from our regiment captured Stewart and Johnson and immediately escorted them to General Hancock. Stewart had been a classmate of Hancock's at West Point, and when brought into his presence was quite crestfallen. Hancock, to relieve their embarrassment, stepped forward and extended his hand, saying, "How are you, Stewart?"

Stewart declined the proferred hand, saying, "I am *General* Stewart of the Confederate army, and under the circumstances I decline your hand."

Hancock replied, "Under any *other* circumstances, I should not have offered it."

Matters soon became gloriously mixed, and it was impossible to find anything resembling organization. A few here, a few there, fighting under anything or anybody, or nobody, or not at all. The provost guard did all in their power to arrest stragglers and runaways — that is, within certain limits. They didn't dare get too near to risk their carcasses in such a melée. After a while, finding that there was no probability of any further organized attack and not caring to continue in the desultory mess going on in front, I meandered up the hill to the Lendrom house and sought lodgings for the night in the shed.

But I anticipate matters slightly, as there was much desperate fighting between the charge of the morning and the selection of lodgings in the afternoon. The Rebels fought like devils, seeming to despise danger. Before 10 A.M. they made no less than eight charges to retake the salient, showing the tremendous importance of the place. At one time they came on flying *our* colors. We held them at every point and made them pay dearly for their attempts.

We were held in a vise. We certainly couldn't advance, to retire was almost as difficult. We did all that any body of troops could do or would do under like conditions. We held our own, but to do this amounted to nothing.

The 6th Corps did arrive, but it was too late so far as making an advance on the second line. The entire Rebel Army was on the alert, and the weight of it concentrated on this portion of the line. Lee was determined to retake the "Horse Shoe" [Mule Shoe].[2] Hancock's determination was no less rigid. To extricate himself from the trap without a fearful loss of life while daylight lasted was not possible.

And so for the entire day the fiercest fighting waged; the oldest soldier has never witnessed its like. Lee's forces made charge after charge. Lines didn't give way, they *melted* away. The dead lay in heaps and others took protection behind them. Pandemonium swept right and left, and the earth was literally drenched in blood. Confederates sprang over the works and fought with the bayonet and clubbed musket till they were pinned to the earth. Federals hurled themselves over and pushed the lines back a few rods, but were soon swallowed up by the rebound.

From daylight till dark this terrible fighting went on without intermission. An attack was made on Lee's right and left, but he paid no attention, knowing they were only feints, and he didn't dare draw a man away from Hancock's front. Hancock sent Brooks's brigade to assist the 6th Corps when it was hard-pressed. It had just been served with fifty rounds of ammunition. It rushed to the front with a yell, and in ten minutes lost 110 men. Who will say this is not carnage infernal? This is only a sample of the day's events, and nothing but the arrival of darkness prevented much more.

When the fight waxed fiercest around the Horse Shoe, a section of artillery rushed up and unlimbered within pistol shot of the Rebels. Before even the second shot was fired, twelve of the artillerists had been mowed down. In another ten minutes, horses and men were so nearly wiped out that the cannon had to be drawn back by hand.

All around that salient was a seething, bubbling, roaring hell of hate and murder. In that baleful glare men didn't look like men. Some had lost or thrown away hats and coats. Some were gashed and cut, and looked like tigers hunted to cover. Darkness alone brought an end to the carnage, and men who had scarce tasted food for twenty-four hours, or slept for twice that time, dropped to the ground. "Sleep, the twin sister of Death" could not be distinguished from him now as they lay side-by-side on the wet, cold bosom of Mother Earth. Not wet with water alone. War is a leveler, like death; the best and the meanest blood here mingled.

Than General Hancock, there is no greater. Yet today I made the amusing discovery that he has *lice*. It was with a species of profound rapture that this truth dawned upon me. While taking his lunch of hardtack and coffee this morning, he became quite animated. The cause of this was an insect, and an order for a "search and seizure" was immediately issued. It proved to be one of the largest specimens of louse flesh known to naturalists. For size, it was in keeping with the general's magnificent physique. (If, as has been asserted, "all flesh is grass," General Hancock may be said to be a load of hay.)

But these bloody precincts are not the place to indulge in seeming levity. This has been a most awful day, and if there has been any benefit commensurate with the loss of life and limbs, I cannot see it. This is all the comment I have to offer on this day's work.

## May 13th.

In the morning we discovered that Lee's lines have been shortened and strengthened, leaving us in possession of "the Angle"[3] and of more dead than we have ever seen. A large detail was sent out to bury them — a very disagreeable duty.

After attending to our dead we returned to our regiment. Our division was ordered to the left of the Angle and remained there till near nightfall, when we moved to the extreme right and threw up breastworks on the flank. We'd just completed them and thought we were safe for the night when we again moved to the left, and passed the night. This moving from right to left, and left to right, must be what one writer has reference to when he speaks of Grant as, "Raving up and down the line."

Our force was strengthened tonight by the arrival of the Corcoran Legion.[4] We were mighty glad to see them, although they were not ready for action till the priest had absolved them. Although I take no stock in this performance, under the circumstances it was quite impressive, and their chaplain came much nearer the front than most dare to. But I don't blame them much, for chaplains have no real business at the front in time of action.

## May 14th.

We were moved to the left and massed in rear of the 9th Corps, which was ordered to assault the Rebel works. But soon we found we had "changed ends," and if any charging were done, *we* would do it. The 9th Corps had been quietly removed and we were now at the front, with skirmishers out. We waited in line of battle an hour or so, advancing a short distance without discovering the enemy. We soon called in our skirmishers and fell back to a quiet place and passed the day.

We stood sorely in need of both quiet and rest, having been continually on the march and fight since the night of the third of May. My endurance has been so outrageously taxed that I sometimes envy those who have laid down their lives; they sweetly sleep while we toil on.

At night our regiment was sent on picket, and after we went out our division (Birney's) moved again. Mighty sure we are that General Hancock will never be accused of that masterly inactivity that has been charged to McClellan. We move so often that it is no easy matter to keep run of our command unless we stay with it every minute. It is suspected that the Rebels are preparing a demonstration on some weak point in our line, or going to retire from here altogether. The losses on our side thus far are terrible beyond imagination. Our division left camp with 7,000 men and we now are reduced to a skeleton of 2,500. Such decimation of our ranks and the fact that we are not more than twenty miles from our first encounter has had the most pernicious effect on morale.

This has been an example of Grant's hammering generalship. That he does understand the flank business is abundantly attested, because he did flank the enemy at Mine Run. *All* he will gain will be by outwitting the enemy with flank maneuver. Then why all this slaughter?

### May 15th.

Were on picket all day and expected to remain there till we were set upon by rebellious subjects of Uncle Sam bent on homicidal intent. We saw some of them hanging around as though desiring an introduction or something. If they came any nearer, we could promise them a cordial reception. Along toward night we were relieved, just in time for other troops to tangle with our visitors.

We had just reached our division inside the works when the Johnnies appeared on the ground, making hideous sounds as they came (this being considered a very important factor in Rebel tactics). Our pickets fell back promptly and tried to draw them out, but they wouldn't come, except to the edge of the field in front of us, where they stood and grimaced and yelled like monkeys.

Our situation today is somewhat peculiar. We are facing the same way as the Confederates were on the 12th, and they are now menacing us from the same direction from which we then threatened them. Having failed to get in here by frontal assaults, they are now trying to get in from the rear, but we have anticipated their designs and conformed our lines to this expected order of things.

This must be the most valuable piece of real estate in Virginia, judging from the effort put forth to possess it. We pass the night in the Rebel works, which are divided off into square pens for the better protection of the inmates.

### May 16th.

The 2nd and 6th Corps massed on the Rebel flank, while the others moved off in a southerly direction. Here now was another flank movement, which compelled Mr. Rebel to get up and dust. Why this wasn't done some days ago is a problem whose solution I cannot undertake. So Spotsylvania is ours, and not by might, but by the simplest rule of warfare.

# Battle of Cold Harbor

## May 17 – June 9, 1864

*May 17th.*

We remained there until midnight, when we moved out under the starlit sky, and no halt was made until this morning, when we hauled up not far from a plantation known as the Anderson House.

Orders came to lay aside the emblems of war and rest our weary carcasses. We have been in harness since the third of May, night and day. Nearly two weeks in the immediate presence of death and the enemy, and in that time have scarcely had our clothes or equipment loosened, or our guns out of our hands. We haven't had the shoes off our feet, and a little *ablution* would be worth more than all the *absolution* of all the priests in Christendom.

Since this campaign commenced there has been no fooling, no boys' play. It has been a campaign of earnest, deadly combat, and he who hasn't had his fill of blood and thunder hasn't kept with his command, or else he is a hog. I have seen in the public prints many expressions like the following: "eager for the fray," "spoiling for a fight," "anxious to meet the foe," "the army is all enthusiasm." I shall knock the romance all out of this business by remarking that these are only gush from the pen of a wretched scribbler who knows not what kind of gibberish he is dispensing. These phrases look well in print — much better, indeed, than does the language of the real military man when he sees them paraded as *facts.*

It is quite the common thing to hear people speak flippantly of a small fight or skirmish in which "only a few" have fallen. How quickly their tune would change if one of that few was their child or their brother! This is the only way to gauge sorrows and losses: take them home and make them a personal matter. Battles must cost the life and limbs of someone, and to that someone, though ten thousand should fall, it can be no more disastrous. Each one dies for himself, and the pangs of death are not mitigated by going in a crowd.

*May 18th.*

Nothing worthy of notice. We did an amount of resting that would seem incredible to anyone who doesn't know how tired we are. We washed a little, slept much, and instituted a war of extermination against the ubiquitous louse. As for eating, we ate all we could get our hands on. This, however, is not an implication that we were gourmandizing, for the country doesn't furnish much.

### May 19th.

Passed most of the day quietly until 5 P.M., when we heard heavy musketry fire in the direction of Fredericksburg. While cudgeling our brains to think what it could be, we received an order to "fall in immediately in light marching order." Fortunately for our comfort, we gave this order the most liberal interpretation and took along what we could.

We found the scene of conflict a short distance away on the Fredericksburg Turnpike. A portion of Ewell's corps had gained a position in our rear where our wagon train is in park, and the Rebels, inspired by thoughts of full bellies, had attacked our forces. They were wading into the 1st Maine Heavy Artillery. The 1st Heavies were 1800 strong and presented a splendid front to the foe — much larger than any brigade of ours — but this was their first experience on the battlefield and they didn't understand how to take advantage of the situation. Being novices in the art of war, they thought it cowardly to lie down, so the Johnnies were mowing them flat. Had our arrival been delayed only a short time, they would have been nearly annihilated. The Rebel loss was insignificant, indeed I don't know that they lost any until our arrival. Being simple and cowardly enough to lie down and take advantage of the situation, we lost but two men in the time the other regiment had lost over 200. We not only took advantage of trees and hillocks, but we dug trenches with our tin plates and bayonets.

No less than four attempts were made to pierce our lines before morning, but we resisted successfully and gave not an inch of ground. Sometime after the wee small hours, the Rebs stampeded, leaving their dead, wounded, and vedettes on the ground for us to care for. The latter were asleep when we became acquainted with them, little dreaming it was the voice of the enemy in their ears. We just followed down the line and scooped them in. They woke up sufficiently to know that the order to "fall in!" came from Yankee lips, not their own officials. We captured not less than 500 men in this way and left the dead and wounded on the field, the latter being no better than dead.

### May 20th.

Finding no other sign of the enemy, about 10 o'clock we were ordered into camp. In doing so, we passed over the field where the 1st Maine made their first fight, and here we found an excellent chance to replenish our wardrobes. They had just come from the defenses of Washington and had several changes of clothing and diverse other extras.

Before reaching camp we passed by General Grant's headquarters, where about 2000 prisoners were lying around loose. One young upstart whose vealiness stuck out at all corners informed us that "we'uns would get terribly punished if we persisted in following General Lee." This specimen of juvenility was a more suitable subject for a primary school than for the army. However, many of the Confederate soldiers are of this type, while another large squad are nearly old enough to graduate from life's school.

We remained in camp just long enough to get dinner, then moved round into a grove in rear of the division hospital. Here we stayed till midnight, when we struck out again. None could tell where morning would find us.

### May 21st.

At daybreak we halted at a crossroad near Massaponax Church, only ten miles from Fredericksburg. We can't get away from Fredericksburg, no matter how far we march! After breakfast we resumed our march and during the forenoon crossed the Richmond and Fredericksburg Railroad at a point called Guinea Station. This was where Stonewall

Jackson crossed the boundary line between this world and the next and uttered the words, "Let us cross over the river, and rest under the trees." We are mighty glad he isn't here now to bother us.

The next place we struck was Bowling Green, a very pretty little village surrounded by beautiful farming country. At this town we found a jail with four prisoners in it, sentenced to death. We liberated them and did some other things not to the liking of the citizenry. We also found a lot of hams here, which we appropriated to the use of the government.

An apothecary shop was gutted because we disliked the chin music of its proprietor. His family had also taken the bucket from the well so that we could get no water, and refused to produce it. An examination of that shop after we paid our respects showed that they were not as smart as they thought. We stuffed our haversacks with medicines until we resembed walking apothecary shops. Later, as I was overhauling my store of drugs, with a view of handing them over to the surgeon, Colonel Merrill reprimanded me, saying, "It is no part of a soldier or a man to rob these impecunious people of medicines." This was a deuced strong reflection on my manhood, and I proceeded to make some very pointed remarks concerning a couple of ducks that the colonel's cook was at that very moment preparing for his palate. I see no great difference between the sins of stealing medicines or ducks, but Colonel Merrill is a lawyer, and he doubtless can discriminate.

After resting awhile — long enough for the colonel to dispose of his ducks and his scruples — we crossed the Mattapony River at Milford's Station. As the foe is supposed to be near, the first troops over formed in line of battle while the rest of us massed in rear of them and quietly passed the night.

### May 22nd.

Sunday. Advanced about a mile and threw up some breastworks. After this, we were set to cutting slashing, although there is no need of it. (Lee's army is at Chesterfield, about ten miles away, and in no danger of attacking us.)

### May 23rd.

At daylight we were in harness and soon came to "Po City," a busy, bustling place of four log huts and a couple of sheds. The entire population (two women) turned out and received us with arms akimbo. If they'd known of our approach, it is probable we should have received a regular ovation of decayed hen fruit. We passed through the "city" in good shape and continued our march until noon without discovering any signs of the enemy.

Marching a mile or two farther, we came upon the 5th Corps in line of battle. We formed in rear of them, but were ordered to the front. Doing as directed, we moved out beyond them and formed in line in a belt of woods, in front of which was a large clearing rising slightly to a crest and then falling away to the North Anna River. On top of this crest stood a body of Confederates who disputed our further progress. Over this river they had some very formidable works. As this was a position of importance, we could expect fierce resistance.

As soon as we were all in line, a charge was ordered and executed. A grand rush was made for the crest, and it was but a few seconds' work to cause a radical change in the enemy's position. We were soon studying the pattern of their coat tails and we went in hot pursuit under a pitiless storm of shot, shell, and we know what not. Our momentum wasn't checked in the least by the fusillade, and we pushed onto the banks of the river.

With our being so close onto the Johnnies, few of them could gain the bridge so they jumped into the river. Some succeeded in swimming across, but most fell under our fire. It is safe to infer that few of those on the northern bank of the river escaped. Company I lost one man killed and one slightly bruised. This is phenomenal when I remember the tempest of old iron we waded through.

We lay on the bank of the stream and blazed away till dark, then moved back onto the crest of the hill and threw up some works, which we occupied the rest of the night.

Our 1st Brigade crossed over at Taylor's Bridge and gained a footing on the enemy's flank, causing them to vacate their front line. We thought this was key to their entire line, but in this we were seriously mistaken. They had not less than three lines of works, in a peculiar formation like a letter V with the point on the river. Although the 2nd Corps was on one side and the 5th Corps on the other, the point wouldn't let go its hold on the river, and we couldn't seem to make any headway.

IN THE TRENCHES. *Harper's Pictorial History of the Civil War.*

### May 24th.

All the forenoon we were digging and strengthening the line of works we had thrown up. Contrary to all expectation, the Confederates didn't disturb us although we were within easy range of their guns. Perhaps they had no ammunition to spare.

At noon we were ordered forward. We left the works and double-quicked to the bridge. Just before we reached it, the Rebel batteries opened a furious cannonade, but we passed over to the southern side and formed in line of battle. Batteries were arranged with special reference to this bridge, making a crossing extra hazardous, but a portion of the corps was over there and must be supported. We effected a crossing in the face of a murderous tempest of missiles and without losing a man; nor was the bridge damaged, strangely enough, even though a large number of guns were trained on it and they hit all around it within a radius of a mile.

At 2 P.M. we were ordered to make an advance, and a dangerous one it promised to be, for we were literally "in the face and eyes of the enemy." Had we gone forward in the usual line of battle, there would have been some cheering items for the Richmond daily "wallpapers." Our method was to push forward one company at a time, thus attracting less attention. The Rebels also might have some doubts as to our real intentions. As each company found its place in line, it commenced to entrench and was soon under cover. Thus our entire line was advanced to the front an eighth of a mile, and our regimental loss was one: Lieutenant Noyes of Company G. A solid shot passed through his body, and, astonishing as it may appear, he lived for over an hour afterward.

After this line of works was completed, we remained in possession of them the rest of the day and night, and drew rations. After dark another line of works was thrown up nearer the front. This last line took under its protection the house of a divine who must be a person of "culture and means." He and his family had found that his duty lay in another direction, and at the first gunshot had left precipitately.

This man of God has not been slow in securing a share of the *world's* goods. He probably has more business capacity than faith. His effects were all there in the house, and we could pick out such as suited our needs. I fell in love with a choice bit of china plate, and a union was effected in a few seconds without benefit of clergy. It is in keeping with our mission to destroy his kind of theology as quickly as possible. A theology that sanctions slavery savors too strongly of Satan to be tolerated. The religion of Jesus Christ has nothing in common with the auction block or the lash. Two-hundred years of slavery have not elevated the nigger or his master. The only advancement has been in the way of *un*natural selection; the line of demarcation between white and black is not as positive as true virtue demands, but is dimmed by a kind of neutral tint that cannot but be regarded with suspicion.

By reference to my map I found we are now only seventeen miles from Richmond. So, we are rapidly nearing the Rebel stronghold and might reasonably expect to be thundering at its doors in a few days, or weeks at the most.

### May 25th.

Laid here nearly till night, when we moved in rear of the 9th Corps, where it was expected the Rebs might strike after dark. We weren't at all sorry that they chose not to, as it was a pokerish hole. They could have massed a heavy force in front under cover of a dense growth and rushed us before we could duck them.

### May 26th and 27th.

It was afternoon when we were ordered to relieve the 9th Corps from the front. This position we occupied till midnight, when we silently moved away. We recrossed the North Anna, burned Taylor's Bridge, and started again down the flank. By this time it was daylight and we halted in the road for the teams to pass. This flank movement, like all the others, is because we can't walk over Lee's army and must therefore go round it. It is hoped that this move will place us very near Richmond, and as soon as the teams were out of the way we started. We didn't stop long enough even to make coffee or eat. We hauled up in an open lot after dark and were told that we had fifteen minutes to make coffee. This was truly a refreshing piece of intelligence! Here we were at night, in enemy country, with neither wood nor water.

Soon after this the column started, and most of it marched until midnight. Gus Bradbury, Jack Brine, and the writer formed a partnership to promote the interest of the trio named. We halted *our* column and decided to have refreshments of hard tack, pork, and coffee. Sadly, the last item had to be dispensed with, we having neither matches nor water. So we lay down in the leaves and slept like babes in the woods.

### May 28th and 29th.

Our trio started out in search of the army. We conjectured, and rightly so, that they were not many miles ahead. We started in the direction we supposed they had taken, but after only a couple of miles we came to a corner. Now we were in a dilemma, for there was no sign to indicate which road the column had taken. We deliberated a moment and then decided to go to the right. We happened to strike it right and soon came to the headquarters of our division. We didn't arrive any too soon, for the head of the column was just starting out as we came in. We marched until 3 P.M., when we crossed the Pamunkey and massed in rear of the 6th Corps.

A line of earthworks was soon in progress, for we didn't feel safe without it. We stayed here till noon of the 29th, when we moved out onto the Richmond Turnpike. Here again we started a line of works, but moved on before completing them. (We worked hard enough to have *owned* them.) A cavalry reconnaissance had discovered that we could advance a piece further to Hawes's Store. We did so, and found no resistance.

We set a lively pace, trying to keep up with the cavalry. After a mile or so, we turned square to the right and went through fields and woods, pastures and bogs. Another mile brought us to the enemy's works across the Totopotomoy Creek — an insignificant stream with marshy banks, difficult to get over. Of course, the first thing we did was to throw up some works and throw out some pickets, then lay down for the night, as we had but little else to do. We also had but little to eat, and the question of food has become as serious with us as with the Rebels. We captured one Reb not long since whose entire stock of food was a haversack of meal, the dryest kind of fodder, with nothing whatever to season it.

### May 30th.

We had no fighting today and rested until night, when a picket detail was called for from our regiment. Some of us contrived to get lost on the way to division headquarters but managed to find our way back to camp. About 10 o'clock Burnside, who is on our left, opened on the enemy in fine fusillade with some mortars. This set off picket firing, which lasted all night. The lines here are very close, and mortars are the most effective weapon for such short range.

### May 31st.

No cessation of hostilities. We endured and returned the enemy's fire till noon, when we were ordered forward to stop it or make it worse. We moved out on the right, crossed the creek, and after a short struggle, pierced the Confederate line. However, as we were not supported on either flank, we very soon discovered that we had no business on that side of the stream, and if we didn't get back we should arrive in Richmond several days in advance of the army. Our movement to the rear was executed with great dash. In fact, we nearly dashed our d——d brains out, getting out of this scrape without being gobbled. The row was short and sweet, and we warmed ourselves up in good shape.

At night we were back holding the line we adopted the day we came here. In addition to this setback, we are hungry and despondent. For several days we have been getting what Paddy gave his drum: hard knocks and nothing to eat. Rations of all kinds are difficult to obtain, and for the past week we have been hard put to keep body and soul together.

### June 1st and 2nd.

The first sound that greeted our ears this morning was a most dismal howl on our right and in front, quickly followed by the most scalp-lifting, blood-curdling shrieks. We found that it all emanated from a drummer of the 4th Maine who thought it would be an excellent joke to dress up in a suit of gray that he'd come across. Supposing him to be a genuine "butternut," our men commenced to pepper him. Hence the yelling and screaming. Some of the troops fell in and took arms, thinking there was an attack. It was a decidedly serious joke, one that nearly cost him his life and undoubtedly taught that sheepskin pounder a lesson he will not soon forget.

After this rumpus, quiet reigned. We were too tired and hungry to make any noise or exert ourselves. At night were transferred to the 1st Brigade and started off on another flank movement, marching the entire night.

There was no halt at morning. We kept right on until about noon, when we hauled up at a place called Cold Harbor. It was anything but cold now. We formed line of battle under a hill and remained till after dark, when we moved up nearer the front and were posted in the woods as a reserve. A drizzling rain set in, much to our annoyance.

### June 3rd.

This morning at daylight, Barlow's division (to which Birney's was acting as a reserve) charged the Confederates and were repulsed with frightful slaughter. We fell back to an open space in rear as the ground around us was ripped with shot and shell. Why we were not torn asunder is one of those unfathomable mysteries of war. We dug holes in the ground and, ostrichlike, hid our heads, leaving the rest of our carcasses exposed to any missile coming our way.

It was reported that Hancock's corps lost 3000 men here in ten minutes. Our company lost only two. If this estimate of Hancock's loss is correct, this is worse than Spotsylvania.

No further attempt to advance was indulged in. Not that Grant wouldn't have continued the work of slaughter, but the officers and men in the ranks refused to budge. We were tired of charging earthworks. Many soldiers expressed freely their scorn of Grant's alleged generalship, which consists of launching men against breastworks. It is well known that *one* man behind works is as good as *three* outside the works.

This fight was near Gaine's Mill, a place made famous by a great battle fought by McClellan in 1862. The old soldiers among us recognize many familiar spots. It is a dreadful hole.

Some of us had to go out on picket. We sought shelter behind several rocks and thus avoided receiving a deposit of lead in our carcasses.

### June 4th.

We remained in this line of works all day and apprehended as much danger from filth as from bullets. There is only one redeeming quality here — an apple orchard. Also, in the attic of an old house nearby we found something resembling beans. A further acquaintance confirmed our suspicions as to age. We tried to render them edible by boiling, but one might as well boil shoe pegs.

Near to, and belonging to this house, is a log pen occupied by what was once a human being, but now the saddest and most hopeless wreck I ever saw. His food has to be passed through a door near the roof. No clothing can be kept on him and no one can approach him. His hair and nails are of an almost incredible length, and he reeks with filth. I hope some merciful missile will find its way into his hut and end his misery.

At night a great many pickets went out, and such dodging and ducking was enough to throw one all out of joint. The enemy seemed to be everywhere, and we didn't know which way to turn. Sometime after dark we were ordered in and told to report to our regiment, an almighty indefinite order, for we had no more idea of its whereabouts than we did as to when Queen Victoria last pared her corns. Stacy and myself decided to stay put until morning and seek the regiment by daylight, there being a series of corps, division, and brigade badges by which we can find any command without asking questions. It is a difficult undertaking to find one's command after dark in an enemy's country. Some of whom you inquire don't know, others don't care, and a few have just enough pure cussedness in them to delight in misdirecting you.

### June 5th.

Soon as the light was strong enough we struck out for our regiment and soon ran afoul of them near where we were laying a few days before. Nothing unusual transpired during the day except for the transfer of the 3rd Maine veterans to our regiment. Those who won't re-enlist are to go home in a few days, and a happy lot of mortals they are. It makes me positively sick to see them! My term of service will not expire until August 6, 1865, a trifle over a year from now. The way things look now, it is a ten-to-one chance that I will expire before my term does.

Along toward night we moved down the line by the flank and came to some breastworks built by our troops two years ago. We didn't occupy them, but moved out to the front and commenced to march and countermarch in the dark. No one seemed to know where we were, or why we were there. It was a miracle we weren't gobbled, wandering around in the dark, with Johnny Reb all around us. I venture the assertion that old Tommy Eagan was at the bottom of this ridiculous order and that a large quantity of whiskey had recently disappeared down his Irish gullet. (This same Eagan is a firm believer in the doctrine that there is no sense in buying meat, since half of it is bone, when one can buy whiskey with *no* bones.)

After doing this for an hour or so, we formed in line in the woods and were ordered to throw up some works. A few of us did try to do so, apprehensive of an attack, but others declared they wouldn't turn a spade till they'd had some sleep.

### June 6th.

Went out on an exploring expedition and soon came to an old house, which upon being demolished showed, to our astonishment and joy, a lot of sweet potatoes. How they escaped notice from the famished Rebs is beyond my knowledge. By a most singular coincidence, we drew fresh meat in our rations also, so we feasted on our potatoes and beef.

After strengthening the inner man, we went out to strengthen our line of works, and kept at it all the forenoon. In the afternoon a detail was sent to bury the dead killed on the third. All firing was suspended while this melancholy work went on. The enemy's pickets are very near us here but seem to be peaceably inclined, giving us but little trouble.

### June 7th.

We put in the day adding to the works as if we intend to stay awhile. The Confederates were in sight the whole length of the line, except in front of our division where there is a heavy pine growth.

While lying down reading this morning, I got wind of something that caused my salivary glands to react and my heart to palpitate. It was whispered that there is a sour apple tree flourishing nearby. In my haste, I ignored danger and was soon greeted with the *Whish! Whish!* of the festive rifle ball. I concluded it was less disagreeable to die by the bullet than by scurvy, which is making such inroads into my health, and managed to pick a quantity of the fruit. Fruit and potatoes are said to be the best remedies for that malady.

### June 8th.

Our labors today were similar to those of yesterday. The line of works we are building bid fair to extend all the way to Richmond, if our men aren't all picked off by sharpshooters first. Several men inside the works were killed, while the pickets, who were much nearer the foe, were unmolested. There seemed to be a fatality lurking in certain spots along our line and no one could tell just where the missiles came from, except that it was from above every time. It was decided that this must be stopped. Accordingly, one of our "independents" was invited to reconnoiter the spot. He betook himself a short distance to the rear and watched. It wasn't long before Mr. Reb made his whereabouts known, but he was so covered with leaves that no eye could discern him. Our sharpshooter drew a bead on him and something dropped, that something being a six-foot nigger whose weight wasn't less than 300 pounds.

This put an end to the firing and we soon commenced trading instead. The Rebels have plenty of tobacco but precious little of anything else. Rations have been scarce for us too, for no readily apparent reason, so we cannot let them have much.

When we have nothing else to eat, we fall back on the following decoction: Take a pail of water and broil it until it is brown on both sides. Pour into this one bean. Simmer this a while. If it will not simmer, it is too rich and you must put in more water.

*June 9th.*

About the same routine as yesterday. It is really getting dull after the fierce activity of the last five weeks. Not that we don't need rest and quiet, and would be glad to have it under other circumstances, but we all well know that the rest we are enjoying can only be for a very brief period. Suspense is oftentimes far worse than action.

And action must come. Richmond must be ours. Grant promised he would have it on the 4th of July.

# The Siege of Petersburg Begins

## June 10 – August 6, 1864

### June 10th.

Quiet up and down the line. There was some picket firing, otherwise no one would have a shadow of suspicion that two immense armies are confronting each other. Firing on our front has ceased, so we go in and out as we please. Extended our works to the left.

### June 11th.

All quiet on our front, except the sighing of gentle breezes through the pines. One year ago this very day we broke camp for the Gettysburg campaign. Though we are far short of our goal, still it seems that military matters in Virginia now wear a more cheerful aspect for us. A year ago Southern feet were on our soil, and it looked dark, for Gettysburg was the darkest hour this nation has ever seen. But it was the darkness before the dawn, as Lee's cause has waned from that battle, and he has never won a decisive victory on Northern soil. We have faith that the proud bird whose wings spread over our standard will yet have the filthy secession buzzard under his feet.

### June 12th.

Nothing aggressive on this part of the line. At night a lot of us went on picket, and another flank movement began. We were drawn inside the works at midnight, and after all the troops passed we struck out down the road toward Richmond.

We overtook the column about five in the morning while they were halted for breakfast at St. James Church, a little wooden structure in the forest. The church was occupied by soldiers, some of whom had disfigured the walls with obscene language and pictures. The most conspicuous decoration was a toast to General Grant, nominating him for the presidency.

It ran thus: "U.S. Grant: May he be hung, drawn, and quartered: Hung with the laurels of victory, drawn in the chariot of peace, and quartered in the White House at Washington." When my one good optic fell on the first part of this sentiment, I thought that some infernal crayback had been making free with our Ulysses' name, but further perusal allayed my suspicions.

Our coffee was barely cool before we were ordered to go on, and on we went, coming up with the advance about 10 o'clock. We passed today the old, tumble-down cottage of one of the signers of the Declaration of Independence, Stephen Hopkinson. How the old man's bones would rattle in his box if he could see how fast old

Virginia is going to the "Demnition Bow Wows" in her blind infatuation for states' rights. She has become so stricken and poor that it will take a hundred years for her to recover.

We continued our march all day, passing through some fine country and some as mean as ever a grasshopper starved on.

### June 13th.

Started this morning from a place, name unknown, if indeed it had any. Virginia, as indeed the entire South, is very indefinite as to localities. Settlements are scarce, towns and cities fearfully so, and the nearest one can identify location is to signify the county or court house. In our wanderings today we crossed White Oak Swamp and the Richmond–York River Railroad, the latter near Savage Station, the scene of one of McClellan's engagements during the famous "Seven-Day Fight." Continuing our journey, we came to and crossed the Chickahominy at Meadow Bridge. Soon after, we went into camp on top of a hill. (History is repeating itself with a vengeance, as we are following McClellan's old route with great fidelity.)

### June 14th.

Had orders to get ready to move about 9 A.M. We had no idea we were so near the James River. Although we had observed masts in the distance, we had supposed they belonged to transports in some of the tributaries of the James. Our surprise may be imagined then, when after a short march, we found ourselves on the bank of this historic stream and a number of transports awaiting us. Our division was soon aboard one, the *Eliza Hancox*, and in a jiffy was landed on the south side of the river at Wind Mill Point on the plantation of the Rebel General Wilcox. After we were across, we moved up to the house of that celebrity and went into bivouac.

Some indulged in a "swash in the wet." Others found a more congenial occupation harvesting the general's abundant supply of early vegetables. We had to tear down a large barn to procure wood enough to cook these treats. We cannot eat the stuff raw; we have already perpetrated outrages enough on our stomachs.

Spent a very comfortable night. How could we possibly endure this infernally hot, humid climate without the deliciously cool evenings?

### June 15th.

We were ordered to get out at daylight as we had no rations. General Hancock didn't move with his accustomed celerity. About 10 A.M. we started on the road to Petersburg, fourteen miles away. General Hancock's instructions were wrong, and he stumbled and blundered around so that we didn't reach the vicinity of the city till dark. We then seemed to be wandering around without any aim. We marched and countermarched until we began to think we would pass the entire night in this way.

We finally located near some heavy earthwork captured by Butler this P.M., and having drawn rations, lay down for the night.

This is a very powerful line of works, comparable to the defenses of Richmond, and if the Johnnies can't hold them, they must be poorly manned.[1]

All night we heard the whistling of the engines as the cars came from Richmond loaded with troops for Lee. Surely he now knows that Petersburg, not Richmond, is Grant's objective. By morning the works at Petersburg were fully manned and bristling with bayonets ready to deal out death. Our feelings may be imagined as we listened and reflected that every carload of Rebels is so much the more for us to contend with.

## June 16th.

This morning showed us our close proximity to some towering earthworks — the ones captured yesterday. I was admiring the valor of our troops who had captured them when my cogitations were brought to an inglorious termination by the explosion of a shell over our heads. Our Southern friends were opening the ball.

Captain John Perry, who was in command of the regiment, was gouged in the leg and compelled to retire. A few others were disabled and went to the rear. Captain Ben Pennel now assumed command, and we earnestly pray that he will prove an abler leader than Perry. A worse one he cannot be.

At 6 A.M. we moved to the left and formed in line in front of a Confederate redoubt not far from the Avery House and near where the Rebel works covered the Petersburg and Norfolk Railroad. We supposed we were to entrench there, and this was General Hancock's order. The idea of deliberately inviting annihilation was not our intention, but old Tommy Eagan, of our brigade, thought differently. He desires two things: to add another star on his shoulder straps, and to wreak vengeance on his old regiment, the 40th New York (or Mozart Regiment), whose term of service expires in two days. Some members of this outfit have been obnoxious to the gallant Tommy, and probably he thought it an excellent chance to repay them.

As soon as we had formed in line among the felled timber and stumps, he ordered us forward to attack a breastwork well-manned and containing artillery. The Confederates didn't wait for us to commence the attack, but opened on us with extraordinary briskness. And here for the first and only time I saw a cannon ball in motion. Stacy and the writer, standing side by side, were looking intently at the Rebel works when we saw a puff of smoke, and in it we could see the ball. This was so fascinating that we kept our eyes on it although it was coming straight for our heads; we were riveted to the spot. All of this occurred in a very few seconds. Before I could utter a word, it passed between our heads and bedded itself in the stumps behind us.

The charging party consisted of the 40th New York, the 99th Pennsylvania, and the 17th Maine. As the 40th has but two days more to put in, they decided to place themselves in as safe a place as possible and only swung around under the cover of the line of works in our front. They had small notion of butting their heads against Rebel shells in such a senseless movement. Tommy Eagan is a third rate idiot. It is a wonder that the men didn't rebel and not move at all, and a still greater wonder that so few were wounded or killed. Circumstances favored us somewhat and we took advantage of the situation, hiding our heads behind stumps and logs, and thus sheltering ourselves from the storm of shot and shell.

We failed to drive the foe from their entrenchments. We crawled back to our starting place and again formed in line, supposing we were to entrench as General Hancock ordered. But old Tommy gave another order to advance! The 40th New York just swung itself round by a left wheel and took refuge behind an old line of works.

We swung over another works, and here occurred some grand and lofty tumbling. We piled over the works in a most unmilitary manner. On the side toward the Rebels was a body of troops lying flat on their faces in the dirt. We knew nothing of them till we mounted the works, and were then in too much of a hurry to stop for an introduction. In the common danger, we waived all courtesy and jumped right down onto them, regardless of landing place. They took our sudden arrival with surprising good grace. A kick in the head is preferable to a bullet in the head.

All day we held the position and hugged the earth with wondrous persistence. The hours crept on like snails and it seemed as if night would never come. It was suffocatingly hot, and we baked like the festive bean. The Rebs were so near that we couldn't lift hand or head without danger of having it perforated. Sometime during the afternoon old Tommy Eagan, who got us into this scrape, received a dig in the region of his kidneys, which deprived us of his company. With astonishing complacency we watched him dragged to the rear. If any tears were shed, they were tears of joy mingled with the hope that his wound will keep him away till our terms end.

A little before sunset we were ordered out. We *backed* out, one by one, hoping our movement would not be noticed by the Johnnies. A grand charge was to be made all along the line and thus wind up the show for the day. Our division was to act as a reserve and we were stationed near where we started, not far from the Hare House. As our troops advanced, the musketry fire was just terrific, and I thought that if the loss of life bore any proportion to the noise, our army must be melting away like butter under a July sun. It was a continuous roar, now dying away, now swelling like the surf on the shore. Our advance was a dismal failure, although a trifle more territory was gained.

The Rebs fell back to another line in rear and couldn't be dislodged, so nothing more was done and we passed the night on the estate of one O.P. Hare.

## June 17th.

Put under arms at daylight and about 7 o'clock were ordered out into the front line of works. We moved part way and then waited a long time for the troops who were in there to crawl out one by one. There is but little space between the enemy lines and ours at this place; just a narrow ravine separating us, and our friends across the way keep up a continual fusillade. For a man to raise his head is equivalent to signing his death warrant. As soon as the other troops got out, we crawled into their places, and although there was a storm of lead flying about, we contrived to get in without losing a man in our company. We now had a chance to pay back Johnny Reb. We have some excellent sharpshooters, in no way inferior to the Rebel article, besides being much better armed.

Soon after our arrival, it was again our misfortune to be without a regimental commander. Captain Pennell was instantly killed while watching the effects of the sharpshooting. He had supposed himself screened from view in the grapery of the Hare House, and probably he was, the bullet being a chance one. It is said, "misfortunes never come singly," and Captain Moore, whom the writer once threatened to drop an axe on, was next in line of succession. But he only held it long enough for another to be appointed; Major Hilbraith of the 20th Indiana was assigned next to the command.

After dark the 2nd Division of this corps (the 2nd) crawled up the ravine in our front, and by a sudden rush on the enemy broke through their lines and sent them flying. It was but a few moment's work to clear the entire line, and this we proceeded to do.

## June 18th.

About daylight we moved forward in line of battle, intending to charge the entire length of the line. As we emerged from the woods, we found the Confederates had completely evacuated the area. Instead of a charge, we simply took possession. We could see them clawing over the hills towards Petersburg, and if we could have gone on, we would have kept them going. Instead, we were ordered to halt and throw up entrenchments. When the Johnnies discovered this, they ceased running and commenced digging in, right in plain sight, on Cemetery Hill.

Each regiment sent out one company to cover its front, and Company I was chosen as skirmishers for our regiment. We harassed them for a spell, but their sharpshooters secured a lodgement so near that they had us right in their sights. We advanced to the crest of a hill in a field of oats and concluded that if we could establish a position there we might check these fellows. It was soon discovered, however, that our position was incompatible with keeping a whole skin, so we retired behind the crest, and thence to the rear of the hill. Here we discovered a patch of ground with a lot of "garding sass." The very thought of fresh vegetables made me throw away all caution. I ambled up over the hill to a shed near the garden entrance. No sooner did I appear than I was met with rifle shots from some unknown party occupying the trees in front.

When the firing started, I spotted a line of our skirmishers lying flat on the ground. They ordered me to "get down!" Two years service in the field have taught me the art of self-preservation, so the advice was entirely gratuitous. In this position I crawled along worm-fashion to the pea patch and soon filled my haversack, remarking to a fellow who was doing the same, "Let us have peas."

I grabbed as many beets and squash as could be carried by the tops and, with my haversack, told myself to "git." I proceeded to crawl out on my belly. On the way, I encountered Billy Patterson. Now, Billy, seeing the writer fairly groaning under his load of goodies, decided to "go and do likewise." In vain I pointed out the dangers. He declared that he was going into the pea patch at any risk. But the instant he appeared over the hill, a bullet struck his belt buckle and he went hunting grass in a very unceremonious manner, the breath knocked out of him. He didn't care to run that risk again. He was suffering from a pain in the "abandon," as an illiterate person once said.

When I reached the post, it had lost one of its complement. Jimmy Taylor had been hit in the head and, although living, was unconscious and fast passing away. I found Stacy doing all he could to put space between him and the enemy. He was burrowing for dear life, expecting any moment to join Taylor. We laid our dead to one side and with heavy hearts finished our works of protection. It was intensely hot, the dirt was baked hard as a rock, and bayonets were our only tools. After several laborious hours I was finally able to cook the stuff found in the garden, but it didn't taste as I'd hoped. The experiences and labors of the day had killed my appetite.

Along toward sunset we took care of Taylor's body, after removing such mementoes as could be sent to his family. The firing was so lively that it wasn't safe to go to the rear, and we suffered severely from lack of water. It was evident that the Rebels were heavily reinforced at this point.

This morning we had them on the run, and had we moved, Petersburg would have been ours. A goodly number of our men have fallen. I call it murder, for whoever ordered this halt is to blame for our predicament. And now we were to be sent forward again, only to be hurled back, torn and bleeding. A curse on those responsible! Company I, being on the skirmish line, didn't have to participate in this latest charge, but we have seen our share of death this day.

After dark we threw up some works in front of our skirmish line. The Confederates also built one, and when morning dawned we found ourselves in uncomfortable proximity, in fact, so near that a stone could easily be thrown from one to the other. This state could not long endure, and the Reb sharpshooters suddenly cleared our part of the line. We moved out and formed another line a few rods in rear of this dangerous section, remaining out all night on the skirmish line.

### June 19th.

After sunrise we were relieved from the picket line and went a short distance to the rear. A place had been left for us on the works — rather a place for us to build up. We labored under several disadvantages, the chief one being lack of timber for the breastworks. This could only be procured in front, beyond a piece of ground dominated by Rebel sharpshooters. We were fortunate not to lose a man from Company I while running the gauntlet.

A fellow named Stearns, in Company C, was hit in the neck and expired almost instantly. He lived just long enough to gasp, "Tell Mother I died happy." Rather a sudden way to finish one's pilgrimage, and yet much preferable to the lingering tortures to which others have been subjected. It will seem strange to some that this young fellow in the very bloom of manhood and health could say he died happy. We who know the dreadful suspense and nervous strain of war do not wonder that, when he realized he was through it all, he should say he died happy, for he left no wife or little ones behind him.

Today one of our men was wounded in the *bayonet*. On May 5th, another was wounded in the testament and still another in the diary, neither of whom had his usefulness impaired thereby. The last named individual might have lived a good many years more but for his subsequent attempt to stop a bullet with his arm, which didn't work so well.

### June 20th.

Nothing for excitement except that a few men were picked off by sharpshooters. A feeling prevails that sooner or later this experience will befall us all. So we have an indefinable dread, our nerves subjected to a continual strain which we know cannot end till the war ends, or we are wiped out.

In the evening a division of darkies relieved us and we moved back a mile and bivouacked for the night. Rumor has it that we are going to rest here for two entire days.

### June 21st.

Rations were served to us and then we started out to destroy the Weldon Railroad, but soon changed our minds. A force of the enemy was there ahead of us, and their intentions did not look peaceful. We contented ourselves with looking at them with inutterable ferocity. Not at all astonished at our audacity, they commenced to throw things at us. Our officers pretended we were on the wrong road and ordered us away from there. We were on the wrong road all right, unless we were in search of destruction or a trip to Richmond as prisoners.

Being quite late when we extracted ourselves from this mess, we moved back to the Jerusalem Plank Road and formed in a line with our right near the Jones House. It took a long time to get located, as the trees were very dense and there was a great deal of underbrush to dispose of. We laid here till midnight, when we were ordered out in front. We went over a road cut through the woods and found a line of works thrown up. The 2nd Division of our corps had already been out there all day, and we are eternally grateful for their hard labor in throwing up these works.

An attack is expected at every moment, so we are kept under arms and ordered to stay awake. This last order we obey, but of what use are pickets if those in the works can have no sleep or rest?

## June 22nd.

The 2nd Brigade of Birney's division, and the whole of Barlow's, were sent but a short distance in front to establish another line and throw up some works. Everything went on swimmingly for a time, and we began to relax. General Barlow was so confident that he advanced some distance beyond his command to a little brook into which he projected his feet. A Rebel yell at his elbow brought this refreshing performance to a sudden end. Seizing his stockings and shoes, the general fled to the uttermost parts of the field, the Rebels at his heels. He reached the works only to find that the Confederates had made a savage onslaught on them at this point. His right wasn't much better, and the Rebs were fast turning it, causing what General de Trobriand called "von grand skeedaddle." Men were flying in all directions, some to the front (but not voluntarily). Death filled the air like snowflakes in a winter storm. Most of the men sped in the direction of the works behind which our company reposed. When we found them coming, we did wonders trying to urge them to stand fast. We soon became alarmed, for words of encouragement didn't seem to check them, so we added copious threats to punch them with the bayonet if they didn't turn about and check the Rebs. Our apparent bravery was the result of our fear that if they didn't stand, we should have to do so.

The Union line was in a condition to give our Confederate friends a very sultry reception if they persisted. A masked battery was just trembling to get a crack at them. But the Rebs evidently reconsidered and dropped the pursuit. Our troops in front were too demoralized to attempt any counter movement and were withdrawn inside the works.

General Hancock is away, or this disagreeable affair would never have taken place. General Barlow is chiefly censurable for the entire transaction. It is an open secret that Barlow isn't just right in his head, and his performance lends strength to this insinuation. The most stupid private, and we have legions of them, would know better than to push a column out in this way, no connection right or left and both flanks in the air.

## June 23rd.

Sometime previous to daylight we were ordered out front and formed in line of battle in the cornfield where yesterday's combat took place. Just as the gray mists of morning lifted, we charged across the field to the edge of a belt of woods, ending up slightly in advance of yesterday's position. We found here a line of rifle pits partially completed. These we finished and occupied for the rest of the day. An attack was expected at any moment, but no movement of any consequence was made.

We found in this field the body of one of our officers who fell in the previous battle. There were indications that while he lay wounded he was murdered for his clothes. The Yankees are, no doubt, a low-born set, but we have never been charged with murdering a man for his clothes.

At night all was quiet except for the festive mosquito and the mournful whippoorwill.

### June 24th.

All still on this part of the line. Not so, however, on our right. Up there the country rebounded with the boom of cannon. Went on picket at night in the works we'd occupied the day before yesterday. No attack was made, although we were in constant expectation of one. The Confederates seem to have abandoned all idea of driving us from here, and we of going. In consequence, picket firing has virtually ceased.

Our sorest need is water, for all we have is derived from digging holes in the ground with our bayonets and dippers. Perhaps it is just as well that we have so little, for bog water is not the most healthy beverage in the world. If we were to drink our fill of it, our systems might soon be filled with malaria.

### June 25th.

Nothing of thrilling interest on this part of the line. To the right of us, at the Avery house, picket firing was quite brisk.

We were relieved from picket duty at night and returned to the regiment, near the Jones house — the dirtiest hole in the entire United States. But there was one mitigating circumstance here; we found an ice house. We were far from slow in putting the ice to good use. That is to say, we had the *crumbs* and the rest of it went to the hospital. Little as we had, it was a great thing, the weather being hot, dust nearly suffocating, and the water poor and scarce.

### June 26th and 27th.

Two quiet days. Too sultry to be otherwise. Were I at home, I certainly would be cooling my heels in the Atlantic. There is not so much as a rill or wavelet here. To our right, instead of quiet there is an infernal din and racket. All the noises we cannot account for seem to be located up on the James, and we confidently expect a grand old row up there at no very distant date.

At night we were pushed out into the front line of works and kept there until morning. We suspect we were a decoy to draw out the Rebs so that our masked battery could get a crack at them, but they refused to cooperate. The Confederates left us alone, and had the mosquitoes done the same we should have enjoyed a reasonable degree of comfort.

### June 28th.

After daylight we moved back to our old place in line. "Silence reigns with a terrible uproar." General Warren has planted a battery of 32-pounders on the right of the Jerusalem Plank Road, facetiously naming them "The Seven Sisters." This entire family is noisy and quarrelsome. Not a peaceable one among them.

In the afternoon a detail was sent out to clear a spot for a new camp. We have for several days been crouching here in the open, where the sun can rake at us for

BATTERY BEFORE PETERSBURG. *Harper's Pictorial History of the Civil War.*

fifteen hours out of every twenty-four. Clouds of dust fill the air at every move we make; chewing gravel is an ordinance now, as much as eating "peas on a trencher." Our pork quickly becomes rusty and rotten, and our beef maggoty, unless eaten as soon as drawn. Any change must be for the better. The spot selected has been burnt over and is enough to smother us, but there is shade. We desire above all things to get settled *somewhere* long enough to dig a well, our great and overwhelming need being water.

### June 29th.

Moved out this morning and commenced building at once. The orders seemed to indicate that we would tarry here some days. Yet it doesn't speak well for our judgment that we should be so often deceived by rumor. We no sooner built our tents and put bunks in them, when an order came to "Pack up and move immediately!"

We didn't move a great distance, only enough to nullify all our labors in the new camp. We were so indignant that we decided to be less hasty in the future, and govern ourselves by the needs of the hour.

Our new position is superior enough to make us forget our pain and disappointment. We are in the front line and have lots of shade and a good chance for a well.

### June 30th.

No firing on this part of the line, and at 10 o'clock we were mustered for two months' pay. One year ago today we were mustered at Taneytown, Maryland. No doubt Lee's hordes do not now sing "Maryland, My Maryland" with quite so much relish as they did a year past. Our position with regard to the enemy is much improved since that date. We now have them driven to the wall, and it can only be a question of time when they must collapse.

### July 1st.

At the first sign of dawn the bugle blew us out of bed. We naturally expected a row; however, no demonstrations of a hostile nature occurred, only a disturbance at the "oat field." There was scarce a moment all day when there wasn't a jolly racket going on up there. Rumor has it that two brothers who own farms near the oat field are waging ceaseless war on the Yanks. Though ridiculous, it is mighty uncomfortable for those within range.

### July 2nd.

No fighting, but incessant firing in front of the 18th Corps, where colored soldiers are posted. The Southern chivalry regard their presence as an especial insult, so the gentlemen of African descent have to lay low. I must confess that *our* love for the Negro soldier isn't overwhelming, due largely to the fact that he has been spared at our expense, and his appetite pampered, when it has been most difficult for *us* to get anything to eat. He is not to blame, but as the subject of those attentions he becomes also the subject of our envy.

### July 3rd.

An inspection of arms was ordered, and we put ourselves in condition to perform. For some unknown cause it didn't come off. It was Sunday, and the chaplain of the 20th Indiana expounded the Word as we sat in groups under the trees. I'd conjecture that he preached to not less than 100 quarts of baked beans. When Voltaire said, "A minister is five feet above contradiction," he could not have had *this* clerical quack in view. Perhaps he is better pictured by Holmes's description of katydids as "saying an undisputed thing in such a solemn way." Stale platitudes, religious commonplaces, and cheap stories fell from his lips in a melancholy drizzle. After listening to this fellow for an hour or so we were dismissed, and passed a comfortable day.

### July 4th.

It would seem that a day crowded with historic memories, as this is, would not be allowed to pass without trying to add luster to it. We expected that something extraordinary would be attempted to arouse our latent patriotism. However, nothing has occurred, and I don't remember a quieter day at the front. I recall, though, that this is the day General Grant promised to eat his dinner in Richmond. There seems to be a hitch somewhere.

### July 5th.

It is so hot that the vim is all out of us. We went on picket and had a very peaceable day of it. We were relieved at dark and returned to our old place, where we abandoned ourselves to a general looseness, as we have no fear of an attack.

### July 6th.

Hot as blazes, and this is no idle phrase. The sun must be several million miles nearer the earth than when it went down last night.

One circumstance did occur that added so much to our comfort as to make the day memorable: we drew *beans*.

In the afternoon I flew in the face of Providence by tramping up to the Plank Road, where the lines are so close together that one could easily throw a brick over our line to the Confederates'. In fact, that is exactly what the men were doing when I arrived. Bricks make good ammunition; they are comparatively cheap and can do duty many times. Whenever the supply dwindled the men replenished it by firing at a couple of nearby chimneys.

There is a brisk trade in tobacco in this neighborhood. The Rebs seem to have an unlimited supply of it, which they gladly trade for anything to eat. The news literature of the day is exchanged as well. We split a stick, insert the paper in the slit, and toss it across to the Confederate lines. (When there is any news that might encourage the other side, however, we cut it out before the exchange is made.) There is perfect freedom in this place. We go in and out as we please, and there seems to be an era of good feeling inaugurated, which if allowed to grow unchecked would shortly end this war.

Just in rear of our line here we are building an immense fort. The concealing brush will be removed when the work is complete, giving our chum Johnny a considerable surprise. Similar works are being constructed at other places.

### July 7th.

Hot enough to cook an East Indian brown, and it is quiet — except for the "Seven Sisters," who grow garrulous with age. The dreadful heat reduces our pugnacity so that it is no easy matter to get up a row.

### July 8th.

Building forts and other impedimenta to obstruct the free locomotion of Johnny Reb. A heavy wire stretched the entire length of our line will send them sprawling on the ground if they approach. They will rise just in time to get tripped by a second line, and then by a third, which will plunge them into a ditch. The same state of things stares us in the face if we attempt to force ourselves on their notice. Neither side has omitted any device whereby his brother might fall to rise no more. We hear some of the tallest kinds of swearing — regular three-story, bay-window cuss words slung around — as our own men stumble over the impediments in going to and from the front after dusk.

Captain Bell, of the 20th Indiana, was hit today by a fragment of shell and died within a few minutes. He was formerly a Rebel, and deserted to our side. Captain Bell was highly respected by his own men, and his loss deplored. He was a brave fellow.

### July 9th.

We were sent on picket directly in front to give warning of anything suspicious. As nothing of this nature was undertaken, I have nothing to chronicle. It was the lightest guard duty we have done for months. Although wholly unnecessary, it was not tiresome because we had no restraint, no shoulder-strap gentry to put on airs and order us about.

### July 10th.

From the racket this morning, the Rebels apparently inferred that this was evacuation day, and with this silly notion in their noddle they undertook to enter here. When they found the entire Yankee army still on hand to receive them, they retired quite as promptly as they had advanced. This was not our day for receiving such calls.

## July 11th.

The 6th Corps made some movements this morning, and at noon we were ordered to get ready to "move immediately," but the order to go did not come until midnight.

At sunset, the usual time for exchanging pickets, our detail moved out across the cornfield and was treated to some Rebel attentions. No one was hit, and we were not long in vanishing into the woods. Here, the ground had been recently burned over and the smell and the smother were sickening. Clouds of cinders and charred leaves were kicked up at every step.

During the night we were kept in a state of lively suspense, for we could distinctly hear voices and frequent rustling of leaves in front. Had the sounds approached us we should have either opened on them or taken ourselves out of the way. When morning dawned we found that the line in front of us wore blue, not gray. By some blunder, our line lapped over this one. This was a very stupid thing and might have resulted in serious disaster.

## July 12th.

The 6th Corps headed for the Shenandoah Valley and our corps (the 2nd), with Hancock commanding, was ordered to replace them in the line. At noon we were relieved and returned to the division, which seemed to be supporting a cavalry force that was reconnoitering toward the Weldon Railroad. This was the locality where we tried a movement a few days ago. They met with no better success than we did. Our division remained in this position the entire day and night. We enjoyed a good rest, although it was rather difficult to find a space large enough to lie down in amid the scrub oak.

## July 13th.

Turned out at 7 and received orders to get ready to move. Somehow we were given the impression that we were in for a long one. We moved — about a mile — and went into camp in rear of everything except the teams. We were held there as a reserve to go where most needed. Aggressive movements seem to be abandoned for the present, and we were instructed to build quarters.

A rumor prevails that the Rebel army has gone up into the Shenandoah Valley to menace Washington. The 6th Corps will make it an interesting trip for the Johnnies. With Sheridan to help them, we are confident that the Rebels' attention will be fully monopolized.

The Rebs have succeeded in wrecking several miles of railroad leading to Washington and probably transferred the rails to this vicinity, repairing the Weldon Railroad (which *we* had destroyed) as far as Yellow Tavern. This structure, like so much of Virginia, is dilapidated and dreary. This seems strange in a country boasting of its wealth and culture: no mills, few schoolhouses, no carriages, but few of the comforts of life so common in the North. Yet they call us mudsills, greasy mechanics, hirelings, and diverse other titles. It is not from necessity that they are deprived, but from sheer *ignorance*. Nature has been very lavish in her gifts to the South, but too much dependence on the darkey and too much intimacy with them has lowered the standards of decency and morality and made its people effete. Yet they are prejudiced to such a degree that they don't see this. They rely on the nigger to manage the farm and to procure food, so although there should be a bountiful abundance, we find elegant ladies and their entire familes sitting down to hoe-cake and ham, hoe-cake and ham, day after day. This is because those high-toned whites do not know how to cook and think it degrading to practice the culinary arts.

(Why this bread is called hoe-cake is unknown to me unless it is because of its resemblance to that article in thinness and hardness. It appears to be a mixture of flour and water baked solid. As a change from hardtack it is quite palatable; as a steady diet it would be simply execrable.)

It is argued by some that this state of things has been brought about by the war but it is just as easy for these people to lie as to breathe. Perhaps they are ashamed of their stupidity and so they say that they had things differently "before the war." Their barbarity to our wounded and prisoners is in keeping with the spirit of cussedness that leads them to sell their fellow men, even their own offspring by slave mothers. Time after time, the Southerner's own children have been forced upon the auction block although they are as white as the children by his lawful wife. The strong argument here to justify slavery is that the nigger is not human. This might do if the Southerner's conduct were in keeping with his theory, but it isn't, and it cannot be reconciled with the various shades of color we behold in the slaves.

There are some great moral and physical questions involved here that it is not pertinent to discuss too freely now.

### July 14th.

Six men from each company were detailed to work on a big fort on the Norfolk & Petersburg Railroad intended for the rear line of defense. There has been a conspicuous paucity of grub of late and we are so reduced in strength that we didn't feel a mite like working. So, we sat around in the woods and rested our carcasses until noon. After dinner we went out and dropped trees till midnight, when we were allowed to lie down for a couple hours of sleep.

### July 15th and 16th.

About 3 P.M. were turned out and ordered to fell trees on all roads leading into Petersburg. Kept at this until noon when a stop was made for dinner and to draw whiskey. We continued chopping until midnight. After a short respite, we were turned out again at 2 A.M. and arrived at camp around four. We thought it surely indicated an emergency, but it was nothing of the sort. It was simply the antics of a canteen of whiskey under the waistcoat of Steve Graffam, who had charge of the detail.

Being overloaded with bug juice, he mounted a stump and essayed to give us a speech, which began thus: "What did Abraham Lincoln say?" At this point, he lost his balance and plunged to the ground, remarking as he went, "Well, he did." What the rest of this extraordinary harangue would have been was left to our conjecture. The commencement had given promise of something stirring.

We were allowed to sleep as long as we liked, and when we arose on the 16th we were glad to find no movement. The rest of the day was spent working on our quarters, raising them up and otherwise improving them, thus adding to our comfort and our sanitary condition.

### July 17th.

A full inspection was ordered at 1 o'clock. This kept us busy all the forenoon, for a full inspection means a lot of cleaning up.

After inspection I visited Dr. Hersom at Division Hospital, nearly every ward of which is occupied by the sick, not the wounded. The scurvy is making horrid inroads into our ranks, while malaria is holding high carnival amongst us. Hundreds of men, myself included, amble around on legs as raw as a piece of meat. This condition is the result of having little or no vegetable food. We exhausted all the local gardens weeks before. Even then, but one man in ten managed to get a mouthful of vegetable sustenance. We live mostly on *promises* of potatoes and "desecrated" vegetables, as one illiterate fellow used to call them. But each of us gets so little of these that it is only an aggravation. Not only the morale of this army but its health is fast disappearing.

### July 18th.

An attack in front was expected and everyone was put under arms at daylight. We are in position to be sent to any portion of the line, from Appomattox River on the right to the Weldon Railroad on the left, but the attack was never made. For this we shed no tears. Those of us who survive the next thirteen months may yet see the end of this early rising and fighting. However, if the mortality continues as it has in the last two and a half months, there is not a ghost of a show that any of us will again behold the old Pine Tree State. This regiment left Portland with 1040 men, including officers. I have seen all but 200 of these melt away from one cause or another.

Some of the absent have been killed. Some have died from wounds and disease or have been discharged on these accounts. Others are bumming at the hospitals, while a few have been bold enough to desert in the conventional way, thus showing a kind of courage that would have kept them in good standing at the front. Undoubtedly, some men are in Rebel prisons.

### July 19th.

Were sent out with a detail to dig a covered way, or road, from a point near the Avery mansion to Jerusalem Plank Road, where a new fort is just completed. The road is designed to protect the teamsters. If it weren't built, we would be compelled to carry our rations on our backs a long way. The average teamster does not court danger, and his visits to the front would be scarce indeed without this added protection.

At night we returned to camp, having done work enough at least to pay our taxes in old Virginia.

### July 20th.

Heavy firing in the picket line to the right of the Hare House, otherwise all was quiet. Being so far from the front, we can't tell what is going on. Firing ceased after a while and we busied ourselves as usual around camp.

We are in a growth of pines very near the Prince George Court House, and a more dreadfully hot, dry place it has not been our misfortune to see. This is a miserable section of Virginia, and as destitute of water as the Sahara.

### July 21st.

Not a military thing to record, only the usual morning fusillade in front of the 18th Corps. Other reports than those of firearms reach us from the front, ones that make us desire to share some of their danger that we might also claim some of the concommitant luxuries. While we revel in an abundance of pork and hardtack, it is said that they are

FIRE-PROOF (OR BOMB-PROOF). *Harper's Pictorial History of the Civil War.*

kept on rice, canned fruits and meats, potatoes, pickles, and dessicated fish and vegetables. However, lament is useless.

### July 22nd.

A second dose of digging the same covered road where we were the day before yesterday. We did just as little work as possible, for we have no strength.

Some of us visited the 5th Corps, which is in front of us in bombproofs.[2] No gun invented thus far can send a missile through these embankments but there does appear to be some danger of their falling in and crushing the life out of the men inside. They are also low and damp.

### July 23rd.

Our camp is quiet enough to suit anybody. To break the monotony an inspection is held occasionally, but as long as Colonel Merrill has command, we have no fear of needless drill exercise. Colonel Merrill has great sympathy for the men; in fact, he is as tender-hearted as a woman. This would not be the case if Major West, or Mattox, were in command.

I was visited by an old friend from Saco this afternoon, a Dr. Moore. I enjoyed his visit much and hope to see him again soon. I still have some of the sugar I purchased from him before leaving Saco. It has done good service, too.

## July 24th.

Went on fatigue again in the covered road, which when complete will be one mile long, twelve feet wide, and six feet deep. We shall shed no tears when it is done. The scurvy is doing its work, and we are so weak that any exertion takes the vim all out of us.

We also are sadly in need of a suitable place to bathe and wash our clothing. The pond we wash our clothes in is lousy — worse than the clothes themselves in this respect. In addition, the pond has received such generous deposits of soap and dirt from our clothes that the water is more in need of a washing than the garments are. It is the color of skim milk and the consistency of soft soap.

To those not acquainted with the habits of lice and their astonishing tenacity of life, my story of lousy water may seem a lie, but it is strictly true. Water has no effect on army lice unless it is boiling.

We dug away till night, when we returned to camp to pass a few hours in scratching and smarting.

## July 25th.

Profound stillness prevailed here this morning. Later in the day we had a drill, just to keep our hand in — it pleased the officers and didn't hurt us.

## July 26th.

The usual quiet prevailed until noon, when we were suddenly ordered to get ready to leave at 3:30. Because of a delay in distributing rations, however, we didn't set out until nearly five. We moved in the direction of City Point, then turned to the left toward the Appomattox River. We crossed at Point of Rocks, and sometime before morning crossed the James River at Turkey Bend, where we bivouacked till daylight.

Some of us did not cross till considerably after daylight, being too weak to stand such a long and hurried march. So we decided to refresh ourselves with a little coffee. We no sooner had it ready when along came a few of the provost guard, led by a *thing* on horseback who ordered his posse to kick over our coffee and further ordered us to "Move on. Quick!"

I didn't tear myself to pieces to comply, so Mr. Flunkey yelled, "G——d d——n you. You act like you don't mean to hurry!" The thermometer of his wrath rose several degrees at my deliberately slow movements, and he drew his cheese knife. He made several threats to decapitate me and then lunged and drove it into my knapsack with such force that I staggered and almost fell.

My companion supposed I was injured and instantly drew a bead on Mr. Provost. Had I not shown immediately that I had sustained no real injury, I am positive that Jack Brine, my comrade, would have scattered the brains of this fellow into the surrounding woods like so much rubbish. Seeing the box he was in, the provost put spurs to his animal and departed in haste. *We* moved on at our leisure.

## July 27th.

The mists of morning were just rising and imparted a somber tint to the scene as we formed in line of battle and awaited orders. A chill pervaded the atmosphere, in keeping with the solemnity of the moment.

A portion of the brigade was deployed as skirmishers, supported by the rest of the division. A move was immediately made on the enemy's position, scattering them in a precipitate flight, leaving their skirmish line and four 24-pounders to fall into our possession. The skirmishers might have saved themselves, but instead tried to save the guns. They failed to do either. This was an excellent beginning for us.

A further advance on our part was unsuccessful. The Rebs made a stand, and as no reinforcements were sent to our aid, we fell back. A strong picket line was then thrust out, with Gregg's cavalry in advance, armed with the Spencer repeating rifles. These weapons made it exceedingly lively for the Rebs because they can discharge sixteen bullets at one firing.

A friend of ours from Saco was in this cavalry. He came over to visit this night. He pointed out some of the localities nearby made famous earlier in the war. Malvern Hill is about 2½ miles away. That is where McClellan gave the Southrons an unmerciful whacking and slaughtered them by the hundreds.

### July 28th.

The Rebels did some firing in our front, but our gunboats on the James replied and also opened up on Fort Darling. a little farther up the river. About noon we moved out onto the Newmarket Road, the Rebels having fallen back to some powerful works on Chapin's Farm. At the same time, Sheridan's cavalry and the 2nd Division of the 2nd Corps moved out on our right flank and attacked the Confederates but found them too strong to be dislodged. As we couldn't accomplish anything by staying, we fell back into a clearing and rested till after dark.

About 9 o'clock in the evening we started on a movement, whither or wherefore we knew not. We hadn't gone far when we discovered a deucedly familiar look to the area. We soon arrived at, and crossed, the James, then followed a southeast course to the Appomattox, crossing it at Broad Way. The night was spent marching, and in the morning we hauled up where the City Point Railroad crosses the road to Petersburg, one of the worst places in Virginia. We suffered from heat, thirst, and infinite dust.

### July 29th.

Stayed in this abominable hole all day. The cool of evening came at last and we moved on. To our dismay, we soon found ourselves right in front and ordered to relieve a division in the 10th Corps in the vicinity of the Hare House. Here we were ordered to sit with our accoutrements on and not to go to sleep under any circumstances. Most of us succumbed to sweet dreaming despite the edict.

### July 30th.

Our slumbers were terminated as abruptly as though Gabriel himself had tooted his horn in our ears. The most infernal din and uproar that ever greeted mortals crashed around us. Earth and heaven were rent by an explosion that would have done credit to several thunderstorms. Some of us shot into the air and came down again to find the old planet still left, or enough of it to stand on as we took a look around. We scrambled for shelter from a storm of shot and shell that came hurtling around and over us. Such a scampering and tumult only found its parallel in the Rebel lines, where Burnside's mine had been exploded, sending a couple of hundred Confederates into the "unfathomable hence" in a jiffy. (Like most of my comrades, I entertained grave doubts as to the existence of such a mine. These doubts were now dispelled.)[3]

EXPLOSION OF BURNSIDE'S MINE. *Harper's Pictorial History of the Civil War.*

The explosion of this mine, together with the discharge of one-hundred shotted guns, the yells of the charging party as they attempted to enter the breach in the enemy's works, the screeching of the Rebels, and the general confusion were enough to destroy the nerves of everyone.

The general movement was made by parts of the 5th and 9th corps. They truly entered the mouth of Hell when they charged here. Birney's 10th Corps and "Baldy" Smith's 18th Corps supported them, and had things been properly managed there is little doubt of our complete success in carrying the lines at Petersburg. Instead, we suffered the most mortifying defeat and useless slaughter.

After the Rebels had time to collect their wits, some colored troops were thrown in, but *no* troops could stand this deadly fray. The time for support was the instant the mine was sprung; a grand rush at that moment would have swept the Rebel lines away. As it *wasn't* made then, Lee had a breathing spell and he soon let loose such a withering fire on our lines that no troops could stand before it. Cemetery Hill, the objective, was a sheet of flame. Every gun in the defense of Petersburg swept that spot. Men went down like grain before the reaper. The hole made by the explosion was filled with wriggling humanity, and the Rebels poured every form of missile onto them. Escape was impossible, except for an individual now and then who managed to crawl out.

The Rebels soon turned all their fire on our colored troops, for whom they have a special hate. Who can describe the horrors of heat and thirst as the wounded lay in the broiling sun? The Confederates allowed none of the courtesies to these troops, which they might have extended to white men. But on this occasion they didn't allow us to render aid to white or to colored. The suffering of the wounded was indescribable, for the sun has never shone any hotter in Virginia. Nearly all who were wounded died before night. Darkness mercifully lent her aid, and we sent out details to bring in any survivors.

The Union loss in this affair is frightful, and when we consider the paltry results, it degenerates into *murder*. We didn't gain a foot of ground, a prisoner, or a gun. We sacrificed hundreds of lives and all we got for it was confirmation of the rumor that Burnside had a mine.[4]

After witnessing this carnage, we were allowed to return to our old camp of reserve. Heaven knows, we have been into enough of this business since May 4th.

### July 31st.

All is as quiet as if no battle had been fought, and an inexperienced eye would detect no sign of our having been out of camp. A flag of truce was sent out this afternoon to enable us to bury the dead and bring in the wounded, if any still survive. The Rebs wouldn't recognize the flag, however, nor allow any cessation of hostilities. Nothing can be done until the Rebels recognize the truce.

### August 1st.

Under marching orders all day but didn't move. We don't know what new phase of the enemy's condition or attitude led to this order. Whatever it was, it amounted to nothing this day.

All we seek is a change of camp, for this is an intensely sultry and filthy place, and with nothing to do the hours drag wearily. Time is divided into small portions devoted to eating and sleeping; some prefer gambling. Occasionally an overdose of tanglefoot relieves the monotony.

### August 2nd and 3rd.

No move, but we did have a diversion of a more agreeable nature. The paymaster put in an appearance, and it wasn't long before we paid a visit to the sutler. The remainder of these days has been devoted to a frantic effort to fill an aching void. Heaven knows we need the fill-up. Men have actually been known to eat a dozen sutler's cakes at one sitting, and other things to match. No wonder the chronic diarrhea gets such a grip on some of them.

### August 4th.

We are compelled to resort to the oft-repeated phrase, "all quiet" — not on the Potomac alone, but in front of Petersburg. It may be reassuring to the country to know that

General Grant is doing all he can to put down the rebellion — by smoke. It is said he smokes nine cigars a day and fills the interim by sucking the stubs.

I have noticed nothing in Grant's conduct to lead me to suppose he cares a straw how hot it is, or how many are wounded. It is my humble opinion that he thinks no more for wounded men than the angler does the worm wriggling on his hook. If he has ever visited the hospitals and dropped a word of praise for the sick and wounded, there is a serious omission in the records. How different, this, from President Lincoln — kind old soul, tender and full of sympathy, as though the boys are each his own.

### August 5th.

Some of us made a most important and timely discovery today; we found a sour-apple tree. If at the time Mrs. Eve met the serpent she desired apples as much as we did, and needed them as much, I don't blame her at all. But I have my doubts as to her *needing* them, for Earth was young and Eve hadn't been punished with ancient salt horse and rusty pork as we are. This fruit was a real blessing and I felt relieved as soon as I tasted it. The apples were "as manna to the hungry soul."

### August 6th.

Just two years today since I enlisted; not less than a century has been crowded into this time. These two years will be fresh in memory for as long as reason holds sway. Forget them I never can, and never *want* to. The fact that I am now in the enjoyment of life still is because I have a remarkable tenacity for life and great endurance. Although suffering from malaria and other disease, a kind Providence has shielded me from shot and shell.

# Autumn Siege of Petersburg

## August 7 – December 31, 1864

*August 7th – 11th.*

Nothing of sufficient importance to record. There was some picket firing, a little cannonading, and the usual routine of sounds, but it disturbed us not, any more than it would the sphinx of Egypt. I had settled down to the conclusion that we are out of the way of Rebel missiles, but this morning (the 11th) encountered a shell wending its way down here, on murderous thoughts intent.

*August 12th.*

We were told to pack up and move immediately. An order of this kind always goes right to the stomach and bowels (and those who are thus exercised retire precipitously to commune with themselves). We were soon on the road to City Point. Arriving there, we went into bivouac in rear of Grant's headquarters. We are intensely curious as to our ultimate destination, but nobody cares to enlighten us. Some think we are going farther south; one of our officers has heard we are going to Washington; another is positive a division general said it will be the opposite direction.

*August 13th.*

About 9 o'clock I wandered down to the wharf to see if I could sniff out any information. More bummers, sutlers, and teamsters were gathered there than Lee has men in his whole army. Miles of transports have brought provisions for our army to be stored in acres of sheds. Just one-half of these provisions would be more than we get, for we are sparsely supplied of everything.

After returning to the regiment I drew rations — a couple of salt mackerel. Either these are intended as a treat or we are going on a sea voyage. How to construe this development is a problem.

At noon we were ordered to board transports in the river. Most of us thought we were going into the Shenandoah and we began, in fancy, to feast on the abundance of that section. An officer heard General Mott say we are to leave Virginia.

Never were we so puzzled or mystified. Our division (Mott's) boarded the steamer *Highland Light* and dropped down into line with the rest, and it was not till after dark that any light was thrown on the subject of most absorbing interest to us.

A tug came alongside and brought an order to General Mott to move to Deep Bottom at 10 o'clock. So this much was settled, and at the appointed time we

AN ARMY TRAIN — SUTLERS' WAGONS. *Harper's Pictorial History of the Civil War.*

were steaming up the James, arriving at Deep Bottom, or Jones's Neck, about 1 o'clock. We recognized the place as being the scene of our exploits of July 27th.

We made noise enough to be heard clear to Richmond. The tide was running out rapidly, and we were late. It was with great difficulty that we could get near enough to the shore to land. But after a deal of fussing, fumbling, and swearing, matters were regulated. We landed, and bivouacked till daylight in a field near the river. If the Rebs had known we were coming, they might have made it a trifle smoky. Their spies must have been as bewildered as we were when they saw the transports drop *down* the river. It was a well-kept secret until we were far away from the shore. Every one of our boats could have been sunk in a few minutes if they had known what we were about.

## August 14th.

An order to advance came at daylight. We hurried across a field and to a belt of woods. We then moved a bit to the left and front and came to a line of works put up by our 2nd Division on a previous visit here. We stopped for a few hours, losing several men by stray bullets. After a while we moved back to a line of old works. During the day, the 1st Maine Heavy Regiment had a slight engagement and lost their colonel. This was all the fighting of any consequence.

## August 15th.

A skirmish was indulged in this morning but was of short duration. A couple of gunboats came up the James and made matters somewhat lively in Rebeldom. These old monsters have such perfect range that they never fail to put a shell just where they want it *every* time.

About 9 o'clock we moved up and massed our brigade in the woods in front. After convincing ourselves there was no immediate danger we lay down in the grass and waited further orders.

The order soon came to "send the heaviest regiment on picket." This meant none other than the 17th Maine, and a few moments later we were ambling along the New Market Road, a highway leading straight into Richmond. We formed on the edge of a cornfield of good dimensions. The Confederate pickets are on the opposite side, near enough to cause us much trouble should they be so disposed. Perhaps our boldness amazes them. A battery on their left *did* insist on showing us some attention, scattering missiles in our neighborhood. The only visible effect of this was to make us take up as little space as possible on the ground. (If some of us had smaller feet, the task of condensing ourselves at such times would be much simplified.) The bullets whisked around us in a manner positively threatening, but no one in our company was hit. Again, the gunboats opened on the Rebels, putting an end to this affair.

### August 16th.

A charge was ordered at 10 A.M., but it ended in smoke and not much else. On an advance into the cornfield, a shower of bullets flew around our heads. We had no protection but corn stalks, but not a man was hurt. This was nothing short of miraculous because the air was full of flying devils, whistling and screaming around us, cutting cornstalks and grass as clean as a scythe. We halted in our advance, and the Rebs ceased firing.

We stayed here till 5 P.M., when the threatened charge was made by Birney's 10th Corps. This corps was on our right and held several roads leading to Richmond. When the charge was made, we opened fire on the "chivalry" in front to hold them and to support the impression that the charge was general.

Birney's troops captured three lines of works and many prisoners. Two Confederate generals — Sherrard and Chambliss — were killed. Coincidentally, the last-named lived only a few miles from where he was shot. The Rebs made two unsuccessful charges to recover the works, then a third one resulted in their favor.

At dusk each side finds itself about where it was in the morning. We had hoped the distance between us and Richmond would be shortened several miles today, but this hope, like everything else since this campaign began, proved to be a disappointment.

### August 17th.

We were relieved from the front and sent to the reserves. It is very quiet here, and we are determined to do all in our power to keep it so. We immediately built some breastworks from cordwood lying nearby. Though they are not shell-proof, they will keep out bullets.

In the afternoon a truce was entered into for the usual purposes following in the wake of a battle. Hostilities were not resumed when the truce ended. About ten in the evening, we heard heavy firing toward Petersburg and noticed a glow in the heavens as though the entire city were in flames. A report soon circulated that Burnside's corps has entered and burned the city. The mania for lying has extended even to official circles. What the actual cause was we never heard.

### August 18th.

*Only* one more year to serve, if I continue to live. One must have as many lives as a cat to hope to live through what is, no doubt, in store for us.

Captain Hobson returned from the North today and resumed command of the company. This pleases us immensely, as he is very popular with the old men (that is, the original men from Camp King).

In the afternoon Rebels attacked in front and on our right. One movement was real, the other a feint, but we didn't know which was which. Neither was successful, but the skirmish gave us a chance to return some of the old iron and lead sent over here a few days since. When the fight opened, we were advancing into the cornfield to within supporting distance of the picket line. Hostilities ended with the daylight, and we remained out with the pickets, making a strong line of twelve men on a post, the usual number being four. About 9 o'clock we laid down for the night, but were turned out at ten and silently stole away. We very soon discovered by the landmarks that we were en route for Petersburg.

Soon after crossing the James we were halted, and in five minutes each man was sleeping just where he fell, too weary to unfold a blanket and thankful to have a chance to doze unmolested, something we hadn't done for several nights.

### August 19th.

Were put in motion as soon as it was light. We soon crossed the Appomattox and then followed the line to the Hare House, where we arrived about noon. Now it commenced to rain quite hard, a rather unpromising condition for men who don't have any shelter and but little idea as to *when* we will. After marching and countermarching an hour or so, we piled into some breastworks recently vacated by the 9th Corps, who have gone down to support the 5th Corps at Weldon Railroad.

### August 20th.

An uncommon quiet day, but the night compensated for it. The Rebs opened all their batteries on us, but the only casualty was one man killed in the 20th Indiana. We felt quite safe, unless our bombproofs caved in. After shelling us for a few hours, and wasting enough matériel to have fought a respectable battle, they "leff us be." We have known for some weeks that the Rebs are heinously under-provided with ammunition, so we cannot understand such an outlay of ammunition on their part.

### August 21st.

A heavy cannonading in the direction of the Weldon Railroad. It is reported that the enemy attacked the 5th Corps near Yellow Tavern (an old-time hostelry five miles below Petersburg) and got badly mauled.

Nothing happened in our vicinity until night, when a lot of deserters came in from Finnegan's brigade. They represent the 10th Florida, but their speech betrays them as Irish. Their blood-curdling oath — "Be Jabbers!" — never originated in Florida.

They were escorted to headquarters and a general sent word to Finnegan to "come over and take charge of your brigade!" Of late, deserters come in so often from his brigade, and at such unseasonable hours, that our officers are disgusted. These Celtic "patriots" probably found the lack of grub in Rebeldom not to their liking and decided to come back to the land of plenty. Candor compels me to admit, though, that they are by no means the only ones who mistake potatoes for principles.

### August 22nd.

If it isn't quiet here, I don't know the meaning of the word. There is not even the sound of the borers, which some of the timid ones assert are mining under Fort Sedgwick just as Burnside did under the Rebel fort near the oat field. Personally, I have no faith in the story, although there is a prevalent suspicion that something of the kind is underway. The officers cater to the suspicion by keeping but a small detail in the fort, so that if it did go up, the loss would be comparatively small.

Three more disgusted Rebels came in today for a more plentiful allowance of fodder. Rations are so poor and scarce over there that even prison fare is a luxury to them. We took them in with a good will.

### August 23rd.

Were routed out before we had accomplished our forty winks. Three o'clock in the morning is a decidedly unfashionable hour to get up. This business of retiring at ten and starting up in the wee hours has been going on for days and puts us in anything but an amiable mood.

A few deserters came in today who reported that their brethren were about to elevate Fort Hell, our cozy breastworks, with several tons of powder. The fort was vacated for a time, but, finding it didn't go up, we were ordered in again.

There was the usual amount of firing in front of the 18th Corps. If any Yankee raised his head above the works, he was greeted with a *Whiz! Whiz!* More men have been hit in this oat field than in any place three times its length along the line. The infernal scoundrels on the opposite line appear to have had no corresponding loss.

A piece of woods directly in front conceals a body of enemy sharpshooters. We could easily have battered it down days ago, and now are reaping the effects of our folly. The Seven Sisters could reduce the place to pulp in short time if only the order would be given.

### August 24th.

Every private in this army, of ordinary intelligence, knows more of war by actual experience and observation than any general knew at the commencement of this war. So, all things considered, McClellan made better showing than General Grant has up to now. Be it said to his everlasting credit that McClellan was a humane general and tried to avoid useless slaughter of his men. Now, with Grant in command, we have been in front of Petersburg as long, aye longer, than McClellan sat in front of Richmond, and yet we hear of no such senseless chatter as we heard about McClellan.

The quiet here now we regard as only a lull before another tempest. We are preparing for forward movements and strengthening our line for any attacks the enemy might make. We have a large detail at work on the City Point Road, making gabions, facines, and rolling breastworks, these last being the latest product of engineering skill. So far as I know, they have not yet been brought into use although I have seen many times when they might have been of considerable utility. Besides all these appliances, we sappers continue to dig so that we can pass from point to point without exposing our persons to danger.

### August 25th.

Nothing unusual till noon, when we were put under arms and executed the most extraordinary movement, worthy of a Wellington or a Napoleon and calculated to inspire the Southern Confederacy with mortal terror. We fixed bayonets and marched from right to left, and then, ducking down out of sight, returned to the right and repeated the maneuver. This performance was carried on until the Rebels must have decided that we have added at least 20,000 fresh troops to our force. We were fain to stifle our merriment at this absurdity. The Rebels kept right on with their cooking and other duties, utterly indifferent. They didn't even salute us to show an appreciation of such high strategy.

At night the Rebs showed us something of a truly strategic nature. They cut off a portion of our corps on the Weldon Railroad, gobbled up nine pieces of artillery, and took several prisoners. Our men had moved too far out and broken their connection with the rest of the corps. This isn't the first time we have sustained such a loss from this cause. It should teach all concerned the importance of keeping the flanks well-covered. If ever the teachings of experience were purchased at a ruinously high price, it is ours this summer. My soul is so permeated with sad memories as I think of it that I have been obliged to swallow my Adam's apple several times before proceeding with this narrative.

### August 26th.

Quietness is making us careless. We mount the works and sit there for hours reading and playing cards, anything to kill time. The Rebels have been equally loose, and this pleasant state of affairs might have continued indefinitely but for a dirty trick played on the Rebs by an old Dutchman in charge of the battery presently occupying Fort Sedgwick.

A bevy of females from Petersburg visited Fort Heaven (the Rebel fort opposite Yankee Fort Hell). They mounted the parapet and were chatting and laughing and having a good time generally. This so excited the envy of that eater of Limburger and sauerkraut that he sent a few little tokens of regard their way. Such scampering to get under cover, and such unearthly yelling, has not been often equalled. "Then rose the cry of women shrill / Like goshawks screaming on the hill." (Whatever goshawks may be — I know of no bird by this ill-sounding name.) I don't think the ladies were favorably impressed with Fort Heaven, notwithstanding the high-sounding title of that pile of Virginia mud.

### August 27th.

No firing today, and our men and the Johnnies have been playing cards and trading all day. There is a large tree midway between the lines, and thither the card players and traders ply their arts. The Rebels have obtained some silver money, and in the excitement of this discovery we nearly forgot our differences. We readily scoop in their shekels. Grub is trumps with hungry men every time.

During our trading today, we learned there is to be a big ball in Petersburg at night. We didn't deem it prudent to attend in a body, but chose a representative. Sam Bishop of the 17th Maine has procured a butternut suit from one of our card-playing friends and will attend the ball. We had to dictate strong orders to our big mortar, which has been in the habit of dropping shells most anywhere in the city every day for the last two months.

### August 28th.

The pickets, urged on by certain sons of Belial who doubtless fear an era of good feeling, commenced a lively firing at daylight. Supposing it to be an attack, we prepared to give our foe a worthy reception, but it proved to be only a fusillade. About seven, generals

Hancock, Mott, and de Trobriand visited our line to ascertain the wherefore of all this rumpus. This might appear akin to locking the stable door after the horse has been stolen. One thing is certain, no taint of cowardice or neglect of the troops in either of these worthies can ever be whispered. Braver officers than Hancock or de Trobriand I have never seen. At night we went on picket, and as there was no firing, we passed a very comfortable evening.

### August 29th.

On picket, and the Rebels tossed a few pieces of old scrap at us. No damage was done, no thanks to them. After a while their ammunition dried up, and we moved to the front to do a little trading. The money being exhausted on both sides, we gave sugar, salt, and hardtack for tobacco, of which they seemingly have an unlimited supply.

It was quiet again until night, when there was a lively artillery duel. The air was full of shells flying both ways and blinking like a host of monstrous fireflies. Most of this shelling was done by mortars in the oat field.

### August 30th.

Quiet again, and we have resumed trading under the big tree. The Rebels must be in a most precarious condition as regards food. While I was under the tree, a captain came out and asked me to sell him something to eat. As I had nothing but a piece of flabby salt pork which had been lying in the sun several days, I replied I hadn't anything fit to sell. I described the pork, telling him it was in camp. He requested me to procure the same immediately. Judge of my surprise when, with nervous haste, he clutched it as a starving dog would a bone. What could they be feeding on when a commissioned officer deems such stuff edible?

Why men will stay in the Southern army and support such a tottering cause is almost incomprehensible. Doubtless the chief reason is pride. Having enlisted, it requires more nerve to desert one's comrades than to face deprivation and death. And so they fight and suffer on, hoping that somehow deliverance will come. Our own cause sometimes has a leaden hue, but it is *bright* compared with theirs.

### August 31st.

We were mustered for two months' pay, and trading is still brisk, as if no thought of danger or treachery is apprehended. The supply of tobacco seems inexhaustible. We are getting on such good terms with our Southern friends that we can hardly conceive of tearing each other's eyes out again.

### September 1st.

Turned out at 3 A.M. It could as well have been at eight, as our batteries didn't open on the Rebel works until then, keeping at it until about noon. This was nothing but a waste of ammunition, and the Rebs showed good sense in not taking any notice. But it caused their officers to issue orders to stop all friendly intercourse with the Yankees. Too much contact with us is having a demoralizing effect on Lee's army. They are fast discovering how they have been duped. Most every night lately, Rebel pickets have found their way into our gopher holes to sit for hours cursing their leaders for continuing the war after resistance is in vain. We agree with them and clinch the discussion with a generous supply of coffee and cakes. Although these are sutler's cakes, and not fit to feed to hogs, we have no evil motives in offering them. The Johnnies seem to relish these abominations named cakes, and we wish to show we hold no ill will toward *them*, only toward the matter of secession.

We are all heartily sick and tired of slaughter and blood when we know that a slight concession on both sides could have settled the matter long ago. If left to us privates, we'd make short work of it. Perhaps we can accomplish more by cakes and coffee than by bullets.

There *is* a set in the North who would give Jeff Davis all he asks for in the South, and a generous slice of our territory as well. This infatuation of these Copperheads is beyond my comprehension. It is largely men of one class — drunken corner loafers — who favor the South. And they are mostly, if not wholly, Democrats. This by no means proves that all Democrats are Rebel sympathizers, for many of our best generals and soldiers are dyed-in-the-wool Democrats. But there are two kinds of Democrats, war and peace, and I think that the war element of the party are virtually Republicans in their sentiments.

### September 2nd.

Not an ounce of powder has been exploded today that I know of.

This morning I procured a copy of the *Richmond Examiner*, a daily sheet devoted soul and body to the Confederacy. It is a two-page concern, and small at that. (One of the Petersburg dailies is printed on common wallpaper.) The *Examiner* is filled with brag and bluster. It professes the greatest confidence in the ultimate success of the South. This is only the merest pretense, for the Rebels are almost daily compelled to yield ground somewhere. This paper wouldn't have been forthcoming, but the Johnnies were very anxious to get a paper of ours and knew of no way to get it except by exchange.

### September 3rd.

We have quiet again today. It seems hardly credible that two hostile armies are facing each other here.

### September 4th.

Quiet still prevails. We have news of the fall of Atlanta, accomplished by General Sherman. Atlanta is a highly important position for the Rebs, but of no specific importance to us except to keep them out and break their communications. It is the converging point of several railroads and the seat of many of their ammunition manufacturers.

Sherman must have exerted remarkable pressure, yet his losses were insignificant compared with ours here outside Petersburg with no such victorious results.

A salute of 100 guns was fired tonight to mark the event — and they were not blank cartridges. The Johnnies responded feebly, then quiet settled down over the field for the remainder of the night. The fall of Atlanta makes the Rebs more sparing of their ammunition. *We* feel tonight as if a heavy weight has been lifted from our shoulders. Every Rebel stronghold that falls is a great step toward the return of peace.

### September 5th.

This day the draft is to be enforced in the North, to fill the last quota called for by President Lincoln.[1] I have it from good authority that it is now exceedingly unhealthy up there. Drafting develops diseases hitherto unheard of in otherwise healthy men. In the absence of more serious maladies, a broken heart or a white liver will do. (One fellow reportedly claimed an exemption on the grounds that he was the "only child his mother had to support.")

There was some firing in the afternoon. I was on picket with Jose and Marble, and nonintercourse was the order of the day. So many of Lee's men have come over and forgotten to go back that "Uncle Robert" deemed it necessary to issue orders to this effect.

Rebel deserters are so plentiful that we are often at our wits' end to know what to do with them or how to care for them. It is not uncommon for them to arrive in squads of twenty or thirty. Nearly one-half of the Rebel army is presently commissioned officers, and an entire brigade sometimes numbers only three hundred men. The deserters complain that food is so scarce and their cause so utterly hopeless that they cannot suffer it any longer. If we keep on yanking them in at this rate, we'll have their entire army in a few weeks, or months at most.

Patriotism starts from love of self. We don't love any country any better than we do ourselves, and our reason for loving it is because we expect a benefit nearly equal to the outlay we make for our country.

Just previous to our exchange of pickets tonight, I went out and had an interesting interview with a young Johnny Reb. At first he was so scared, fearing I would gobble him (though we were on his own ground), that it was difficult to get him out of his hole. I assured him I merely wanted to trade. He was uncommonly well dressed, evidence that his wardrobe was recently supplemented by clothes from a fallen comrade. He had one desire that outweighed all others — to get something belonging to a genuine Yankee.

I had on a particularly shoddy cap and I noted he wore a fine one of English make. He seemed perfectly satisfied with the exchange, even though it was not a fair bargain. The usual Southron is alert to our devious character in sharp trading, but this young lad must be new to the practice.

It would be difficult to invent a story about the Yankee so absurd that the average Southerner would not gulp it down. Many still hold the childish notion that we have horns, blue bellies, and sundry other peculiarities. Even the Richmond papers print such myths. An old woman at Cold Harbor came near to having a fit when one of our men (to whom she had remarked, "I thought you'uns had horns") raised his hat to disclose a good-sized wen sticking up through his hair. She was so overcome by the sight that she had to be helped to a seat.

### September 6th.

Rainy and cool. About 9 o'clock we were relieved from picket. We only stay out twenty-four hours now. It is so uncomfortable on post that we prefer to go more often and not stay so long. In rainy weather the water in the saps lies three to twelve inches deep, and mud is everywhere. These narrow trenches act as sewers and receive all the surface water, turning our hardtack into sodden dough and assisting the onset of rheumatism. Our coffee is diluted, our sugar and salt dissolved, and our pork flabby from the drenching.

### September 7th.

We can record the usual firing today in the oat field. The troops who man our lines there don't know the luxury of standing up straight. From dawn to dark, and into the night, it is crack! bang! zip! and whish!

### September 8th.

The Confederates took it into their heads today to have a diversion with Grant's railroad. They don't take kindly to the fact that we have obtained a controlling interest in the Weldon Railroad. With this supply route cut off, flour has advanced to one hundred dollars a barrel in Richmond, and other articles have risen in proportion. Virginia's tables may. still be rich in *plate* but they are poor in *provender*. One thing secession has accomplished is to show the Southrons how few things they actually need.

### September 9th.

As there was nothing in particular to do, ninety men were detailed to level a lot of old breastworks near Fort Warren.

One other item made the day memorable. Old Tommy Eagan, recovered from his wounds of June 16th, returned to us today. I recall no special sin, committed severally or collectively, that merits such punishment. My hope was that we'd seen the last of his old Irish mug, but Fate was against us. He is in quest of another star on his shoulder straps, and I fear that his reappearance may be the signal for a new era of drunken foolhardiness.

### September 10th.

Three o'clock found us out and under arms this morning. A few Rebel picket posts on the right of the Jerusalem Plank Road were in a threatening position. Either they or we must move, and quickly. The 20th Indiana, the regiment selected to do the job, was supported by the rest of Birney's division (including our company). The 20th crept up to within a few paces of the Confederates. At the signal, they rushed the snoozing Rebs.

We captured about a hundred prisoners and contrived to leave thirty of our men inside the Rebel lines. This was the result of a misunderstanding by which several of our posts advanced when they shouldn't have, and daylight found them in this peculiar position. They could neither advance nor retreat. Some surrendered at once while others held position until dark, keeping up an incessant jaw with the Rebs in front of them. After a while the firing died out. The "common trash," of which I was one, laid low and let them blaze away. After dark they were able to retire back to our lines.

During the engagement, Colonel Michal of the 20th Indiana thought he would do something a little extra. He owned a bright red shirt and a pair of white pants, which he wore as undress uniform in camp on hot days. These he donned, then mounted the works, parading back and forth in an exasperating manner. His men, who worshipped him, begged the colonel not to expose himself so recklessly. He refused to come down. In but a few minutes, he who would not heed the entreaties of his friends or the dictates of his own reason listened to the persuasive eloquence of a minie ball, which tore its way through a vital part. The entire affair took less time than it has taken me to write it down. He died in less than two hours.

Colonel Michal was a general favorite on account of his fine soldierly bearing. Although not connected with him officially, I knew and liked him much. It seems as if some evil power drives some folks to their own destruction. Colonel Michal's was one of those cases.

At night, Jim Jose, Joe Paine, and myself went on picket from Company I. No sooner did we emerge from the opening in the works than a Rebel bullet deprived us of the company of Lieutenant Hobbs. He wasn't killed, only slightly wounded. The rest of us finally reached our destination in safety. After getting settled down we made the Confederates take a little of the sauce they have been peddling to us. The consequence was incessant firing all night.

### September 11th.

An armistice was agreed upon, both sides being sick of the restraints of the past twenty-four hours, when we stared Death square in the face every time we raised our heads. It is not much fun to be kept strung up to such a pitch. The armistice was of short duration, for the Reb officers ordered a resumption of firing. Their pickets sang out, "Get down inter yer holes, Yanks. We'uns are goin' to fire." Having allowed us time to get under cover, they opened fire.

A thundering clatter was kept up on both sides till night, when a cessation was called to allow pickets to be relieved. An agreement has been entered into that, hereafter, this should be the rule. It is a singular feature of this war that we should allow a cessation of hostilities so as not to injure each other. We pelt away all day and when night comes on, we suspend firing and commence to banter and laugh at each other till pickets are relieved, and then go at it again. If there is so much fraternal feeling among the men — and there is — then let *all* firing cease and let the leaven work.

### September 12th.

No safety today except in hugging the works vigorously. An incessant fire is kept up and it is deliberately inviting death for one of us to leave the works to go to our tents, just a few feet away. No one has been hit, but it has been thump! thump! thump! all day long. There must be tons of iron piled outside the works.

### September 13th.

Not contented with picket firing, the Confederates kept up a brisk fire from the works also. Two men from the 20th Indiana were instantly killed this morning while asleep in their tents. I fully expected that one of our own men would catch it, but we have reduced the art of "gophering" to a science. To gopher is to dig oneself into the ground. In military parlance, this would be called a "sap," but I prefer the Western phrase. Mortar shells fly into the works occasionally, at which times we get *out* in double-quick time. But the Rebels don't enjoy this sport alone. Our old Dutchman in Fort Sedgwick (alias Hell) has dropped several disagreeable visitors inside the Confederate works.

Fort Hell never appears in general orders under this name. It was derived in this way: General Baldy Smith rode up one day after it was completed, and seeing the name "Fort Sedgwick" on the sign, yelled "Fort Sedgwick! Fort Hell!" The name was immediately adopted. Although it is a dangerous place, its occupants never take it to heart. We sit around smoking, playing cards, and eating, as though at home — accustomed to the many missiles dropped in our midst.

### September 14th.

The Johnnies attacked our lines in front of the 18th Corps. They were handsomely repulsed, and with heavy loss. Our part of the line was not affected in the least.

One man in our regiment was incapacitated from labor today. Lots of men are hankering for a chance to get hurt just enough to get a respite from the front. There are others whose nervous systems are braced up by gazing through a bottle. There is wonderful recuperating power in a bottle, when properly manipulated.

At night went on picket, and there was firing all night, though it amounted to nothing except a waste of ammunition. Each man was required to carry out one hundred and fifty rounds and dispose of them before morning. (This helps explain the continuation of the war, and where the money goes.) Some men fired them all at the Rebels; others made rockets and mines of them rather than fire them at Rebeldom. We seldom hit a man during the day, and certainly don't stand much show of doing so at night.

### September 15th and 16th.

Noise and racket enough to drive a man distracted. There is one mitigating thought: we can stand it as long as the Johnnies can. They are as disgusted as we, and if their officers consulted them, there would be no more fighting. But, as the Rebs are the aggressors, they cannot be expected to make peace overtures.

The Confeds are dependent on foreign supplies. Even the clothes on their carcasses, except those stripped from our dead, come from England, as well as most of the necessities of life. Old Granny England has done all she can to aid them except to come out openly in their support.

Today the hungry Rebs made a raid on our cattle at Coggin's Point on the James and carried off 2500 head. We don't relish this, for we have yet to see the time when we had too much beef.

### September 17th.

Went on train guard about a mile in rear of the works and almost out of the sound of guns. Life at the front allows no rest, night or day. The change to the rear is much appreciated. No shells screaming, no bullets whizzing through the air. After a month at the front, I know how to appreciate a little rest. I am as happy as a deluded hen setting on a dozen china eggs.

### September 18th.

Raining hard, but I was not uncomfortable. A canvas covering over the hay stacks on which I reclined gave me protection.

One of our men was killed while on picket in front of Fort Hell today. He was hit in the back, but had strength enough to get back to the reserves and in a laughing way remarked that he was hit. Everyone supposed he was joking until he fell to the ground and the unmistakable pallor of death settled over his handsome features. His name was Cale Miller, and no more loved member of the company ever breathed.

How often are the ties of friendship severed by the cruel hand of war. One after another is cut down and hurried out, and I am left to mourn and wonder how many more will be called. My immediate circle of friendship has not been invaded by death since the first day in the Wilderness, when Frank Sweetser and Fred Loring fell. A Richmond paper once boasted that we "would plant 50,000 Yankees in Virginia."

I have no doubt but what this promise has been fulfilled to the letter. The world regards our fallen men as martyrs or heroes; *I* live to write their obituaries.

### September 19th.

Still on guard at the train and feeling much like "a cat in a strange garret." Having been so long at the front, I do enjoy the respite from danger but I begin to miss the excitement of the front. The boom of guns and bursting shells, the whirr of the gentle minie, have become so much a part of me that it does not feel quite right to have them stopped altogether. It is difficult to get accustomed to the sounds in the rear: carpenters, blacksmiths, teamsters, and commissaries. The teamsters make more noise than all the rest of the army. Their command of "army Latin" is absolutely astounding. Their bravado disappears when business takes them near the front, however.

A good pair of legs is a good investment when a retreat is inevitable, also in foraging on the march. The fact that I am here scribbling is proof conclusive that mine have never stood still and seen their owner abused. The short-legged fellows, or "rat detachment," need good underpinnings, for in marching we have to take three steps to every two of the "cranes," or long-legs. Notwithstanding this discrepancy, we rats don't furnish half so many recruits for the hospital as do the cranes.

### September 20th.

Returned to the front and am not so well pleased as I thought, for I do love my ease. Matters here haven't changed much during my absence, and little of note to record. There is less firing. This is as it should be, for to shoot men down, situated as we are, is nothing less than murder, and it amounts to nothing in settling this question.

### September 21st.

Word reached us that Sheridan gave old Jubal Early a tremendous thrashing in the Shenandoah Valley on the 19th. Early had the advantage, but he fell back. Sheridan pursued him for miles, his only orders being "Smash 'em! Smash 'em!" And smash 'em they did. A total rout was reversed and victory wrenched from defeat.

We fired a 100-gun salute in honor of the event.

### September 22nd.

On picket. One year ago today I was at Culpepper Court House and having a splendid time. Cannot say the same for today. We had an interview with some Johnnies and found them sore over the drubbing Sheridan has recently administered. They hoped the diversion over in the Shenandoah would lessen our grip on Petersburg and Richmond. The 6th Corps has been away in the valley some time, and now there is an excellent prospect that they will be returning to us soon. We certainly need them here.

### September 23rd.

Rainy and uncomfortable. We should have fared badly enough in camp, where we have small shelters — out here we have none, and but little fire. On picket our only tent is the sky, and it is leaking badly now. We munch hardtack and raw pork, washing it down with cold water. Some malignant persons intimate that our bread is some left over from the Ark stores. If this is so, it only goes to show that contractors in those days were as mean as they are now. It is some satisfaction to know that Noah's contractor was drowned; ours still lives.

One year ago today our recruits joined us at Culpepper. There were seventeen of them; only three remain. Most are dead, others in Libby prison. The three still alive and present are Marble, Brine, and Sawyer. Marble was wounded last June, but has recovered. Brine was saved by an infernally cheap watch bought of a swindler. A Rebel bullet struck it and glanced off, saving his life — not that this in any way exculpates the swindler.

### September 24th.

Not much excitement. I should like something to crack the dullness as I am sick and tired of looking over the wasteland of red clay between us and the Rebels. Nothing visible but dirt. Heard this afternoon that Sheridan is still pursuing old Jubal Early and his troops, and caught up with them at Fisher's Hill and laced them nearly out of their boots. At last account the Rebs were en route for Richmond via Gordonsville, and Sheridan was in hot pursuit. It has the appearance of having the tables turned now. Jubal has another chance to translate the English language into his peculiar vernacular, or such portions of it as have a profane sense. But he has good reason to swear if anybody ever did. For a general of his standing to get soundly thrashed twice inside of a week must cause a desire to express himself in the most emphatic language. He is the most thoroughly thrashed general in the Confederacy.

Good news comes thick and fast now and encourages our fainting hearts. We have laid here so long and accomplished so little that, if things drag along in this way, we stand a good show of being old men ere the Confederacy collapses. Another hundred guns were fired tonight to quicken the Rebel memory. It is quite probable that none of the rank and file of the Rebel army knows of their defeats. No reply was made to our salute, so probably their ammunition is as low as their spirits. The Rebels must now be satisfied that they cannot break our hold on the valley.

### September 25th.

This morning is quiet enough to suit even a sick person. Although there is heavy firing on our right, I don't locate it nearer than Fort Darling. There is a battery at the Howlett house that (in connection with the above-named fort) keeps our vessels of war from advancing up the James above Deep Bottom. If Butler's Dutch Gap Canal[2] ever gets completed, it is expected to obviate the difficulty by leaving Fort Darling high and dry. But for these things Richmond must long ago have succumbed to our combined land and naval forces. The gunboats alone can compel a capitulation in from two to four hours.

We are not over ten miles from the city, on the north side of it. Richmond is in a tight place and Grant has no idea of relaxing his hold until he has choked the life out of it (the life of the Confederacy being Lee's army). Here we are, sitting like two dogs confronting each other and watching for an opportunity to give the other a telling bite. This figure is suggested by a cartoon on an envelope issued in the early part of the war in which the two sections are represented by a miserable cur, Jeff Davis, trying to get a bone over which a huge mastiff, General Scott, is keeping guard. No doubt Jeff Davis is a cur, and I hope to see him get his deserts under Scott's successor, Grant.

### September 26th and 27th.

Heavy firing up on the James. We hope our gunboats will soon reach a position where they can silence the Rebel batteries. Dreary's Bluff is a high point of land on the James, and Fort Darling is on top of this, dominating our section. From there, all the movements of our fleets can be observed long before they get within firing distance.

Went on picket both nights, and it was quiet and peaceable. No firing except for the purpose of disposing of the surplus cartridges we are ordered to take out every night — not less than 150 rounds to a man.

### September 28th.

About 8 o'clock we were sent out on a detail cutting timber for a corduroy road near the Norfolk and Petersburg Railroad. Several of us cared more for grub than work and devoted our time instead to hunting up a sutler. When Hooker commanded this army we had a surfeit of food and drink, but we haven't received a full ration, such as the government allows, in more than a year. All the eatables I could find was a solitary box of sardines. I pitied its loneliness and took it under my vest. The sardines soon went the way of all the earth, and precious little strength I derived from them.

About sunset we were returned to the front and put under arms on account of an attack on the colored troops on our left. At the same time, a furious mortar shelling was commenced in the oat field. Knowing that this was simply a tickler to draw attention, we didn't move a step in that direction. The disturbance was of short duration, and by half past ten we were stowed away under our blankets.

### September 29th.

On this pleasant morn we were turned out most abruptly and ordered to move at 4 o'clock. We were soon ready except for striking tents, then lay around expecting the order to go, but no order came. The 18th Corps (General Ord) attacked the enemy at the Weldon Railroad, capturing fifteen pieces of artillery and 500 prisoners. At the same time the 10th Corps (Birney's) attacked them at Deep Bottom and dusted them out of their entrenchments. We heard they were in full retreat toward Richmond, closely followed by Birney, who was then in possession of the New Market Road. The Rebels rallied in time to halt our forces before they reached the second line, not more than four miles from Richmond.

### September 30th.

Under orders to march, but not until other troops relieve us. We lay around all day waiting further orders, which we didn't get. At night the enemy attacked on our right and was repulsed with heavy loss. About the time of this attack the 5th Corps (General Warren) attacked them near Yellow Tavern and fought till 9 o'clock in the evening, when the Rebels fell back toward the South Side Railroad. This road runs from Petersburg to Lynchburg via Burkesville, where there is a junction with the Danville Railroad running southwest from Richmond. Both roads are well-guarded, as the life of the Confederate capital depends on them. Originally, four railroads ran from Richmond to the south and east. We have entire control of one and a strong foothold on another. All the Rebel supplies have to be hauled by teams subject to cavalry raids. If we can possess the other two, down comes Richmond, and her walls and bulwarks become worthless.

### October 1st.

The division moved toward the railroad at 7 A.M. and headed south through the rain. I was highly indisposed and unable to march any distance, so Colonel Hobson sent me to the sutler's for guard duty. Lieutenant Usher sought this relief on my behalf, and his kindness was much appreciated, for guarding the sutler's stores is so much better than being out in the cold rain in my feeble condition.

Not long after the division's departure, we heard heavy firing, which continued all day. A report came back that General Warren had been killed, but this sad intelligence proved to be untrue.

At night the Rebs attacked some colored troops near the Jerusalem Plank Road. Some of these colored individuals received a sudden discharge from the war as a result. I am not able to say that I feel quite as badly about this as if the same number of white men had succumbed. I desire that their freedom should be established but don't consider that freedom involves social equality. If to them it means the liberty to foist themselves on our society, it also means to us the liberty to decline to entertain them. They might be just as good, just as clean, just as intelligent, and possess all the qualities of gentlemen, but they are a different species of bird. Still, there are many situations where I would prefer a smart, well-behaved colored man to a white man of the *opposite* character.

I have to acknowledge that my principal reason for disliking them now is *jealousy*. The colored troops have been much favored of late, and *we* have been contemptibly ignored, hence my feelings are not especially fraternal. If a division of white troops had been favored thus, I would be equally indignant and just as outspoken about it. This resentment is widespread. It is almost impossible for a nigger cook or bummer to pass on horseback or mule without being the subject of abuse, sometimes of violence, though the latter is infrequent.

### October 2nd.

Still could hear heavy firing in the direction of the Weldon Railroad. On the front just vacated by our division (Mott's), there was considerable cannonading, although no attack was reported.

I was again on guard at sutler Wineberger's. Humphrey's division have just drawn their pay and kept us busy furnishing them with edibles. The day's receipts were over $1350, mostly for crackers, cheese, and cakes — more properly called "condensed cholera" because of the condition that directly results from ingestion.

Likewise did the 2nd Division eat, and the profit on them was over $1000. Once started filling their bellies with something besides rusty pork and hardtack, the men don't seem to know when to stop as long as money or credit holds out, at which time a rigid fast begins. Some men have been known to offer a costly watch to the sutler for just one fill-up. (In at least one case, this would not be a particularly good bargain for the sutler. J——m C——k, for instance, can easily eat the value of two watches at a sitting.)

### October 3rd.

Almost perfect silence now prevails, and it is rumored that the enemy are evacuating. (Just *why* anybody should think the city is being evacuated is not clear.) At 8 o'clock the quiet of the day was broken by a most furious racket, but by 9 o'clock quiet had settled down on camp again.

Some of the sutlers, having no goods to sell, packed their goods when the uproar broke out and perambulated deftly in the direction of City Point. Not so with Wineberger; he decided to stay a while longer and risk a little more. He *has* to stay, or also go off and leave his goods, for he cannot procure transportation for love or money.

### October 4th.

We sold $1000 worth of stuff at the sutler's today (or more properly $200 *worth*, for which he received $900 in profit.) At the sutler's suggestion I acted as clerk when a rush began. After a short while he notified me that he would attend to the money-taking, as some scrip had disappeared from his box. A $20 bill had suddenly decamped, either by theft or mistake. If stolen, I had done it. This imputation could not be rested under with dignity, and he quickly apologized when I objected to the accusation.

At night another little tilt occurred with our friends over the way, and they got the worst of it. They charged our lines near the Jerusalem Plank Road and were repulsed with heavy loss. Among the prisoners was a brigadier general who professed to have surrendered voluntarily. The kind of gum he was giving us wasn't being chewed on this side of the fence, for we know that Southern gentlemen only come in by force or fasting.

There were indications earlier in the day that there is fighting beyond Petersburg. Perhaps our troops have penetrated to the South Side Railroad. Here behind the lines, we have no reports from my division, but seeing some pontoons moving in that direction, we conclude that progress has been made and that a crossing of the Appomattox above Petersburg has been effected.

### October 5th.

After a fight, the sense of rest and peace that comes over a body is something marvelous — like a reprieve from death or deliverance from great danger — and valuable in proportion, for the chance is that it will not occur again. True, I haven't done much active fighting of late, but I have had enough in the season just past to make me desire peace forevermore.

This day was spent in the service of the sutler of the 110th Pennsylvania. Being a liberal sort of fellow, not like old Wineberger, he broke open several cans of turkey, duck, mutton, and beef, and commanded me to exercise my culinary skill immediately. Having been on the verge of starvation for many moons, I needed no second invitation. We soon sat down to a dinner fit for the president. The contrast between this sutler and ours is glaring; ours is not only too mean to feed us, but too mean to feed himself.

My division came back at night and took position near Fort Sedgwick. I was glad to hear their familiar voices ascending in some choice cuss words as they stumbled over the guy ropes of the sutler's tent in the darkness.

### October 6th.

Our troops were coming in all the forenoon and moving out into the works in front. The Rebels took no notice of their arrival. I learned that no casualties have befallen our men in Company I, except that a tree fell across the spinal column of "Sissy" Rounds, nearly breaking it. (This wasn't needed, for it was none too strong anyhow.) He recovered sufficiently to get into camp.

At noon those of us at the sutler's were ordered to join our command. "Old Hentz" feels safe now that our division is back, which only goes to show that he has a power more confidence in us than we have in him. Honest or not honest, I can't forget or forgive the devilish cheating we endure at his hands and have no compunction in helping myself to anything I can get hold of.

### October 7th.

On fatigue building bombproofs as a protection against mortar shells, which are getting to be mighty common.

Two years ago today I left Fort Stanton for active service in the field. I little thought at the time that I should be here now or that the war would have continued this long.

### October 8th.

Nothing of special interest occurred. In fact it was an unusually quiet day and we passed the time "laying around loose," which phrase has considerable meaning when used here. In military affairs it indicates a general unbending of the usual stiffness and strain, a time when we lay aside "buckram and starch." Some slept, some played cards, some wrote letters, others devoted the time to cooking and eating, the latter occupation being the only one some care to engage in. The only drawback to their pleasure is the lack of something to keep the jaws going. We have several men who can eat three days' rations in one.

### October 9th.

Painfully quiet down this way, but noisy enough on the James. This has no effect on us except to arouse our curiosity to know the extent and the locality, and whether the results are favorable to us or not. We have a strong desire to know the reason for such a liberal outlay of ammunition and whether or not the channel of the James is entirely obstructed so that it has to flow through Dutch Gap Canal. This triumph of engineering skill seems to give our Secesh friends no end of anxiety and concern. They vent their rage as often as possible on those who are engaged in its construction, especially the niggers. The Rebels well know that when that canal proves a success, at that instant Fort Darling becomes useless as a defense for Richmond and the city will be at the mercy of our gunboats.

Setting aside the hope of foreign intervention, the Rebels by now can hardly keep a corporal's guard in the field. But the Rebel army is densely ignorant, and their ignorance is only equalled by their confidence in their leaders and their faith in final success. On the other hand, we *Yankees* (not the Irish, English, Dutch, or any other foreign element) are readers and thinkers and have no blind faith in anyone. We judge for ourselves, and no amount of brow-beating or blarney can move us a hair. If the difference in the mettle of our two armies were as marked in *our* favor as the difference in knowledge, we would make quick work of it. But unfortunately for us, the measure of Rebel ignorance is not the measure of their courage, but rather the reverse. They are brave, or reckless, just in proportion to their ignorance.

## October 10th.

The Rebels shelled us a little today but no one was injured. Sometimes we don't care a straw for it all; other times we don't care a straw to live any longer. My mind reverts to the days in the last two years corresponding to these dates and then I take courage and hope that I have not much longer to endure these experiences. Two years ago today we were in the confines of Washington and Lee wasn't many miles away. One year ago we were just breaking camp to skeedaddle toward Washington with Lee on our flanks. These facts are mentioned for the benefit of those (would be) prophets who insist that we have gained *nothing* and have made no progress southward. In addition, they openly declare the war a failure and demand a halt.

There are in the North a lot of dough-faces who are never happier than when a chance is offered to them to get down on their marrow bones and fawn on their slave-owning friends of the South, acknowledge their infinite superiority, and pay their respects and ask pardon for being born outside the limits of Rebeldom. Indeed we have such a case in our town of Saco, where one aged citizen is so affected when the Secesh suffer defeat that he hies himself to bed and indulges in a fit of sickness. His son-in-law has similar symptoms, each competing with the other in the grief business. If they could only know with what contempt they are held by the Rebels!

## October 11th.

In the matter of firing we have been the aggressors today. But we have no compunctions of conscience on account of it. The Confeds replied with mortars, the only missile that amounts to shucks, situated as we are. Shot or shell fired point-blank doesn't hurt anybody unless they happen to be away from the works, but mortar shells, especially if fired in the daytime, are the visitors who make us wish we were "not at home." Two men were instantly killed today by the explosion of one of the above named death-dealers. They heard the report and both looked up. One had the back of his head torn off while the other lost the front of his head.

This region is dangerous and demoralizing. Not only this, it is disgustingly filthy and hasn't a single redeeming quality. The hours we pass on picket or asleep are the only ones when we know comparative comfort. But on picket there is no protection from mortars. Some of them are rude enough to invade our holes without the ceremony of an introduction or an invitation. At such times we make a hasty exit.

## October 12th.

Quiet today, but an arrival occurred which gave us precious little satisfaction. It was none other than Colonel West, who has been away since May 5th, when he was wounded in the leg in the Wilderness. His advent was the signal for Lieutenant Colonel Merrill to "get up and dust," his resignation having been sent in time to take effect when West arrived. West was promoted colonel by jumping over Merrill. However, this was not the reason given for Merrill's resignation. Colonel Merrill said it was on account of "domestic affairs of a delicate nature requiring immediate attention." It wouldn't have been consistent with honor or dignity to remain under this new relationship. Colonel Merrill should have had the promotion; he has earned it. He came out of Portland as lieutenant colonel, with West as a major. The latter, who is ambitious and unscrupulous, has left no stone unturned to make Merrill appear at a disadvantage. Consequently, they have never had the most ardent attachment for each other.

None of us think that Merrill is excessively brave, but he has the respect and affection of the men to a marked degree. He is a humane gentleman and too tender-hearted for a fighter, although he has stuck by us through the thickest of it. West we admire because of his military tact, and Colonel Merrill for qualities of the head and heart no less conspicuous. To these latter Colonel West is a perfect stranger. He is a very pompous individual who acts as if he thinks the Creator exhausted his inventive power in making *him*. His contempt is unbounded for all who are not up to his standard of military knowledge. This is all he excels in, and he deems all other matters as nonessential.

I can attest to Colonel West's character as I have had a little experience with him in the past. The last time I had an interview with this aggregation of "fuss and feathers," he left in a frame of mind not conducive to deep or abiding friendship, and I well know that if an opportunity presents itself, I will be made to remember this little affair. Notwithstanding the airy way he has, West is a thorough military man, quick as a flash to comprehend the situation and anticipate orders. He has an eye like an eagle. One time on dress parade, when he saw a man way down the line whose coat was partially unbuttoned, he yelled: "That man on the left, button your coat." Not one person in ten thousand could have detected this little discrepancy at that distance, there being only one button out of order. His own clothing is faultless.

Our Mr. West has returned and we can hope for no more rest. Now every moment not spent in drill or fatigue duty will be devoted to policing camp, polishing guns, and wearing our clothes out with excessive brushing. Under Colonel Merrill, red tape was relegated to a back seat. He allowed the broadest latitude consistent with the good of the service. West should have a professorship at West Point; the field is too dirty for such a paragon of neatness. He *is* consistent, inasmuch as he never requires of us any more than he does of himself in this respect.

## October 13th.

We had every reason to believe we were to be blown into the "unfathomable hence" in a jiffy today. But, for some reason unknown to us, the enemy softened and decided to let us abide on the shores of time a little longer. I attribute this failure to annihilate us to wet powder or fuse. No doubt exists in my mind of their disposition toward us — to diminish our numbers is nothing less than a religious duty.

During the afternoon some troops moved down from the right and occupied the works at the Jerusalem Plank Road. The Johnnies saw them and accelerated their movement by dropping a few "whistlers and screechers" among them. We also were favored with a few tokens of their esteem, which flew harmlessly overhead or lodged in the works in front. There is much heavy firing in the direction of Richmond. It is pound! pound! all the time, day after day, week after week, and this has been going on for nearly four months. About all we have gained in this time is an extension of our lines to the left. We have held our own and know we are slowly encircling the doomed city, so slowly that it seems as if we must be compelled to surrender the job to the next generation. No other general has taxed the patience of the country as Grant has. We are progressing on the hypothesis that "a continual dropping will wear away a stone." A continual digging and pounding and fighting is, we hope, wearing out the Confederacy.

## October 14th.

To a listener of the racket this morning it would appear as if a heavy musketry fire is going on — a big battle or a lively skirmish. But it is neither; it is just picket firing. We don't know what ails our friends across the way, nor do we care. Probably some bad news has reached them (and they have heard but little else of late) and they take this way of showing it. We give them as good as they send. It is probable that they have no idea how much ammunition we have to peddle out. Persons of ordinary mental caliber might have guessed that it was practically inexhaustible from the tremendous amount we put out in various ways.

## October 15th.

Colonel G. Washington West, being desirous of perfecting the regiment in drill (something which everyone must see the necessity of — we have been out *only* a little over two years), made application to headquarters to have the regiment sent back to the rear about a mile, urging his "old wound" as a barrier to his longer stay at the front. So we were moved back to the vicinity of Parke's Station and hugged so close to a piece of woods that no matter how high the Rebels might perch, they cannot get a sight at us. Consequently we can defy them, but in a tone so low the Rebs can't hear us. In doing this we follow the suggestion of one of our number from the "rooral deestrics," who, when we used to open fire on the Rebs, would say in a ludicrously solemn way, "Don't aggravate um, for God sake. They may fire at us."

This new situation is by no means what we desire, but it is an improvement on Fort Hell. There is no danger — that is in its favor. Then, there is plenty of wood and water, the woods in our rear being full of old camps and wells. At Fort Hell it is dry and dusty as a dust pan, and hot enough to boil eggs.

Back of us are the wagons, and then a picket line for protection. We should not be greatly surprised if we are called upon to repel an attack from this quarter any hour in the day. If so, there might be a third Bull Run, for by some accounts, it was teamsters and civilians who caused the first Bull Run.[3]

## October 16th.

So quiet we heard the church bells in Petersburg. Hence, I infer it must be Sunday. The sound causes a huge chunk of hardness to lodge in my Adam's apple. If a tear meanders down my cheek, who shall accuse me of weakness?

I do confess to a feeling of homesickness. Many of us were accustomed at home to spend a goodly portion of Sunday in church, and it seems as if it would be quite nice and refreshing to be there again. Here, the observance of the day is generally of the most farcical character. We now and then go through the forms of service, but Sunday is no different from any other day except that the inspections are more rigid than on secular days. Homesickness is only an incident. It is not caused altogether by thoughts connected with worship or church going; filthy pork and mouldy hard bread, which are so large a portion of our commissary supplies, are enough to make a hog homesick. As nothing better is furnished, we are compelled to eat it or go without.

We had no drill or inspection today, but at night a large detail was called for to go on picket. It took nearly all of us. A few invalids were left behind for camp guard. The locality to be picketed was at the angle on the left of the Plank Road. It is an extremely dangerous place when there is picket firing. Then it is all one's life is worth to move around. Although there was supposed to be no picket firing today, one of our men was shot while going to the rear for water. These miserable Rebel devils, whom some claim are too chivalrous to do anything of a mean or treacherous nature, are the quintessence of double-dealing and treachery. All talk to the contrary is nonsense and drivel. Several times of late we have agreed on an armistice and had a right to consider ourselves secure, when the first thing we know, down goes a man. Something severe should be done to teach them the sacredness of a truce.

I can recall only one instance where anyone on our side has been guilty of such dastardly conduct (although opportunity has not been lacking). I have many times tried to cover these acts with the mantle of charity in the belief that the privates in the Rebel army are not as venomous as the higher grade of Rebel, and that in many cases they are simply the tools of those in authority. But it won't go down. No one *compels* them to attempt to scatter our brains around when we are reposing special confidence in them and trusting in their honor. When their officers order them to fire at us, it would be a very easy matter to miss their mark by over- or under-shooting.

### October 17th.

Tolerably quiet. We had another case of Rebel treachery today. One of our men was out trading with a Rebel this morning when the report of a musket was heard and down went our man. The lines are very near at this point, and a parcel of anything could be thrown from our lines into theirs (or, as one fellow remarked, "so near we can shake anything at them"). Shooting the man was deliberate *murder*.

For several days past a fight has been carried on with bricks, so we are not in doubt as to what nationality is opposed to us here and represented by this missile. Although it has been many times asserted that no foreigners are employed in the Confederate service, and that the South would rather not win their independence than do it in this way, we are proof of the falsehood. Some of our men have been treated to "a clout in the head" or a "belt in the gob," these being in vogue among the Milesians.[4] I am proud to say we fully cancelled our obligations to them and gave them clout for clout. Though this is unconstitutional warfare, we should be remiss in our duty if we didn't return what they lent us. We can carry it on as long as they furnish us with bricks. This must be the remnants of Finnegan's Brigade across the way, for brickbats come as natural to an Irishman as ducks take to water, or as a Dutchman eats sauerkraut.

Somehow I don't crave death in this way. It isn't my idea of glory at all.

### October 18th.

No bricks or shillelaghs today. It is as quiet as a country churchyard. This date marks another milestone passed: we are ten-months men today (having only ten months left of our enlistment). But the *shorter* our time, the *longer* it seems, and the more impatient we become. There is a good chance even now that we may die from a combination of circumstances and a load of buckshot. Thus far I have rejected all inducements to become an angel but my chance for exemption seems to diminish as my time decreases. Still, every day of quiet like this helps out, and I hold my breath from day to day, praying that something may turn up to put a more hopeful aspect on the case.

*October 19th.*

If there is anything new under the sun I am in ignorance of the same. At the front, picket firing and mortar go on lively. Today, through the courtesy of Adjutant Verrill, we obtained a copy of Colonel Merrill's farewell address, which we prize very highly. Knowing his kindness of heart, it isn't difficult for us to believe he meant what he said. It is a neat little gem that reflects credit on its author as well as on ourselves. His sympathies have always been with the men, in our trials and hardships, and he tried to lighten our burdens on every occasion.

The address reads as follows:

Special Order 71

The War Department having accepted my resignation, tendered in consequence of pressing claims of a private nature, my official connection with this regiment is terminated. For nearly twenty-seven months we have been associated together, and together shared the privations of field and march; of bivouac and trenches. At Fredericksburg, the Cedars, Chancellorsville, Gettysburg, Wapping Heights, Auburn, Locust Grove, Mine Run, Spotsylvania, North Annah, and during the long seige of Petersburg, you have attested your devotion to the Union and the glorious cause in which you have been engaged. On the hillsides and valleys of the Old Dominion we have laid to rest many of our brothers and made indeed *sacred* the soil of Virginia.

How shall I speak of the noble sons of Maine who, in the suppression of this accursed rebellion, laid down their lives on the altar of our country? Pickett, who sank to rest ere his sword had once been drawn on the field of battle; the noble and large-hearted Waterhouse, beloved by all; the self-sacrificing Johnson, who at Chancellorsville fills an unknown grave; the ardent and impulsive Fogg; and the modest Dyer; the brave and determined Sawyer; and Brown, whose whole life was devoted to duty; Noyes and Roberts; and the gallant Benny Pennell; and the boy hero, Bosworth. They are gone, and forever, but while we live we will keep their memories green.

The heroism and bravery and persistent devotion to duty of the men of this regiment needs no fulsome praises. Upon their banners they have inscribed the record of their deeds, and with their bayonets written their own history. To one and all, both officers and men, I must say farewell. May the god of battles watch over and protect you, and return you in honor to our dear old Pine Tree State, with peace throughout our *whole* country firmly and irrevocably reestablished.

Signed,
C.B. Merrill

The general tenor of this address I like. But I must file exception, as the lawyers say, to one of these remarks and decidedly object to another. First, I wish to express my unqualified disapprobation of the remarks relating to Lieutenant Brown. Of all the tattling, lying, fuss-creating creatures I ever encountered, this Brown takes not only the cake, but a whole bake shop. If this is *duty*, then Colonel Merrill said truly that his "whole life was devoted" to it, and I have thus far labored under a misapprehension as to the meaning of the term. Colonel Merrill must have had some other person in mind when he penned these lines.

The other phrase to which objection is made is: "the boy hero, Bosworth." What he ever did to merit any special notice is beyond my knowledge. I have heard of "posthumous taffy" and think we have it here. Bosworth died from a wound received at Wapping Heights, but I never knew of any special display of heroism on his part.

### October 20th.

During the day it was quiet, but in the evening the Johns made up for any excess of inactivity. Those who sat in the front-row seats received many tokens of affection from across the way. Our mortars in and about Fort Hell reciprocated these tokens. At night went on picket again. It begins to look as if we have not wholly escaped the dangers of the front. I should much prefer a permanent position at the front to so much picketing in such a hole as this. The Rebels can enfilade our line as it is some distance in advance of the main line, thus subjecting us to a front and flank fire and a continual menace.

### October 21st.

On camp guard. An unusual stillness prevails. We hear no firing but this by no means proves there is none, as certain atmospheric effects might prevent us from hearing it. This was an inexpressibly happy day for one of our men. He went home, and to *stay*. He was a nine-months man who deserted and, having been caught, was sentenced to serve out his time in our regiment. This was little better than death, but Fate was propitious; he escaped all the darts of the adversary. O happy day to him, and although I am in no wise a sharer in his good luck, I am highly pleased to see even one escape from this place. We all want to go bad enough, but not enough to allow the Rebels to leave on any other than an honorable basis: a laying down of their arms and acknowledgement of rightful authority. I also entertain an overwhelming idea of being in at the death of the Rebellion and seeing the men who have withstood us humbled and the leaders made to know that treason is o-d-i-o-u-s.

### October 22nd.

Nothing special today, but at night a lusty old row was kicked up between the Rebels and some niggers on our right. Although exceedingly lively, it turned out to be nothing but picket firing. The Rebels never can forgive the insult of our putting niggers in front of them. They have also met several times in action, and this did dreadfully exasperate the chivalry.

It must be confessed that my own antipathy to these "gem-men ob color" isn't so very much below that of the Rebs, but it might not be safe, or prudent, to give expression to such treasonable ideas. It was hinted that by arming them we might save a few white men, but if there has been the slightest dimunition in the death rate among us on this account, I have yet to hear of it. It is said the Rebels at one time contemplated arming them, but on second thought they decided to let the nigger become the digger while the whites continue to manipulate the musket.

### October 23rd.

It dawned on us that it was a Sunday when a full inspection was ordered by Colonel West. He never has any divine services for he doesn't believe in "sepulchral cant." There is no hypocrisy about our Mr. West, whatever else he is. He is a despiser of sham, and our chaplains' services are but little else — a mockery and insult to the Almighty.

Went on picket about 4 P.M. near the Plank Road. There was constant firing, and if we hoped to keep our heads on our shoulders, we had to be very careful to keep low. That we should be perforated seemed absolutely certain. Throwing out vedettes was not to be thought of, as they would have been riddled through in ten minutes. It was precious little satisfaction to know that Mr. Johnny Reb had no more privilege in this respect than we did. A continual popping kept up from dark till daylight.

### October 24th.

We lost two commissioned officers in our company today, and with but one bullet. The missile passed through Captain Hobbs's lungs and lodged in Lieutenant Widden's shoulder. The captain, who had just been promoted to this rank, died in five minutes.

### October 25th.

Got up early, expecting to be soon on the road. We packed up, but hour after hour passed and no order came. Thus the day wore away, with us lying in the dust up to our ears. the heat and suspense were almost unbearable. Which of these three ills is the worst — the heat, the dust, or the suspense — I am hardly prepared to state. By moving a few yards into the woods we could have avoided much of the dust and the heat.

During the day the teams arrived with fresh rations and ammunition. The artillery and teams also came up from City Point and moved toward the left, setting in motion a fresh rumor that we are going to make a heavy attack somewhere on the left. But we have seen enough of Grant to know that what we *expect* of him is just the last thing he will do. (It is pleasing to most men to play the prophet, and the less they know, the more positive they are.) At night, we laid down no wiser than we were last night, at which time I would have bet quite a sum that we should not be here *now*.

### October 26th.

About 2 o'clock we started for the left, keeping well to the rear, following wood roads till we came to the Gurley house. From there, we went outside the line of works and followed the Weldon Railroad a short distance, then bivouacked for the night. The 1st Maine Cavalry were nearby, and some of our Saco friends from that regiment came over to visit. They have orders to be in the saddle at daylight, but it looks very much like rain might interfere with the arrangements. Whenever this army plans a movement, it is almost certain to storm. Our orders are a good barometer.

### October 27th.

Routed out at 3 A.M. and were informed that we had a half hour to get breakfast. It was dark and drizzly and we were in a sour mood for marching, but we moved down the line of railroad a short distance, then turned to the left and passed the Wyatt house, following the Vaughan Road to Hatcher's Run, which we reached about daylight. Here were the enemy's outposts, from which we had to force them to retire. They went over the run at Armstrong's Mills. After crossing the stream, they attempted a stand behind some works, but we moved them on, taking the works and some prisoners. We then deployed all over the field and through the woods to assure ourselves that we were not getting into an ambuscade.

While skirmishing through the fields we encountered another of those solitary and solemn figures of which mention has been made before. My suspicions were immediately aroused. Her aspect was sepulchral, reminding me of ghosts and restless spirits. My opinion is that she was a confounded Rebel spy taking account of our strength. Her ghostly appearance would soon have become real if we'd been allowed to pepper that solemn female. It is very strange that this apparition has appeared yet a third time, perambulating always in the opposite direction with downcast eyes and measured tread, apparently seeing nothing, yet seeing all things.

The Rebels continued to fall back, and if it was a trap they were setting, it was a deep one. About 4 P.M. they halted at the Boydtown Plank Road. We soon formed in line of battle, ready to go for them. Our cavalry dismounted and took a position in the field to the left and rear of us. Notwithstanding all our caution, we were now in a tight place. The Rebel batteries had range of our cavalry and began dropping shells, causing the horses to plunge and rear in a manner suggesting an early stampede. We were nearly surrounded, and the Rebs, thinking they had us, commenced to close in to "bag the game." They initiated a furious onslaught on the weakest point of our line, which was McCallister's brigade. It was soon worsted. The Rebels, essaying to follow, found themselves in an uncomfortable position, for at that moment Pierce's and de Trobriand's brigades executed a movement on each flank, charging as they went, thus opening a way for McCallister to get out of the mush.

There was now a lull in the storm; the Rebels had been worsted and fell back. Much to our amazement, we held the line. I was confident at one point that we should all pass the night in Rebeldom. There was nothing to be gained by occupying such an advanced position once the Rebels retired, so we fell back and occupied a narrow road. We threw up a light line of defenses constructed so we could fight, or flee, from either side.

So ends the fighting of this day. About 7 in the evening went on picket. It was a most dismal and comfortless night. Rain fell continually, and we were soon drenched and shivering with cold. There we sat, wearily watching for the enemy, who was, no doubt, doing the same. After an hour or so, the detail was recalled to escort the ambulance train back to the Gurley house, where a hospital has been established.

The march was too much for some of us, and we sprawled by the roadside to snatch a moment's rest. Stacy, Simpson, and myself bivouacked under a big tree whose spreading branches offered a partial shelter. It was past midnight, thus our pause would be of short duration. It was take what we could get and make the best of it. We were so weary that we hardly noticed the rain.

### October 28th.

We three under the tree were rudely roused by a Rebel yell accompanied by a discharge of musketry close at hand. They had been working round all night to the right of our line, intending to capture us in the morning. Just at this point in the game, a little diversion was created by General Warren. The Rebels were hindered in their impetuosity, but not until they had thrust the 5th Corps back some distance. The 9th Corps had also been placed in position to aid us in case of need, but the reception given them by the 5th Corps was all the Rebels wanted at one session and they didn't get far enough to strike at the 9th.

Stacy and I were all forenoon trying to find our division. At the Yellow Tavern (of which Virginia boasts many, all looking the same and bearing like names) the provost guard stopped us, but finding we belonged to the 2nd Corps and were steering in that direction, he sent us on our way, and we soon joined the division at the Gurley house.

Soon after our arrival an order was issued to build camp. Materials were plenty, and in two hours a camp was well under way. Then the order to build was superseded by another to "move immediately." We were soon back on the flats we had occupied previous to all this movement and tents fast thrown up. The Gurley house would have been a desirable campsite, but this devilish hole has nothing to recommend it except its contiguity to fuel.

### October 29th.

Spent most of the day policing grounds and trying to make them presentable. We also devoted some time to getting ready for colder weather, as we might winter here. We have long since abandoned the hope of taking Richmond this season. Grant's laconic telegram that he would "fight it out on this line if it took all summer" could now be extended to "all winter, and God only knows how much longer."

We heard today of a pretty smart affair recently played on the Rebels. One hundred men from Barlow's division executed this bold movement. They contrived to get inside the Rebel lines even though the pickets were but a few feet apart. The main line was penetrated and four guns spiked. In their plans, this was but the prelude to greater mischief, but the Rebels rallied and set upon them, capturing 75. The rest of the men regained our lines. I have heard much of Rebel pluck, but it has never risen to the dignity of such actions as those of Barlow's men, the *New York Day Book* or any other lying Copperhead sheet notwithstanding. I challenge the Rebel admirers in any section to produce an instance of so daring a character as this. The Southerners' deeds of valor heretofore have consisted mostly of such affairs as hanging Union sympathizers or banishing them, throwing trains from the track, trying to spread pestilence in our cities, and planning the destruction of New York and other Northern cities. This by no means completes the list of outrages, but it is enough to show the nature of their "chivalry." If such deeds are any evidence of elevated culture, or pluck, then I am thankful that the Yankees have none of these qualities. Rebel pluck may be well enough in its way, but *we* have a chance to see its peculiarities far better than people who sit in New York, writing for Copperhead sheets. For the credit of humanity, I do sincerely desire to find an apology for some of the Rebel deeds, but can only attribute such behavior to the old spirit of intolerance and encroachment engendered by slavery.

### October 30th.

Nothing going on in the morning, strange as it may appear. It is like the ways of Providence or the decisions of a petit jury — past finding out. A dress parade was ordered at 5 o'clock, but that order was countermanded by one to march. We broke camp at dark and moved into Fort Rice, a large work on the right of Fort Sedgwick.

After getting straightened out we laid down for the night, but the Johnnies kicked up a bobbery, shelling our line vigorously and showing strong symptoms of attack. We prepared to receive them, but they didn't come. After an hour or so we retired again, this time with good success.

Being now at the front, it is our duty to sleep with one eye open. This is the more incumbent on some of us because certain others make such a business of sleeping that it takes a long while to wake them up. When an attack threatens, it is necessary to nearly shake the life out of them before they can realize what is wanted of them. If all of us were so somnolent, the Rebel army could walk in here any night after 10 o'clock and steal everything, including the sleepers. One fellow in our company can lie down anywhere and sleep soundly as a babe. It matters not that his head lies in the dust or ashes, or that his mouth is wide open and the flies go in and out like bees while the hot June sun pours down on him. How I envy such oblivion.

### October 31st.

As soon as the first streak of dawn appeared I turned out to take in a view of this old pile of dirt. Our opportunity to take a squint at the enemy is better from here, although he keeps himself mostly beyond our ken. It is the same on our side. All I could see outside the forts was a brigade on reserve near the Avery mansion.

Fort Rice is a large, bombproof earthwork manned by Randolph's battery, and now by the 17th Maine. Although this battery is from Rhode Island, the men comprising it are not of such contemptibly small calibre as those who relieved us at Fort Stanton years ago. Randolph's battery rendered us marked services at Gettysburg, so we have agreeable companionship here.

We have a sap running from here to the picket line, and a covered road to the rear. The officers and sutler have their tents outside the fort, the privates inside. Everything is painfully neat, nuisances of every kind being strictly prohibited. Although we have to pack ourselves in uncomfortably thick, we are not too close to be neighborly.

Some have become *too* neighborly after cultivating an acquaintance with the commissary whiskey. Tonight while soup was being prepared, a fellow from Portland, who was seeing a menagerie of snakes in his shoes, insisted on committing a nuisance in the soup kettle. Not being partial to that kind of seasoning, I resorted to forcible methods to prevent him from cutting up in this way. Such creatures are a nuisance, and it is no easy matter to tolerate them sometimes. Our conscripts are almost wholly of this character.

### November 1st.

Except for an occasional blaze from the pickets there is no firing. This popping away at each other has become so common as to excite no comment. It is quite certain that the Rebs will not attack us openly, the forts being so arranged that such a move would be courting annihilation. We can fire cross-ways and every other way, and should the Rebs get in they couldn't stay five minutes. We often wish they would be thoughtless enough to try it, though.

### November 2nd.

Firing from big guns up on the right of us at intervals during the day. At night went on picket and were caught in a rainstorm. This is our usual luck, and deviation from this rule would be regarded as an evil omen. By midnight our holes were about half full of water. Said holes are four feet deep and connected with a sap, which certainly is rightly named, for during a rainstorm it *saps* water from the adjoining lands, making cess-pools of our holes. Picketing is bad enough here under the most favorable conditions.

Wood is worth a great deal. All we use on picket we carry on our backs, so only the smallest fires are possible — just enough to boil coffee or to broil a bit of meat. Our picket detail is formed a half mile to the rear, near a woodpile from which each man is to take a stick — this to last 24 hours. During rainy days we drink cold water and eat raw pork — a nauseous mess (though not so *gnaw*seous as tough, raw beef.)

### November 3rd.

Rainy and as cold as it could be and not freeze. There is no approach to comfort. Everything wet and drooping, making us long for some of the hog pens of New England. While hope keeps us company, it is well, otherwise life would be indeed bitter. Two men who were forsaken of hope died from homesickness today.

### November 4th.

The weather cleared off. Being relieved from picket (and misery), we devote the time to a remodeling of our houses, putting in fireplaces and making other preparations for colder weather. All is quiet on our front, and we go in and out as we please, which is very careless of us, for the lousy Rebs are ever treacherous.

### November 5th.

Very cool and raw; I expect to soon chronicle the first snow storm of the season.

The clouds rolled away without fulfilling the promise of the morning. Quiet remained unbroken all day. Went on picket at night. Here all was quiet until the Rebs undertook to play ball for an hour or so with someone on our left. The air was alive with mortar shells blinking and winking on their errands of destruction. One exploded in the center of our fort; another struck an embrasure and knocked the colonel's tent down flat. He was up in the fort at the time, thus preventing another vacancy in the list of field officers of this regiment.

### November 6th.

Only the occasional crack of a picket's rifle reminds us of the war. This is one of the loveliest days imaginable, but I am not in a mood to appreciate it. When I reflect on this horrid war and the amount of destruction and desolation at every hand, I can but feel sad. This section would be lovely except for the fact that the iron heel of war rests on it like an incubus. Is the old ship of state worth it all?

Most of our men have left mothers, wives, and sisters behind them, and it is hoped that they hold the virtue of their own relatives high enough in esteem to prevent them from violating the women of a foe. I notice no disposition on the part of our men to treat Southern women any differently from what they would ask of the Rebels if the tables were turned. The leaders of the Rebel hordes know this perfectly well, but like wily politicians they arouse hatred by an appeal to the tenderest ties and the strongest prejudices, claiming that the South must fight to protect their women from outrage.

Southern leaders have dragged the low-bred whites into the war by representing to them that if *we* are successful the niggers will be put over the likes of them. Just why this should so startle the poor white is not clear, for the blacks have always been over the poor whites, or preferred to them. The rabble-rousers also industriously circulate a story to the effect that we will enact laws to compel them to marry the former slaves; that we will ransack and rob their houses, ravish their women, and in every conceivable way injure and insult them. So these ignorant creatures have been led to fight and suffer. Instead of fighting for a holy cause, they are actually fighting to perpetuate their own degradation by bolstering up the institution that has already reduced the poor whites of the South to a condition far below that of the nigger.

### November 7th.

A year ago today we crossed the Rappahannock at Kelly's Ford and had a brush with the enemy. Since that time our course has been toward the south, with no backtracks except at Mine Run. Last year it was the custom to advance a short distance and then fall back, often without any fighting to speak of. This was demoralizing because we knew it must all be gone over again. Each time, the Rebels would follow us back. After a while we would recover our equilibrium and go for them again. Thus, the ball was kept in motion. Some people elevated this boys' play to the dignity of "strategy."

Since our Ulysses has been in command, there has been no ground for complaint in the matter of following them up. As for boys' play, or strategy, I do not recall any particular instance of either under his administration to date. He believes in brute force, not in strategy.

An attack is anticipated, and we are kept under arms tonight. Some officers are so excessively timid and suspicious that they would keep us under arms all the time were they in command. Part of this stems from too much caution, another part from too much cowardice, and still another from too much canteen.

### November 8th.

Presidential election, and we have the privilege of casting a ballot for "Honest Old Abe." The day passed without much excitement. The vote in our regiment stood as follows: Lincoln 190; McClellan 40.

The disparity in the number of votes is said to have been caused by a failure of the Democratic State Committee to furnish ballots — a remarkable oversight. It would come nearer the case to say they failed to furnish *voters* rather than *votes*. The South doesn't want McClellan either. Even if they had voted for him solidly, he still wouldn't have been elected. The *Richmond Examiner* calls him "that nose of wax," which must be quite comforting to those Democrats who thought that by putting him in nomination they would appease the South.[5]

The Rebs evince the most intense interest in regard to the election. I more than suspect they had some hopes in connection with McClellan's election. The convention that nominated "Little Mac" declared that "the war is a failure." But the people endorse Mr. Lincoln, and his reelection means a continuance of the war till rebellion is driven from the land.

### November 10th.

Two years ago today Burnside relieved McClellan of the command of the army. The result of the election two days since has relieved him of the notion that he is to occupy the White House.[6] By request of the people, Uncle Abe will manipulate the reins a spell longer. It is now settled for four years, and McClellan's defeat is as good as a Union victory. All hope of any terms short of surrender must now have left the Rebel heart.

### November 11th.

There was "right smart" firing today. The Rebs need a vent somewhere, but in view of the scarcity of war material, they would show better judgment by saving their ammunition for a time when it counts for something.

This afternoon generals Hancock and Mott visited Fort Rice, and I visited the Avery house, where General Miles and the signal corps are stationed. This mansion was a fine old plantation before the war, with spacious grounds beautifully laid out, but now it is in a state of painful dilapidation: fences burned, hedges cut down, grass trampled, and the house showing signs of decay. From the top of the house a vast view of the surrounding country can be had, even into Petersburg. This city, like Charleston and Fredericksburg, has paid dearly for its part in the secession scheme. Fully one-quarter of the city has been riddled by shell and is uninhabitable.

At night, when pickets were relieved, a battery opened on us as we came through the opening in the works. We were taken entirely by surprise, but should have known that we couldn't count on peace and quiet forever. "For ways that are dark and tricks that are vain" the heathen Chinee is not a whit ahead of his "Melican" brother of the South.

### November 12th.

A quiet day on the whole. We learned, officially, the result of the election. That friend of humanity and champion of human rights, Lincoln, is again at the helm of the ship of state. A better or truer man was never entrusted with power. This must put a quietus on any Rebel expectation of dictating, or even suggesting, terms.

A Reb who had not passed the vealy period of youth, and who thought himself *smart*, mounted a pile of dirt and called over, "How many rails can Abe Lincoln split in a day?"

Scarce had the last word left his mouth before the reply came hot and quick, "He can split enough to ride Jeff Davis to hell!"

A shout went up from both sides, and Johnny Smart hunted his hole. No doubt he would have been glad if he could have pulled the hole in after him.

### November 13th.

On picket with my tentmates, Blaisdell and True. They are two pretty good fellows, the first being too simple and mean to be otherwise. Vice generally *costs* something; hence, Blaisdell is generally good. The other man is True, both by name and by nature. There is no room under his ribs for meanness. He scorns to do a mean thing or to put himself in any ambiguous position. He is one who can always be depended on where duty calls.

Nothing of consequence occurred, and we were relieved at night. It is Sunday, and by being on picket we escaped a full inspection. We heartily despise an inspection of whatever kind, unless Major Hobson is the inspecting officer. He is not *too* critical, and we try to stay on his almost-blind side.

### November 14th.

Not a gun heard the entire length of the line. If something exciting doesn't happen soon, we shall get as careless as ever. It is quite warm here even this late in the season, and it isn't agreeable to be hived up inside the fort.

### November 15th.

"How little we know what a day may bring forth." Yesterday was so quiet one could almost hear a pin drop. Today there is enough noise for 500 boiler factories, an incessant firing of mortars.

At night we went on guard. It is picket or guard every two days, consequently we obtain only the minimum of rest. If I live to get out of this show, I will do nothing but sleep for at least three weeks.

### November 16th.

General de Trobriand visited the fort today. He is an old Frenchman whom the men "delight to honor." He is always familiar with us and has a good word for our regiment, saying "Ze 17th of Maine ees von dam splendid battalions."

He is an exile from la belle France, having concluded when Louis Napoleon seized the throne that, "What France admired is not good enough for France." In consequence of this liberal expression he found it risky to tarry longer.

Some member of his family has been in the French Army for over four hundred years. Military life is thus a natural thing to him, an instinct.

One morning when he came down to Fort Hell, the Rebs dusted his coat for him in good shape, and he exclaimed with much vehemence, "The dam Rebels they fire thirty gun at me. They killed one horses and wounded two horse at my headquarters." I always enjoy his company immensely and feel honored in being under command of such a distinguished personage.

### November 18th.

Today we are nine-months men. For twenty-seven months we have endured the dangers, the hardships, and the privations of war. Why we are not dead or wounded is not easy to explain. The battlefields of Virginia, from Fredericksburg to Petersburg, bear the testimony of the sacrifices this regiment has made, and yet our losses are comparatively small.

Since we entered the service many changes have occurred, many promotions made for "gallant and meritorious conduct." So says the record, but I am convinced that, in eight cases out of every ten, promotions are the result of *favoritism* purely. I venture the assertion that more than one officer has canceled a pecuniary obligation by bestowing promotion. Many men will crawl and cringe awfully for a corporal's berth, and turn themselves inside-out for a sergeant's warrant. "Princes and lords are but the breath of kings," says someone; I should like to know *whose* breath these fellows are.

It is idle chatter to mourn or rave about it, and I try to smother my indignation and comfort myself with these words: Sorrow endureth but for a night. Joy cometh in the morning." In just nine months we shall all be retired to private life.

An order to lay in four days' rations and to get ready to move brought my cogitation to a sudden termination. We also received sixty rounds of ammunition.

### November 19th and 20th.

Thought we'd surely be on the way by this morning, but we waited in a fever of expectancy all day. Went on picket at night with Osgood and Wescott, and while we were out, not only the windows, but the *doors* of heaven opened. How it did pour.

Right in the midst of it the two worthies with me lay in the mud and slept. Some people can sleep anywhere — and fortunate it is for them too.

This dreadful night came to an end at last. Daylight was a welcome guest on the morning of November 20th, though it still rained. We devoured our pork raw, and our coffee was made by just soaking it in cold water. Good or bad, we could build no fires. Thus we passed the day until the next set of victims came out to relieve us.

### November 21st.

A rain of this severity and duration is quite uncommon in Virginia. There will be a drought in Heaven if it doesn't soon end. The houses we live in are not adapted to long storms. Our fireplaces, so called, are just large enough for a coffee pot to set in. Timber for building is only to be had by hauling long distances, and as it is mighty uncertain when we might have to light out, we don't care to invest too much labor in shoring up our kennels.

### November 22nd.

About noon the orb of day came out, and it was never more welcome. The Rebs, far worse off than we as to food, raiment, or shelter, mounted the works to bask in the sun and dry their tatters. Compared with them, we are comfortable indeed.

Picket duty seems to have got round to us again, and at night I went out with Colby, Blaisdell, and Osgood. It didn't rain, but the mud abounds and "sticketh closer than a brother."

### November 23rd.

Fair, but so cold thermometers won't stay on the nail. The arctic wave chews our ears and noses. During the night thirteen Rebs came in to get warm and decided to stay after seeing the good things to be had at the sutler's. (We make it a point to visit the sutler whenever Johnny comes to see us.) Nearly all the wood is over here, and the grub too. Under ordinary circumstances I would despise men who desert their cause for such flimsy reasons, but when men know, as these do, that their cause is hopeless and that all their sacrifices are thrown away, it then becomes both right and sensible to desert.

The real grievances of the South are ridiculous. Not one in ten of the Rebel army can tell what all this mess is about, nor can the most rabid Rebel name an act of injustice on the part of the federal government previous to this war. On the other hand, for the sake of keeping peace and preserving the union, we overlooked so many grievous insults from the slave powers that they have come to regard us as so many cowards. Over the last forty years the slavocracy has held over our Northern Democracy, or "dough faces," a threat to dissolve the Union. It had become a matter of comment that when South Carolina took snuff, every Northern Democrat had to sneeze, fearing that if he withheld this tribute the Union would at once be smashed.

### November 24th.

This day has been set apart by the president as a day of "thanksgiving and praise." If anybody can tell me any occasion for gratitude or praise, I shall be greatly indebted to him. Since the recurrence of this festive occasion one year ago, many changes have taken place, many familiar faces have passed away, many voices have been hushed, their lives sacrificed.

As for me, I momentarily expect death or some other calamity in which this horrid war abounds. ("Horrid" is primarily a female expletive which, when emanating from a female mouth, may mean anything or nothing, generally the latter. But I use it in no such limited or vague sense. I attach nothing short of its full meaning, and even then find it inadequate.)

I *am* thankful that the days of slavery are ended. In the multitude of my troubles I have well-nigh overlooked whatever of good has fallen to my lot. I hope that next Thanksgiving will find me safely at home. This is my last one in Virginia, at least, come life or death.

This forenoon we had a divine service, so called. The afternoon was spent watching the northern horizon for a shower of luxuries suitable to the day. In vain did our mouths water and our imaginations riot in visions of roast turkey and mince pie. As these things have been promised, their nonappearance disappoints us immensely.

### November 25th.

A very uninteresting and quiet day until afternoon, when our much-expected dinner finally arrived. In size, it wasn't worthy of notice. I wrote to a friend in Massachusetts: "We are to have roast turkey today, and I expect my share will be about one feather." I was grossly in error, as we had not less than a quarter of a pound apiece and ⅛ of a mince or apple pie, ¼ of a doughnut and the same generous allowance of ginger snap, a fraction of a seed cake, four apples, and a bunch of grapes.

This was delivered to us about supper time. Shortly thereafter I went on picket with Monroe, Blaisdell, and Silk. This gave us all night to dispose of our feast. We revelled in luxuries as much as half an hour, rolling them under our tongues the way some people are said to roll sin. And there was more or less sin mixed with it as we thought how much of this stuff people in the North can gorge themselves with.

### November 27th.

A good deal of firing somewhere, but on this part of the line such a serene and holy quiet prevails that we heard the church bells in Petersburg and the clock strike seven, the hour for our usual Sunday inspection. Some officers strictly observe this practice, and it's not for us to know why the contents of our knapsacks wouldn't look as well on Saturday as on Sunday.

### November 28th.

On picket with Monroe, Wescott, and McKenney. It is barely possible that the Almighty might have made skull cavities containing less brains than these three, but I doubt it. Another day in the society of these worthies may the Fates and Furies never bestow on me.

### November 29th.

We were finally relieved by men from the 9th Corps. On reaching camp we found that an order awaited us to "move immediately."

We bivouacked near the Petersburg and Norfolk Railroad, at the same place we always stop when going on a southern trip. We expect a fight either at Hatcher's Run or the Boydtown Plank Road. This division is so often selected for these rapid transit expeditions that we have earned the title "Birney's Flying Infantry," a name by no means inappropriate.

### November 30th and December 1st.

Moved about seven on the 30th, and after marching five miles or more went into camp near Fort Cummings, situated not far from Yellow Tavern. This place is extraordinarily filthy and it "smells mighty loud." It was almost with surprise that I awoke the next day to find myself in the same place where I laid down; I had neither died with the cholera nor been toted off by vermin.

We had rumors of a move all day and so were prevented from cleaning up or doing many other necessary things. We did pull down a few logs in the stockade. The more we pulled down, the more dirt and lice we found. It was enough to turn the stomach of a turkey buzzard. There were old bones, decayed meat and vegetables, mouldy bread, lice, and other foreign matter.

Night still found us at this place. We had made it perceptibly cleaner by then, and slept better the second night.

### December 2nd and 3rd.

Another day of rumors, but no movement till night, when we moved far enough to finally get out of that filthy camp. On the third we commenced building a new camp, thinking that we might pass the winter hereabouts, if Providence, the Rebels, and General Grant will permit.

This camp gives promise to outstrip all previous efforts at architectural display. We even have a brick fireplace with a shelf over it in our cabin.

BUILDING HUTS. *Harper's Pictorial History of the Civil War.*

### December 4th.

Sunday, but we pursue the work on our houses, as we are out of doors and there doesn't seem to be anything better to do. We are liable to be caught in a snowstorm any time now. We also have a strong incentive to work in the form of a positive hint from Colonel West that a cessation of work will provoke a full inspection.

### December 5th.

We made some considerable progress in building. During the day we had a visit from Jordan and Kendrick, who have been in hospital — one at City Point, the other not far from Washington. This addition to our group resulted in not less than six to a bed. We contrived to *spoon* ourselves in after a fashion, and by laying motionless managed to get through the night without kicking anyone through the tent. Our tents furnish comfortable cover for three; all additional company is a big inconvenience.

### December 6th.

If we could only bear in mind the uncertainty hanging over military matters, we should save ourselves much vexation and no little labor. None of us had an idea when we rose up and resumed building operations today that we should be routed out so soon. By nightfall, the finishing touches were going onto our houses. Stacy and True had gone after eaves boards, and I was up behind headquarters getting pieces of brick for the fireplace. While there, I heard an orderly ride up to Colonel West and give him an order to move at daylight.

I slept most of the night with one eye open, mostly because of the banging of the dippers and guns belonging to the troops moving in to relieve us. Even though they couldn't sleep they needn't have made such a racket that no one else could either.

### December 7th.

Turned out at 4 A.M. and at nine marched a short distance to the Jerusalem Plank Road. We struck the road just as a rain storm struck *us*. General Warren had command of the force, which consisted of the 5th Corps and Mott's division of the 2nd Corps. We marched all day, and at night crossed the Nottoway River and soon went into bivouac on a patch of ploughed ground. (A nice place to camp after it had rained all day — soft as feathers.) Pickets are posted on the bank of the river, which is very narrow. We have been warned that there are guerrillas in the area. It is one of the darkest nights I ever knew; nothing can be seen beyond the fringe of trees skirting the river, whose dark current rolls by in silence. It is very difficult for the poor pickets straining their eyes and ears to catch the faintest sign of danger. Of course, no guerilla could see us any better than we could see him.

This day's work represents an entirely new departure in the tactics of the army. For us to boldly strike out, put a day's march between us and our supports, and bivouac here, with a river in our rear, is an astonishingly reckless movement. Such actions have never been popular at headquarters heretofore.

We are very surprised that we have penetrated enemy country to such an extent and not encoutered any Rebs. Either Lee isn't cognizant of this move, or cannot prevent it, or else has a little plan of his own involving our destruction. It is with dreadful misgivings that we lay down to sleep, having never before been out overnight in such an insecure place where death seems to lurk in every thicket.

### December 8th.

Were on the warpath at an early hour and this time were used some better than on the previous day. We were detailed for train guard and had our knapsacks carried in the train. Not less than twenty miles were gone over without encountering the enemy. On the way we passed the Sussex Court House, a large brick building, and near it a dilapidated jail and tavern, companion fossils. Doubtless many have been sentenced to death in the old building and executed on the gallows behind it. But something found in the garden of the old tavern interested us far more than any question of history or law. It was a lot of cabbages, a luxury that tempted us so sorely that we jumped the fence. Beneath the shadow of the old gallows, on which many a poor nigger doubtless was hung for stealing less, we gathered our cabbages.

We halted for the night near the Weldon Railroad. As we went into bivouac, we heard the cavalry hooting and yelling, showing that some deviltry was afoot. This diabolical noise continued all night, but they were not molested, although they have torn up several miles of track of the most important road connecting the Rebel capital with the South. More than half the Rebel supplies come over it, and we have destroyed over ten miles from Ream's Station to Stony Brook.

Thus far, our division has done nothing but march, keeping in supporting distance of the cavalry. At night we were on camp guard, and most of the men went out hunting supplies. This section seems to be well supplied and to have enjoyed immunity from pillagers. The Philistines are now upon them, though, and they stand an excellent chance to lose all they regard as sacred and secure.

Our advent has been so sudden as to give them no chance to conceal anything, not even their feelings. Some of the more remote farmers did get wind of our approach and they drove their stock away and buried whatever they wish to preserve. One fellow we ran afoul of during the forenoon thought he had secured everything, but the ubiquitous Yankees soon found the hiding place of his vegetables and made free with them. He sought relief from the provost marshal, and while portraying his losses to that worthy, happened to glance in the direction of his premises, where he discovered that his hams — several hundred of them — were walking off with the Yanks. This was the last feather, and he burst out, "G——d d——n my soul, there goes my hams!" If he had offered his prayer on *our* behalf it would have been more to the point.

It would be well for some of our men if another article had *not* been found. The natives call it apple jack. It consists of cider boiled down or evaporated so as to render it intoxicating. Many who imbibed it today soon lost the power of locomotion and fell by the wayside, stupified. We had to leave them, of course, and this was the last seen of them alive. While they lay in this state of stupor, a party of Southrons came upon them and nearly severed their heads.

No doubt the perpetrators of this dastardly act have been robbed. Many things have been taken from mere wantonness by thieves who steal just for the sake of stealing. These people are thoroughly exasperated and might be expected to desire revenge, but our men have committed no murder, and the revenge should have assumed some other shape. Some of ours who had fallen from fatigue and sickness were also murdered. Innocent and guilty fared alike until something like seventy had suffered death. The Southron hatred is broad enough to embrace the whole Yankee race.

I cannot get much rest this night as there is a great deal of racket and considerable foraging. Sheep, pigs, fowl, and sweet potatoes in abundance have been found and feasted upon.

### December 9th.

At daylight we went for the railroad and struck it at Jarrett's Station, commencing operations on a large scale. We arranged ourselves along the track and turned it over like a furrow, then passed along and took another hold. As fast as we turned it, the rails were detached from the sleepers, which were then piled up and set afire. The rails were heated and bent into fantastic shapes around the trees. We facetiously call these "Jeff Davis's neckties."

We kept up this fun for fifteen miles. We also destroyed all the culverts and bridges in a most thorough manner, not leaving one stone upon another. A construction corps would find one solid month's work putting this road in running order again.

A halt was made at Bellfield, and as soon as we had eaten we started out again to destroy the bridge over the Mehekin River. On the opposite side of the river is Hicksford, North Carolina. Here we encountered our first opposition and some strong works commanded by none other than A.P. Hill — a guarantee that this was no inferior force. We immediately retraced our steps and went into bivouac not far from the river.

During this time a drizzling rain kept falling and finally turned to sleet. Some of us are heinously unprovided for in the matter of foot covering, being nearly barefoot. We got our tents up by 10 o'clock, drew half rations, and laid down for the night. We are feeling extremely hollow, as we've had nothing but half rations since this march began and have to depend on foraging to make up the difference. We are at least fifty miles from camp and lying down in the snow and wet, hunger gnawing our stomachs. What more is needed to make us miserable? It seems we will surely freeze our feet before morning.

### December 10th.

Turned out in good season this morning, and each of us having put ourselves outside a couple of hardtack and a dipper of slosh, we set fire to a barn full of cotton and soon destroyed the fleecy mass. It belonged to an old minister who is ungodly enough to believe in human slavery. We felt justified in punishing him for his sentiments.

We then struck out in a northerly direction and waded through oceans of mud, making but little progress. Being shoeless and in a dilapidated physical condition, I gained admission to an ambulance train and rode nearly all day in company with an officer and a leg of pork. The latter I hung on to like death, for I have the appetite of a cannibal.

We continued about fifteen miles and hauled up somewhere in the woods, but don't know precisely where, as our maps are blank from Bellfield to Sussex Court House. After reaching our place of bivouac, I built a fire and commenced pork-packing. Slice after slice disappeared under my vest. A grand fill-up was the order of the day. I then retired for the night, to sleep — to dream, perchance, of pig.

During the night, Colonel Byles, of the 99th Pennsylvania, and his adjutant were perpetrating one of the foulest outrages upon two defenseless women whose house was within our lines. These women were compelled to submit to their infamous proposals or have their house burned down and themselves turned out into the bleak December.

Had this been the work of privates, said privates would have suffered death. The nearest tree would have been requisitioned, and it would have been just punishment. But old Byles is an officer, and was drunk, as is his custom.

### December 11th.

Started again at daylight on the same route as yesterday. After marching about four hours, we arrived at the Sussex Court House, where we found something calculated to set our bile in motion and to keep us on the march. We came across several of our men murdered and their bodies stripped. Some of the residents were seized, and not being able to prove an alibi or explain certain suspicious circumstances, they were hung in the Court House yard.

After the majesty of the law, or mob, was vindicated, we set fire to the Court House, which held many valuable records. General Warren now issued an order to burn all the houses along the road within two miles of it on either side. By nightfall there were at least one hundred families homeless. It was a sad sight to see women and children wailing and running about with no shelter in the cold December night. The hellish work was finally consummated and we moved on, crossing the Nottoway River and immediately bivouacking.

I rode nearly all day, having "thrown up the sponge" quite early in the morning. The few ambulances would have been literally crammed if all had ridden who *claimed* to be unable to march, but as only a limited number could ride, those who found themselves debarred suddenly renewed their strength and pushed on. Had I been subjected to this choice, this diary would in all probability have ended a day since. Being on excellent terms with the surgeon, it needed only my statement to convince him that it was necessary for me to ride. As I was stowed away in the ambulance, I noticed the faraway expression on the countenance of one who was turned away and I couldn't help feeling a shade of sadness permeate my soul. Once in, my position was maintained against all attempts to oust me — either by force or by strategy. Only once was my position endangered; an officer desired admittance, and if I hadn't been taken for one myself, I'd have been ejected from the ambulance. I sent a fiendish chuckle down into the innermost recesses of my sleeve as I heard Dr. Hersom remark, "He can't come in. There are two officers here already." This streak of good luck was the result of a couple of trades whereby I have procured an artilleryman's coat and felt hat. Whether Dr. Hersom mistakenly thought that there *were* two officers in that ambulance, or whether he said what he did to favor me, he no doubt saved my life by letting me ride this day.

A small enemy force put in an appearance soon after we bivouacked but were encountered by the 9th Corps, sent out to aid us on our return.

### December 12th.

Turned out early and were soon on the march again. The ground was frozen solid, and we skipped along lively although many of us are still shoeless. Two in our company haven't even an apology for shoes, others have only the uppers and heels. Jim Osgood wears seven pairs of socks in lieu of boots.

Our picket line was reached about noon, and we were soon under protection of our defenses. When we reached our late camp, on which we expended so much labor and skill, we found it flattened. We must look elsewhere. General de Trobriand took us outside the lines and put us in a camp in a low, damp place. (It is intimated that our French commander has meandered out here more to find a good supply of frogs than to find a good campground. The nature of the ground selected certainly gives color to the report.) At dark we rejoiced to get four days' rations, which forms the basis of a rumor that we are going to move again right off.

### December 13th.

Have a strong impression, as the Quakers say, that we are going to move. General de Trobriand went off early to look up a campground and was gone all the forenoon. Upon his return, he ordered us into a large pine grove nearby. The day was far spent by this time, and we had only time to cut brush for beds and to put up shelters. This campground promises to repay us for losing the last one — everything is fresh and clean and bathed with the sweet incense of hemlock and pine. We have plenty of wood and water, an abundance of timber, and a frog swamp not far off. General de Trobriand, however, objects to our using his name in connection with frogs. Not long since, he remarked with great vehemence, "Ze 17ths of Maine says I eat frogs. I *do not* eat frogs!"

### December 14th.

We are now a good healthy distance from the front. Our troubles are more likely to come from the rear.

At an early hour this morning we commenced to build our camp. Timber being abundant, we made excellent headway, cheered by the hope that we will very soon be comfortably situated for some time.

### December 15th.

All in a huddle this morning, as there were rumors of a move. To build or not to build; that was the question. Whether it were better to endure the ills of lying out-of-doors, or take axe, and by cutting timber, end them. We decided to go on with the work.

It was soon ascertained that all the moving there was to be was to move one of our houses, which projected a quarter-inch beyond the rest. After much deliberation it was decided to put the building in line. Now the crisis is past and the country is safe.

### December 16th.

Everything has been settled. Red tape has won a victory, and now that the houses are all in line we are at liberty to push ahead with the building operations. I deem it wise to leave out some of the extras that I put into our last house, being heartily tired of working for nothing. Besides, this way we'll be able to move in sooner.

### December 17th.

Nothing special going on, so we continued building and improving camp. At night we disposed of our last morsels of food, and some had no supper at all. No government under the sun ever made such generous provision for its soldiers, and yet we profit but little from it. We are continually robbed by the villains who handle our rations. They enrich themselves at the expense of our health and comfort. Month after month, our beans, rice, potatoes, candles, peas, and other vegetables have been withheld. If we received their equivalent in bread, I would not complain. Instead, our bread also has diminished until it is now less than two-thirds of a ration. Here we are at camp close to a railroad station where there are thousands of boxes of bread and other things, yet we have nothing to eat. I can fully endorse the prayer of David, when he said of a certain class, "Let Satan stand at their elbow when they are judged." David had had some army experience in his day.

### December 18th.

Sunday, and of course it would be grossly improper to draw rations on this "sacred day." Although we didn't desecrate the day thus, a full inspection was held at one o'clock. Such piety. Today I wrote home, and made use of this remark: "Just eight months from this day I shall be a free man once more, if I live. Then I'll trouble you for something to eat, something to fill up the immense hole in my stomach caused by three years of starvation."

### December 19th.

Rations were issued this morning, and devoured about as soon as received. At night the sutler issued tickets, in obedience to Colonel Hobson, who told him that the army was not created solely to make sutlers rich and that a failure to comply would be followed by dismissal. When the colonel sets his mouth in motion, it doesn't stop short of its object. He complained for the fiftieth time to General de Trobriand of the paucity of our rations. This so vexed the old man that he threw up his hands and rolled his eyes, exclaiming, "O Connil, you will come here and complain some day when you have one louse on your shirt."

Our credit at the sutlers is good, but butter sells at eighty cents per pound, fifty cents for cheese, twenty-five for a dozen crackers. It doesn't take long to exhaust a credit of sixteen dollars a month in currency worth only thirty-three cents on a hundred.

Went on fatigue embellishing the headquarters of General de Trobriand. The work is light and easy.

### December 20th.

On picket with Reed, Osgood, and McKenney — not the most agreeable trio in the land, but one cannot choose his company on picket, only in his tent or mess. We were posted on the Vaughan Road near the Wyatt house in an open field. By the time we were fairly posted it commenced to rain. Having no shelter but a log to sit *upon*, we were soon in a most wretched plight. We felt very much like disposing of ourselves for old, dirty rags, and passed the night in a state of severe depression and intense desire for daylight. Wet daylight is preferable to wet darkness any time.

### December 21st.

We didn't melt or wash away after all. Near noon it cleared off, and we dried ourselves. It was to me a very dull day, and I was excessively happy when relief came at night. In our haste to reach camp, we cut across lots and soon found ourselves in a swamp, floundering knee-deep. There is a large thread of truth in the old adage,"The longest way round is the nearest way home," paradoxical as it may seem. We would have saved ourselves much fatigue, and reached camp at least an hour sooner, if we had stuck to the road.

## December 22nd.

I had nothing to do this morning, but after "dinner" went on duty policing camp, a performance that, although necessary, still seems like "labor vainly done." To sit quietly would be much more to my liking than to be kicking up dust and smoke sufficient to suffocate the whole country. Good health depends on a vigorous policing of camp, though. Old bones and mouldy bread festering in the sun and exhaling villainous odors are neither agreeable nor healthy.

## December 23rd.

At 11 o'clock we were ordered out to witness an execution of an Englishman charged with "desertion with intent to betray."

He had left our lines a little to the left of Fort Sedgwick. Near this point our line projects toward Rebeldom, forming an angle. The fellow started for the Rebel lines, but the night being exceedingly dark and much firing going on, he got turned round to the left and ended up in front of the angle near some old chimneys on the Jerusalem Plank Road. Supposing himself at the Rebel lines, he mounted the works and yelled, "Don't shoot! I'm a Yankee deserter with important information for headquarters!" He was accommodated with a speedy visit to headquarters, but the "important information" died on his lips when he found himself facing his own brigadier general. His crime was compounded by the fact that he was a British emissary.

The day of his execution has been a raw, uncomfortable one, and every bone in me rattled as I waited the slow movements of the cortege. It might not be right to want to hurry another human being out of this world, but the longer I thought of his treachery and the lives it might have cost, the more I wished for his immediate execution.

He didn't seem to share my feelings and tried to delay the business in every way. He threw the bandage from his eyes at least twenty times. He would take off his coat and walk around, then put it on and sit on his coffin. In a moment, he would hop up and throw it off again. This he did time after time till my patience was worn threadbare.

The woods were only twenty paces in his rear and the undergrowth so thick that no mounted force could have pursued him. If he were shot running away, it would be no worse than his sentenced fate. I held my breath as we watched his gyrations, but he made no attempt to flee.

The marshall and chaplain finally lost patience and informed him that no more fooling would be allowed. With this, he submitted to the bandage, and in a few moments his body was riddled with bullets. It was a great relief when it was over. I was chilled all out of shape and my teeth chattered in their sockets. I was soon back in camp, hugging the fire.

## December 24th.

Our spirits took an upward turn today in consequence of a rumor that another Rebel stronghold has fallen. Eighteen thousand prisoners and a large quantity of arms and ammunition fell into our hands as trophies. I confess to a lack of faith in this story at first, thinking it one of those scaly yarns so often preceding a move. Too many such lies have slid down our necks like some sweet syrup. Fewer lies and more bread would suit much better! Patriotism, like religion, is closely allied to a full belly and comfortable quarters; also a clean, warm bed is not incompatible. Patriotism is all well enough under some circumstances, and it should ever be inculcated in the young, but it should be done by those who *practice* what they preach. The ones who prate of patriotism have none of it under their vests. This kind of chin music sounds fine in speeches, and looks exceeding fine in print, but I have observed that a few days' abstinence from food and water will in most cases cause the fires of patriotism to burn very low indeed. At this time we are so hungry we can think of nothing but food.

### December 25th.

"Merry Christmas" has no significance to me. I had no work to do, so the time was passed answering letters. This condition of repose is the reward of being on guard at the sutler's. This post is a very desirable one, as the clerk and yours truly are on most friendly terms, so I fare well. We have signals by which we know when the time comes for a "wave offering." The subscriber whistles Penny Royal tunes and is promptly rewarded by seeing a hand thrust through the aperture in the tent, loaded with eatables. This man Furlong is from Massachusetts and not of the same breed as the sutler, who is a Baltimore Dutchman and too mean to feed a flea.

### December 26th.

Commenced to drill three hours per day. Our officers have made a discovery of immense importance: "Inactivity is destructive to good morals." To demonstrate that they will have little cause for concern, I will list our round of duties: cooking and cleaning dishes three times a day, wood to cut, tents to keep in order, guns and brasses to scour, clothes to wash and mend, guard and picket duty, fatigue duty, and more or less to do for the officers.

One consoling thought looms up out of the dreariness. If we have to drill, some officers must drill us. This falls to the lower officers, yet they are not the instigators of this folly. Our higher-grade officers play cards, swill whiskey, and generally raise the devil.

### December 27th.

We cut timber for a corduroy road to Patrick's Station. Finished at 4 o'clock and returned to camp. Old Virginia never had such good roads as those we are building here. We also have opened some new ones not to their liking, for we often obliterate old landmarks of considerable importance, besides giving the owners no compensation for land damages. If ever a readjustment takes place, it will be a difficult task, as so many deeds and records have been destroyed at the various courthouses.

### December 28th.

Nothing of special interest happened except a corroboration of the earlier report of the fall of Savannah. A salute of 100 guns was fired in honor of the event. The official announcement was read on dress parade, but having heard this information before, we received it unenthusiastically.

### December 29th.

Considerable firing up the James, probably at Dutch Gap. The Johnnies hold a special spite against the workers in that enterprise and omit no opportunity to annoy them.

Our guns are trained on them, ready to retaliate. In consequence, a tremendous racket was kept up all day.

### December 30th.
Went on picket near Hatcher's Run, where we had the rumpus in October. The trees are all battered and bruised as if nature has been on a rampage. The Rebs are picketing on the west side of the run on the Vaughan Road and are anxious to trade but afraid to approach us. They are dressed (if such I may call a condition so near nudity) in old carpets and pieces of quilt — anything that will cover them.

At night one of them finally came way in and reported things as looking mighty dark in the Confederacy since Sherman reduced Savannah: Butler is threatening Wilmington; Thomas has just given Hood a sound drubbing; Early has been trounced by Sheridan, who has advanced on Gordonsville, tearing up the Virginia Central Railroad and destroying the James River Canal.

Such a series of disasters is enough to destroy anybody's spirit, and I can only wonder why they cling so tenaciously to a lost cause. Deserters are numerous, and all tell the same stories of deprivation and want, and of lack of confidence in their leaders and their cause.

### December 31st.
On picket for the last time in 1864, and may the Sovereign of the Universe, or whoever managed our affairs this past year, be praised. He who has done his duty and suffered all the dangers, cares, anxieties, vexations, fears, and doubts, and come out whole is a lucky dog indeed.

During the year just passed there have been some of the most terrible battles on record since the world began, with an appalling loss of life and limb. The Union loss is estimated at 60,000 men. All this to attain a position that could have been reached with but trifling loss.

# Winter of 1865

## January 1 – March 4

*January 1st.*

A new year dawns, the third in the service of my country. Hope and fear mingle — hope the war will soon end; fear that however soon it ends, I might not live to see it. These fears are reduced to an absolute certainty as I consider that the confounded Rebels are as defiant as ever. Though I know that much of this is bluster, I also know that the battles still to be fought will be like worrying a wounded tiger in his death struggles, determined to injure many of us before the finale.

The blows dealt by Sherman, Sheridan, Thomas, and Farragut are staggering, but Jeff Davis and his minions still seem to be defiant, though there is an undercurrent of "peace by negotiation" now manifest. We expect peace shortly after the opening of the spring campaign.

*January 2nd.*

Went on fatigue, cutting wood for the officers. Supplying the officers doesn't help us much nor produce any special tokens of favor. Somehow it seems as if every one who receives a promotion speedily loses all feeling for those in the ranks.

*January 3rd.*

Had a battalion drill by Major Hobson in the afternoon. This exceedingly senseless and disagreeable performance was executed somehow, but we had no heart for it, nor did our "Major Billy." After drilling for the prescribed time, we returned to camp to find we had company: Kendrick, Jordan, and Gus Bradbury. Not being subject to service and free to depart whenever they see fit, they like to come up and look around, knowing that no harm will befall them. I envy them their privilege and often think that I would be willing to endure a pretty good thumping for the sake of enjoying the same freedom.

*January 4th.*

Heard heavy firing last night, and it continued after daylight with unabated fury. We suppose it to be the Rebels paying their respects to Butler's Dutch Gap, which is a great eyesore to them. The Confederates tried to run rams down the James but our gunboats pursued them back to the shelter of Fort Darling, not in time to save them, however. One was captured, the other run ashore.

Rebels who came into our camp today reported that Lee is soon to execute a movement which will astonish the world. *What* it could be is a nine-days wonder to us. That it will be gigantic, none can doubt who see the preparations going on. Lately the Confederates have been making elaborate naval preparations. It is known that they recently purchased two dry goods boxes and an old cook stove, from which two ironclads are to be improvised. This will spread terror to the Yankees and convince the effete monarchies of Europe that the South is entitled to recognition immediately.

It is my opinion that if Lee attacks us here and comes off with a whole skin, he *will* astonish the world. We are anxious for him to commence, in fact, for the sooner he begins the sooner he will learn that our star is now in the ascendancy.

### January 5th and 6th.

Company drill in the morning by that casket of secrets, Lieutenant Usher, who is an awfully mysterious person. He always has some tremendous secret to impart. At least there is no danger of our being overworked by this officer, for he is the very embodiment of comfort. He has oceans of sympathy for us, and we in turn like him well enough to overlook any neglect in the matter of drilling us. In the afternoon of the 5th we had a battalion drill on the flats near the Pegram residence. If ever a dog was sick of hot broth, we are sick of these confounded drills and inspections. In the afternoon of the 6th, Providence interfered and sent a rainstorm, so we had the rest of the day to ourselves.

### January 7th.

Everything quiet here, a condition I hope will continue. So tired am I of the ceaseless Tramp! Tramp! Tramp! and Pop! Pop! Pop! that I haven't much spunk or spirit left. I long for an end sometimes, not caring if it means an end to me.

### January 8th.

A full inspection at 1 o'clock. I have nothing new for the official optics to feast on, and I don't know of any private who has. The inspectors ought to know every hole in our socks by this time. However, we shall no doubt be called upon to gratify their curiosity at least once a fortnight for as long as we remain in this army.

### January 9th.

Had nothing but a skirmish drill this morning, after which we received some distinguished visitors, among them our former colonel, now Brigadier General G. Washington West. He was as bumptious as ever and looked *over* us instead of *at* us. At 5 o'clock had dress parade, with General West as a spectator.

Some person has circulated a story to the effect that in the late fight Mr. West offered his commission for an ambulance (instead of the conventional kingdom for a horse). He had a horse but pretended he couldn't ride him. It looked well in print that "Colonel West was on the field, but his old wound broke out and he was compelled to retire, General Hancock having offered his ambulance to him."

An old wound is a wonderfully convenient thing to have when one is scared out of his seven senses. It is related of a certain valiant official that during an engagement in the earlier part of the war he felt something meandering down his legs and supposed it was blood. But it was darkly hinted by some who were very near him that there was a peculiar fragrance in his vicinity. This is not a reference to West or any officer in this regiment. West was as brave an officer as we cared to see until he was wounded in the Battle of the Wilderness. Before then, he many times offered himself and his wing of the regiment in cases of emergency. He is now in the predicament of the urchin who, having been burnt, dreads the fire. But if everyone who is wounded should become so timorous, the army would have to be renewed pretty often. I blame no one who has been wounded if they do dread it afterward, but if they would have charity extended to them, they must exercise the same toward others similarly situated.

### January 10th.

It is raining hard, as it has done all night. This is a rather alarming state of things, as there can be *no* drill. The officers, having plenty of tanglefoot, are all right, of course. With us, the rain has a different effect.

### January 11th.

This morning a lot of us were detailed for picket. We hadn't proceeded far before I was conscious of the loss. Examination showed it to be my *sole*. Had my brogans been anything but mudscows, they would have been condemned as unseaworthy at the start. This mishap, combined with a hideous shortage of rations, determined me to make a hasty retreat (or as General Hooker once said, "an inglorious flight") in the direction of camp.

The rest of the day I spent writing and making sketches of places hereabouts. This section can boast of nothing phenomenal either in nature or in architecture. Red clay, stubble, and low bushes extend in every direction, occasionally relieved by an old house or tree. It corresponds well with a description I once read of a portion of Cape Cod: "Two huckleberry bushes and a mullein stalk make a grove."

### January 12th.

Had a company drill in the morning and a battalion drill in the afternoon. General West, being minus a command, fusses around us, although he has no more business drilling us now than the Duke of Cambridge has. If he could be where I wish him, it would be Fort Kent, Maine, as far away from us as possible.

### January 13th.

Same old rigamarole. Company drill this morning. In the afternoon had skirmish drill. This was a superfluity of folly, for we have never used it, and I don't know of any who have. In action we are governed more by circumstances than by any forms or rules. If a position is to be occupied, we do so in the most expeditious manner. We don't stop to see if every man's coat is buttoned, or whether one's feet are directly in line with every other man's feet.

### January 14th.

A full inspection by General West. How the State of Maine could ever have held this extraordinary person I cannot imagine. It is well the state has ample territory; a small one like Rhode Island wouldn't know what to do with him at all. His pomposity is wonderful to view, and yet I thought I detected just the least bit of softening today. His inspection wasn't half as rigid as it was when he was a major.

## January 15th.

Went on picket near Hatcher's Run on the right of the Vaughan Road. In front of us in a clearing was a log hut occupied by two women and a little girl, no males present. Virginia is the most prolific place for widows I ever saw. Every woman of marriageable age I have encountered is a widow, only two exceptions being noted thus far.

During the day we called on these lonely females to see how they fared and to inquire whether they had any eatables to sell. Instead of having anything to eat, they were in the most deplorable condition, destitute of everything but a few walnuts. Starvation stared them in the face, and but for our timely arrival would soon have stared them down. We supplied them from our scanty store, enough to last several days. Lieutenant Usher treated them to some cake the like of which not many Virginians have ever tasted. It was a delicious morsel of fruitcake, for which he had paid the sutler the moderate price of *one dollar* per pound. We hope these supplies will last till the commissary department unrolls the regulation amount of red tape and furnishes assistance.

The younger woman recently went to a camp ten miles distant (and this over a villainous road) to procure aid. I heard her telling the old lady she rejoiced when she "saw the old flag once more." This was somewhat ambiguous phraseology and conveyed no hint as to which flag she meant.

The ancient damsel would converse on almost any subject but the war. The minute any allusion was made to the conflict she was seized with acute lockjaw. I inquired whether she had been much alarmed during the late fight in the neighborhood. She replied that she was *not* greatly concerned, as she is over seventy, and if they had killed her they wouldn't have deprived her of much life, she having already passed the alloted age of man. In most respects she appears to be of a philosophic turn of mind — a philosopher in petticoats.

When the shelling was the fiercest she had taken a seat in the chimney (which is large enough to hold the entire family), showing that her ideas as to the power of a shell are exceedingly crude. She had selected the most dangerous place in the house, for a shell or cannon ball striking the chimney would have sent a shower of rocks down on her head.

After trying in vain to get any more information from the old dame, we set the table and took supper with this female trio, then departed to our various posts for the night. All is quiet although we are but a short distance from the Johnnies.

## January 16th.

We returned to camp about 10 A.M. Just a few moments later the "sons of Belial" over in Fort Welch commenced a series of didos that aroused our officers' suspicions as to their intent. We were ordered to be ready to move at any moment. We packed our loose stuff and awaited further developments. As none were made, all fears were allayed. But better to be fooled five hundred times than caught unprepared *once*.

## January 17th.

The forenoon was spent getting ready for the afternoon performance, which was a brigade drill by General West and a division review by Major General A.A. Humphreys, our new corps commander. Being on fatigue, I escaped this circus. I'd rather work a *day* than drill an *hour*.

### January 18th.

Today we are seven-months men. Time drags provokingly slow. A month seems an age.

We received official information of the fall of Fort Fisher and the capture of Wilmington by our combined land and naval forces. Another feather for the back of the Rebel camel. I know by experience how depressing such news can be — all the more so for the Rebs, who are suffering from hunger and nakedness. It is evident now that the boss Rebels made some very important miscalculations in going to war. They overestimated their powers and underestimated ours. Pride now prevents them from admitting it. To cave in after such blood-curdling vows and execrations will be doubly humiliating.

### January 19th.

Out at five this morning and were sent on a detail at corps headquarters and thence to Fort Welch. We were to work on the fort, a monstrous earthwork in the main line, to the right of Fort Cummings. It was a miserably cold day, overcast and gloomy. The very air seemed laden with sadness and uneasiness, as cheerless as a graveyard.

The enemy lines were very near, and we posted a lookout while we pawed around. All the noon was spent frantically searching for enough wood to build a fire to boil a cup of coffee. The day passed miserably, and we were rejoiced to return to our camp at sundown, glad that Fort Welch is not our permanent abode.

### January 20th.

Routed out again early this morning and ordered to report to Chaplain Simpson of the 40th New York, who was going up to Petersburg grave hunting. This is not meant to imply the chaplain is a ghoul; he was looking up the resting places of those who have fallen since last June in front of Petersburg. Each regiment sent a man, and the writer was detailed from the 17th.

Went down to Patrick's Station, but not finding the Reverend Sir at this point, I moved on to Meade's Station. As I didn't find any sign of him there either, I attended to my part of the business and returned to the regiment at noon.

That section of country around Petersburg has undergone an astonishing change, so much so a native son wouldn't recognize any part of it. Every tree, stump, and fence has disappeared, and all the breastworks, except the main line, have been levelled. What was once verdant is now a wasteland of dust and dirt. Enough old iron and lead have been shot here to make a respectable mine of each. Some graves can no longer even be found in this desolate ground.

### January 21st.

Went on picket on the Vaughan Road, near the domicile of the Widow Cummings. Virginia is a dreadful unhealthy state for the masculine gender; every woman is a widow who isn't an old maid. No less than three of this last class, who have "walked life's rugged pathway alone," live here with their mother, the widow. They are all schoolmarms but cannot fit themselves hereabouts for there are no facilities of learning. These pinks of propriety don't condescend to hold intercourse with the vulgar Yanks, and it is amusing to see the airs these simpletons give themselves, although they are as poor as church mice. They call us "mudsill Yankees," "greasy mechanics," "vulgar tradespeople."

May the saints protect us! Their contempt for us is only a reflection of ours for them. Shoddy aristocracy and musty gentility we cannot endure.

It rained awful hard today, and we couldn't keep fires going. We found the Rebels quite anxious to trade. One of them who was posted in the road tried to dicker for an overcoat. He was protected only by a piece of carpet that served as a coat by day and a blanket at night, and he looked like an animated rag bag. The demand for carpets should be good in the South after the war.

### January 22nd.
Having an hour to spare this morning, I called on the ladies I last visited on the 15th. They still have received no supplies except from the various picket details. Red tape must have its way even though women and children starve. The younger of the two women has been into camp three times, to no avail. It is not a light task for a frail woman — or indeed *any* woman — to plod ten miles through mud ankle deep. Had she been some *rich* Rebel, I venture to assert, her wants would have been supplied without so much delay. I saw her return from camp utterly exhausted, but no word of complaint escaped her.

### January 23rd.
It was rainy and cold, and but little doing along the line, only the usual pounding up on the James. I passed a quiet day, and for this reason I rather enjoy a rainy day.

### January 24th.
More firing and pounding, cause and effect unknown to us. At 10 A.M. had company drill, ending at noon. At 4 P.M. had dress parade by General de Trobriand. This conduct on the part of Old Froggy must have been the result of intoxication, for he hasn't been guilty of such silliness heretofore.

### January 25th.
Was on camp guard all day and had a quiet time of it. Although it is Sunday we had no full inspection, so we did get one day of rest. Strange to say, we didn't grow recklessly immoral from lack of drill, either.

### January 26th.
Relieved from guard about 9 A.M. Did as I pleased the rest of the day — and I pleased to do nothing much. I enjoy a day to myself when I am not called upon to do anything and can be a spectator instead of a participant.

### January 27th.
Went on picket at 9 P.M. Very quiet here at Hatcher's Run. The fallen leaves rustled in the chilly air, crackling beneath my boot as I trod my lonesome beat. One bright star bloomed like a deathless flower above the horizon, and in the cloudless sky a slender crescent hung, like a twenty-five-cent scarf pin. Picketing is not especially pleasing under such circumstances; it is solemn, cold, cemeterial, and ghostlike. The gloom of night gives to all an air of mystery and silence.

## January 28th.

Returned from picket about 10 A.M. and rested the balance of the day. There was plenty to do, however, as we were early informed that a full inspection will be held on the morrow.

## January 29th.

Busy as bees all the forenoon, cleaning guns, scouring brasses, and packing our knapsacks for the full inspection by Colonel Hobson, one of the slackest of mortals that ever wore a uniform. This was an agreeable surprise, for we had supposed that G. Washington West was to preside. General West has an eye like an eagle. Any little shortcoming of ours violently agitates that lofty gentleman. He cannot look anyone in the eye, and the lowest man in the ranks can drive him frantic with rage by just staring straight at him for a few seconds. The writer tried this *once*, and West's wrath was terrible to see. His eyes fairly started from their sockets and his teeth almost hung out of his mouth, at which I had to smother a titter. This enraged him all the more, and it is a wonder I was not instantly decapitated.

## January 30th.

Went down to Patrick's Station to see one of our men off who was discharged because of wounds received in a previous encounter. As the train receded from view, a great wave of homesickness swept over me. He is all done with soldiering, while I know not what I have yet to pass through. What a happy day this must be for him.

Many peace rumors now circulate, one to the effect that Alexander H. Stevens and other prominent Secessionists have proceeded behind our lines to City Point for an interview with President Lincoln and members of his cabinet.[1]

## January 31st.

A few of us were turned out at 5 A.M. and sent with a detail to work on Fort Fisher, about two miles from camp. While there, we witnessed some suspicious movements on the other side of a fence. We signaled headquarters, and all the troops were ordered under arms. We were ordered to camp and kept on the alert until sunset, when the scare ended.

## February 1st.

Was out again this morning to see one of my tentmates off on furlough. Some of us don't take very kindly to this furlough business. It furnishes as much pain as pleasure. If I were to go, every moment of the time would be harrowed by the thought that I must soon return to these scenes of destruction and bloodshed. What, then, is a respite of a month, especially as we are now enjoying quiet?

Returned from the station about nine. All was quiet till noon, when we had an order to be ready to move at a moment's notice. (My feelings being variable, I now *did* envy the fellow on furlough.) This was, no doubt, a repetition of the Fort Fisher affair. Someone had heard or seen something he couldn't account for. Where the pesky, lying rumors come from, nobody seems to know.

We didn't move today after all, but the sick were sent off to City Point. This looks suspicious and brings on one of my blue spells, for I do so dread to move.

## February 2nd.

Camp is full of rumors concerning the anticipated exodus, but no move was made this day either. At night we had dress parade by General de Trobriand. This might be regarded as an evil omen, as it is equivalent to a review. So we have another night of suspense and anxiety.

## February 3rd.

There was nothing suspicious this morning, no new indications of a move. In fact, the regular detail to Fort Fisher was sent out. Those of us who remained in camp were permitted to indulge in our favorite pastime — drilling.

At night went on guard duty at the sutler's, my favorite post. I rent the air with the usual programme of Penny Royal melodies and was rewarded as usual. The reasons I prefer this post have already been set forth in these pages. One needs the digestive organs of an ostrich to wrestle with the sutler's pastry, and these I have, although they have been subjected to a dreadful strain.

## February 4th.

Quiet during the day, and we concluded that the move had been abandoned, but were shortly awakened from this dream. An order was received at midnight to be ready to move at a moment's notice. Such an order at such a time entirely upset our equilibrium. We didn't know whether to get up and tear round or lie in bed and rest until definite orders came down. We finally compromised and packed all but our blankets and tents, then laid down again. We had just settled in when we were bounced out again to listen to another order: "Send the sick and those unable to march far on picket."

Lieutenant Usher allowed Stacy and myself, who are in the condition named, to go on picket. As soon as the detail was formed we moved out to the picket line. As the men already there had only been on since sunset, they demurred at being relieved so soon. But being backed up by an officer, we could not be ignored. They packed up their duds and started for camp, but not until they had given us unquestionable proof that they are masters of an uncommonly energetic vocabulary.

## February 5th.

Heard the drums and bugles sound reveille at 3 o'clock and knew something was about to happen. Of course we expected to hold the picket line till the culmination of the movement. Great was our astonishment to receive an order to fall in when the column came along. So a movement down the Vaughan Road was to be executed, and we were to fall in! Here was richness, and no mistake — turning out the sick and weary at midnight, then playing this scaly game on us.

We had only a few moments to consider before we saw the head of the column approaching, preceded by a division of cavalry. As our regiment came along we fell in, and the column moved down toward Hatcher's Run. The ragged Johnny who was on picket in the road fled at our approach, but not till he had emptied one of our saddles.

We soon made a breach in the Rebel line and moved on, crossing the run at Armstrong's Mills. We formed in line of battle in the edge of the woods and laid there the rest of the day and night.

The Rebels tried in the afternoon to sever our connection with the left of our line, near the Smith house, but General Humphreys had anticipated this action and prepared for it by detaching the 2nd Division of the corps as a support to that portion of the line menaced. The Rebels confidently advanced, but were hurled back, leaving most of their dead on the field. Among them was a major general, his adjutant, and the young son of the owner of the farm where we fought. The lad dropped very near his own threshold and we rejoiced that his parents were not there to see it. What would have been their feelings?

The Rebs didn't attack in front of our division. If they had, they would have stood more than an even chance of getting in. We have no works, and had only a single line of battle, so it was a good thing for us that they attacked where they did.

### February 6th.

Routed out at 3 A.M. and packed up, ready for anything. Not long after, we advanced down a road running straight into Rebeldom. We went to the place where they attacked yesterday. Here we massed in rear of our 2nd Division, anticipating that a charge was contemplated. The reverse was true; our generals were afraid of a charge on us, and had sent us to strengthen the line. The 5th Corps (General Warren's) arrived and took our position, thus giving us double the force.

As the Johnnies made no demonstrations, we were sent out at 9 o'clock on a reconnaissance to ascertain their whereabouts. We moved cautiously onto another road, an eighth of a mile or so, then deployed right and left as skirmishers, till we came in sight of the Rebel works. Finding we couldn't draw them out, we faded into some woods and stayed until noon, when we made a further retrograde movement to our line of works, taking a position in rear of them. It was quiet all along the line until 5 P.M., when Johnny Reb made an attack on the 5th Corps on our left and drove them over Hatcher's Run.

At the most critical moment of this engagement we were ordered to double-quick down there to assist them; but were met on the way by an aide from General Warren who curtly informed us, "You are not wanted, and when General Warren desires your assistance, he will ask for it!"

This speech had a very cooling effect on our officers. We didn't shed any tears either. After this, if an emergency arises where General Warren needs our aid, he will probably have to send for us several times before we respond. Considerable bad blood has developed because of this terseness of General Warren's, who actually is one of the bravest and best generals in the two armies. He has few equals, and no superiors in generalship.

We bivouacked for the night, leaving General Warren to fight it out alone and reap whatever glory might attach to it.

### February 7th.

A day as uncomfortable as smoke, rain, and cold could make it. We lay in the mud and slosh and were nearly converted into ham because the smoke from our fires of green, wet pine hugged the ground and nearly smothered us. About sunset the Rebs gave the 5th Corps a vigorous shelling until late in the evening. Sleep is out of the question, so far as the writer is concerned. One eye is still especially sensitive from my previous accident with the branch.

### February 8th.

Morning found us unrefreshed and as short as baker's pie crust. Raw pork and wet hardtack were about all we could get to eat, as no fires could be coaxed from the soggy embers. A portion of the regiment went on a detail building a corduroy road from Hatcher's Run to Yellow Tavern. They lost three men. Two were killed by falling trees; the third tried to lose an axe in his foot.

Most of our woodcutting operations today were on the land of Widow Cummings, whose sable garments would have been fearfully agitated had she known about it. The Rebels who camped here before us hadn't even an apology for a fire, so careful were they to protect the property of this rich Rebel. They even spared her rail fences.

We camped the night near the same place as last night, which we have named "Smoky Hollow." At sunset we began to see tokens of fair weather, and the smoke lifted. We hope to pass a fairly comfortable night.

### February 9th.

Marched about a mile up the line, passing outside of it. Although no charge is intended, we are sure to kick up a row, as the foe is not far off.

### February 10th.

Very cold, and we made no demonstrations. At 10 o'clock went out cutting slashing in front. Having no rations, we were relieved. We could not account for such consideration; hitherto it has not seemed to concern anybody whether or not we have anything to eat. Justice compels me to state, in this connection, that we do have some officers whose bowels of compassion have not quite grown up and who would favor us often if they were at liberty to follow their inclinations.

Perhaps when one is hungry, work is better than idleness, as it diverts attention from an empty stomach.

### February 11th.

Had orders to go out slashing again and to cut down everything in front for a space of 800 yards. Details from other brigades did the same in their front. The pickets were advanced 400 feet, which brought them out in plain sight of the enemy's works.

At 4 P.M. we changed camp, moving about a quarter of a mile to the right, near the Smith house again. How we are trotted round; on the 5th we were on this same ground and have been running around within a half mile of it all this time. We surmise that we are on detached service by the way we are hustled about.

### February 12th.

On fatigue building a redoubt in front of our camp. It is evident we are here to stay some time and are expected to be attacked by the Confederates. They would be worse than fools to attack us here, however.

### February 13th.

As there was nothing to do for the government this morning, we piled up a few logs for a shelter to keep out "the howling wintry blast," which, however, doesn't howl as fiercely here as it does in New England. *There* the phrase has meaning. By sunset we had quite a good house up — much better, in some respects, than any we have yet had.

Somehow I have an idea that this is the last stockaded house I shall build in Virginia. It is certain that the final struggle cannot long be postponed. Spring is virtually here, and in another month the roads will probably be settled. Then the serenity of Bobby Lee will be disturbed, and his communication as well. However, we get an impression from reading the Rebel papers that the prospect looks exceedingly bright to *them*. One of us is laboring under a colossal error.

### February 14th.

Went on picket with Rounds and Joy. We didn't get posted until 2 o'clock in the afternoon. The delay was caused by a change made in the line today. We finally got settled on the reserve, though, and had an uncommonly easy time, not being in any way disturbed although in sight of the enemy.

### February 15th.

All quiet, and we were relieved at noon and proceeded to camp forthwith. After dinner were sent out in front of our line to make an abatis, at which we labored till 5 P.M. This kind of work, though valuable in some places, is worth about as much here as the *fifth* wheel of a coach. It being light work, we didn't care very much, though.

### February 16th.

Today was devoted to building, and we made excellent headway, so as to be ready for the mortar. During the day there was some heavy firing toward Petersburg — why, we know not. It is often the case that people at home hear of events before we do. The first intimation we have of events close by is often obtained from the New York dailies.

### February 17th.

Were paraded to watch an execution. The unfortunate victim was a fellow from the 124th New York. He had deserted and joined the Rebel army. After serving a time in an Alabama regiment he came into our lines as a *Rebel* deserter. So far all went well, and doubtless would have continued so but for the next step in his programme. Having been sent to New York until paroled, he went to a bank to draw his money. Here he had to give his name, and here his play ended. The detectives soon had him, and he was forwarded to his regiment to be dealt with according to law. Sentence was executed this day, at noon, in the presence of this division.

He was thoroughly overcome and could perform the death march only as he was supported by the chaplain. It is a sad sight to see a young man brought to such a doom.

We must enforce discipline or we should soon see our army dwindling away. The late conscripts are almost wholly mercenaries. Remove the penalty for desertion and these fellows would skip. This man knew the penalty and incurred the risk. Now he must endure the punishment.

### February 18th.

On fatigue at the Smith house, our brigade headquarters, building a chimney for one of the staff who occupies an outbuilding. The house itself is no better outside than many a barn up our way, although the owner was well-to-do.

We are six-months men today, but it is a long, long time, in view of probable events. As time grows shorter, it grows *longer*, seemingly. It would be doubly hard to die now when we are so near an end. We have coquetted with death and dallied with destruction for almost three years, passing through so much and escaping.

There may be a thread of truth in the phrase, "Dulce et decorum, est prop patrie mori," but I, for one, confess a repugnance to this kind of sweetness. I'd prefer to be a live dog rather than a dead lion, notwithstanding the latter has loads of glory. Oceans of cheap twaddle have been recited about the sweetness of dying for one's country, but this is not a reference to the speechmakers' own tastes. Theirs are too much after the Josh Billings type of patriotism, which is willing to sacrifice all his *wife's* able-bodied relatives in suppressing the rebellion.

### February 19th.

This day bore a slight resemblance to Sunday, which indeed it was. We had no inspection or parade, though, and some worked on their houses all day.

### February 20th.

Nothing important to notice on this part of the line. There was a thundering racket up on our right. There are but very few days when our ears are not saluted by such sounds, just enough to keep us on the tiptoe of expectation.

### February 21st.

A salute of 100 guns was fired in honor of the fall of Charleston, birthplace and hotbed of treason and secession. At dress parade an official order was read giving the particulars: Two hundred large guns and many small ones fell into our hands along with much ammunition.

After dark a lot of deserters came in. They were especially down in the mouth and reported the rest of the Confederacy to be in the same condition. They expressed the opinion that the collapse of the Southern Confederacy is near at hand, even at the doors. It is rather late in the forenoon for them to finally wake up to that fact. When these fellows came in, a volley was fired after them, in consequence of which we were turned out to resist an attack.

Was on picket since seven this morning with Welch and Paine. There was no disturbance during the day, but the Officer of the Day, who had been taking observations through a bottle, hastened to the front and ordered us to stand up and hold our guns all the time, whether on post or not. We had to make a show of obedience in order to get rid of him. As soon as his back was turned we resumed our indifference and grounded our arms as before. We have been in the business long enough to know our duties on picket. The solemn-faced nincompoop soon returned, though, and ordered us to get up and stand guard. We complied as before.

Lieutenant Cummings, an individual recently elevated to that rank, was also highly agitated today. He hardly allowed us to speak aloud, and came near throwing himself into a fit when Mike Welch climbed a tree to better observe the enemy (or, according to his own vernacular, "to see could he see some o' thim"). Mike is fearfully nearsighted in his ears, and when Lieutenant Cummings in a voice husky with fear called to him, "For God's sake, come down. You'll draw fire!" Mike responded very innocently, "By Jesus, I see some o' thim." This sent a congestive chill down the lieutenant's spine, shaking his whole system and causing an audible titter from the rest of us. Mike soon descended, much to Cummings's relief.

On the whole, this has been rather a spicy sort of day. It is always a good day when we can exercise some of the shoulder-strap gentry.

### February 22nd.

On picket, and nothing happened to disturb anybody. We could see the Johnnies plainly, as they made no attempt to cover themselves. It has become a policy with us to commit no more murder by shooting down pickets when they are on post and minding their own business. They now appear as unconcerned as though we too were Confederates. After dark we can see forms moving around their picket fires like huge black shadows. Were we, or they, so disposed, we could make a fearful slaughter. Thank heaven, we are not disposed.

### February 23rd.

Rainy, and we were relieved from picket about 8 A.M. When we returned to camp, we were filled with stories of a sensational nature. Every deserter has something marvelous to relate, and thus we are constantly agitated and expecting an attack at any moment. Our common sense tells us this is the last place for an attack to succeed. Swamps and puddles abound in our front, and the Rebels couldn't bring men enough to counterbalance this advantage.

### February 24th.

Some more good news. Wilmington, North Carolina, has fallen under a combined land and naval force. Its garrison fell into our hands, also much matériel. At noon we had orders to pack up and be ready to move any moment. It was suspected that the enemy was going to evacuate Petersburg inside of twenty-four hours. That suspicion was just a trifle too previous. Petersburg remains in possession of the enemy, and at night we unpacked and retired as usual, except that half of us must sit up on guard so our officers won't have any nightmares.

### February 25th.

On our front perfect silence prevails, but on other parts of the line perfect Bedlam exists. Heavy firing went on all day, and we supposed it to be opposite Petersburg. At night a host of deserters came in, eighty on our front, fifty of these in one batch. This was doing the desertion business wholesale. When they left the Rebel line their comrades, instead of shooting them, set up a war whoop that would have made a body of Comanches green with envy. Our side responded with all-wool yells and screeches, and for a few minutes one couldn't tell who or what had broke loose.

After the display of vocalism, silence settled down over the scene. It isn't strange that the loss of so many produced such an uproar. Eighty men is more than an entire regiment. We gave the deserters a warm reception, even hot coffee. Here were eighty-six less for us to fight, and we appreciated it.

### February 26th.

Company I turned out at 5 A.M. and went on a reconnaissance in front, an utterly senseless performance that must have originated in some officer's whiskey bottle. If the Rebs had been so disposed, they could have shot every man in our detail. All that could be gained from the reconnaissance was the fact that the Rebs are just where we *know* they are. What restrained the Rebs from wiping out the detail is as much of a mystery as what our men were out there for.

On the appearance of this detail, the enemy's vedettes retired behind their works. After traversing the length of our division front, the detail returned just as wise as when it went out, only that each man knew he had been skirmishing very near eternity. I positively refused to go on this detail, not having been notified the night before as the rest had been.

The rest of the day was destitute of events worthy of mention.

### February 27th.

Another lot of deserters landed in our midst with the same old story of want and starvation to tell. All of them agreed that the Confederacy is played out, but their leaders will never give up as long as they can get a following.

In the evening went to prayer meeting in the chapel of a battery on a hill in rear of us. Chaplain Simpson of the battery conducted the service. There is much religious enthusiasm now among a certain class. As spring draws near, with its portent of severe fighting, the thoughts of many are directed toward their spiritual needs. The crowds that throng these meetings every night *seem* to be deriving much satisfaction therefrom.

### February 28th.

Still raining like great guns, and our only exercise was to go up to headquarters and sign the muster roll. The writer hasn't missed one yet, and hasn't spent any of them in the hospital, on any soft detail, or at home. Because of the rain we did not have the full inspection that usually accompanies a muster.

### March 1st.

A day of rest, as it was too muddy to drill. This evening I attended devotional meeting again. It lasted two hours, and there were many exhortations. It is currently reported that some rivalry exists in religious matters as well as in drill. A certain colonel, on hearing that a Massachusetts regiment was to baptize ten converts next Sunday, ordered his adjutant to "detail ninety men for baptism," saying, "I'll be d—d if I'll be outdone by any Massachusetts regiment." I never heard whether or not the order was executed. Some men will *never* wash unless forced to.

### March 2nd.

Heard no firing today. Our lines are nearly forty miles long, so we don't hear *half* that is going on. Personally, I haven't been under cannonading for a long time and it won't vex me if this continues.

## March 3rd.

Same as yesterday, with the addition of rumors of a move. No doubt the rumor is utterly groundless, but we feel just as uneasy as though we had a positive order. Spring is upon us, and we see the end drawing near.

Today is the writer's birthday, and whether I will live to see another is exceedingly problematical.

## March 4th.

A company drill was undertaken, but we did most everything but drill. It is Inauguration Day, and we didn't propose to work, so we spent the time boxing, wrestling, running, and tumbling.

We anticipate breaking camp very soon. The condition of the ground is such that we have much concern, as appearances indicate that the campaign will open much earlier than last year. One reason for this is that the Philistines be upon us, and we have only a few rods to go to become hotly engaged. Another reason is that we can start our campaign without having to wait so long for trains as we did last year. We can start with several days' rations, and there are plenty more here to load the trains. With such men as Humphreys and Wright to command the corps, and Meade to direct, it looks quite cheerful. I feel a degree of confidence I haven't felt at the opening of any previous campaign. It is well known that Lee and his army are discouraged and disgusted at the Davis management, which in great measure accounts for the wholesale desertions of late. Hence, we expect short and sharp work.

# The Fall of
# Petersburg

## March 5 – April 9, 1865

*March 5th.*

A full inspection, so it is Sunday, surely. Captain Green simply went through the formalities and gave but little attention to details. But this wasn't known until *after* the inspection, so we applied ourselves to getting ready with our accustomed vigor and exactness. As Captain Green comes from the ranks, he knows how thoroughly we despise drills and inspections.

*March 6th – 8th.*

Nothing to break the monotony of camp. We drill some and rave more. Were we ordered to *work*, we would do so cheerfuly, but drill we loathe. The quiet of these days is ominous and the rumors of a move increase.

The Boston *Herald* of the 7th reports that "the Rebel papers are rejoicing over the assumption that Sherman is stuck in the red mud of North Carolina, as sticky as its famous tar."

The Richmond *Examiner* of Friday last says:

The military condition of these Confederate states, after a few years of war, is by no means discouraging. The enemy has but two armies in the field of all the hosts he once had. General Grant has literally stripped every section of country and concentrated all into two armies. In West Virginia he hasn't sufficient forces to protect his major generals in their beds. No rest for the wicked out there [frightful joke]. In Tennessee and Kentucky there are no troops. Mississippi, Georgia, Florida and Alabama have only small detachments, strongly fortified and holding only their own camping ground. In Trans-Mississippi the Confederacy has no enemy. The army around Richmond, and Sherman's army, are all that are left of the hosts who once menaced these states.

These two armies disposed of, and victory and independence are ours [truth, every word of it]. The whole country returns to Confederate authority, and we confront again the frontiers of the enemy's country. Never before has the prospect of final and sure victory presented itself to this people. . . . The enemy has apparently [this is rich] won many successes, but really he has been narrowing down the issues and putting them within the reach of our resources and arms. While scattered over a whole continent, it was impossible to win a decisive victory.

But concentration has, in four years of effort, brought victory and independence within our reach without hazarding our liberties on the issue of battle.

Grant has been drawn to this despite his successes. He has been compelled to denude his conquests and give up the fruits of his victories, and concentrate his armies into two.

Did anybody ever hear such brag and bluster as this? I know well who penned this bosh; it was the cowardly Pollard, the biggest liar and braggart in the country. What folly to print it when he knows that the disintegration of Rebeldom has made rapid and alarming headway.

The *Herald* referred to earlier closes with these comments:

The capture of Chancellorsville by Phil Sheridan is a military advantage gained of great importance. It is less than 70 miles west of Richmond, is connected with it by railroad, is in the heart of the region whence Lee draws his supplies, and is only about 60 miles from Lynchburg. Its capture indicates the straits Lee is put to when he can spare no more than 2000 men in defense of a point which has repeatedly been attempted by us and obstinately held by a large force of the enemy. . . . This new movement of Sheridan's shows in striking manner the value of having all our troops and movements under one military head. . .one who can command, combine, and coordinate, who can seize the opportunity and make all things work to a common end.

The *Army and Navy Journal* of about the same date contains an article touching on the same subject. It says, "The two ablest generals in the Confederacy command its respective armies, and while our own commanders surpass them in skill and our troops are far more numerous and brave, vigorous and flushed with victory, we needn't therefore tremble for the issue. But movements of importance must be speedily looked for." This article shows a remarkably clear conception of the situation, but I disagree with the writer's belief that our generals are more skillful and our men braver. This is Yankee braggadocio and worth no more than the same kind of bosh on the Rebel side. It is simply stolen Rebel thunder. No man who has met the Rebels in the field will make invidious comparisons. As for the skill of generals, no sober men of moderate intelligence will claim that Grant is more skillful than Lee. If this army has ever done anything with even a suggestion of skill, it was before it came under Grant's control.

The Rebel papers quoted from by the Boston *Herald* seem to have no doubt but what Grant will commence operations as soon as the ground becomes dry enough to allow moving of artillery and trains. We have that same notion and are expecting an order to "get up and dust" at any hour.

### March 9th.

Had nothing to do although the weather is "unco fine," as the Scotchmen say. After dinner I was ordered out to drill. Only *five* men were found in camp who were liable to this duty today. It is possible that my bump of conceit is abnormally developed, but I have an idea that I already know all I need or desire to of drill.

## March 10th.

A dress parade at 5 P.M. under Captain Green, who has a strong ambition to be Major Green. After it was over a few of us went down to the battery chapel to meeting. It was a right lively one. Many wanderers returned to the fold, declaring vehemently their determination *never* to go astray again. The value of such declarations can only be determined by giving due weight to the circumstances. Who will fall in this campaign? is the question that presents itself to every one of us with great force and makes us consider whether we haven't something to adjust before going.

## March 11th.

Drill in the morning and review in the afternoon by generals Meade, Humphreys, Mott, and de Trobriand. Here is a sure token of an early departure.

In the evening attended another meeting on the hill and found it the same as on previous occasions. The house was crowded, and many had to go away for lack of room. How fortunate for us mortals that the Most High dwelleth not in temples made by hand and that wherever a soul seeks after Him, there He is to be found. It is singular, though, that so many seek after Him in a crowd. A worship in solitude smacks more of true worship and humility. There were several other meetings in full blaze at the same time tonight, and those who claim to be conversant with such matters say that no such religious wave ever swept over this army before.

## March 12th.

Sunday. A full inspection this morning. In the afternoon Chaplain Lovering came up and held forth, this being the first time he has done so since Thanksgiving up in Fort Rice. Lovering has been at the hospital, caring for those who are sick and wounded in body and not troubling about their souls. Still, Lovering is the best we have been favored with.

Our first chaplain, Hersey, was a disgrace to the regiment, and more so to his profession. He had no sooner arrived in camp than he joined himself unto the "sons of Belial" and could soon guzzle more whiskey than the fattest of them. As he couldn't get enough to drink in legitimate ways, he resorted to illegitimate ones, even to stealing. He also stole a horse when we marched through Maryland in the fall of 1862. On the whole, he acted so much like Satan that his career with us soon ended.

Our next chaplain, Hayden, was taken from the ranks and, as he thought, elevated above *us*. He was a cheap buffoon and a very prince of gas-bags. His alleged preaching and attempts to expound the scriptures excited both pity and disgust. While he expounded the Word, the officers used to sit around and make game of him by telling cheap stories and uttering base plagiarisms of venerable jokes. If there can be a more pitiable or humiliating sight than that of one who occupies so high a calling prostituting the same in such a way, I don't know about it. The officers, seeing what a fool Hayden was and how susceptible to flattery, pasted it onto him so thick that it fell off in flakes, and he began to think himself greater even than Beecher.

The next victim was the present incompetent, Lovering, a person holding the Unitarian faith, which is altogether too high-toned for the army as it is too noncommittal. (We have seen the extremes, for Hayden was a Baptist of the hard-shell persuasion.) I have never heard anything against the character of Lovering, and think him the best of the lot so far. This is damning the man with faint praise, but it is the best I can do. He is unpopular because he keeps aloof from both officers and men, so his preaching is mere emptiness.

### March 14th.

Now the winter of our discontent is about to end, I believe. The sutler was ordered to take himself to City Point today. That we will soon follow suit needs no telling, only we might well go in another direction from the sutler.

### March 15th.

An attack and a move were expected all day. The Rebels across the fields have been acting highly suspicious for two or three days, particularly today. We have an eye on them, and at the slightest sign of a move we are ready to spring on them. It is a little late for Uncle Bobby Lee to undertake any movement of magnitude.

### March 16th and 17th.

No move yet on either side, but so strong is the expectation of one that we didn't drill or have any inspection. A wonderful abstinence — and an evil omen. If the Rebels had a move in contemplation, they probably have not abandoned it but are trying to lull us and take us unawares.

### March 18th.

Nothing of note going on this morning, only a notice that we should go out at 10 o'clock to witness an execution. Being now on the eve of important movements, it becomes necessary to make an example of someone so that we might have a wholesome dread of the fate of cowards and govern ourselves accordingly.

The victim this time was a person whose intellect was in several senses below par, and this is by no means the first such instance I have noticed.

The men who were selected to do the shooting made a botch of it and hit the man everywhere except in a vital part. He rolled on the ground, writhing in agony until the reserve, two in number, were ordered to finish him, which they did by blowing his brains out. It was the most sickening sight I have ever witnessed. Although I have seen men fall in action and seen them mutilated in every way, that was in the regular order of warfare, not deliberate murder. This man was simply butchered by blunderers, and at a time when every man is needed.

If all were treated thus who have ever shown their coattails to the enemy, our ranks would be thinned to such an extent that we should have to recruit before the spring campaign could commence. There is another reason why the shooting was not justifiable: If a man is a coward and can't control himself, he should be removed from the ranks and detailed for some duty he is fitted for. A goodly number of our troops are foreigners who have been impressed into the service. They had no idea of the nature of an oath when they were enlisted, and were in many cases so intoxicated that they didn't know whether they were taking the oath of allegiance or saying the Lord's Prayer. When they came to their senses, they found themselves in some military camp without knowing how they came there. Such men have a *right* to desert, and we have *no* right to shoot them.

I returned to camp disgusted and in a somewhat savage frame of mind. The rest of the day I didn't do anything to distract my attention from this subject.

### March 19th.

Sunday, but we didn't have any inspection. May the saints protect us, for I am now positive that some dreadful calamity awaits us. At 2 P.M. had preaching and at 5, dress parade. After this a band concert ended the day. These are days of unrest; we don't have much peace.

### March 20th and 21st.

Two days of bodily rest. No drill and but one parade.

### March 22nd.

Was detailed this morning to go up in front of Petersburg again to search for and mark the graves of our dead who fell in battle there. We took the train from Humphrey's to Meade's station. Leaving the rail there, we followed the Jerusalem Plan Road to Fort Hell, then followed the works. Also visited the works at Hare house, where our first engagement on this side of the James occurred on June 16th.

Everything there has undergone a complete change. Not a line of works could we distinguish. Every tree and root has been cut and dug out of the ground for wood. The forts were all we could see of a warlike nature. It is now a trackless waste of clay and dust relieved by nothing but a house or two in the distance.

We found nearly all we sought and started for camp about 3 P.M. Our engine ran off the track (an everyday occurrence) and delayed us, so we didn't get to camp till after dark.

### March 23rd.

A grand review by General Humphreys. The wind blew like a young tornado, and dust filled the air almost to suffocation. The uproar of the elements did not in the least interfere with our arrangements, though by the time we reached the reviewing officers (after marching nearly a mile), we looked like Graybacks — there was no tint of blue about us any longer. President Lincoln and Secretary Wells of the Navy were expected but failed to appear. This last-named venerable fossil never has favored us with a view of his flowing beard (which is the only aqueous thing about him).

### March 24th.

Nothing in the wind today, and no wind compared with what we had yesterday. The weather is excellent and the roads dry rapidly. At this time of year the frost in the ground is the only element working against us, though rainy weather almost might put us back now.

### March 25th.

Heavy firing heard this morning in the direction of Petersburg. It rapidly increased in volume, and by 7 o'clock a fierce conflict was going on. An order came from corps headquarters to pack up and be ready to move. This order, coupled with the racket, meant business. Tents were struck and further orders awaited with impatience. They soon came: we were to move out to our picket line and make a show of attack, thereby drawing the Reb attention and preventing them from sending any troops to the point of attack up the line. We also took this occasion to change the picket line so as to better observe the enemy.

We formed in two lines of battle with a heavy skirmish line in front. Our line met heavy enemy fire and retired hastily. It became evident that if we were to advance, we must increase our force. Another line was advanced, but with no better success. The Rebels had all the advantage and we found it no light task to keep our line in place. Never have I seen our men so terribly demoralized, and although the front line was well protected by an elevation in front, they seemed determined to break and run.

While they were thus protected, the second line, in which we were much exposed, was right in a position to catch the missiles that flew harmlessly over the first line. As long as no advance was made, those in the first line had the best of it. If they moved up, we should have taken their place. Besides the danger from bullets, we were subjected to the inconvenience of lying down in water to avoid having our brains scattered to the four winds. In order to keep the front line in place between us and the Confederacy, we resorted to various devices to intimidate them. Colonel Hobson even went so far as to threaten to punch one officer showing a lack of nerve. Colonel Billy threw in an extra inducement to bravery with an elaborate hint that he would presently cause the most intimate relations to exist between his number 13 cowhides and that portion of his anatomy concealed under the officer's coat tails. The effect was marvelous, and he executed a movement of his company with surprising agility.

Notwithstanding all our wallowing in the bog water, we lost two men from Company I, other companies lost more. No further attempts were made to advance, and after dark we returned to camp very unexpectedly. There we learned what the row was all about. The Rebels, under General Gordon, had attempted to capture Fort Steadman and had succeeded temporarily. Before they could utilize their capture, the 6th and 9th Corps were in their wool and compelled most of them to surrender. This event was probably the "great exploit" with which Lee has been threatening to "surprise the world." It is a question which of his movements surprised the world most, his capture of Fort Steadman or his hasty exit from it.

## March 26th.

A little more firing, one man killed and one wounded. Our lines remain virtually the same as yesterday, although the Rebs have made the most desperate effort to recover what we wrested from them. The lines are so near together that neither side can advance without bringing an engagement. We are near enough to carry on a conversation, if it were allowed. The Rebel officers are very strict in enforcing silence.

At night went on picket. Had a nasty time and didn't get posted till 7 o'clock. It was almost painfully quiet all night and the only way we knew there were Rebs in front was by seeing their forms silhouetted in the firelight. They have fallen back, although still near enough for us to hear their fires crackle and snap. We don't care how much they move in *that* direction, as long as they don't come this way.

We have been informed by some deserters that for every Reb who deserts to this side, there are *two* who go home or flee to the mountains. Their ranks must be thinning rapidly.

## March 27th.

All quiet today, and the Rebs fell back to their second line. This made it advisable for us to straighten a portion of ours. We dreaded doing this by day, as the Rebs would be sure to interrupt the peaceful relations existing. Pickets were relieved at 4 P.M., and we didn't "open the ball" until after dark. The Johnnies knew nothing of it until it was too late. They woke to find that we have covered the ground they left by falling back.

### March 28th.

We settled back into the old ruts enough to have a company drill, both forenoon and afternoon. This didn't allay our forebodings, as we well know that these two great armies are liable to clash at any moment. At night had orders to be ready to move next morning with sixty rounds of ammunition and four days' rations apiece, and we retire with a feeling that at last the time has come.

Four years has Virginia withstood the tide of invasion, spurning it from her battlements as the rock beats back the billows. Six times the tumultuous and angry flood has surged against her firm barrier, and six times has recoiled. Now it was McDowell, now McClellan, now Pope, now Burnside, now Hooker, now Meade, now Grant. Grant's great hordes came like the mighty seventh wave, topping all its fellows to crush into ruins the ramparts of Virginia.

At sunset Sheridan's cavalry went to the left in the direction of Dinwiddie Court House, and this gives a clue to the probable location of the entire army.

Here we have been for nearly three years. In plain view of eternity, time and time again we have reached its edge. Each time some of our number fell, but others came off triumphant. Will we be thus lucky again? Each of us (especially the writer) is selfish enough to hope that *he* will be spared. Our numbers are now few and our hearts faint. I retire with these grim thoughts to keep me company through a sleepless night.

### March 29th.

At 4 A.M. we were hustled out and went through the motions of eating breakfast. We packed our possessions and departed from camp, our last winter quarters in Virginia, come what may. The entire army was drawn up on the plain at the left, the telegraph lines were strung, and we soon were following in the direction of Hatcher's Run. We moved rapidly a mile or so, but it soon became necessary to go more cautiously and we began to feel our way.

Thus far no enemy was visible. We inferred we must be swinging out around their right. We have made several advances, each one a wheeling movement, our left swinging toward Lee's right. In the afternoon we swung again, and this brought us around facing toward Petersburg, which indicated that we had begun a turning movement and would probably advance on the enemy at once. We formed in line of battle and threw up some light works. We were almost facing the point we started from in the morning, but as yet had encountered no enemy.

I can give but little idea of our movement here, for we know nothing of the topography of this blasted country, having left the roads a long time ago. Our line has been swinging continually to the left over bog holes, hills, gullies, and fields, through woods and over streams.

General Humphreys and staff made a short reconnaissance in front and on his return ordered an immediate advance through the woods, our left still swinging to the left. After advancing a short distance, we halted. About 5 o'clock were ordered forward again and soon found ourselves floundering through an alder swamp with water knee deep. We struggled around for a half hour, then halted at a Rebel camp that appears to have been abandoned just this morning.

After dark the rain set in, and having been foolish enough to retire without proper precaution of digging a ditch around our tents, we have the alternative of turning out and doing it now or being drowned before morning.

## March 30th.

As soon as we were ready, we commenced another day of swinging to the left (Lee's right), momentarily expecting contact with some portion of Lee's army. They must have fallen back considerably, otherwise we should have encountered them long since. We have tried to penetrate this section several times before and always met with strong resistance.

The water was so deep and the brush so thick that no kind of line could be kept. In consequence, our progress was extremely slow. We had to stop often to close up and straighten the line. At last we came into a clearing near Hatcher's Run, having swung around enough to strike this stream again a short distance above where we crossed it yesterday. Here we struck a line of Rebel breastworks, but they had long departed to their main line, which is very strong.

Up to this time our division hasn't fired a musket or unlimbered a battery. The enemy has offered no resistance, falling back faster than we advance. We'd supposed we would be fighting like Satan by this time, and rather enjoy *this* kind of fighting, hoping for a continuance of it to the end. This present line of works being very near the main line, we didn't advance beyond them.

The rain continued, and we dined on hardtack so soft as to be eaten with a spoon and delightfully flabby raw pork strongly flavored with coffee. We now advanced to within gunshot of the enemy's works and halted again, then advanced one regiment at a time, each in turn receiving its share of Rebel attention. Losses, if any, were very small. We threw up another line of light works, all we could manage, for we have no tools. One can't throw much dirt with hands alone.

Our beds are *soft* enough in this morass. I have secured a bed in the second story of this hotel and am the envy of every man in our company. A small pine tree grows directly in front of my place in line. When I lie on it, it bends just enough to place me in a horizontal position. Its gentle, undulating motion is quite soothing and soporific. It continues to rain, and we are gloomy, cold, wet, and as blue as milk which has been skimmed on both sides.

## March 31st.

Three o'clock found us on our pins and soon plodding our weary way toward the left, following the line through slush and mud the like of which I hope never to see again. After moving a few miles, we halted on the right-hand side of the Boydtown Plank Road. Here we found less mud and a chance to rest.

A portion of the corps, the 2nd Division, were sent further to the left to aid General Sheridan. This accounts for our moving down here. Sheridan is near the Dinwiddie Court House and working this way. A portion of the 5th Corps (General Warren) is on our left, while another division has gone to aid Sheridan.

The Rebs made the most strenuous effort to turn our left all day and get between us and the 5th Corps. They would have succeeded but for the continual firing of the 2nd Division of our corps near the Crow house. The Rebels attacked on our left incessantly and we expected to hear a triumphant yell and see their banners flaunting over our works at any moment, but we were spared this spectacle. At night we moved a few rods to the left so that our regiment rested on the Boydtown Road, giving us an excellent view of the Rebel works for half a mile or more. We drew rations and then two hundred men from our regiment were detailed for picket. I was allowed to remain behind with a few others. We laid down rails to keep us out of the mud and hope to pass a comparatively good night. Rails may not be as soft as mud, but after such a night as last night we like them much better.

### April 1st.

All quiet on our front, and we were moved a trifle to the right. It was not long before the boom of cannon reverberated over the fields on the left. Sheridan's cavalry and the 5th Corps, with Miles's division of the 2nd Corps, are down there somewhere, and we suspect they are stirring up General Lee, or maybe he is stirring them. It is of the utmost importance to Lee that he keeps his lines of escape open.

We waited all day for orders to charge or move forward, but they never came. At night Major Mattox, who was captured in the Wilderness, returned to us. If anybody went into raptures over his return, I didn't see them. Too much bandbox and red tape never enthused me worth a cent.

Another quiet night, but as portentous events are hourly anticipated, we lie on our arms, ready to spring at a moment's notice. The Rebels are desperate, and like the stag at bay, might undertake a desperate venture no matter how foolhardy.

### April 2nd.

We were up betimes this morning and got the impression that something important was about to happen. The very air was laden with this presentiment. It was Sunday and we were in the immediate presence of the enemy. When these two items come together we can expect a fight.

At 1 o'clock this morning the 6th Corps (General Wright) and Hay's Division of the 2nd Corps commenced an attack on the enemy near the Crow house and near daylight carried the Rebel works. The Johnnies in front of the 6th Corps were driven up opposite the 9th Corps (General Parkes), which was holding the line near Fort Steadman. About 7 o'clock General Meade came down the line, and so elated was he that he ordered us to advance without delay. Although Meade is superior in command to all corps commanders, it is from General Humphreys that we take orders. This breach of etiquette may be excused, though, in light of General Meade's excitement attending the successes of the morning.

When we did move forward, we expected a desperate resistance and great loss. It couldn't be much longer delayed. Orders were received to advance up the road and carry the works. Now for a bloody encounter. But a sudden change came over us, for as we gazed at the point we were to attack, a sight met our eyes that nearly unmanned us. Where two minutes before the Stars and Bars had flown, now floated the glorious old Stars and Stripes. Never before have we thought it so beautiful, and a cheer went up that could have been heard in Petersburg. Our yells rose above the din of battle. Cheer after cheer filled the air as we saw its graceful folds waving in the morning breeze over the works so lately held by the enemy and where a few minutes before the emblem of treason was flaunted in our faces.

When the order came to advance, all we had to do was march up the Boyden Plank Road by the flank. We moved with uncommon alacrity and soon came to their entrenchments. These are formidable, having not less than three lines of abatis and two rifle pits before reaching the main line. After getting in, we halted to catch our breath, for we had come up the road almost on the gallop. We then pushed on toward Petersburg, following the works all the way. As we moved along we could see all the old places we have occupied since last June. We soon came to the ruins of the Turnbull house, lately the headquarters of General Robert E. Lee, now a pile of smoking cinders with official documents flying around. (I procured one as a relic: the findings of a court martial in a case of desertion.) General A.P. Hill was killed at or near this house.[1] Some of our men came upon him suddenly, and one of them shot him through the heart. The Rebels buried him hastily, as our army was hard upon them by that time.

We paused here a few minutes and then moved on, stopping next at the place where the South Side Railroad enters the city. Here we laid low behind its embankments and waited for the rest of the army to come up and get into position.

From this point we could see the whole Rebel army huddled in groups on the hill, surrounded by artillery and doing all it could to keep us at bay. Flames engulfed a portion of the city, and the greatest confusion reigned all around. Everything indicated that the Rebs intended to dispute any further progress on our part, probably to give the citizens of Petersburg time to leave or to hide the possessions they couldn't carry away.

Our division had orders to fill a gap in the lines at the Whittaker house, General Mahone's headquarters yesterday, today General Grant's, whose men were fast occupying the grounds.

Mr. Whittaker is a venerable Virginian of the old school. His language and appearance indicate the scholar and polished gentleman, besides being an orator of no mean order. If his word is to be credited, he was a person of importance in the days when Petersburg had won the title of the "Cockade City." He entertained such men as Andrew Jackson, General Scott, and other celebrities of earlier days. We found a crowd of New York toughs insulting and jeering at the old gentleman for no reason except that he was trying to dissuade them from mutilating his property. He stood firm on his doorstep and argued with them for an hour or more, but he might as well have argued with a lamp post. Regrettably, some in our regiment felt called upon to show their ignorance and join in with the rabble, smothering the old man's voice with a foul stream of billingsgate. They seemed to cherish the delusion that their unmitigated bosh was *wit* or *argument*. How cheap and commonplace it sounded when weighed in the balance with the old man's eloquence. He knew what he was talking about and handled his subject with much skill, not for an instant losing his temper. He didn't claim to be a strong Union man, nor was he a rank Secesh, yet he was threatened with violence. Having exhausted all other means of proving him a Rebel, the mob claimed it on the grounds that "Billy" (General Mahone) had used his premises as headquarters. On the same line of reasoning, there are many Union men in Virginia whose homes *our* generals have occupied.

We threw up a small entrenchment in his yard and planted a battery there. This he begged us not to do, saying the Confederates would make no further resistance in this vicinity. After we formed the line in his yard, we commenced a search of the house for valuables but only found a half barrel of shin-plasters and a lot of molasses. The molasses we ate on our bread, the Confederate money we keep as relics, that being the only use we can make of it.

Generals Grant and Wright were on the ground in front of our line, at the end of a shed, talking over the disposition of the several corps. Grant was so completely disguised that none of us were aware who he was till we were close to him. No one would recognize that insignificant individual as the commander of the armies of the Union, numbering not less than 1,500,000 men. Our Colonel Hobson, probably not knowing him, rode almost onto his heels and shouted in clarion tones, "Get out of the way here!" General Grant turned partially round and we all saw who it was. Ninety-five out of a hundred men would have been profuse in their apologies, but not our Colonel Hobson. He just kept right on forming up his lines, and Grant moved out of the way as quickly as if he were the lowest in the ranks. Grant was accompanied by his usual companion — an unlighted cigar stump from which he seems to derive much comfort and inspiration. Had he been some corporal, he probably would have flared up and been very indignant at being thus addressed, but Grant smothered his outraged dignity.

Having formed our line, and there being no farther advance for the time, we looked around us a bit. A good deal of skirmishing was going on and considerable cannonading in the vicinity of the Crater and Cemetery Hill. Clouds and puffs of smoke in all directions toward Petersburg told how fiercely the contest raged. The tobacco warehouses were on fire, having been set ablaze to prevent them from falling into our hands. By dark the flames were raging, and by their light the Rebels made their way to Richmond.

They seem possessed with the demon of destruction, burning all the bridges over the Appomattox as they retreated. Of course these bridges must be rebuilt at the expense of the city or state, and their destruction won't long deter us. By midnight the "defenders of virgins fair and matrons grave" had made an inglorious flight and left the matrons and virgins to look out for themselves. None are left to defend the city except some of the colored population and such whites as couldn't get away or who have sense enough to know that Yankees are human and not the ghouls we are represented to be by the Southern fire-eaters.

Our entire army, so far as I know, passed the night where we had formed in the afternoon, and such a night I have not seen since enlisting in the service. Great things were done this day and "still there's more to follow." So far our loss has been small, none in our regiment.

### April 3rd.

Turned out about six o'clock, and after refreshing the inner man prepared to go in pursuit of the enemy, who left for parts unknown during the night. Bag and baggage has he departed and left no trace.

The 9th Corps entered the city and received its surrender while the rest of the army started off in a southwest direction. We didn't get far before we came to one of the roads on which the Rebels fled. They have fallen out all along the line and in the woods, so great in number it seems a literal fulfillment of the oft-repeated phrase, "the woods are full of them." One entire regiment, officers and all, surrendered to us as we came along. I noticed a perceptible absence of their usual swagger and none of

THE OCCUPATION OF PETERSBURG. *Harper's Pictorial History of the Civil War.*

the enthusiastic expressions of confidence in Lee, which have been so abundant at other times. The inordinate Southern conceit has suffered a thorough collapse.

We marched about ten miles during the forenoon, and at noon came up with our 2nd Division (General Miles), which has engaged the enemy and suffered heavy losses. They have established a temporary hospital near Five Forks. Here we learned that the Rebels have crossed the Appomattox and most assuredly will dispute our passage across that river. We didn't go that way, therefore, and instead moved *up* the southern bank of the river about seven miles and bivouacked for the night. We are jubilant. We have them on the run and victory is in the air. Another thing in our favor is the fact that Lee's army is now cut loose from any regular base of supplies and in a few days will be out of food. Soldiers may thrive a few days on enthusiasm, but horses require oats and hay. Discipline counts for nothing once a certain stage of hunger is reached. My own experience establishes this fact.

### April 4th.

As soon as we were ready we started. Soon after, we received official information of the downfall of Richmond and the evacuation of the Confederate governor. It was immediately occupied by Union troops under Weitzel. General Shepley, of Maine, has been made military commandant.

I could hardly credit my senses or describe my feelings as this piece of intelligence reached us. So these two nests of treason — Richmond and Petersburg — have fallen into our hands at last.

The roads are very bad. Colonel Hobson's horse stepped into a hole and broke his leg, and had to be shot. It was concluded that some road must be corduroyed if we are to make much progress. Large bodies were detailed for this purpose. We cut and laid timber nearly all day, getting over many bad places. We then moved about a mile and bivouacked in a field nearby, feeling very much pleased with this day's work.

### April 5th.

Were turned out at 2 A.M., and at four were pushing along after Bobby Lee and his ragamuffins. We marched until nine and then halted for rations. While we were there, a body of 920 Rebels passed to the rear, having fallen into our hands since daylight. They were covered with filthy rags and represented all the colors of a Virginia landscape, red mud being the predominant tint. I have often wondered why we can't *see* the Rebels better; now I have the answer. If this lot of Rebels had been lying on the ground we could have passed very near them and not suspected their presence, mistaking them for rocks, logs, and dirt.

After dinner we marched until 10 o'clock at night, when we formed in line connecting with the 5th Corps, which is planted squarely across the Danville Railroad. After fooling around a couple of hours, we lay down for the rest of the night. This was a moment of supreme enjoyment for the writer — and one of wretchedness as well. Was ever a mortal permitted to endure such tortures as I have suffered today? Quite early in the day my heels were galled to the bone. The blood dried into the stockings and boots, and when I removed them, the flesh was actually torn from my heel. I thought I had known suffering from this cause before, but all previous experiences have been simply skirmishes compared with the agony of the moment.

The most fearful forebodings for the morrow rack my mind as I wait for sleep to drown the smart and pains of my lacerated extremities. The Rebs made a stand here at sunset and we have orders to attack at six tomorrow morning all along the line.

Even though we arrived so late at our bivouac, a few of our men went to check the poultry interests of this section. They were beset by guerrillas who served them as they had served the hens: cut their throats and plucked their clothing. This game of stripping the dead is a favorite sport with Rebels. If they do it from necessity then I can only say that when a so-called government gets *that* poor it is quite time to go out of business.

### April 6th.

In pursuance of last night's order, we were ready to move at 6 P.M. We advanced down the track a short distance and saw indications of the enemy. Skirmishers were thrown out at once and the main army began to move more cautiously.

General Mott, our division commander, was soon wounded and carried off the field to the rear. General de Trobriand assumed command of the division. For a mile or two we moved rapidly, the enemy making but slight resistance until they came to their line of works at Deatonville, undoubtedly thrown up to detain us till their trains can be pushed out of our reach. For we have now driven them till they are crowded onto their trains, loaded with furniture, plate, libraries, costly wardrobes — almost everything that can be moved. The wealthy of Richmond and Petersburg are fleeing, they know not whither.

As we approached Deatonville (a collection of one house and its attendant outhouses), we were tendered a warm reception and met with considerable casualties. Colonel Hobson was wounded in the thigh and sustained a heavy loss of blood; Lieutenant

Usher, to whom I am much indebted for favors and for my only promotion, was mortally wounded; John E. True, my tent mate, was slightly wounded in the head; Wallace Hodsdon was shot through one lung; and others were more or less injured. Up to this time I had kept up, although every step was torture, making me sick to my stomach. Soon after Deatonville, I commenced to lose ground. Had it not been for stimulants, I should have sunk down by the road and made no attempt to proceed.

We soon had the Rebs in close quarters again, with their large train in sight. Now there was wild screaming and clawing to get out of the way of the confounded Yankees. Our column dashed forward to secure the spoils, but every rock and tree, every fence and hillock, seemed alive and offered resistance. Wagon after wagon was overturned, its contents confiscated and scattered to the winds. The writer wasn't present at the time they were overthrown, but arrived at last. Although elated by the degree of success, I was so tortured that I could truthfully say, "There's nothing in the world that gives me joy."

At 5 P.M. over eighty wagons had been destroyed and their contents distributed, but at the loss of several lives. The guards would jump from their wagons and hide behind some defensive point and pepper us. To think these fools risked their lives and fought like fiends for goods in which they had not one cent of interest; everything in those wagons belonged to the aristocracy. Our men made a lively search for small articles, and in many cases were well repaid.

The pleasure and exhilaration of this day's work were not shared by the writer, however. I kept losing ground, so that by sunset I was at least four miles in rear of the column and with no more idea of the whereabouts of my regiment than I had of what Queen Victoria ate for breakfast this morning. I plodded along as best I could, hoping to get some clue as to the direction they had gone. Luckily for me, I encountered a body of engineers from our corps. As they moved more leisurely and the night was cool, I was able to keep up, arriving at Corps Headquarters about 10 o'clock. The officers have chosen a large house just over a stream called Sailor's Creek. In the rear of the house are 2,000 Rebel prisoners, among them General Ewell and several generals of lower grade. The prisoners go in and out as they please, seemingly much more jolly than their captors. There is no fear of their escaping, for it is useless for them to return to their own army. With us, they have *something* to eat. As for going home, many are hundreds, even thousands, of miles from home and they are too weak to walk far.

Destruction and starvation on one hand, surrender on the other. Still many cling to General Lee with childlike faith.

### April 7th.

Daylight enabled us to get our bearings, and we found ourselves very near our own regiment. I was fortunate in finding a pair of army brogans that had been abandoned, by some providential circumstance. I felt as if I had experienced a change of heart, so great and sudden was my relief. My heart was as light as my purse two days after payday.

We moved on, going through the debris of yesterday's battles for three miles at least. One of our officers found a gold watch, another a gold chain, and still others scooped up abandoned treasure. The Rebs have made the mistake of loading their trains with foppery, but no food. Quite a lot of the aristocracy are fleeing in their own private carriages, but their *goods* are in the army wagons. Hence the frequent delays along the route. If it weren't for this, the Rebel army would doubtless leave us behind.

Their mules and horses must subsist on brush now, and although a mule is the hardiest of animals, many of them have fallen by the wayside to die of starvation or exhaustion unless some friendly hand dispatches them.

We have taken the wrong road, and while our superiors look up the matter I shall elaborate a few minutes more on the subject of the festive mule. He has no more sense of taste than a stone jug and will eat anything containing nutriment. He is especially recommended for his brave appetite, which slights no part of a hill of corn, but masters cob, stalk, and shuck as though it were the most succulent substance.

The mule is a good worker but liable to *strike*, and when he strikes, human calculations fail to find any rule by which to reckon when he will go to work again. I have been through the New York Stock Exchange, once passed part of a day in a boiler factory, and have been on one or two Sunday School picnics — all these are quiet compared with an army mule's bray.

A mule has one more leg than a conventional milking stool. He can stand on that one leg and wave the other three in as many different directions.

Nobody knows what a hard time Noah had with the antediluvian ancestor of the mule. Historians are silent on this point, as on most other points of interest. If he had one on the Ark, it is strange that it didn't eat up everything else.

But we are going. The officers have decided to about-face and get onto the right road as speedily as possible.

Having been so exercised on the previous day, I am already nearly prostrated even this early in the day. Hoping to keep up by lightening my burden, I have parted with one thing after another till nothing is left that can possibly be dispensed with. When a soldier is so weak as to be unable to carry his blanket, it is evident he hasn't much strength left; there are no nights in Virginia when one doesn't need a blanket. My ammunition goes next, for I am determined not to get left again today. We don't expect much more fighting, and if we have any, ammunition will soon be forthcoming.

About noon we came upon the Rebels at a place called High Bridge on the South Side Railroad. This stand was taken to gain time and position, although I should add that if they searched the whole state of Virginia, they couldn't have found a better position. Both ends of the bridge are fortified with strong earthworks, bombproof and able to withstand anything but earthquakes. When we sighted it, we thought we could make no impression on them and that probably the entire Rebel army would be here to offer battle. But we were disappointed, as there were only a few troops and the works didn't have to be carried by assault. We moved along, and they moved along too, after firing the bridge.

The bridge is all its name implies, a stupendous affair. It crosses a valley through which flows the Appomattox River and rests on brick piers 200 feet high with 60-foot spans. So monstrous are its proportions that a train of cars looks like a toy and men appear no larger than ants. We set to work immediately to save it from total destruction, and succeeded, all but for two spans. The attempt to destroy this bridge is another illustration of that devilish spirit of "rule or ruin" that now controls the Rebel army.

As soon as the fire was out we pursued the Rebels, who fled over the road to Lynchburg. They soon found it necessary to make another stand near Farmville.

We drew up in line for an assault, but they had stopped just long enough to establish a skirmish line, under cover of which the main army pushed ahead. It being quite late, we didn't move any farther. Retired "resting on our arms."

### April 8th.

In the morning we discovered that our antagonists had taken French leave in the silent watches of the night. As soon as we could get ready, we went in pursuit, but they had made such excellent progress that we didn't catch up with their rear until 4 P.M.. The enemy must have marched nearly all night and stopped for nothing.

In the afternoon the 6th Corps, which was ahead of us, encountered them at a place called New Store, but the enemy took immediate flight. This encounter served one purpose. It disclosed to us the weakness of the enemy, showing that the Rebel army might wind up its affairs any day.

A report reached us that Grant and Lee are carrying on a correspondence relative to a surrender. We gave but little heed; our credulity has been imposed upon too often to swallow such cock-and-bull stories.[2]

About 4 P.M. we came up with the Confederates at New Store and had a little tilt. They moved on as usual, but just before leaving they played a joke on us. They rolled out a barrel of cold tar and as our men came along, some thought it was molasses. Their dippers will be utterly useless forevermore.

We went no farther just then, but halted for rations, which we finally received about midnight. We then started again and continued to move until about 3 A.M., then went on picket until daylight.

### April 9th.

The reason for all this rushing is now apparent. Lee's army is close at hand. Grant has ordered the rear to close up. We expected to come to a halt every minute, and this was all that kept us going this morning, for we are thoroughly fagged.

# Appomattox

## April 9th and 10th, 1865

*April 9th.*

A day never to be forgotten by those who participated. The Army of the Potomac will remember it as the day of a great victory; the Grand Army of Virginia, though suffering defeat, will remember it as the end of intense suffering and privation. This day is the climax of a four-year war that entailed much suffering and no benefit.

The process of disintegration has been going on for a week. Thousands have surrendered on their own account, as I have already narrated. Now Lee is brought to bay.

About 6 o'clock we heard firing in front. It was quite sharp at first, but dwindled to an occasional shot and in an hour ceased altogether. As it was Sunday, we knew there was every probability of a fight, so we began to brace for it. Having done so, we marched off in the direction of the firing, though it had nearly ceased before we started. We marched along till about 10 A.M. Having gone about seven miles, we turned into a field and halted to get dinner, pausing near a brick house where Meade has his headquarters.

A half hour or so after we came to a halt, the same fellow who reported the story of the correspondence between Grant and Lee yesterday came down the line from headquarters and said he had just heard one of General Meade's staff say that terms of surrender were at that moment being drawn up, which is why we halted here. General Lee had requested a cessation of hostilities for the purpose of conferring with Grant.

· We at once charged him with lying, he being an inveterate newsmonger who is always hatching up something marvelous to regale us with. (The news he brought now was contrary to the discouraging kind he was in the habit of bringing, however.) The story was soon corroborated by more reliable sources, and we began to have some hope, way down in our boots, that something extraordinary was about to transpire.

About 2 o'clock the 2nd Division of this Corps, which was in line on the opposite side of the Farmville and Lynchburg Road, fell in, fixed bayonets, and unfurled colors. Such a proceeding at such a time and place lent credence to the view that something very unusual was afoot. Just then an ambulance came down from Meade's headquarters, followed by an old express wagon trimmed with evergreens. Most of us were of the opinion that it was carrying the bodies of generals back to the Confederate lines, or setting out to bring back some of ours. Others swore they saw Grant in the ambulance carrying a flag of truce. What we most wanted to believe, we couldn't.

No light was thrown on the matter for about an hour until General Meade came in from the front and drove around the lines, shouting lustily, "Thank God! Lee has surrendered!" His frenzy of joy was contagious, and we acted as if we had taken leave of our senses. We shouted, danced, sang, and wept. Bands played, drums beat, flags were unfurled, guns fired, and cannon boomed. We flung our hats in the air and roared until we were out of wind. Some were so overcome they seemed to lose all power of speech.

It was not easy to adjust to the new order of things. All that we have suffered and fought for and almost died for, at last consummated. Three years of suspense and horror were broken in less than three minutes. Had every man in this army been sentenced to death and now suddenly pardoned, I imagine the effect would be similar.

The Rebels added their mite, and mighty little it was, too, for they were too hungry to do much yelling. Although they are vanquished, they are as happy as we, or more so. They are tired to death of being toted around half-starved and half-clad, with no reasonable hope of victory.

After the surrender General Grant sent rations to the Confederates, as they are very destitute. This was the first thing Lee asked for. General Lee has the reputation of being very humane, and yet to gratify ambition he witnessed all this suffering and waited for Grant to admonish him of his folly and ask for its cessation. It is an unholy ambition that thus drives men to lead others to make sacrifices of this kind. Perhaps such a course does not seem inhuman to people who have been accustomed to buying and selling human flesh the way we in the North do cattle and hogs. The most puzzling part of all is that men will follow such a man and expect him to bring them out safely.

Darkness brought quiet to camp, and I retire to rest feeling better than I have since first entering the service. Visions of home and full larders flit across my mental sight, along with images of comfortable lodgings, clean clothes, and the faces of friends from whom I have been long separated.

Hope once more fills the niche so long occupied by Despair.

### April 10th.

It was quite easy to get up this morning. I feel that a load of several tons has been lifted from my shoulders. We supposed General Lee and his army would march out by us today so we could get a near view of them. We think it only fair we be allowed to see, face to face, the men we have met on so many battlefields. And they might want to view us. In this matter our wishes were disregarded, however, and we were ordered to treat them as "erring brothers." They must be spared all those humiliating scenes which a foreign foe would have been compelled to undergo.

The fact that they are not foreigners is not due to any lack of effort on their part. We have already divided our rations with them even though we have no more than *half* rations ourselves. If we are to be so tender, perhaps we should have surrendered to them, for it must be excessively humiliating for these high-toned Southerners to surrender to us mean, craven-spirited Yankees.

It rained this morning but we didn't mind. So good-natured have we become that we would probably even consent to being rolled in the mud. We look now for speedy relief from the restraints of army life and a restoration of the liberty of citizens. This seems especially desirable due to the fact that we are now under such strict guard that one who didn't know better would think we are the vanquished instead of the victors. Do the mutton-headed officers suppose that we will desert *now*?

During the forenoon some of us managed to elude the guard and went out a short distance to see the country, and perchance the natives. We failed to find any in the immediate neighborhood. The only form of animal life we saw was ourselves. We returned to camp wondering why a court house should be established in such a place.

Nothing of *any* consequence occurred for the rest of the day.

# The Long
# Road Home

## April 11–June 11, 1865

*April 11th.*

This day finds us still at Clover Hill, which sweet-smelling locality is adjacent to Appomattox Court House. Here we laid until 10 A.M., when we started for New Store.

Before leaving we were formed in line and had an order read to us from General Humphreys congratulating us and giving some statistics. Statistics are generally dry stuff, but these had considerable interest for they showed what a mere handful of men Lee had at the time he claimed that he was under no necessity of surrendering.

We arrived at New Store about dark. Again we are put under guard, not allowed even to go out for water unless accompanied by a noncommissioned officer. This is mighty galling, but the only remedy is open mutiny, and we have worked too hard for our reputation to blast it all now. While we are thus curtailed in our privileges, the Rebels go in and out as they please — and lots of them don't please to come back again. One consolation is that my time is short, even if I serve out my full term. As we have no more risks to run, the outlook is not so very dismal.

*April 12th.*

Started at 8 A.M., marched all day, and at sunset reached Farmville, an attractive little village on the South Side Railroad. We marched through the town with flying colors and our bands playing national airs — all of which was presumably highly refreshing to the dwellers hereabouts. A portion of the 9th Corps have been here several days and are now guarding some Rebel prisoners. We borrowed rations of them, ours being entirely exhausted. We would have been glad to stay here for some time but fate decreed otherwise. We passed on and bivouacked beyond the town.

*April 13th.*

Raining hard, but we started on the march, and about noon the clouds rolled by. The roads are in a fearful condition, but we made good time and soon hauled up for dinner near High Bridge. Here we waited two hours and then struck out again. We faced a serious problem, for the streams are swollen by recent rains and nearly all the bridges have been swept away. We were forced to improvise one from defunct mules dumped into the stream. After marching a few miles, we came to the South Side Railroad, followed it three miles, then went into bivouac. After getting settled, we drew food and clothing, both of which we were sorely in need of, as we haven't drawn clothes since Petersburg.

### April 14th.

Up early expecting to resume our march. Although some of us are played out, we want to move along as fast as we comfortably can. The condition of the roads is a barrier, but there is another reason for this halt: we might be ordered to North Carolina to assist Joe Johnston in making up his mind. He has been coquetting with Sherman. If we have to go, we are handy to the railroad and could soon join Sherman's forces.

### April 15th.

Passed the day in much-needed rest and repose. Did nothing until night, when we went on brigade guard to keep the men in camp. If they aren't thus restrained there is no telling what dreadful things might be done. I have frequently noticed, though, that the very ones for whom the guard is designed go out as they please, while those who are kept in would do no harm if they *did* go out.

We have some in our company who are good for nothing but to keep bread from moulding. Some men cherish laziness as one of the cardinal virtues — except when eating. We had a fellow of this kind when we first came out. While we were on picket one time this gourmandizer drew, and ate, the rations of his entire tent crew for three days. When we returned we found the beastly glutton with his head bandaged, the very image of sorrow and suffering. I'd have thought a bandage would have been more appropriate on his abdominal region, which he had converted into a commissary department on legs.

### April 16th.

Sunday, and all is quiet, no hostile guns to break the calm. "The face of Nature wore a placid smile." The trees are putting on their spring dress, and we are in a frame of mind to enjoy it all. Never have we passed such a Sunday in old Virginia. Our work is done — well done; success has crowned our efforts. We are encamped in a nice grove on the road to Burkesville and today were taking solid comfort, until in the midst of our rejoicing we were suddenly stunned by news that President Lincoln, General Grant, Secretary Seward, and others have been assassinated at Washington. Can we credit our ears? Is it possible that any man — or *thing* in the shape of man — could lift his hand to strike down one of humanity's best friends? How could He that sitteth in the Heavens remain passive while this hellish deed was consummated? Lincoln, the gentlest soul who ever walked this earth, who has struck the shackles from four million human beings, is now struck down by a cowardly assassin.

No people were ever so agitated and grieved over the taking of one man. Had he been removed by any natural cause the shock would be terrible, but to be struck down in this way is horrible beyond expression. Most of our men are loud in their denunciation of the fiend who did this deed. Billy Patterson desires to "fry his liver before his very eyes." Another would hang him till most dead, then resuscitate him, and repeat the procedure for several days. Thus the men give vent to their rage.

History records no blacker crime. If the murderer was in search of notoriety, he has found it.

Later in the day we had a correction of the rumor: the president was the only one killed. Seward is seriously wounded, but Grant is all right.

One individual who expressed satisfaction at the murder was hurried down to a nearby frog pond and treated to a little hydropathic practice — to so much of it, in fact, that he was taken from the water more dead than alive, coated with green slime and frog spawn. In this miserable plight he presented himself to his colonel to complain about the assault. When the colonel heard the facts of the matter he replied, "They served you right, only it is a d——d shame they didn't drown you!"

### April 17th and 18th.

Learned that there is no immediate prospect of a move, certainly not for a week or two. So we were ordered to build a camp and put up bunks. This and the laying out of company streets took up these two days. We haven't put much effort into this camp because neither the time we shall occupy it nor the time of year demands it.

### April 19th.

We were notified officially of the death of the president. Obsequies are to be held in Washington today. Our flags flew at half mast, bands played dirges, and a salute of twenty-one guns was fired at noon, in addition to which we were exempted from drill.

In the afternoon the writer visited Burksville Junction, the junction of the Danville and South Side railroads, otherwise of no earthly consequence. The place abounds with Rebel equipment and trumpery.

A few niggers were sunning themselves in the streets. They had not known of their freedom until we came this way, and this seems to be their idea of what freedom is about. We not only enlightened them, but enforced the Proclamation, and the government has set up a bakery to feed them. This was the purpose of my visit. I tried to purchase a loaf of bread, a luxury I haven't enjoyed in a long time, and to my chagrin and indignation was told it wasn't for "white trash." Somehow, I had the reprehensible notion that a white man is almost as good as a nigger, but I stand rebuked for my ignorance.

### April 20th.

This day appears to have been set apart in Maine as a "day of humiliation, fasting, and prayer." If an empty stomach is evidence of humility, we can lay claim to an excess of it. Our condition is closely akin to that of a Western editor who grew so thin that he advertised to sell himself for a stove funnel. This is a melancholy condition, but at least it promises to be of short duration.

### April 21st.

Nothing going on today. We did hear a rumor that Johnston has surrendered, but as no official notice has been served, we can't accept the news without some doubts. We have a notion that we might be called upon to go south and induce Johnston to end the drama. If, however, he can see his way to do so without us, that's fine, for we much prefer to go *north*.

This army is virtually out of a job. Sherman's army, which has accomplished the stupendous task of marching through a country that resembles an empty eggshell with both ends stove in, some time since gave out the word that they will "finish Johnston and come up and assist us in reducing Lee to subjugation." They need have no solicitude concerning General Lee, that individual having suffered defeat at *our* hands alone. If there is to be any *assisting* business, we will take a hand in it.

## April 22nd.

After a week of rumors we have at last received official information that General Grant was not among the victims of the assassination.

Was on camp guard all day and had dress parade at night, the first since we left Petersburg. I thought we had seen the last of this senseless rigamarole and I concluded that red tape will not let go its grip till our term of service is finished.

## April 23rd.

Sunday. Major Mattox was seized with an overwhelming curiosity to know what was in our knapsacks and ordered an inspection. If this is the way he's going to carry on, I am not obliged to the Johnnies for releasing him. Dress parade at five ended the day.

## April 25th.

Were routed out by the booming of cannon at a very early hour. I supposed there could be only one occasion for this racket, the surrender of Johnston. After getting up, I learned it was in honor of the president's remains being transported to Springfield. All drill and work were suspended, flags few at half mast, cannon boomed, and officers ordered to wear crepe on the left arm for thirty days. There are some to whom this order is most unwelcome, for their sympathies are with the murderer more than the murdered.

## April 26th.

All quiet, and we were treated to another yarn about Johnston's surrender. We have been imposed upon too many times the past fortnight to give heed. Nothing short of an official order will convince us now.

General Grant has gone down there, and we infer that not much time will elapse before that event will become a part of history.

## April 27th.

One of my tentmates, John E. True, returned from the hospital. He was slightly wounded in the head on the 6th. The slightness of his wound isn't the reason for his early return, though. He feared starvation in a day or two if he stayed at the hospital. So, calling on what strength he had, he sought his regiment. If the Rebels who starve our men in their prisons are worthy of the deepest execrations, what shall we say of our own men who do the same thing?

## April 28th.

On camp guard today and had reliable information that Johnston's surrender is fact, and was made on the same terms as Lee's — which are quite too liberal by three-quarters. What guarantee have we that this contest will not be resumed when they are able? None whatever. My opinion is that every officer, civil or military, who voluntarily took up arms against the government should be banished or forever disenfranchised and prevented from holding office of even the lowest grade. And if he or she put money or subsistence toward carrying on the war against the Union, he should put into the U.S. Treasury a like amount. If this action does not make treason odious, it will at least make it expensive.

### April 29th.

Was relieved from guard at 9 o'clock, and the rest of the day was passed in cleaning clothing, policing quarters, and other such work. Policing camp is a frequent duty. Dirt increases so fast that without continual warfare against it we should soon be buried beneath old bones, carrion, crusts, and decayed vegetables. In even moderately warm weather this soon becomes miserable. For warmth, our present weather is about the same as June weather in New England.

### April 30th.

A full inspection and muster for two months' pay, then a rest. After dinner, half our regiment went on picket. They took no tents, and when it rained as if the heavens had become a colander, they received a dunking, thus proving the truth of the scriptural passage that sayeth: "The wise man seeth the evil and hideth himself while the fool layeth outside and is punished." (I have taken just a trifle of license with the language, but without changing the idea.)

### May 1st.

Clear as a quill, and warm, if not positively hot. Rumor has it that we shall advance on Richmond tomorrow. I can execute this movement with a relish that would have been entirely foreign one month ago today. My objection now is to the *method* of transportation. We assumed the government would send us by rail, but it seems we are to walk. I sweat at the mere thought. Many of us are footsore and weary, and the mercury in the thermometers cavorts in the vicinity of the 80s. But all we can do or say will not change our orders one iota.

### May 22nd.

About 1 o'clock we pulled up stakes and started *homeward*! At last we are on the road, thank Heaven (or whatever controls these things). A march of a few miles brought us to Burkesville, and here we took *rail* (not cars) for Richmond and camped for the night about eight miles from where we started. The mazes and cow paths of old Virginia are so bewildering that we have little idea where we are half the time; we only know we are steering north, and this is all we *care* to know.

### May 3rd.

This day has been prominent in the annals of the army. In 1863 we fought the Battle of Chancellorsville. In 1864 we broke camp for the Grant campaign via the Wilderness. Today we marched to Five Forks and after a short rest moved to Amelia Court House. Court was in session and the town was filled to overflowing with men in stovepipe hats, a quaint affectation of old-time dandyism. Everybody seemed to be talking, probably discussing the events of the past four weeks. It will take an almighty pile of chin to enable them to adjust to their changed condition.

We moved through the town and crossed the Appomattox, then halted for the night, having marched twenty miles. A good day's work for a hot day.

## May 4th.

Marched about ten miles and hauled up for dinner. General Miles was in command of the corps today and didn't hurry us. Still, we covered a good piece of road. Started out again after dinner, finally camping ten miles southwest of Richmond. How I long to gaze on that remarkable city. There seems to be a good prospect that I will do so on the morrow. I can lay down tonight filled with pleasant anticipations and with the glad feeling that we are making good progress homeward. We can reckon on being Washington in a very few days.

## May 5th.

Started about 6 o'clock and marched to Manchester, a dingy, old, rickety, tumbledown place across the river from Richmond. We halted near a large earthwork of Rebel construction on the outskirts of the town. Manchester is a town of perhaps 3,000 inhabitants divided into three classes: men, women, and niggers. The latter predominate. There might be churches and schoolhouses and elegant private residences in abundance, but we couldn't see any, not even one *painted* house. Judging from the standard of neatness one finds in New England villages, I would unhesitatingly say that Manchester is the nastiest place in the U.S.

About sunset I perambulated through its long, dirty street in search of something to eat. Most of the houses had pastry or bread to dispose of to such as could furnish the collateral. Having not a penny, I "went away sorrowful."

One year ago today we commenced the Battle of the Wilderness.

## May 6th.

At 10 A.M. we fell in and marched over to Richmond. It was with indescribable feelings that I entered this city for the first time. It is a wonder that they didn't request us to march around the city instead of through it, in deference to General Lee, who is there now.

The first building we saw that attracted attention was a large brick edifice with a sign informing us that it is the famous Libby Prison, that den of torture through whose portals so many of our men entered, never to return. It is now filled with Rebel prisoners. I involuntarily shuddered to think how near I have come several times to taking lodging there. A short distance away is another building, called Castle Thunder. This too is a prison, but not so repulsive as the other.

We next passed up from the river street into the burnt district, near the ruins of the *Times* and *Examiner* offices. (I trust they have been purified by the fire.) We then passed through several streets of ruins into Main Street and halted a few minutes near the capitol, where Jeff Davis and his Rebel Congress so recently assembled to concoct deviltry.

It was intensely hot in the streets, which detracted much from my interest in the sights. Many fell from the ranks in the incipient stages of sunstroke and had to be left to the care of the natives. Such a heat I have encountered but seldom, and may Satan seize me if I want to again.

Richmond must have been quite a pretty city before it was visited by this awful conflagration. The Yankees cannot have *this* calamity charged to them, for the fire was set by order of General Ewell. If he had the sense of a louse or a tadpole, he would have realized that burning Richmond didn't help the Rebels or injure us. But

RUINS OF RICHMOND — MAIN STREET. *Harper's Pictorial History of the Civil War.*

"rule or ruin" was the policy; if they couldn't hold the city, they were bound that we shouldn't.

General Meade and "Grandmarm" Halleck, along with some smaller fry, stood on the courthouse steps to review us as we passed by.

As soon as we were beyond the city limits we halted from sheer inability to go any farther. As we lay on the grass of the common, one of the sutlers came out to relieve us of our money. Although few of us had any money, there was a great demand for cakes — so much so that the sutler couldn't supply it. "Necessity knows no law," nor did we just then. The sutler realized this as he saw a fellow grab his money box and make off with it. The man hadn't gone far before the contents of the box were flying to the winds. The men soon had it picked up and taken care of. The tables are turned this once. The officers did their best to restrain us, one of them even going so far as to strike a man on the head with his sword, fracturing his skull.

One fellow who was exploring the bottom of a barrel, looking for cakes, became thoroughly wedged in. An officer observed his predicament and commenced a series of blows on the protruding portion of the soldier's anatomy. The fellow, in his haste to extricate himself, caught his arm on a nail and tore it from elbow to wrist.

After a while we moved on and camped five miles beyond the city. A host of young niggers followed us to camp and soon made themselves too familiar. We bounced them up in blankets and made them butt against each other — also against some pork barrels and hard-bread boxes. A couple hours' worth of bouncing satisfied them. One young nigger had an arm broke, and several others were more or less maltreated.

## May 7th.

Were routed out at daylight and started in the direction of Fredericksburg, passing over some extremely good farmlands. Our route lay via Hanover Court House, which we passed during the afternoon. Having crossed the Pamunkey, we marched four or five miles and camped near Hanover Junction. This is familiar ground that has been fought over several times. We passed very near this place on our way south nearly a year ago.

## May 8th.

Routed out at five but didn't get started before ten. The morning hours were passed in the same dignified way as was the evening of the 6th. About 10 o'clock, when the sun shone hot enough to boil us, we started on the march and went four hours without rest. We should have done our marching in the cool of the morning and done our *resting* after ten. There were several cases of sunstroke in consequence.

At Concord we passed a country tavern, a three-story brick building presently without patrons. I am not surprised that the building is of brick; if made of wood, it would take fire from the sun. We marched a few miles farther and bivouacked near a large stream, the name of which I haven't bothered to learn.

Sometime during this day we have meandered into the wrong road, but as it is so late General de Trobriand has decided to wait until morning before attempting to find the right route. It is said that we are about eight miles out of our way. The war being over, it is quite interesting to go over this ground again, and to do so without the constant dread we felt when this was still enemy country.

The stream in front of us is doubtless one of the four which make up the Matapony. They are the Ma, the Ta, the Po, and the Ny. As they all unite into one stream, so they unite in name: Matapony. Rather a remarkable way of naming it. No similar case has ever come to my knowledge.

## May 9th.

Commenced moving at seven this morning. After marching across country a few miles we struck the right road and soon joined the rest of the column. We crossed the Polecat River and came to the Fredericksburg Turnpike about twenty miles southwest of the city. About 12 o'clock we halted for dinner, then continued our march. Crossed the Matapony at Thornburg (another house) and finally camped twelve miles from Fredericksburg. We passed many more familiar places on the way.

## May 10th.

Crawled out of our rubber blankets and put ourselves in marching order. One year ago this day we were engaged in a desperate battle close by here, the Battle of Po River.

About 8 o'clock we started, and noon found us at Fredericksburg, where we halted for the farce of eating dinner without having the faintest suggestion of food, only a little coffee. Afterward we picked our teeth, slung on our knapsacks, and marched into the city, which is in a truly deplorable condition. Fully one-quarter of it has been burned and a large portion of the rest is thoroughly battered. Corners and whole sides of houses have been torn off, windows and doors, chimneys and roofs smashed and perforated. It is sad to see a city so disfigured, and an American city at that.

As we passed down one of the streets we saw General Humphreys and his staff on the steps of a public building, reviewing us. In a moment his ears were saluted with a yell of "hardtack!" This little pleasantry didn't set well with the mighty Andrew, and his face suddenly grew as red as his neck cloth. The fools should know that this action will not bring them any hardtack, only the general's displeasure. General Ward's brigade once tried a similar demand on him and found the fun too expensive.

We soon recrossed the Rappahannock at a point halfway between Fredericksburg and Falmouth. Not a single being except ourselves did we see in the latter town. This cemeterial suburb of Fredericksburg has suffered none from the war, only from age. We moved out over the ground where we camped the first winter, and halted beyond Stoneman's Station for the night.

## May 11th.

Turned out at five, but 8 o'clock found us still on the ground, sweltering. This refreshing condition was the result of that little joke of yesterday — yelling "hardtack" at General Humphreys. That entire division was ordered to stand in line two hours with all their things on while the sun did its best to cook them. The righteous had to suffer with the wicked. Our division didn't stand in line but we had to wait for them while the sun mounted to the zenith in hot haste, so hot that it seemed nothing short of a miracle that we were not converted into soap grease.

About 9 o'clock we started, and marched a dozen or more miles in the direction of Fairfax Court House. We went into bivouac just in time to get our tents up before one of the heaviest showers I have ever seen. While the downpour beat through the tops of our tents, little Mississippis were industriously working their way under us, wetting everything.

## May 12th.

When the sun rose in the morning his beams fell on a sorry looking lot of mortals who felt as if they were not far from being *im*mortals. We partially dried our tents and clothes, and at 9 o'clock were again on the way to Washington. We marched almost continually until 5 P.M. On inquiry of an aged citizen of this section we were informed that we are no nearer Washington than when we started this morning. We must have been traveling around in a circle all day, or else we have just encountered an ignoramus or a colossal liar. This is a kind of crablike progress that we don't think desirable just now.

## May 13th.

The exercises of this day commenced with the band playing a new and most exasperating tune: "Sweet Home." The prospect of getting there is anything but cheerful, taking yesterday's advance as a standard.

After wallowing around numerous quagmires and following cow paths for several miles today, we struck the Orange and Alexandria Railroad at a place called Burke's Station. Learning that we were then only twenty miles from Washington, we began to revive.

We got bewildered again before night, however, and wandered around for some time. We finally came out into an opening and soon hauled up for the night at Annandale, only five miles from Washington. Somebody has been lying to us again with regard to distance.

If old Blinky French were at the head of this column, I shouldn't wonder at the slowness, for he almost invariably contrives to get off the track. (If one could fancy a bulldog come into man's estate and wearing coat and hat, one would have an apt idea of Frenchy's physique, but it wouldn't do to judge his intellect by this standard, as I'm convinced that the dog would show points of superiority.)

### May 14th.

Sunday. No move today, and I didn't use more than two handkerchiefs bemoaning the fact, either. This is the twelfth day that we have been confined to an exclusive diet of hardtack, and a half ration at that. All this time we have been on the march — eight hard breads a day to sustain us for twelve to twenty miles of marching. A well man can easily devour his day's ration at one meal and not exert himself dangerously. Some men do eat all at one meal, saying that they much prefer one *meal* to three *aggravations*.

At ten o'clock we had an inspection of arms, after which we drew a ration of fresh beef! We ate this in a jiffy, and finding it did not throw us into convulsions, we went out to where the cattle had been butchered and cut the melts [spleens] from the entrails, but they didn't satisfy. I have never heard before of eating such trumpery as melts, but necessity drives us to sample this disgustingly filthy mess. Shame on a government that treats its defenders this way.

The afternoon of this day we passed as we pleased. Some of us made soup from bones that others improvidently threw away. We try to fill up on slops, but call it *soup* because that title makes it seem more filling — besides, it sounds more genteel. We boiled the bones in juice flavored with salt, bog onion, and pepper. (Bog onion is a small root whose flavor is akin to the larger bulb.)

We have marched from Burkesville to Annandale, nearly two hundred miles, in twelve days, and over the most infernally hot and rough roads.

### May 15th.

We moved today from Annandale to Four Mile Run, halfway between Annandale and Washington. We went into camp near Bailey's Crossroads and close to Munson's Hill. We arrived about noon and soon thereafter, much to our enjoyment, drew rations of beans, pork, bread (both hard and soft), coffee, and sugar. A good square meal.

Our arrival on the ground was the signal for the advent of numerous vendors of pastry (so-called), but as most of us had no currency, neither side was enriched or impoverished thereby.

### May 16th.

"When fair Orient in the heavens appeared" uprose this writer and took a walk on the surrounding hills. These heights command an extensive view, including part of Washington, Fairfax Seminary, and other points. I discovered also that a railroad creeps along the base of the hill, so I dismissed any fears of further short rations. After coming down from the mount I heard rumors that we are to move to Bladensburg dueling ground in order that Sherman's army (which is approaching) can occupy our present site. If it is a matter of need, I don't object to moving. If it is to show preference, I decidedly object. After all, we are already settled down; let *them* continue moving to Bladensburg or elsewhere.

### May 17th.

The weather is extremely hot, with the thermometer roaming around the 90s. Nothing worthy of note going on, and if there were, I haven't life enough left to notice it.

If we were now pursuing Lee, or being pursued by that gentleman, there would be some tall straggling. It is not enough that we frizzle and fry, but the authorities must add to our burdens by promoting Major Mattox to colonel. Having in his system an inordinate love of show, he orders us, old soldiers all, to drill several hours each day. He has sent to Maine for all the old, tattered battle flags we have cast aside. He also has ordered new caps and silver figures and letters, and new chevrons for the noncommissioned officers. As one want creates another, I expect he will soon add paper collars, white gloves, and other finery. We might even carry gold-headed canes and part our hair in the middle, put on eyeglasses, and, if need be, we can lisp.

### May 18th.

Today we appear to be three-months men, provided we are requested to serve our entire term, which may the good Lord forbid if He has any pity for the creatures of His hand. I hope that no more than three *weeks* will elapse before we become citizens again. One report is that we are to be mustered out just as soon as blanks can be procured and filled out.

### May 19th.

Orders received to muster out all troops whose term of service expires prior to October 1st. This net surely scoops me in and increases my impatience greatly.

At night went on guard with Sawyer and Whitten at brigade headquarters on the hill in front of camp. Soon after we got posted a tremendous shower fell. Having no shelters, we took refuge under an army wagon. (Red tape doesn't allow us to take shelter under the fly of the general's tent. It is delicious to know that this distinction will soon come to an end, and, so far as shelters and beds go, we shall have as good as we can pay for.)

### May 20th.

Were relieved from guard and crawled down to our tents. The rain ceased sometime during the forenoon. Shortly after, I had a visit from an old tentmate who left me after the Battle of Chancellorsville over two years ago. He has since served his country in the hospital. As he came from a place where all sorts of supplies are to be had in abundance, I naturally supposed that he would bring some little dainty to share with us. But he didn't. Rather, he compelled me to put myself to great straits to offer hospitality. The contents of my larder are very meager, but by diligent search enough was found for a meal. We enjoyed ourselves as ladies do over their "mild Souchong."

My friend had moved on Washington in a highly dilapidated condition after I last saw him. Arriving there, he took to bed and was shocked beyond expression to find himself in the bed where another of our men, Moses Moody, had died of smallpox only three weeks before.

At night we had a dress parade and inspection of arms. After dark it commenced raining again, and by morning the mud was ankle deep.

### May 21st.

Was on guard at General Pierce's headquarters on an exceedingly lofty elevation from which I could literally look down on the people. The rest of the regiment is on picket near Munson's Hill. There is some compensation like this; like corns, this evil is a blessing because it makes us forget the greater evil and foolishness of drill and parade.

### May 22nd.

There would be as much sense in going on picket in Maine. There is no enemy here, but there are strong indications that the windows of Heaven are about to be raised for our benefit. Let it pour! Plenty of mud and water are impediments to drill, and somehow rain seems to sharpen the wits and bring out the ludicrous as dry weather never does.

Today was devoted to cleaning up and getting ready for a review in Washington. At night we had dress parade and a sorting of men to see who looks fit and nice enough to go on review. Orders are to have the companies composed of men who are all nearly the same height, a great *show* being uppermost in the skull cavities of our officials.

### May 23rd.

The lines were formed at 7 o'clock, as ordered last night. In a short time they were on their way to the city. Being an intensely plain person with a strong tendency to corpulency, I was left in camp. This is one case where an excess of adipose tissue is not a detriment.

I am left in charge of a camp guard composed of short men. While we cool our heels under trees and tents, the long fellows are sweltering on their way to the city. There have been several times when shortness has been a decided advantage. Many a missile of death and destruction passed over my head, which an inch more in height would have sent crashing through the seat of my intellect.

### May 24th.

Sherman's army passed through our "sweat box" on their way to Bladensburg to camp. There isn't room enough for both these armies on this side of the Potomac, I am convinced, until those braggarts learn better than to taunt *this* army with being "bread and butter men," a most insulting term, considering the circumstances. Their impudence was promptly hurled back into their teeth when they ventured to insult us as they passed by. Hot words were followed by blows and then by a resort to firearms. Two were killed and several wounded. After this little exchange, all ammunition except two cartridges each was taken away from us.

It was exceedingly exasperating to have that army taunt our army with the above-mentioned epithet. Sherman's army, above all others, has been favored with the fat of the land, and their march to the sea has been without interruption, while we, on the other hand, have been subjected to the most rigorous hardships, hard fare, and hard fighting. Their covert sneer at the fighting qualities of this army was one we didn't choose to let pass in silence. I have no desire to underestimate the services of Sherman's army, but we will be careful that they do not lacerate our reputation.

### May 25th.

About 6 o'clock this morning went on picket on Munson's Hill. Each corporal has thirteen posts, and these are so far apart that by the time he has relieved the last post it is almost time to relieve the first post again. The posts extend from Munson's Hill to Bailey's Crossroads — not less than three-quarters of a mile.

### May 26th and 27th.

Returned from picket on the 26th, coming in by the road rather than cross-lots as we went out. It has rained so hard these past two days that we cannot go out to drill. As I have a constitution that has carried me through three years of carnage and exposure, I have full confidence that I shall survive this.

### May 28th.

An inspection of arms at 5 o'clock by Colonel Mattox, followed by a dress parade by the same bundle of exquisiteness and red tape. A concert by the band finished the exercises of the day. Our muster rolls were completed tonight and sent to headquarters, which is a refreshing piece of intelligence.

### May 29th.

Battalion drill from eight till nine. We then laid 'round till dress parade, when we had another spell of torment infernal. Colonel Mattox is determined to make a show even if he displays only our skeletons. I am fully as determined that I will not be killed to gratify his vanity when home is almost in sight. I don't care to look nice and have a holiday air.

### May 30th.

The 2nd Corps was reviewed by generals Hancock, Humphreys, Meade, and Mott, as well as President Andy Johnson. This was my first encounter with the last-named individual. He has a very prominent nasal organ that has an upward tendency as though it were indulging in a fit of lofty scorn for matters terrestrial. It has the look of one that is trying to get away from an unpleasant odor. If current rumor is true, his own breath is sufficiently pungent to cause this recoil.

After the review we retired to camp feeling very hot.

### May 31st.

Had a battalion drill of the men who are to be sent home, that is, our original members. It seems as if we never shall get started. We are at the mercy of a thousand rumors that we can neither accept nor reject, but each one sets our hearts to fluttering.

### June 1st.

Today was set apart by President Johnson as a day of fasting and prayer. Consequently no drill was ordered. At night had a dress parade during which a man from Company K dropped dead in the ranks. This was nothing short of cool audacity and defiance. He had been complaining of not feeling well for a day or two, but the medicine man pronounced him well and refused to excuse him from duty. Tonight he showed his contempt for the medical faculty by dropping dead without consulting them further.

### June 2nd.

Company drill in the morning, then no more till night, when we had dress parade.

Some portions of old Virgina are intensely lovely under certain circumstances, but this is not the section nor these the circumstances.

### June 3rd.

Thank Heaven, our muster rolls have been returned complete, accepted and approved, and a certificate of their correctness forwarded to headquarters. All we now lack is transportation, and we expect this within thirty-six hours. We hear that there are two transports at Alexandria, ready for whoever is first ready to go. As I am in that interesting condition I don't know why I may not go. It taxes my patience immensely to endure the slow motions of those who are in no hurry to relinquish their authority.

### June 4th.

Nothing to encourage us this day. We were ordered to scour our guns and brasses and not to allow any dust to stick to us. At night we had a full inspection. A notion prevails that we may depart on the morrow, and our bandbox colonel fears we might not look as well as he requires if we don't polish up late into the night. How in the name of common sense does he suppose we will march four miles on a hot day in June with the dust ankle deep and not destroy every vestige of cleanliness?

### June 5th.

About 9 o'clock an order came for us to be in Washington at 7 o'clock. At last we move! It seems like a dream, and I don't know but what our exuberance of spirits is quite as great as when Lee surrendered. We needed no second beat of drum or blast of bugle to cause us to fall into line.

General Pierce addressed us briefly. He paid us a glowing tribute for our good conduct *in* and *out* and hoped we will make as good citizens as we have soldiers. He congratulated us that we have been in at the death of the rebellion and have won an enviable reputation. He ended with a touching allusion to our long and honorable connection with this division and this brigade. In conclusion he said he hopes we will long live to enjoy the benefits of the government we risked so much to save.

In response to this speech we gave him three cheers, and he called on the rest of the brigade to give "three cheers for their old companions in arms, the 17th Maine." When this was all over we turned our backs on our old comrades and started for Washington, four miles distant. The 1st Maine accompanied us for two miles, then the 20th joined us, and together we journeyed into the city via Long Bridge. At the end of the bridge we halted for a rest, then formed in column by company and marched up Pennsylvania Avenue to the Capitol. We then turned left to the Baltimore depot.

With what different feelings I now stood here from what I felt nearly three years before when I landed on this same spot. We who are left are now to quit the scenes of war and retire to private life, our warfare ended, our work done.

When we reached the depot we were as filthy as pigs with dust and sweat. The day was intensely hot and the dust stuck to us like flies to a glue pot. No one who sees us would suppose us to be paragons of neatness. The fine brass has become dim and the glory has departed from our attire. The soil of Virginia has always shown a wonderful affinity for Yankee clothes.

After lolling around at the station for an hour or so we heard that the train was ready. But where was it? All we could see were some open coal cars nearby, and into these we were ordered. Here was a grand tumble, to be sure. Perhaps this is the best the railroad can do. If so, it speaks volumes for their carrying capacity. There being only one line from Washington to Baltimore, it might be taxed to its utmost to furnish even this poor accommodation.

About 4 P.M. we boarded our "rolling palaces," and at five we left the seat of corruption commonly called the seat of government. In about three hours we found ourselves in Baltimore. After waiting there a while we were walked across the city and piled into some cattle cars. (If it were cold weather this might have been more agreeable.) It was nearly daylight again before the last of us were wedged in.

## June 6th.

Left Baltimore very early in the morning. If we continue in this rapid way, we shall get to Maine about the time the snow flies.

A tedious delay occurred at Havre de Grace, after which we moved along smoothly, reaching Philadelphia about noon. Here we were cordially received and marched to the old Cooper Shop, where we were treated to a lunch of very nice quality: bread, ham, sausage, pickles, cheese, coffee, and cake for dessert. Before commencing on these viands we enjoyed a protracted session at the sinks.

Philadelphia has been called the "soldiers' paradise." Its people seemed to know just what we needed and how much we needed. Nothing seemed too good for us. If I could have found some place here where my exemplary conduct would be considered as an equivalent for board, I might have continued my stay in the city. But no such opening presented itself so I decided to push on.

We were next presented with some little tracts containing a lot of stale platitudes and advice, notably a caution to look out for sharpers who will try to inveigle us out of our wages. How the said sharpers could possess themselves of what we don't have is not made clear.

As soon as all had satisfied their appetites we started for the Jersey and Amboy depot. The people all along the route turned out, acting very much as if they had never set eyes on a soldier before. Flags and streamers were in great profusion. Our passage through the city was one continuous ovation, almost burdensome in its profuseness.

We crossed the river on a ferry and were soon on our way to Amboy, where we arrived about 8 P.M. From there we took the steamer for New York, reaching there about midnight. Our officers went ashore, leaving us on the boat asleep.

## June 7th and 8th.

I thought we had encountered some mighty mean men during our previous stay in this section, but I yield the palm to the creatures who have charge of this boat. Early on the morning of the 7th we were ordered ashore by the captain, who threatened to carry us back to Amboy if we didn't comply with his order at once. This discomposed us slightly, but we finally rallied sufficiently to tell him that we should await the orders of our officers, pending which he would *not* take us to Amboy or anywhere else. This took the wind out of his sails.

Not long after, Colonel Mattox came down and ordered us ashore. We went down to Castle Garden and had a lunch. I ate the bread and skipped the soup and then concluded to take a cruise to see the sights, among which I noted Trinity Church, City Hall, Barnum's Museum, Mr. Astor's Tavern, and other points of interest.

Our sightseeing group had not been out long when our officers decided that they had blundered in letting us go. Some other fellows were sent out to recall us, telling us that the boat was to start right away. We hastily returned to find that we had been hoaxed. But the end justified the means, and I recognize the wisdom of thus early recalling us if they wanted to start at the regular hour.

We drew a ration of the softest kind of bread and the fattest kind of pork, boiled. After this we laid around until four and had a "rum time" of it — that is, such as desired it. Quite a lot of the men imbibed freely. At 5 o'clock we were all on board the steamer *Empire State*, of the Fall River Line, and were soon on the way to Newport, where we arrived about 3 A.M., glad to be on terra firma once more.

There must be some demoralizing influence about steamboats. Their crews are always permeated with a malignant, cussed hatred for all who wear the Blue. Although this steamer is one of the largest in the line and one of the most elegant, we passed the entire night on the uppermost deck, exposed to wind and weather.

We landed as soon as anything could be seen in the early morning light and took cars for Boston, where we were marched out to the Beach Street barracks to stack arms. Our officers supposing that it would not be possible to procure transport before night, we were allowed to go out.

Colonel Hobson came down to meet us, as did an old friend of mine who had offered me the *last* act of kindness on the day I left three years ago and now performed the *first* such act in Boston. He took me to an eating saloon and bade me order just what I most desired. I had a most vigorous appetite and was soon munching sausage and the usual accompaniments.

Despite earlier expectations, it was soon ascertained that transportation could be had immediately, and we moved down to the Boston & Maine station. As soon as we boarded we were whirled away to Portland, which we reached about 6 o'clock. We moved into the depot amidst the ringing of bells, the firing of cannon, shouting of the crowd, and every demonstration of gladness. An immense crowd assembled to greet us and they pressed us so hard that we had some difficulty even getting off the train. We could almost pray to be saved from our *friends*.

A line was formed at last and we were received by a military escort, all the civic organizations, ex-officers, and wounded (the latter riding in carriages). With these, we paraded through the principal streets of the city. All along the route, the houses, stores, and public buildings were decorated with bunting, evergreens, and flowers. "Virgins fair and matrons grave" waved handkerchiefs, and bouquets were showered down upon us. Our reception here put in the shade all previous welcomes. This was as it should be, for this is our own state and many of the troops in the regiment come from this city.

At City Hall we stacked our guns in the gangway and had a collation. This being disposed of, we were treated to some chin music from Colonel Roberts, Chaplain Lovering, Governor Israel Washburn, and some others. We then marched to the old city hall and lodged on the bare floor! It is too filthy for a dog to lie on. What a sudden collapse to our bubble of glory.

### June 9th.

Glad to get up as soon as daylight showed itself. About nine o'clock we marched out to Camp Berry (formerly Camp King) and were put under guard as though we were prison birds. Some from Saco and Biddeford took French leave and struck out for home. Myself and some others procured passes and were soon approaching old Saco.

It was with no small emotion that I neared the place I left nearly three years before. Here we are, some with whole skins, and some not so whole. Others have been left behind. For myself, I can only wonder that there is a bone left in my carcass when I think of the wholesale carnage through which I have passed. *My* bruises are inward.

It is all over now, and I can only regard it as a hideous dream — the smoking ruins, the sodden field, the trailing banner, the slaughtered thousands and wailing families, the roar of cannon, the Rebel yell and the Yankee hurrah have all passed away and we again return to peace.

## *June 10th – 11th.*

Returned to Portland from Saco and prepared to be mustered out of service. This day Uncle Sam refused to feed or clothe us any longer, so we were thrown on our own resources. Pending our release, though, we were put under guard and given mouldy bread and rotten pork, which were promptly stamped into the mud. After this we acted so badly that they were glad to hurry up and get rid of us.

Just before noon we marched to Portland and turned over our guns and equipment (those of us who were not foolish enough to buy them). After this, we hung around waiting for the paymaster. He didn't get to Company I before midnight. Those of us from Saco had a stage waiting to convey us home, where we arrived about 2 A.M. on Sunday, June 11th, 1865 — a happy set of mortals.

And thus ends my military career and diary, the troubles incident thereto and the observations thereof. No pencil can do justice to this theme. How, then, can one of my limited capacity do that for which the brightest intellect is so poorly equipped?

Had I entered into the minutiae of my experiences, I could have filled ten books like this with incidents but have deemed it better to keep within a reasonable limit. What is related in these pages I vouch for as my own experiences and those associated with me. It hasn't been altogether agreeable to record these events; the experiences of a three-year campaign of active warfare are vouschafed to comparatively few, however, and in later life I expect to derive considerable satisfaction in recalling them to mind.

This book is written for my own amusement. Let those who may read it "lay the critic's glass aside and tread upon their lettered pride." This journal claims nothing of merit except truthfulness. None have been screened, none belied, but an attempt has been made to do exact justice to all.

# Roster of Company I
# 17th Maine Regiment

*Below are the names of the original members of the company and their military standing.*

☆ Captain William Hobson — Successively promoted to Brev. Brigadier General. Wounded April 6th, 1865.

☆ First Lieutenant P.S. Boothby — Didn't see much service. Promoted as adjutant of regiment. Dead.

☆ Second Lieutenant J.O. Thompson — Promoted captain of Company K. Resigned at or near Brandy Station, latter part of 1863, on account of conscientious scruples — alleged.

## Sergeants

☆ S.S. Richards — First Sergeant. Wounded at Po River, May 11th, 1864. From Saco. Promoted captain.

☆ F.C. Adams — Second Sergeant. Wounded at Gettysburg and Wilderness. From Saco. Promoted captain.

☆ J.C. Libby — Third Sergeant. Mortally wounded December 13th, 1862. Died a few days after. From Biddeford.

☆ C.C. Cole — Fourth Sergeant. From Oxford. Promoted captain. Very fine soldier.

☆ O.D. Blake — Fifth Sergeant. Retired to hospital and was returned later, reduced to the ranks. From Biddeford.

## Corporals

☆ C.J. Goodwin — First Corporal. Promoted to first sergeant.

☆ S.C. Jenness — Second Corporal. Reduced to ranks.

☆ A.C. Parkhurst — Third Corporal. Remained in field short time.

☆ C.H. Parcher — Fourth Corporal. Promoted lieutenant, Company K.

☆ J. Boothby — Fifth Corporal. Died from homesickness.

☆ E.F. Tibbetts — Sixth Corporal. Not with us after Chancellorsville.

☆ A.A. Robertson — Seventh Corporal. Killed at Gettysburg.

☆ J.M. Paine — Eighth Corporal. Reduced for desertion.

## Musicians

☆ J.P. Atkinson — Died at Fort Stanton.
☆ W.H. Atkinson — Remained till term expired.

## Teamster

☆ Edward Sweetser — Died at Fort Stanton.

## Privates

☆ Allen H. Abbott — With provost guard most of the time.
☆ Levi D. Allen — Deserted in Virginia, from Fort Stanton. Not recovered.
☆ Robert Benson — Wounded at Locust Grove. Company cook, generally, when not employed as officers' cook.
☆ Thomas Brand — Wounded at Gettysburg. Promoted to sergeant. Away sick considerable.
☆ T.C. Bradbury — Rheumatic. Promoted to sergeant. Present about all the time.
☆ Aug. F. Bradbury — Rheumatic. Present or accounted for most of the time.
☆ Stephen Bradbury — Wounded in Wilderness. Sick considerable.
☆ Cyrus Buker — Company cook, generally. Fell over a shadow and was disabled.
☆ James M. Brown — Away much. Loved rum more than country.
☆ James B. Brown — Died at Sandy Hook, Md., June 1863.
☆ I.M. Boothby — Discharged without seeing much service.
☆ J.C. Blaisdell — Present most of the time. Had an uncommonly brave appetite.
☆ Thomas Blaisdell — Away much after the first year.
☆ Thomas S. Clark — Hostler, also great facial contortionist and whisky guzzler.
☆ James S. Clark — Noted only for gluttony. Could eat four men's rations.
☆ Zenas Chase — Officers' cook. Also proprietor of "Zenas's Spoon."
☆ F.S. Deland — Brought away but few scalps. No active service.
☆ T.W. Emerson — A bloodthirsty brave — in his mind.
☆ Daniel Foss — Discharged at Camp Pitcher on account of sickness.
☆ Charles E. Goodwin — Rheumatic. Killed in the Wilderness, May 6th, 1864.
☆ J.H. Goodrich — Well. Killed at Chancellorsville, May 3rd, 1863.
☆ Newhall Guptill — Well. Died at Camp Pitcher.
☆ Isaac Grant — Strong aversion to fighting. Face indicated conviviality.
☆ John Grant — Did better. Stayed nearly all the time. Killed in the Wilderness, May 6th, 1864.
☆ Joseph Hill — Wounded at Locust Grove, November 1863. Didn't return.

| | |
|---|---|
| ☆ Daniel Hill | Died of fever at Camp Pitcher, January 1863. |
| ☆ John Haley | Below criticism. Poor fighter. Attained successful mediocrity as a soldier. Present all the time. |
| ☆ W.S. Hodston | Rheumatic. Wounded April 6th, 1865. Good soldier. Shot in the lungs. |
| ☆ S.J. Harmon | Stout. Very noisy, ignorant, and absent-minded. Wounded in Wilderness. Died at Fredericksburg, May 1864. |
| ☆ A.J. Hodge | Transferred to battery. A notoriously coarse person. Good riddance. |
| ☆ H.G. Holmes | Away about half the time. Always had a spasm of virtue when under fire. |
| ☆ Mell Irish | Rupture and varicose veins. Better mimic than soldier. Clever person. The poor farms are filled with them. |
| ☆ Ed Jaques | Discharged on account of sickness from Fort Pitcher. Very free and easy at expense of others. |
| ☆ C.A. Jordan | Wounded at Gettysburg in leg. Did no further service. |
| ☆ J.W. Jose | Wounded at Petersburg. An excellent soldier. None better or braver. |
| ☆ Ambrose Kenney | Deserted on the "Mud March," January 20th, 1863. |
| ☆ J.W. Kendrick | Wounded twice. Promoted twice. A great sufferer, in his mind. |
| ☆ J.A. Kilham | Varicose veins. With the teams and provost much of the time. Killed at the North Anna, May 23rd, 1864. |
| ☆ George Kimball | Wounded at Gettysburg. Present most of the time thereafter. |
| ☆ J.E. Leach | Rheumatic. Pig with the same snout as Kenney. They took flight together and were seen no more. |
| ☆ George W. Libby | Discharged early in the term. Don't know any cause. |
| ☆ John G. Libby | Killed at Chancellorsville, May 3rd, 1863. Good fellow and good soldier. |
| ☆ H.H. Libby | Alias "Hardbread." Had an insatiable appetite for hardbread. Sick much but showed excellent *grit*. |
| ☆ F.A. Mitchell | Mortally wounded at Gettysburg. A good soldier and a good man. |
| ☆ M. McGrath | Teamster, with all the instincts of the craft, including great piety when near the front. |
| ☆ J. McKenny | Played out years "before the war, sah." Put in Ambulance Corps and hit in the toe. |
| ☆ Moses Moody | Died of smallpox and came near to scaring another man to death with it. |
| ☆ Hiram Patterson | Varicose veins. Promoted to corporal, for reasons best known to officers. |
| ☆ William Perry | Varicose veins. Hostler for doctor. Was himself a pack mule when on the march. |
| ☆ T. Perkins | Very shaky in action. At some other times very drunk. Wasn't built right inside for a soldier. |

| | |
|---|---|
| ☆ W.H. Pillsbury | A *prodigious* eater. And not very well most of the time, but very religious. |
| ☆ Ben Ross | Teamster. Not violent as a patriot, except at the mess table. |
| ☆ Walt Rounds | Met with various and sundry ills. A very good soldier. Promoted twice. |
| ☆ G.S. Richardson | Piles. A great wit, and aggravator of simple ones. Would make a mule whicker. |
| ☆ Eliphaz Ripley | Died from an excess of green peaches and other causes known to himself. |
| ☆ John H. Roberts | Mortally wounded at Spotsylvania, May 12th, 1864. A good soldier. |
| ☆ Charles F. Sawyer | Another good one. Slightly wounded at Locust Grove, November 29th, 1863. |
| ☆ John H. Simpson | A most eccentric person. Dirty as he was brave. |
| ☆ Jarry F. Smith | Company cook. Died at Camp Pitcher, January 1862. |
| ☆ Owen Stacy | Promoted sergeant. Hit in the heel at Gettysburg. An excellent soldier, very odd. |
| ☆ Al Smith | Good record. Killed in the Wilderness, May 6th, 1864. |
| ☆ T.B. Sanders | Fought two battles and then hunted a soft place for the rest of his term. |
| ☆ J.F. Sweetser | A good fellow and soldier. Killed in the Wilderness, May 5th, 1864. |
| ☆ Benjamin F. Small | Discharged with very limited experience as a soldier. |
| ☆ Josh W. Small | Most always sick. Suspected of eating soap and other choice edibles. |
| ☆ Edwin Small | Most nerve of any man in the company. Didn't know fear, or had a great facility for concealing it. |
| ☆ W.A. Small | Last and least of the Smalls. Liver all bleached out. Had "left his girl behind him." |
| ☆ W.E. Strout | Good man. Died young, before eating many rations. |
| ☆ Josiah H. Sturtevant | An ornament to any company. Was transferred to colored regiment as an officer. |
| ☆ George Tasker | Killed in the Wilderness, May 6th, 1864. Not especially energetic. |
| ☆ S.G. Usher | Promoted lieutenant. A very mysterious person. Mortally wounded April 6th, 1865. Died *whispering*. |
| ☆ W.S. Waterhouse | Promoted corporal. A good soldier. Wounded in the lip at Spotsylvania, May 12th, 1864. |
| ☆ George Whitten | Rheumatic. Taken prisoner at Chancellorsville. Away two or three times. |
| ☆ Lewis G. Whitney | Killed in the Wilderness, May 6th, 1864. |
| ☆ C.M. White | Served about half his time and then procured a discharge. |

| ☆ David A. Wentworth | Killed in the Wilderness, May 6th, 1864. |
| --- | --- |
| ☆ John Wentworth | Didn't stop with us long, or take many chances. |
| ☆ Thomas R. Warren | An old man and a tough one. Served long and well. Knocked out lots of *boys*. |
| ☆ John Wildes | Consumptive. A scrawny old maid. Looked like an Egyptian mummy. Tough as a boiled owl. Discharged. |
| ☆ William Lamberton | If he was good for anything but lying and swearing, there is a gross omission in the records. |
| ☆ Nahum Pillsbury | A remarkably good feeder and somewhat given to *pie*ty. |

End page from the original journal.

# Appendixes

# Appendix A

## Background on McClellan, Stanton, and Sickles

### George Brinton McClellan (1826–1885)

After the disaster of Bull Run in July of 1861, the army was a shambles, sprawled along the banks of the Potomac around Washington. To compound the problems of defeat and chaos, terms of service for the 75,000 volunteers would expire a fortnight after the battle of Bull Run. It was feared that the Confederates, arrogant and flushed with victory, would march on Washington and find the capital easy prey.

The North sprang to the crisis. Men signed up and were hurried to Washington. Soon the number of troops doubled, though they were more a mob than an army, untrained and undisciplined. A general was required who was capable of molding the raw recruits into soldiers with a strict conformity to military principles.

All eyes turned toward a new hero, General George B. McClellan, as their savior and an equal to Lee. McClellan had gained some prestige in the Mexican War, and had studied modern methods of warfare in Europe during the Crimean War. His special training fitted him admirably for the monumental task. Although he had acquired the nickname of "the little Napoleon," he did, in fact, possess enormous charisma and inspired almost blind idolatry in his officers and men. Unfortunately for the country, he was not a great general, and his military performance was always flawed by his hesitation to act decisively and to follow through. His talent for planning massive strategic campaigns could have made him invaluable in Washington, but his role was cast as a soldier in the field. Nonetheless, McClellan's organizational ability served the country well, and the Grand Army of the Potomac emerged as a proud, unified force. He breathed spirit and soul into the men, and they soon chafed for action.

In November General Scott, the elderly and ailing general-in-chief, retired and McClellan took over. This delayed him still further while he begged for time to work out the new problems of command. Lincoln became impatient.

McClellan refused to move, overestimating the enemy's strength and underrating his own army. Lincoln pressed harder for action, convinced that the army *was* ready and haunted by the financial situation in the country, which threatened bankruptcy. Finally, January 27, 1862, Lincoln issued his General War Order No. 1, ordering an advance of all the armies on February 22. In particular, he insisted that the Army of the Potomac should move upon Manassas (Official Records, Army, 1 ser., V, 41).

McClellan continued to urge his plan to transport the army by water to the lower Rappahannock or to Fort Monroe and advance on Richmond from the east. Lincoln reluctantly consented but demanded that sufficient troops be left to ensure the security of Washington.

As McClellan advanced up the peninsula from Fort Monroe, the Confederates were waiting for him. Heavy rains and impassable roads added to his troubles. He bitterly complained that Washington did not support him with enough supplies or troops. On May 31 and June 1 his army took heavy fire at Seven Pines and Fair Oaks but he managed to take up a position almost at the gates of Richmond. He immediately began building bridges to bring McDowell's promised support across the swollen Chickahominy. Instead of McDowell, Jackson came. On June 26 McClellan suffered another disastrous defeat and fled back across the bridges he had so recently built. The Confederates pursued until McClellan finally took a stand and defeated them at Malvern Hill (Seven Days' Battle).

McClellan was becoming increasingly unpopular in Washington. The president and Halleck, now general-in-chief, were tired of his demands for reinforcements and his constant excuses for defeats. But his greatest enemy in the government was Secretary of War Edwin Stanton. McClellan had considered Stanton a friend before Stanton became Secretary of War, and warm relations even continued between them for a few months after Stanton's appointment. Stanton assured McClellan of his desire to furnish all necessary matériel, but he grew impatient with McClellan's failure to show results. McClellan became more and more distrustful, and the breach widened. Adverse editorials appeared in the press, believed to have been instigated by McClellan, accusing Stanton of being responsible for McDowell's withdrawal of forces in the Peninsular Campaign. These attacks enraged Stanton, and in August 1862 he joined Chase and others in the cabinet to force Lincoln and Halleck to remove McClellan from command.

On August 3 the Army of the Potomac was assigned to General Pope's Army of Virginia, and McClellan was detached from command.

After Pope's resounding defeat at Manassas, McClellan was again called on to reorganize the army and prepare defenses for Washington. He rode out to meet his troops and was greeted with an overwhelming ovation. There was no doubt where the loyalty of the army lay.

Again, after the battles of South Mountain and Antietam, McClellan failed to press his advantage and Lee safely withdrew his army across the Potomac. McClellan did not follow until October. Early in the month Lincoln ordered him to fight, and on October 13 the president asked him, "Are you not overcautious when you assume that you cannot do what the enemy is constantly doing?" (Official Records, 1 ser., vol. XIX, pt. 1, pp. 11,13).

On November 7 Lincoln ordered McClellan to turn over his command to General Burnside and to proceed to Trenton, New Jersey, to await orders. McClellan never held command again.

It is unfortunate that McClellan took command at the start of the war, for it is always true that such commanders receive the sharpest criticism. But it is also true that he was a poor tactician. Nevertheless, whatever blame or praise historians give him, they all agree that it was McClellan who breathed fire and spirit into the Grand Army of the Potomac. Thanks to him, Grant took over a disciplined, expertly organized military machine.

## Edwin McMasters Stanton (1814–1869)

Stanton had already proven himself a capable civil and constitutional lawyer at the time he defended Daniel E. Sickles at a controversial murder trial and gained a reputation in criminal suits as well.

His success in representing the United States in the California land cases in 1858 — fraudulent claims to lands allegedly deeded by Mexico prior to the Mexican War — brought him national acclaim and an appointment as attorney general under Buchanan.

Returning to private life during Lincoln's early months as president, Stanton was vindictive in his criticism of the administration. When McClellan took over the army in 1861, Stanton became his legal advisor and (supposed) friend. He openly expressed to McClellan his contempt for Lincoln. At the time he was also legal adviser to Secretary of War Simon Cameron, and helped frame the report recommending the arming of slaves. Lincoln took umbrage at this and removed Cameron immediately. Inexplicably, Lincoln then appointed his severest critic, Edwin McMasters Stanton, to replace Cameron as secretary of war on January 15, 1862.

There is no doubt that Stanton was capable, energetic, patriotic, and an inspired administrator, but he was also abrasive, suspicious, and conniving, and he meddled constantly in military affairs. He continued his friendly relations with McClellan for awhile but eventually became impatient with the general's dilatory nature. McClellan grew suspicious that Stanton sought his removal. Attacks in the press naming Stanton as the one responsible for the withdrawal of McDowell's troops in the Peninsular Campaign were attributed to McClellan. Stanton then insisted on McClellan's removal.

Stanton invited the hatred of various groups. He brought the press yapping at his heels with his strict censorship of the news. His excessive powers of arrest were often capricious and frightening to the public. Soldiers and civilians alike hated his arrogance, his brutal and unjust treatment. Stanton's severity at the trial of Mrs. Surratt and his charges that Jefferson Davis was implicated in Lincoln's assassination were held in disrepute. Rumors grew that Stanton himself might even be involved. Historians agree, however, that the secretary had grown to respect Lincoln and deeply mourned his passing.

President Johnson asked Stanton to remain at his post but he soon was in conflict with both Johnson and the cabinet over his radical ideas on reconstruction. Outwardly, Stanton remained in harmony with the president at cabinet meetings, but Johnson soon realized that Stanton was plotting behind his back. Johnson became convinced that Stanton was responsible for the insubordination of General Sheridan and other commanders, so he called for the secretary's resignation. Stanton refused, contending that the Tenure of Office Bill, just passed, prevented his removal from office; he would stay until "expelled by force." He ordered the arrest of Adjutant-General Thomas, secretary ad interim, then barricaded himself inside the War Department building, posted a guard to insure that the department records were not seized, and took up residence there for several weeks. On May 26, 1868, he finally accepted the inevitable and resigned his post.

He was an able lawyer and a tireless administrator, but his temperament and the disclosures of his disloyalty and duplicity detract from his record. Shortly before his death he admitted that Johnson's reconstruction program closely followed the one planned by President Lincoln.

## Daniel Edgar Sickles (1825–1914)

Congressman, soldier, diplomat — so reads a biography of Haley's hero, Daniel E. Sickles. He was also a colorful, controversial figure.

Sickles was admitted to the bar in 1846 and elected to the New York legislature in 1847. He was appointed counsel for the city of New York but resigned to become secretary of the United States delegation in London.

Returning to America, he served in Congress from 1857 to 1861, residing in Washington with his wife and little daughter. It was during this period that Sickles gained national notoriety. On February 27, 1856, he accosted Philip Barton Key, son of Francis Scott Key, on the streets of Washington and calmly and deliberately shot and killed the young man for attentions paid to Mrs. Sickles. What followed was a landmark case where the defense, for the first time, used the plea of temporary insanity. Interestingly enough, it was Edward Stanton who conducted the Sickles defense and achieved the acquittal.

Although a staunch Democrat, Sickles offered his services to President Lincoln when war broke out. He returned to New York and organized the Excelsior Brigade, rising to the rank of major general. In 1863 he took command of the 3rd Corps at Chancellorsville and is credited with stopping Stonewall Jackson's advance.

His last campaign was at Gettysburg. Meade informed all his officers that he planned a defensive, not an offensive, strategy. He ordered Sickles to hold a position covering the Round Tops. Sickles decided to advance to the Peach Orchard. (Haley describes this bloody battle in his journal.) Meade arrived on the scene and personally ordered Sickles to retreat, but a violent attack led by Longstreet prevented this. By nightfall Sickles had lost half his men, but he did stop the enemy's advance with but slight loss of ground. Shortly afterward Sickles was shot, and his right leg was hastily amputated on the battlefield.

Meade's reports later sharply criticized Sickles for disregarding orders. Sickles's military career was now at an end but he continued to serve his country as a diplomat. In 1867 President Johnson appointed him military governor of the Carolinas but removed him in 1867 as he found him "too strenuous in execution of his duties."

In 1869 Sickles was appointed minister to Spain, but the complications of the Cuban problem proved too much for him. Again, his actions earned him unfavorable notoriety and he was called the "Yankee King" — hardly proper for a diplomat. While in Spain he met and married his second wife. This marriage proved unsuccessful, and after seven years Sickles returned to the United States alone.

His next public office was as chairman of the New York State Monuments Commission in 1876. Once more his temperament brought trouble crashing around him. He was relieved of duties for mismanagement of funds, and it was in this period that he wrote a letter to John Haley calling for help from his old comrades in arms: "I thank you for your sympathy, and would be grateful if you, as one of my good soldiers, would organize a movement of those who served under me to come to my relief now, in my troubles. . . .No time should be lost."

On May 16, 1914, the "old, irresponsible and cantankerous gentleman" died of a broken heart, stripped of honor and money. The one remaining testimony to his efforts is beautiful Central Park in New York City.

# Appendix B

## Battles in Which the 17th Maine Regiment Participated

*1862*     Fredericksburg (December 13)

*1863*     Chancellorsville (May 14)
Gettysburg (July 1 – 3)
Wapping Heights (July 23)
Auburn (Oct. 14)
Kelly Ford (Nov. 7)
Mine Run (Nov. 26 – 28)

*1864*     Hatcher's Run (Feb. 5 – 7)
Boydtown (March 31)
Totopotomy Creek (May 28 – 31)
Cold Harbor (June 2 – 4)
Seige of Petersburg (June 15)
Locust Grove (July)
Burnside's Mine (Aug. 9)
Deep Bottom (Aug. 10 – 14)
Battle of the Wilderness:
    Po River (May 10)
    Laurel Hill
    Spotsylvania (May 11 – 15)
    Fredericksburg Turnpike
    Todd's Tavern

*1865*     High Bridge (April 6)
Sailor's Creek (April 6)
Fall of Petersburg (April 2)
Appomattox (April 9)
*DISBANDED OFFICIALLY MAY 26, 1865*

# Chapter Notes

## Prologue

1. In the spring of 1862 it looked as if the Union Army might have victory within its grasp; by late summer, it was feared that defeat was imminent. Lee was reported to be in Manassas with 120,000 troops, and the Confederates were about to move on Arlington. The Washington coterie gathered by Stanton and Chase, who had been seeking the removal of McClellan as commander of the Army of the Potomac, circulated a petition among Lincoln's cabinet demanding McClellan be recalled and Pope made commander-in-chief. Stanton and Chase succeeded in getting the cabinet to favor the document and intended to present it to President Lincoln with the ultimatum he either fire his general or lose his cabinet.

At this auspicious moment General Pope wrote to Halleck, general-in-chief of the army, saying that the "unsoldierly and dangerous conduct of certain Army of the Potomac officers has created an impossible situation." There were certain officers, he said, who maintained that the Army of the Potomac would not fight and that they were demoralized by the withdrawal from the peninsula. Pope strongly advised Halleck to bring all the troops back to Washington for reorganization "to avoid great disaster."

2. McClellan considered the war a "gentleman's fight," not one aimed at bringing the South to its knees. Also, he found the thought of the abolition of slavery appalling. He predicted all kinds of dire consequences, even to Negroes serving in the army. Nevertheless, when Lincoln issued the Emancipation Proclamation, McClellan sent an order throughout the army saying it was the president's civil authority to make policy and the army's duty to enforce it.

Loose talk at McClellan's headquarters filtered back to Washington. One particularly offensive remark — attributed to Major James J. Key, a member of McClellan's staff — caused Lincoln to order Key to Washington. The major admitted to saying, "We didn't capture Lee at Sharpsburg, because the object of this war is that both armies shall be kept in the field till they are exhausted, when we will make a compromise and save slavery." Key was immediately dismissed from the army.

Although Key was the author of the statement, McClellan was blamed for allowing such talk to take place. It was well known that he secretly favored this approach to the conduct of the war. Lincoln was shaken in his staunch support of McClellan and henceforth doubted the general's loyalty.

The tenor of the war was changing. Lincoln had committed himself to a war of revolution with attendant harsh measures to win the conflict. McClellan's position became daily more untenable. Finally, Lincoln had no recourse but to remove him as commander of the Army of the Potomac. On November 7, 1862, McClellan was ordered to turn his command over to General Burnside. He never served in the field again.

## Chapter 1: Camp King, Cape Elizabeth

1. Sibley tents were the small, pointed tents used by the soldiers in bivouac, as opposed to the larger, flatter-roofed tents used in camp.

## Chapter 2: Off to the Land of Dixie

1. Plug uglies: nineteenth-century street gangs in New York City, so called because of the plug hats they wore. The term came to be used for any kind of gangster or ruffian.

2. Billingsgate: coarse or abusive language. Billingsgate was a London fish market.

## Chapter 3: The Chase Is On

1. Number 18 pontoon: an extremely large boot. Haley goes into greater detail on the size of Captain Martin's feet in his November 2 entry.

2. On October 21, 1861, the Federals, through gross mismanagement, were routed with great slaughter at the battle of Ball's Bluff, Virginia. They suffered 49 killed, 158 wounded or taken prisoner, and 714 missing.

      McClellan, uneasy about Lee's movements across the river, had ordered Brigadier General Charles P. Stone to cross the Potomac at Harrison's Island in what is known as a reconnaissance in force. General Stone sent Colonel Edward D. Baker over with a few regiments to scale the heights at Ball's Bluff. A bloody ambush awaited them, and the Union soldiers were cut to pieces. Baker was killed.

      Bitter memories of Bull Run were still vivid in Washington at the time. Also, Baker was a close friend of Lincoln. (The president had named his second son after him.) A committee was formed to investigate the affair, as rumor had it that a Federal officer with Southern sympathies had engineered the ambush. Suspicion fell on General Stone. Although Stone was never accused, he was imprisoned, and though later released, was never cleared.

      Ball's Bluff was a place of "unhappy memories" to any soldiers of the Army of the Potomac recalling the slaughter of the ambush on October 21.

3. Notes: Probably these were I.O.U.s.

4. Haley goes on at this point to defend McClellan. These paragraphs were obviously written with benefit of hindsight, inserted into the field diaries by Haley as he wrote his account in later years: "And right here I should like to have an explanation of this conduct on the part of Washington. McClellan had been urged forward in pursuit of Lee and had perfected a plan for the destruction of Lee's army. Having reached a point where the movement was about to culminate successfully, he was summarily disposed of, superseded in June or July by John Pope. That spread-eagle had, by a method not yet understood, got himself into a most inextricable snarl [at the second battle of Bull Run], nearly sacrificing his army and the capital as well. The government was then glad to recall McClellan, who came up as cheerfully as though he had not been misused and fought the battle of Antietam, compelling Lee to seek safety in flight. A tardy pursuit followed, which I have been detailing. McClellan claimed it was necessary, and perhaps it was, to the success of his plans, which were pretty well matured when the official axe fell.

      "Some said he had been too dilatory, although after Antietam President Lincoln despatched to him, 'God bless you and your whole command. You have done better than could have been expected.' A general in command of a great army, maneuvering to defeat another great army, cannot always divulge his plans, especially when he knows the administration in Washington is surrounded by spies. But the administration in Washington was influenced too much by some of its satellites, as the sequel to this showed. It is almost certain that if McClellan had been retained in command another month, I should not have to record the bloody repulse of our army at Fredericksburg under the patriotic but incompetent Burnside.

"Burnside succeeded McClellan not by choice but on order of the commander-in-chief. Since this change was an insinuation that McClellan's route to Richmond wasn't favored by the administration, the new commander chose another route. Instead of going by way of Culpepper, he struck lower down the river toward Fredericksburg, leaving Lee to follow. A little strategic movement was resorted to by which it was hoped to deceive our Southern friend into a belief that we were going right down to Richmond. If we could reach Fredericksburg while the Rebels were lying here, we should be in Lee's rear and he must either hurry off towards Richmond or fight at a great disadvantage.

"Our division going to Waterloo was part of this strategic performance, and as soon as this was done we ambled back again, having accomplished but little. Burnside had succeeded in planting a part of his force at Fredericksburg and that was all. It didn't secure the prize."

See the Appendix for further discussion of the career of George B. McClellan.

5. General Ambrose Burnside was a man called upon to take on a job that he was woefully inadequate to perform. He presented a friendly, dignified appearance, although he was constantly fumbling with his clothing. He always wore a short jacket, tightly belted around his portly stomach, and a bell-crowned hat that somewhat hid his famous shaggy whiskers. Burnside's name, slightly rearranged, is *sideburns*, and he is perhaps best remembered for having given his name to that style of facial decoration, of which he sported fine examples.

Haley reflects the blind idolatry of McClellan felt by most of the army at this time. It is easy to imagine the painful conflict encountered by the ordinary soldiers as they tried to abruptly transfer their loyalty to a new commanding officer. However, Haley's sense of justice compelled him to acknowledge that treachery by McClellan's irate followers made any success on Burnside's part nearly impossible.

## Chapter 4: Fredericksburg

1. When Burnside reached the banks of the Rappahannock opposite Fredericksburg, he found the pontoons missing to build bridges for his supply trains to cross the tricky water. The Army of the Potomac waited and waited, giving Lee plenty of time to line up Rebel soldiers on a high elevation on the opposite bank. Here the Confederates sat and watched the enemy mulling aimlessly around. At long last the pontoons and materials arrived, and on December 11 Burnside went to work to build his bridges. The Rebels opened a murderous fire. Burnside sent word to the townspeople that he would lay Fredericksburg in ashes if they did not ask the Rebel soldiers to leave. Although the mighty Army of the Potomac lay in clear view, the inhabitants chose destruction. Over 100 Federal guns answered Rebel fire, but still the Confederate sharpshooters knocked down the engineers building the bridges. It was like shooting fish in a barrel. Burnside kept up the cannonading, pulverizing the town but doing little damage to the Rebel troops.

The engineers finally floated Union infantry across the river on the pontoons, and the Rebel resistance ended. A triumphant Burnside marched into the town with flags flying and bands playing.

2. The summer of 1861 was a discouraging period for the Federals. The crushing defeat at Bull Run, and in September another southern victory in Missouri, cast a gloom over the North. At this time Colonel James A. Mulligan of the 23rd Illinois was sent to a tiny corner in upper Missouri called Lexington. He brought with him his own regiment of Irishmen from Chicago (called the Irish Brigade), a regiment of cavalry, a regiment of Missouri militia, and some light artillery. In all, Mulligan had not more than 3,500 men. His orders were to hold the line of the upper Missouri and prevent the state's Secessionist government-in-exile from seizing the territory.

The Confederates sent General Sterling Price with an army of 18,000 Missouri state guards to chase out Mulligan.

Jefferson City was the closest Union base. It was commanded by an officer with the unlikely name of Jefferson Davis. Davis was unable to go to Mulligan's aid. When word reached the brigade, Mulligan's fellow officers begged him to make a speedy retreat. He scornfully replied, "Begad, we'll fight 'em. We enlisted to fight, and fight we shall."

Price, with his superior numbers, soon surrounded Mulligan and cut off his water supply. Two days of fierce fighting ensued, but the feisty Irishman was forced to surrender on September 20. He had suffered 100 casualties; he and his men were all taken prisoner.

Later in the war a full complement of men proudly bore the name of the "Irish Brigade," bringing glory to its banner.

3. The Battle of Malvern Hill took place July 1, 1862, during the Seven Day Battle in the Peninsular Campaign. McClellan had executed a brilliant retreat to Malvern Hill, Virginia, and the Confederates were in hot pursuit. General D.H Hill, commanding one of Jackson's divisions, misunderstood a signal to advance and attacked the crest of Malvern, which was bristling with the Federal cannons.

In *Reports of the Army of Northern Virginia*, vol. 1, p. 186, Hill says, "Tier after tier of batteries were grimly visible on the plateau, rising in the form of an amphitheatre."

The expected artillery never came to Hill's aid, and every assault met a bloody repulse. Night closed on the combatants, and near nine o'clock the battle slackened. The repulse of the Confederates was complete, with a loss of over 5000 men, while the Union loss was only one-third that number. Never before had Lee conducted a battle so poorly conceived or executed.

4. "We hoped in vain, for we were not relieved that night," added Haley. "It was no part of General Franklin's plan. He sought only to defeat and destroy Burnside and reinstate his friend McClellan, and he wouldn't hesitate to destroy us to accomplish this. General Burnside was not a suitable person for so large a command and had been jumped over several 'elder and better soldiers.' In addition, the idol of Franklin and others ('Little Mac') had been unhorsed twice within a year, an unpardonable crime. Franklin's plan, as it developed, seemed to be to weaken Hooker's column, although it occupied the worst place and needed the strongest support. This was done by borrowing a division of Hooker's as support for Franklin, who would then withdraw his force and use his 'support' as the *attacking* party. This insured Rebel success on the left and set the Rebels free to send much of their force on the right to help overwhelm the grand division of Hooker in the center, thus making success for Burnside impossible.

"Admitting that the Rebel works were strong and well manned, I am in possession of enough facts to prove that they could have been carried and held with a much smaller loss than we sustained. Even the mere handful of men sent over by Franklin penetrated two of General Lee's three lines at this point. Had they been promptly supported, they could and would have held their own and flanked the enemy from Marye's Heights. A single division, perhaps brigade, thrown in at the right moment at Hamilton's Crossing would have accomplished this. Breaking both wings of an army is the surest way to make it fly, but neither wing of the Rebel army was broken."

5. On August 29, 1862, General Pope was beaten at the battle of the Second Manassas (or Bull Run) and fell back to Washington. He was relieved of command and his troops transferred to McClellan's Army of the Potomac. Pope blamed his defeat on Major General Fitz-John Porter's failure to carry out orders and attack Jackson *before* Longstreet joined him. Pope accused Porter of "disobedience, disloyalty, and misconduct in face of the enemy." A court martial was convened, and Porter was found guilty and cashiered on January 21, 1863. In 1879 a review of his case reported in his favor, and on August 5, 1886, he was reinstated as colonel of infantry without back pay and placed on the retired list August 7.

Throughout his court martial Porter maintained that Pope's orders were contradictory and impossible to execute because Longstreet had already joined forces with Jackson. Pope's testimony read: "I believe. . .that at 5 o'clock in the afternoon of the 29th General Porter had in his front *no* considerable body of the enemy. I believed then, as I am very sure now, that it was easily practicable for him to have turned the right flank of Jackson, and to have fallen upon his rear; that if he had done so we should have gained a decisive victory over the army under Jackson before he could have been joined by any of the forces of Longstreet" (*History of the Grand Army of the Republic*, p. 186).

History bears out Porter's version and proves that Pope's accusations were false. In *Reports of the Operations of the Army of Northern Virginia*, vol. 2, p. 8, Longstreet says: "Early on the 29th the columns were united, and the advance, to join General Jackson, was resumed. The head of my column soon reached a position in rear of the enemy's left flank."

6. Zouaves were soldiers in volunteer regiments whose dress resembled the French Zouave uniform — a picturesque Oriental style.

## Chapter 5: The Mud March

1. The Union army was a mostly volunteer force during the first three years of the war. This resulted in a flexible sort of discipline. The soldiers were willing to serve faithfully but wouldn't tolerate an officer who "got too big for his britches." On the whole, a spirit of comradeship existed between officers and men. By 1864 the flavor of the Union army had changed, however. The draft was instituted, and it brought into the army a very different kind of soldier: usually poor and illiterate, often an immigrant grabbed as soon as he stepped on American soil.

A draftee with money could buy a substitute or (for $300) gain a commutation of his service until caught in some future draft. The quota of draftees from each state depended on the number of volunteers — enough volunteers, no draftees. Thus, the bounty system reared its ugly head. The richer towns and states offered as much as $1000 per man. The bounty offer was intended to produce volunteers but instead created only the poorest type of soldier.

The bounty system in turn led to the substitute broker, similar to the waterfront crimp, who scoured the seediest neighborhoods for victims. The broker would coerce a drunk to sign over his bounty, then shunt him off to an army station before he sobered up.

Some bounty men did serve faithfully and well but many others became bounty jumpers. These men took their bounty, joined a regiment, deserted, and signed up again and again. If caught, they were promptly executed, but this threat did little to deter men who had lived all their lives as criminals.

There was nothing more detested than the bounty jumpers. Guards were posted to stem the tide of desertion — 7300 in 1864 — and army discipline became harsh, often barbaric. The old camaraderie died and the gap between officers and enlisted men widened. Volunteers who had once been proud of their outfits counted the days, even the hours, until their enlistments were up. Pressure was brought to bear on the volunteers to reenlist, but most of them lived only for their last day of service.

## Chapter 6: Chancellorsville

1. The rest of this entry for May 2nd appears to be a later explanation added later by Haley.

2. Haley goes on to elaborate on Stonewall Jackson's character: "Jackson was, undoubtedly, the Confederates' most valuable general, not excepting Lee and Johnston. He was a host in himself, as good as 40,000 men. His name in connection with a movement was a guarantee of success. He possessed great executive abilities and powers of perception. He had planned and executed this and a score of other movements, always disastrous to our side. He was a bigot, an oddity,

without feeling, a stern and uncompromising disciplinarian who cared for nothing but personal success. No amount of suffering on the part of his men counted — they were as chaff.

"Nor did he appreciate feeling or bravery in others. Most brave men *admire* courage in others. Jackson is quoted as saying to an officer who captured some of our men, 'Why didn't you shoot them?' The officer replied, 'I couldn't bear to, they were so brave.' Jackson snapped, 'Shoot every one of them! I don't want them to be brave.'

"The writer is acquainted with a fellow who was captured on a foraging expedition and brought before Old Jack, who said, 'Where were you captured?'

" 'Ask your own men.'

" 'How many have you in your party?'

" 'Not over forty thousand.' (If the fellow had said five thousand, he would have come nearer the truth.) This impudent answer made old Stonewall fly around, for he didn't care to be caught napping.

"Jackson had some strange habits. He sucked lemons continually, when they were to be had, and refused to eat pepper, saying it made his left leg weak. (This is proof of a weak spot in his *head*.) General Ewell always believed in his lunacy and said, 'I never saw one of his couriers coming without expecting an order to assault the North Pole.'

"Thus, we draw from his intimate friends some insight into his peculiarities, which in one less exalted would have been positively ridiculous. Indeed, before the war Jackson had been an object of mirth and derision. His career as a military man was thus brought to a sudden termination. He was carried back to old Wilderness Tavern, and there we leave him while we snatch a few moments' repose and prepare for tomorrow."

3. "Fredericksburg was the key, and Lee and Hooker both realized this," Haley adds. "Hence, General Hooker's orders to Sedgwick to hold it until it was certain we had them on the run. For the same reason, Lee made plans to draw Sedgwick away from this stronghold so he might repossess it. His plans worked to a charm. When the Rebels appeared to be fleeing, Sedgwick, thinking he had them, gave chase immediately and abandoned the works, which were occupied at once by the Rebels. And now the retreating party returned and hemmed Sedgwick in on three sides, the river on the fourth. Sedgwick held on long enough for General Benham to lay pontoons. It was over before Hooker had knowledge of it.

"General Sedgwick was the very soul of patriotism and doubtless thought he was doing a splendid thing that would justify his disobedience of orders. But it is certain that if he had obeyed orders, this disaster would not have occurred."

4. Haley continues: "It is somewhat singular that at the very time we were alarmed about the Rebels pounding on us, they were also making preparations to 'git.' This was the meaning of their increased activities. They were about to go to Richmond by the most direct route, while we were headed toward Washington."

5. Pills to curb diarrhea, but ingesting such large quantities would instead bring on a violent attack of diarrhea unless an antidote was promptly administered.

6. "Four of Company I were taken prisoner and marched to Richmond, where they were paraded through the streets with women and children yelling 'Yankee scabs' and hissing as they passed. Two of them made themselves ridiculous by pleading for mercy. They very soon learned that the Rebels have more respect for a foe with the courage to stand out in defense of his side than they do for a crawling, spunkless booby. They were incarcerated in that formidable structure known as Castle Thunder, which, with its companion Libby Prison, rivaled that sultry location the Rebel women would have willingly consigned them to."

## Chapter 7: March to Gettysburg

1. Haley added the following summary: "This same movement was undertaken last year when Pope was in command of our army. McClellan brought Pope's army (which was fleeing in confusion on Washington) and met Lee at Antietam, defeating him and releasing the North and Washington from this menace. It may surprise some that a general of Lee's ability should so soon repeat this disastrous movement. Lee probably would not have attempted it if McClellan had been in command. After the failure at Chancellorsville and Hooker's conduct there, Lee had no fear of *him*. It was the most natural thing in the world to think he could walk right through Hooker's army. He was now on his way — to New England, for all we knew. He had some days' start on us and was now in the Shenandoah Valley."

2. Nine-months men: The first volunteers were enlisted for nine months. Actually, they were state militia called temporarily into federal service. Lincoln then issued a call for three-year volunteers. These men were mustered directly into federal service and their states had no control over them.

3. Haley at this point added an interesting sidelight to his original journal, pointing out several inaccuracies in Whittier's 1864 poem about the legendary Barbara Frietchie: "Frederick City was the home of Barbara Frietchie, a venerable dame of four score and ten whose name is immortalized as one who dared raise her country's flag when men were paralyzed with fear by the Rebel presence.

" 'She took up the flag the men hauled down,' says the poet. This may be true, but so far as the reference to Stonewall Jackson, it is *pure fiction*. Jackson never entered the city, but turned square to the left before reaching it and marched up the stream.

"Such an individual as Barbara did reside here, and she did have a little flag stowed away in a bureau drawer. A relative, a Secesh who often felt the lash of her tongue, relates that Rebel soldiers were Barbara's special abomination. She used a long staff in walking and with this poked some Rebel soldiers who had straggled over the brook and sat down to rest on her piazza. She evicted them promptly, exclaiming, 'Off! Off! You lousy Rebels!'

"Jackson's route lay outside the city and separated from it by a small stream over which hung the piazza of her house. The road on which the Rebels marched turned off and followed the stream and, thus, the column passed her house on the right. So, all day long through Frederick street there was *no* sound of marching feet.

"Those who profess to believe the whole thing a myth can visit the graveyard in the rear of the church. Caspar and Barbara Frietchie both sleep there, having lived to a good old age."

4. "General Halleck, chief in command at Washington, issued certain orders which General Hooker felt he could not comply with and he asked to be relieved. His request was complied with promptly for, no doubt, it was Halleck's intention to force him out. This was a critical time to change commanders. Swapping horses in midstream was a transaction strongly condemned by Mr. Lincoln. We didn't know at the time the points of difference between General Hooker and the Washington obstructionists. We simply heard he had been 'relieved at his own request.'

"General Halleck could not boast of anything but a special unfitness for the position he held, and it must always remain a mystery to those who knew Mr. Lincoln's keenness of perception that he allowed this old woman in breeches to meddle continually with the generals in the field."

## Chapter 8: Battle of Gettysburg

1. History has criticized Howard for the disposition of his troops. The terrain required massing a heavy force of his troops on the right of the First Corps. Instead, he attempted to hold the whole stretch by a thin line and, in effect, left his soldiers unprotected. Nevertheless, Howard fought hard and helped to hold Cemetery Hill.

2. Sickles was a congressman at the time of the incident. He shot the seducer, Philip Barton Key (son of Francis Scott Key), on the streets of Washington. Sickles was acquitted in a celebrated trial on the basis of "aberration of mind," the first time this defense had been used. See Appendix for a biographical sketch of Daniel Edgar Sickles's life and career.

3. In writing his final version of the journal, Haley added his analysis of the events of July 2: "It has been reported that General Sickles was guilty of disobedience of orders in forming his line, and that by so doing he lost the field and came near losing the entire battle. Furthermore, that but for the personal bravery of Sickles, Meade would have preferred charges against him. The facts are that General Meade was very angry because Reynolds had brought on a fight here. Hancock had sustained his action, and Sickles had moved out to a point much in advance of the line Meade *pretends* to have selected. Although we had lost the field, we had held Longstreet's troops long enough to enable others to secure and hold Round Top, the key to our position.

"General Meade had not discerned the importance of the position. In fact, he knew little or nothing of the section and was not only timid, but jealous as well. At a council of his corps commanders he had said, 'Have your own way, but Gettysburg is no place to fight a battle.' He had also said to General Sickles, 'Oh, you are *always* imagining that you are going to be attacked.' Almost at that instant, the enemy opened on Sickles in the very attack he had feared and which I have just chronicled. Had General Sickles obeyed Meade's orders in relation to position, there is no doubt that we would have been a defeated army by nightfall, and Washington in greater peril than ever before.

"Meade is not entitled to much credit for the results of these two days' action. Generals Reynolds, Hancock, Howard, and Sickles were the principal actors. Generals Birney, Gibbons, Humphreys, Warren, Weed, and many more all did nobly. And to them the country owes a debt it can never pay, although it may not show its gratitude."

4. Haley here inserts "A Veteran's Tale" to better illustrate his recollections: "This scene has been depicted so well in verse by an eyewitness that I give it a place here."


A Veteran's Tale

A hundred guns — yes, fifty more —
Rained down their shot and shell.
As if from out its yawning door,
Drove the red blasts of Hell.
The hiss! The crash! The shriek! The groan!
The ceaseless iron hail.
All this for half the day.
It made the stoutest quail.

But sudden far to left we heard
The bank strike up and lo!
Full in our front — no breath was stirred —
Came Hancock, riding slow.
As slow as if on dress parade.
All down the line to right,
And back again — by my good blade —
Was ever such a sight?

We lay at length — no ranks could stand
Before that tempest wild;
But on he rode with hat in hand
And looked and bowed, then smiled,

Whatever fears we had were gone
At once, that sight you know
Just made us fifty thousand more.
All hot to face the foe.

You've heard the rest. How on they came
Earth shaking at their tread;
A cheer, our ranks burst into flame.
Steel crossed — the foe had fled.
Yet still that dauntless form I see,
Slow riding down the line.
Was ever deed of chivalry
So grand, O comrade mine?

## Chapter 10: Winter and Spring of 1864

1. See the description of Edwin M. Stanton in the Appendix for an explanation of "Stanton and his coterie."

2. Here, Haley added an explanation of the long-anticipated move to Richmond: "It is claimed that when General Grant first took command and plotted his campaign to Richmond, he was strongly opposed to the overland route, preferring to go by the peninsula. In his final change of plan, we see Stanton's hand. Had the first plan been followed, it would have been an endorsement of McClellan's plan, and this could not be admitted for an instant. Sooner than do this, they would rather sacrifice a hundred thousand lives and countless millions of dollars. So, Stanton was still the power behind the throne, and he would never forget what McClellan had written to him from the peninsula, 'I tell you plainly, if this army is saved, it owes nothing to *you*. You have done your best to sacrifice it.' So it was settled, in Washington, that the campaign to Richmond was to be overland."

## Chapter 11: The Battle of the Wilderness

1. Haley's optimism of the first and second had evaporated by May 3. Perhaps his doubts were premonitory, for the battle of the Wilderness was a strange conflict where neither side won or lost but where both claimed victory. Terrible and deadly it proved to be, resulting in a Union loss of 15,000 men and a Confederate loss of over 8000.

Grant crossed the Rapidan on May 5, 1864, with 116,000 troops, 50,000 horses, and a 4000-wagon train. Lee waited in the woods with only 60,000 soldiers, but knowledge of the Wilderness gave him the advantage despite the superiority of Union numbers. How he must have chuckled as he watched Grant's cavalry and heavy artillery come up the road. He had only to wait and the Wilderness would entrap them.

The Wilderness was twelve miles wide, six miles deep, and bordered the Rapidan. Here, a dense, nearly impenetrable growth of tangled brush and stunted trees replaced what at one time had been tall virgin timber, long since cut down for the smelting pots of nearby iron mines. It was a vast, dank, evil place of brush, swamps, dangerous ravines, and clawing under-growth — no place for artillery and cavalry, and certainly *no* place for a battle.

Grant's plan was to push through the Wilderness as rapidly as possible, outflank Lee, and force a battle on open ground beyond. Lee had no intention of allowing this maneuver. The odds were all in his favor, and he was determined to shut up Grant in the Wilderness.

This was a new kind of war for the Army of the Potomac. There was no grand pageantry of battle on open fields, no dashing cavalry or display of generalship. From officer down to private, the men entered the darkness of the Wilderness with foreboding. In this terrifying place, each man soon found he must depend on himself for survival and he cursed both the war and Grant.

The cavalry and artillery were soon withdrawn, and men relied on their muskets and their wits. A thick blanket of acrid, black smoke from thousands of guns firing night and day was trapped under the trees, and soon a man must reach out and touch his neighbor to know whether he was still there. It was a battle where they never saw the enemy and all fired continuously at shadows in the fog. The woods blazed and thousands of wounded cried out, trapped by fire, which was more dreaded than an enemy bullet.

Night brought little surcease from battle, and three bloody days and nights ensued. When it was over neither side laid down its guns or admitted defeat. Grant led his men out of the thickets and onto the road to Spotsylvania, another nondescript dot on the map of Virginia, where ten days of battle would prove even more terrible than the engagement they'd just left.

The war was never the same. Grant's objective was to cork up Lee in Virginia and keep him from ever taking the initiative again. Thus, Grant claimed the Battle of the Wilderness as a victory and he continued in the months to come to "hammer, hammer, hammer" until the Confederacy would finally lay down its arms in pure exhaustion.

2. Haley goes on to editorialize about Grant's strategy at the time: "Lee's audacity fairly paralyzed our generals, and he knew this. Grant was well enough acquainted with the lesser number of Lee's troops to know that he could hold Lee's main army here and still spare a force to work on his flanks. But nothing of the kind was attempted, and I am totally at a loss to account for his conduct.

"Grant seemed to have no orders to give, nor did he authorize anybody else to. We could have engaged all of Lee's men and still thrown a Union Army toward Richmond. Instead, we find Meade, on the first day, chattering about 'preventing the Rebels from getting back to Mine Run.' Why he expected them to run in that direction is a matter concerning which I am in Egyptian darkness. Lee, with only 58,000 men and but little protection, had none to spare to get in Grant's rear at Mine Run, especially if Grant kept him well occupied in front and on his flank."

## Chapter 12: The Battle of Po River

1. Haley goes on to assess the results of the long wilderness struggle: "History will record the fact that these days witnessed one of the bloodiest and most destructive battles ever enacted on this hemisphere, and the worst of this memorable year of battles. The Dogs of War never grappled more fiercely at each others' throats than here in the Wilderness.

"Lee didn't attain a positive victory, and the results were a grievous disappointment to Grant. Disillusioned by the bloody experience of the past few days, he might by this time have come to the conclusion that another route offered a better solution to the question of how to get to Richmond.

"Lee had checked us by seizure of the Brock Road and had us bottled up in the Wilderness, but Grant's army was far from crippled. He might have failed to drive Lee back, but the road around Lee was still open. Grant had been feeling for a weak place in Lee's line, as a pugilist approaches his antagonist, but he didn't find it today. We weakened Lee by no less than 10,000 dead and wounded. Grant's losses in these two fights just recounted added up to 35,000!

"I am well aware that in making such a statement I am inviting violent criticism and abuse from the admirers of Grant — would-be historians who cater to the popular clamor for an idol. Having taken George Washington as my guide in this matter, I shall not be intimidated. My distinguished example chose to cut down a cherry tree rather than tell a lie. In this respect I resemble the immortal G.W. (though personally, I would rather tell a thousand lies than cut down a tree; in fact, I don't know but what I'd make it fifteen-hundred lies if it was much of a tree)."

2. "A few weeks later," Haley writes, "we found him posing as a worthy example of 'Christian fortitude and resignation.' A Christian commission had caused to be printed a tract relating the circumstances of Wardwell's dying a peaceful, happy soul. In fact, Cy Wardwell didn't die at all but lived on to test the Christian fortitude and patience of whoever might thereafter be blessed with his society."

## Chapter 13: Spotsylvania

1. "And now, while the troops are forming," Haley continues, "let us for a moment glance at the situation.

"The Rebel army was strongly entrenched about Spotsylvania Court House and directly across Grant's path. In the last two days, Grant went up and down the line, seeking a weak spot to break through. Strangely enough, he selected the very strongest position in Lee's lines. I can only account for this on the grounds that it was central, and if successful, Grant could turn his troops right and left and rout Lee. Accordingly, he ordered Hancock to attempt it. Hence we were massed here within a half mile of this salient in Lee's line.

"If such a movement can be considered as necessary or proper, Hancock was, of all men, best fitted for such a desperate venture. In rain, mud, and darkness he pushed men over and past what most regarded as formidable obstacles even in daylight. Men plunged into swamps and were entangled in thickets, but an hour before daylight they were in line ready for the movement."

2. The Mule Shoe, so named because of its shape, was a gigantic salient a mile deep and half a mile wide. It didn't run in a straight line but formed two tangents joined by a loop of entrenchments bulging out toward the north in an angle named the Bloody Angle. This was the most difficult part of the Mule Shoe to defend, and if Grant could break through here, Lee's army would be cut in half. Haley mistakenly refers to this salient as the Horse Shoe.

3. May 12, 1864, saw the climax of the first phase of Grant's Wilderness campaign at the Bloody Angle in the battle of Spotsylvania.

The Angle was a bend in the entrenchments called the Mule Shoe, and the strongest salient in Lee's defenses. There was nothing remarkable about the Angle except that the worst fighting of the war took place there. All who fought there could never adequately describe the horror of the day. Bodies piled so high that men walked across them. In the savage hand-to-hand combat, the men fought so closely that they felt one another's breath fan their cheeks. All day the battle continued. Skulls were crushed by muskets. Men were stabbed with sword and bayonet. Weapons became so clogged with gunpowder as to be useless. Neither side could advance. About midnight Lee retired to his planned positions and finally abandoned the Angle.

The Federals poured over the breastworks and claimed an empty victory, won at a terrible cost: over 7,000 Union soldiers killed and the Confederate losses even heavier.

This battle marked a turning point in the war. From the Bloody Angle on, Grant would wage one long, nightmarish battle.

4. Corcoran Legion: Corcoran was born in Ireland in 1827 and emigrated to the United States in 1849. When the call for troops went out in 1861, he organized the 69th New York Regiment. This regiment distinguished itself at the second battle of Bull Run but Corcoran was taken prisoner. In 1862 he was released in an exchange of prisoners and promoted to rank of brigadier general. He returned to New York and raised the so-called Corcoran Legion, a regiment of "fighting Irishmen." The legion fought valiantly in Virginia and North Carolina and were credited with checking the Rebels at Norfolk. In 1863 Corcoran died of injuries sustained when he fell from a roof at Fairfax Court House.

## Chapter 15: The Siege of Petersburg Begins

1. "Getting into Petersburg, at this point," Haley adds, "would have been a comparatively easy task. If only we had been there, it is reasonably certain we could have obtained possession of the city.

"Hancock's alleged motive for failing to start — that we had no rations for over a week and he didn't want to push his men — might have some element of truth, but it was not *the* reason. He was considerate of the comfort of his men, but if he had known what was at stake, he would never have delayed. It is claimed that neither Meade nor Hancock had any knowledge that Grant intended to capture Petersburg.

"From my observations I don't believe Grant had planned to go into the city. I may sound bitter, but to have done so would have brought things to a focus too suddenly for Grant. By carrying the city this day, thousands of lives and limbs could have been saved. Just as thousands of lives would not have been spent if Grant had landed his army here on transports instead of fighting his way through the Wilderness."

2. The bombproofs that Haley refers to so frequently were square holes with logged roofs dug in the breastworks where the men took shelter from the shelling. Trenches outside Petersburg ran over five miles, and on every knoll or hill stood a fort (crudely built affairs of earth and logs with small openings for the guns). Mortars were placed in open pits in the rear of these forts, and still further back were the bombproofs.

3. Burnside's Mine. By July 30, 1864, Grant's constant pounding on the Rebel works had failed to weaken them, and when Burnside presented the plan for the mine, Grant listened attentively; it might succeed. If it did, it would place Grant far to the rear of the Confederate lines and he could march on to Petersburg. With the capture of that city, Richmond would soon capitulate and the war would end.

The idea for the mine germinated from a remark made by a private in the 48th Pennsylvania. The 48th was a division of miners from Schuylkill County — coal country — and their commanding officer, Lieutenant Colonel Henry Pleasants, was a mining engineer. The private was peering directly across at the Rebel works through a slit in the Union fortifications. "We could drive a mine shaft right under them and blow 'em to kingdom come." Pleasants overheard the remark and took the idea to Burnside. The two men immediately set off for Grant's headquarters.

Meade and Grant discussed the idea with a group of army engineers, who ridiculed the plan. Meade's caustic remark was, "At least it'll keep the men busy." Grant finally gave Burnside and Pleasants permission to proceed, promising the cooperation of the army engineers.

Not only did Pleasants not get any help from the engineers, they did their best to obstruct him. He persevered. He planned a strongly timbered shaft five hundred feet long, five feet high, and four feet wide. Although Grant ordered the shoring timber, none arrived. Pleasants's men demolished a bridge and raided a nearby sawmill for the wood. Wire for the long fuses never materialized, and again Pleasants improvised. As work progressed, several other regiments were pressed into service. The tunnel slanted uphill, away from Rebel eyes. A long line of men carted the dirt away to the woods behind Union lines to hide all evidence of excavation. In three weeks Pleasants was ready to dig a 175-foot shaft right under the Confederate redoubt above the end of the tunnel, where the explosives would be placed.

By this time the Rebels were aware that a tunnel was being built but couldn't locate it. Pleasants had the 320 kegs (each containing twenty-five pounds of explosives) carried in and the fuses wired in place.

At this point plans went awry. Burnside had rigorously trained a division of colored troops to rush in immediately after the explosion and sweep through the crater to the ridge behind Rebel lines. This division had not been used in building the mine and were fresh and ready. They were extremely proud of the honor and learned their orders quickly. At the eleventh hour Meade warned Grant that such a maneuver would bring the wrath of every abolitionist and radical Republican in the North down on his head; they would accuse Grant of deliberately sending in the colored troops to be slaughtered. Grant agreed and told Burnside he must choose another regiment.

Burnside was known for being a gambler, and he chose to have division commanders pick straws. The task fell to the worst possible choice, Brigadier General Ledlie's division.

The fatal match was struck but the fuse failed to explode the charge. Two officers volunteered to enter and relight it. Finally, at 4:45 in the morning, a solid mass of earth rose two hundred feet in a black cloud of smoke and blazing powder. Union artillery opened fire, and Ledlie's hapless and reluctant division advanced slowly. The Confederate works were now a huge crater, one-hundred fifty feet long, sixty feet wide, twenty-five feet deep. Instead of rushing forward through a paralyzed enemy, Ledlie huddled in the crater while other divisions piled in behind him, creating total chaos. Some men were trampled to death; those Rebels who were left alive sprang in and bayoneted others.

Burnside continued throwing in troops, and at 7 A.M. he finally ordered in the Negro division. Although the Rebels had recovered by this time and were pouring artillery fire on the crater, the colored troops advanced bravely toward the crest, then fled in disorder through the crater when met by a particularly deadly artillery barrage. The exploded earthworks became a slaughter-pen, and it was soon as impossible to retreat as to advance. Over four thousand Union men were killed or captured by the time the fiasco of Burnside's mine ended.

4. Haley sums up the disaster: "The whole experiment was the result of jealousy and cowardice, combined with inefficiency and gross intoxication. Several cases of official incompetency were later developed by a Court of Inquiry."

A Court of Inquiry was held to look into the Burnside mine disaster, just as Haley states. A casual reader might conclude that the affair was a fiasco and that the blame should rest solely on Burnside's shoulders. Historians state, however, that the plan had merit and a chance of success. The mine was superbly engineered and, though the element of surprise was mitigated, the Rebels still had not been able to determine the exact location of the mine. In fact, both Rebel and Federal soldiers joked about its existence, only half-believing that such a massive operation could go on undetected.

Burnside chose a Negro division not used in the excavation work. He trained them well, and they were fresh and eager to prove themselves for the first time in battle. Their orders were to sweep through the breach made by exploding a charge of powder in the tunnel and rush to the ridge in rear of the Confederate troops. The troops were determined to do so. Meade interfered, requiring Burnside to substitute another division for the Negro troops twenty-four hours before the time set for exploding the mine, which spelled disaster for the plan. Burnside's method of drawing straws for the substitute division was ridiculous, and, unfortunately, the "winner" was a division known for lack of valor and discipline. The same men had also worked on the construction of the mine and were already exhausted.

After the disaster Meade tried to get Grant to court-martial Burnside, but this Grant refused to do. Meade then initiated a Court of Inquiry. It was well known that Burnside was both an inveterate gambler and a heavy drinker. (So, too, were many other officers but they were not the ones under investigation.)

The Court of Inquiry allowed Burnside to take a leave of absence. He was never recalled to duty and resigned his commission at the end of the war.

## Chapter 16: Autumn Siege of Petersburg

1. The draft riots in the North festered and boiled over into massive rebellion in New York City after the passage of the Civil War Enrollment Act of 1863. Most of the participants were men from the laboring class unable to pay substitutes to serve for them in the army. On July 13 a mob stormed the draft headquarters, overpowered police, firemen, and militia, and vandalized

hotels and restaurants, even tearing up railway tracks. For four days the city was under seige. Property losses totaled 1.5 million dollars. On July 15 picked troops from the Army of the Potomac were sent in to restore order, and on August 19 draft drawings once again proceeded peacefully.

2. In 1863 General Butler assembled a large contingent of colored troops to cut a canal at a bend in the James River between Appomattox and Richmond. Upon its completion the canal would be five-hundred yards long, sixty feet wide at the top, and sixty-five feet wide below the surface.

It was hard, dangerous work, and the men were under constant fire from bluffs along the river, but the project neared completion in December 1864. All that remained was to place a charge that would remove the bulkhead holding back the river. On New Year's Day, 1865, the twelve-hundred pounds of gunpowder were detonated, but the bulkhead collapsed and refilled the gap. The Confederates were quick to follow up on their advantage and swept the area with their firepower. The project was finally abandoned and termed a military failure.

3. In the summer of 1861 the North was convinced the rebellion would be short-lived. The people and the press clamored for one good battle to end the ridiculous Secession.

General McDowell knew his Union troops were green, untrained men, but the pressure convinced him to confront General Beauregard (the Confederate general who had pounded Fort Sumter). So on July 16 McDowell marched to Manassas Plain, twenty miles outside Washington, where Beauregard waited on the other side of a little river named Bull Run.

Athough the Union soldiers were unseasoned troops, they dug in their heels and fought as well as could be expected against the superior Southern forces. But when an orderly retreat was initiated, McDowell's men broke and fled back toward Washington.

At this point a ridiculous affair took place. The citizens of Washington, anxious to witness the battle, had poured out of the city in their holiday clothes and carrying picnic baskets. As the soldiers overran them, they fled for their carriages. Soon a bridge over Cub Run collapsed from the excessive weight of fleeing soldiers and spectators, and a gigantic traffic jam stretched for miles.

4. Milesians: natives of Ireland.

5. At this point Haley goes on to quote more extensively from the *Richmond Examiner* article and to vilify the paper's editor, saying, "But let them listen to Pollard, the foremost editor of Richmond:

Those people in the North who sympathize with the South, or affect any consideration for it, may be divided into three classes. First, we enumerate the (so-called) war Democrats. They affect great virtue, on account of their opposition to Abraham Lincoln, but are quite ambidextrous on the subject of peace, all they have ever said in favor of a termination of the war being nothing more than the whine of hypocrisy as from time to time the military successes of the South have extorted it. While playing their part against A. Lincoln, in fact they have no higher aim than partisan effort or public plunder. They attempt a popular compensation for this in pretending a virtuous attachment to a "constitutional union," occasionally throwing into their opinions a little spice of blackguardism about 'extreme men in the Confederacy.' These opinions are well exemplified in that infamous sheet, the *New York World*, and that nose of wax, McClellan. We find the editor of this sheet one day emptying his pot of filth on Mr. Lincoln, and the next making a sort of amends and squaring his accounts with the vulgar by low and untruthful flings at the South, and [by] a style of double entendre that shows a wonderful proficiency in blackguard scholarship. The life of this party is equivocation. [It is] an example of Yankee morals and a damning evidence of the incoherency and nothingness of the so-called Democratic party of the North.

"After speaking of another class less obnoxious, he concludes with this grand display, or outburst, of verbal pyrotechnics:

It is very easy to sit in a cushioned chair, with a full stomach, and sympathize. The South wants no such sympathy or display of sentimentalism. She asks for her justification in the eyes of God and man, and disdains a pity that, denying it, offers a comfort that dishonors her. She will be content with *no* abridgment of her rights. She has no claim on mawkish charity, no beggar's plea for the half-pence and broken dishes of Northern philanthropy.

   "Now here's richness, a statement of the case which would do credit to Micawber, that 'prince of gas bags and boss of verbose twaddle and high-sounding inanities.' Much allowance must be made for Pollard; he couldn't help talking that way. This brag and bluster is as natural to a Virginian (especially an editor) as it is for a hen to cackle. His editorials, and a book he wrote after his incarceration in Fort Warren, were nothing but one continual whine. It is a thousand pities he was ever exchanged; he should have been kept in 'durance vile' as long as there was a breath of treason in his cowardly carcass."

6. One can sympathize with the erosion of Haley's idolatry of McClellan. Heretofore, McClellan had always stood for a vigorous pursuit of the war, but now he campaigns against Lincoln on the platform of immediate cessation of hostilities at any cost. This Haley could never condone. Haley never wavered in his stand against Secession at *all* cost. Also, he worshipped Lincoln and saw McClellan's weak bid for the presidency as traitorous.

## Chapter 17: Winter of 1865

1. "This part of it was true," Haley goes on to explain in a later addition to this diary entry. "There was an interview but nothing of a conciliatory nature was done. The Rebels discovered that the North was determined to yield nothing of its demands that the South should lay down her weapons and return her allegiance to the Union. The terms the Rebels demanded involved an entire abandonment of *our* cause. The Rebel ideas couldn't be entertained for an instant. So the Commissioners of the Southern Confederacy returned to Richmond with an uncomfortable-sized insect in their ears. They learned that the U.S. didn't recognize any nation of that name, and instead of being Commissioners of the Confederate States they were simply citizens of the United States in rebellion. This bit of information must have acted as a wet blanket on them, for there can be but little doubt but what they had expected to succeed in getting some sort of recognition."

## Chapter 18: The Fall of Petersburg

1. April 2, 1965, General A.P. Hill of the Confederate army had returned to duty after a brief leave to recuperate from an illness. Upon his arrival on the field he found his men under heavy enemy fire and he rode up to rally them. Just two minutes after his return, a Federal bullet struck him down. He was buried on the outskirts of Richmond, and after the war his men erected a monument to mark the spot where their beloved general lay.

2. "Nevertheless there was a thread of truth about negotiations between Grant and Lee," notes Haley. "Grant had sent a communication to Lee saying that he desired to shift from his shoulders the responsibility of a 'further effusion of blood.' Lee claimed to be equally anxious but didn't think the time had come to surrender, as he was still in condition to prolong the contest for some time yet. A more infamous lie was never uttered, for wasn't General Lee's army at that very moment fleeing before us like sheep before wolves? They were half-starved — and their horses were worse, staggering along and falling by the roadside. The men had grown so thin that an overcoat or blanket had to be thrown over them to produce a shadow. How much longer was General Lee to keep up this unequal contest? If General Lee didn't know that he was lying like Satan when he penned that message to Grant, then he was an infatuated old man."

# Bibliography

*Bibliography*

Bache, Richard Meade. *The Life of General George Gordon Meade*. Philadelphia: Henry T. Coates
      & Co., 1897.

Beath, Robert B. *History of the Grand Army of the Republic*. New York: Bryan, Taylor, and Co., 1889.

Confederate States of America, Army Dept. of Northern Virginia. *Reports of the Operations of the
      Army of Northern Virginia*. Richmond: R.M. Smith, 1864.

Cooper, Charles R. *Chronological and Alphabetical Record of the Engagements of the Great Civil War*.
      Milwaukee: Caxton Press, 1904.

d'Orleans, Louis Philippe Abert. *History of the Civil War in America*, vol. 3. Philadelphia: Porter
      and Coates, n.d.

Porter, Horace. *Campaigning with Grant*. New York: Century Co., 1897.

Swinton, William. *Campaigns of the Army of the Potomac, 1861-1865*. New York: Charles Scribner's
      Sons, 1882.

WILLIAM SILLIKER, JR.

Freelance writer Ruth Silliker lives in Saco, Maine, with her husband. Two children and three grandchildren live nearby. She unearthed John Haley's chronicles in 1981, while researching another project at Saco's Dyer Library, and was so taken with her serendipitous find that she put aside other interests — including work on a history degree and painting "in the Grandma Moses style" — in order to devote all her time and energy to editing this engrossing memoir. She has written articles on a number of subjects over the years, and after leaving John Haley and the Civil War, she shifted her focus by nearly a century and thousands of miles to research the Pacific battles of World War Two.